Claiming the Union

This book examines southerners' claims to loyal citizenship in the reunited nation after the American Civil War. Southerners – male and female, elite and nonelite, white, black, and American Indian – disagreed with the federal government over the obligations citizens owed to their nation and the obligations the nation owed to its citizens. Susanna Michele Lee explores these clashes through the operations of the Southern Claims Commission, a federal body that rewarded compensation for wartime losses to southerners who proved that they had been loyal citizens of the Union. Lee argues that southerners forced the federal government to consider how white men who had not been soldiers and voters, and women and racial minorities who had not been allowed to serve in those capacities, could also qualify as loyal citizens. Postwar considerations of the former Confederacy potentially demanded a reconceptualization of citizenship that replaced exclusions by race and gender with inclusions according to loyalty.

Susanna Michele Lee is Associate Professor of History at North Carolina State University, where she specializes in nineteenth-century American history, especially the Civil War and Reconstruction. She received her BA in history and psychology at the University of California, San Diego, and her MA and PhD in history from the University of Virginia. Lee has taught at the University of Virginia, the University of North Carolina at Greensboro, and Wake Forest University. Active in the burgeoning field of digital humanities, she has served as the project manager for the digital archives *The Valley of the Shadow*, *The State of History*, and *North Carolina in the Civil War Era*. Lee has received fellowships from the Smithsonian's National Museum of American History and the Virginia Historical Society. She has also participated in a National Endowment in the Humanities summer seminar on the ethnohistory of Indians in the American South at the American Indian Center at the University of North Carolina at Chapel Hill.

CAMBRIDGE STUDIES ON THE AMERICAN SOUTH

Series Editors:
Mark M. Smith, *University of South Carolina, Columbia*
David Moltke-Hansen, *Center for the Study of the American South, University of North Carolina at Chapel Hill*

Interdisciplinary in its scope and intent, this series builds on and extends Cambridge University Press's long-standing commitment to studies on the American South. The series not only offers the best new work on the South's distinctive institutional, social, economic, and cultural history but also features works in national, comparative, and transnational perspectives.

Titles in the Series

Robert E. Bonner, *Mastering America: Southern Slaveholders and the Crisis of American Nationhood*
Ras Michael Brown, *African-Atlantic Cultures and the South Carolina Lowcountry*
Christopher Michael Curtis, *Jefferson's Freeholders and the Politics of Ownership in the Old Dominion*
Ari Helo, *Thomas Jefferson's Ethics and the Politics of Human Progress: The Morality of a Slaveholder*
Susanna Michele Lee, *Claiming the Union: Citizenship in the Post–Civil War South*
Scott P. Marler, *The Merchants' Capital: New Orleans and the Political Economy of the Nineteenth-Century South*
Peter McCandless, *Slavery, Disease, and Suffering in the Southern Lowcountry*
Johanna Nicol Shields, *Freedom in a Slave Society: Stories from the Antebellum South*
Brian Steele, *Thomas Jefferson and American Nationhood*
Jonathan Daniel Wells, *Women Writers and Journalists in the Nineteenth-Century South*

Claiming the Union

Citizenship in the Post–Civil War South

SUSANNA MICHELE LEE
North Carolina State University

CAMBRIDGE
UNIVERSITY PRESS

32 Avenue of the Americas, New York, NY 10013-2473, USA

Cambridge University Press is part of the University of Cambridge.

It furthers the University's mission by disseminating knowledge in the pursuit of education, learning, and research at the highest international levels of excellence.

www.cambridge.org
Information on this title: www.cambridge.org/9781107015326

© Susanna Michele Lee 2014

This publication is in copyright. Subject to statutory exception and to the provisions of relevant collective licensing agreements, no reproduction of any part may take place without the written permission of Cambridge University Press.

First published 2014

Printed in the United States of America

A catalog record for this publication is available from the British Library.

Library of Congress Cataloging in Publication Data
Lee, Susanna Michele, 1975–
Claiming the Union : citizenship in the post–Civil War South / Susanna Michele Lee, North Carolina State University.
    pages   cm. – (Cambridge studies on the American South)
Includes bibliographical references and index.
ISBN 978-1-107-01532-6 (hardback)
1. United States – History – Civil War, 1861–1865 – Claims. 2. Confiscations – Confederate States of America. 3. United States. Commissioners of Claims. 4. Unionists (United States Civil War) – Southern States – Reparations. 5. African Americans – Southern States – Reparations. 6. Women – Southern States – Reparations. 7. Citizenship – United States – History – 19th century. 8. Compensation (Law) – United States. 9. United States – History – Civil War, 1861–1865 – Confiscations and contributions. 10. United States – History – Civil War, 1861–1865 – Moral and ethical aspects.   I. Title.
E480.5.L44 2014
973.7′41–dc23   2013035746

ISBN 978-1-107-01532-6 Hardback

Cambridge University Press has no responsibility for the persistence or accuracy of URLs for external or third-party Internet Web sites referred to in this publication and does not guarantee that any content on such Web sites is, or will remain, accurate or appropriate.

To my brothers, Ray, Jonathan, Ben, and Robert.

Contents

List of Tables	*page* x
List of Figures	xi
Acknowledgments	xiii
Introduction	1
1 "We have Fought the First Skirmish": Loyalty and Citizenship	12
2 Men's Union: Fixing the Standard of a Union Man	39
3 Women's Union: Reckoning with the Female Union Man	67
4 Former Slaves' Union: Bestowing Charity or Rewarding Loyalty	90
5 The Colored Union: Being All Things to All Men	113
Conclusion	133
Appendix A	139
Appendix B	146
Notes	171
Bibliography	227
Index	247

Tables

A1. Senatorial Votes in the 41st Congress on Southern Claims Divided by Region   *page* 139
A2. Total Votes in the Senate in the 41st Congress by Region   142
A3. Votes in the Senate in the 41st Congress by Political Affiliation   142
A4. Number of Claims Reported by State and by Year   143
A5. Number of Cases Reported Allowed and Disallowed by Year   143
A6. Amount of Claims Reported Allowed and Disallowed by Year   144
A7. Allowed Claimants in Union Military Service   144
A8. "Aid and Comfort to the Enemy" in the Disallowed Claims   145

Figures

1.1.	Orange Ferriss, c. 1860–1875	*page* 25
1.2.	James B. Howell, c. 1860–1865	26
1.3.	Thomas Nast, "Rising of the Dead," 1874	32
1.4.	Thomas Nast, "Stand From Under!" 1878	35
1.5.	Thomas Nast, "Probabilities," 1878	36
2.1.	"The Union As It Was," 1874	64
4.1.	Benjamin Sterling Turner, c. 1875–1894	101
4.2.	Gaylord Watson, "From the Plantation to the Senate," 1884	102
5.1.	Terrill Bradby, 1899	128

Acknowledgments

We all have stories that we tell of ourselves to reveal who we are, where we've been, and where we're going. In college, my story had been that I was self-sufficient, putting myself through school with little financial assistance by working thirty hours a week. One of the many benefits of the study of the past is that it challenges our understandings of ourselves in the present. In my history classes I learned to question such simplistic narratives of individual achievement. I realize that I am indebted to the many people who shaped my personal and intellectual development.

My mother raised five children on her own – no easy task I'm sure. She too has stories, stories that stretch from India to Indonesia to England to America. As the lone daughter, I always longed for a sister as a child, especially when I was outvoted for movies. Still, my brothers, Ray, Jonathan, Ben, and Robert, to whom I dedicate this book, were bright spots in my childhood and are continuing sources of inspiration in my adulthood.

At the University of California, San Diego, where I completed my undergraduate studies, Steve Hahn and Stephanie McCurry sparked my interest in southern history and inspired me to pursue a life of inquiry and research. Marathon rounds of meetings and grading have not diminished the allure of discovery and knowledge that I first encountered in their classes. Other faculty, including Rachel Klein, George Lipsitz, and Pamela Radcliff, introduced me to new ideas and theories. My first chance to live the life of a scholar came through a summer research program. Lisa Lowe and Yen Le Espiritu in the Ethnic Studies Department generously sacrificed (what I now know are precious) summer hours to guide my first research project.

At the University of Virginia, where I earned my PhD, my advisor Ed Ayers taught me to appreciate the rich texture of southern history. His attention to a range of voices in his scholarship, teaching, and service has served as a model in my understandings of the past as well as my negotiations in the present.

The example he sets of seeing the possibilities of a work rather than merely its limitations guides me as an advisor and a critic. His vision and innovation continue to inspire me.

I benefited from the expertise and counsel of many scholars during my time at UVA, including Reginald Butler, Scot French, Michael Holt, Nelson Lichtenstein, Chuck McCurdy, Deborah McDowell, Peter Onuf, Brian Owensby, Dylan Penningroth, Stephen Railton, and Holly Shulman. Gary Gallagher's teaching and scholarship have been instrumental in shaping my understanding of the Civil War. Grace Hale encouraged me through her scholarship and teaching to focus on big questions. Cindy Aron helped me to realize that white women's claim that they had no story was in fact their story. My dissertation writing group – Danielle Culpepper, Valerie Garver, Bob Katz, Dayo Mitchell, and Sharon Murphy – kept me on track and in good spirits. Dayo, in particular, has been a writing partner, a sounding board, an exercise buddy, a valued advisor, and always a dear friend. I am fortunate to have studied southern history at an institution that overflowed with southernists, including Charled Irons, Watson Jennison, Andy Lewis, John Riedl, Josh Rothman, Brian Schoen, Aaron Sheehan-Dean, and Amy Murrell Taylor, from whom I learned much about the South.

Friends and colleagues from my Greensboro days have remained steadfast even though many of us are now scattered. Bill Link and Michelle Gillespie, at the helm of SHOPtalk, provided me with an intellectual community of southern historians as I completed my dissertation. Bill's advice and friendship have been especially invaluable, and in many ways he served as a second advisor. My summer reading group, consisting of Damon Akins, Peter Carmichael, Mark Elliott, Benjamin Filene, Tom Jackson, Watson Jennison, and Lisa Levenstein, affords opportunities for good books and good conversations. I don't know two more caring people than Lisa Levenstein and Jason Brent, who do so much for so many people.

The Smithsonian Institute provided funding that made a year in Washington, DC, possible. I look fondly on my tenure at the National Museum of American History as a time devoted solely to digging through dusty papers in the archives and writing away in my basement apartment without teaching or service obligations. Pete Daniel played a key role in making my residence in DC one of scholarship and fellowship and also of beer at Tuesday night happy hours.

The Virginia Historical Society, the National Endowment for the Humanities, and the History Department and the College of Humanities and Social Sciences at North Carolina State University also provided funding that made this book possible. Mike Green, Clara Sue Kidwell, Malinda Maynor Lowery, Theda Perdue, and the participants in the Ethnohistory of Indians in the American South summer seminar helped me to reorient my thinking on Indians in the Civil War South. Matt Hulbert worked so efficiently on a research project related to this book that I understand why faculty in the sciences are tempted to keep their graduate students so long. Michael Fitzgerald, Amy Rose Guest

Acknowledgments

Pryal, Watson Jennison, John Riedl, Josh Rothman, and Amy Murrell Taylor all read parts of the manuscript and provided invaluable advice. The staff at the National Archives in Washington, DC, and College Park, Maryland, especially Reginald Washington, showed me the ins and outs of the records of the Southern Claims Commission, Court of Claims, and Congress. I would like to thank Lew Bateman at Cambridge University Press for seeing value in my manuscript and the editorial staff for making the process smooth and seamless.

Colleagues at North Carolina State University, including Jim Crisp, Craig Friend, Blair Kelley, Judy Kertész, Julie Mell, Lauren Minsky, Nancy Mitchell, and David Zonderman, have made Raleigh an intellectual home, if not a physical one. As someone who prefers to write about dead people, I find myself especially inspired by Kat Charron's dexterity in doing justice to the people she interviews and studies. Jonathan Ocko has done more than seems possible to protect the research and educational mission of the History Department in trying economic and political times.

Bik-Na Han, Haivan Hoang, Anita Jain, and Olivia Martin Butler were fast friends in my younger days. We have gone separate ways, but I think of them often. Bik-Na in particular opened her home to me when I felt I had no place to go. Jeff McClurken, Natalie Ring, Josh Rothman, and Kirt von Daacke are what make the Southern the Southern. The Anything But The Book Bookclub, to which Gretchen Engel invited me, has introduced me to the joys *of not* reading the assigned book. Sheridan Lea has made many things clear to me, including that a PhD does not bestow immunity from ridicule, that I am apparently an irresistible target for hip checks, and that family is so much more than a blood connection. Having her in my life has done many things that cannot be adequately enumerated, not the least of which has been bringing out maternal instincts I never suspected I possessed. Suzanne Jennison, Watson Jennison, Alex Jennison, and Grace Sterling welcomed me into their family. They are absolutely crazy, which is what I love about them.

Watson Jennison is sometimes maddening but always amazing. Without him, I would not be as good a scholar, teacher, or person. He has changed my life and the stories I tell about myself, the past, and the future.

Introduction

The scratching of pen against paper signaled something at once mundane and momentous. "What is your name, your age, your residence?" asked Harvey Risk, a representative of the Southern Claims Commission. "My name is Mary Blackburn.... My age is about forty-five years. My residence near Middlebrook," the claimant responded. The commission awarded compensation for property losses during the American Civil War to southerners who could prove they had been loyal citizens. Special Commissioner Risk recorded testimony to be forwarded to his superiors in Washington, for which he earned ten cents per folio. For Risk, the deposition was one among many taken from claimants and witnesses who came before him. For Blackburn, her dealings with the commission marked her recognition as a loyal citizen and her right to claim the Union as her own. Blackburn, a formerly enslaved woman, presented herself before the commission in 1874 requesting $476 for two horses, two cattle, bacon, flour, a saddle, and two bridles appropriated by the Union army in 1864. She had been born into a society that had demeaned her as a chattel, not a person, let alone a loyal citizen. Appearing before the special commissioner and having her perspectives and experiences documented was a small moment, but an important one nonetheless – one that signaled an acknowledgment that she mattered in the affairs of her nation.[1]

The special commissioner offered relatively little in his questions that resonated with Blackburn's perspectives and experiences as an enslaved woman to explain how she belonged in the Union or how the Union belonged to her. Reading through the interrogatories devised by his superiors, the special commissioner asked Blackburn: "Were you in any service, business, or employment, for the confederacy?" No. "Did you ever have charge of any stores, or other property, for the confederacy?" Never. "Did you ever subscribe to any loan of the so-called Confederate States?" Nothing. "Were you at any time a member of any society or organization for equipping volunteers or conscripts?" No.

The special commissioner dutifully recorded a string of negative responses to these and other irrelevant questions originally designed to ascertain whether or not a white man had been a loyal citizen.[2]

Blackburn's presentation of herself as a loyal citizen and her claim of the Union as her own posed a problem. The commissioners imagined loyal citizens as white men who had opposed secessionist politicians at the ballot box and had fought Confederate soldiers on the battlefield. As a former slave and as a woman, Blackburn seemed the antithesis of the loyal citizen. Southern citizenship in the antebellum era had drawn on the logic of mastery. White southern men possessed independence of thought and action made possible through their mastery of themselves and their household dependents. The slave, as subject to the mastery of another, represented the antithesis of the citizen. Women occupied an analogous position in their dependence and their incapacity for self-government.[3] In their postwar dealings with the federal government, how did former slaves, who had possessed no relationship to the state, or women, who accessed the state through their fathers or husbands, prove that they had been loyal citizens?

Blackburn managed to interject her perspectives and experiences as a former slave and a black woman to claim the Union on her own terms. "How many children have you?" the special commissioner inquired to identify heirs eligible for compensation. "I had ... three children, named John F. Patrick, Philip Patrick, and George M. Patrick," responded Blackburn in the same manner as numerous white women who had appeared before her, but she continued, "they were sold to a trader and carried off.... My children were quite young when sold." Blackburn offered her interjections, which were totally beside the commissioners' point, because she linked the forcible separation from her children with her loyalties to the Union. "I felt a willingness to help the cause of the Union at all times, because of the manner in which my children were torn from me." She transcended the limitations of the special commissioners' questions and clarified how a former slave and a black woman with no relation to the state could qualify as a loyal citizen.[4] The commissioners ultimately accepted Blackburn as a loyal citizen, but her explanation of her embrace of the Union as a rejection of the oppressions of slavery escaped their notice. They simply recognized her as a loyal citizen with very little commentary. In their report to Congress, they referred to her children, torn from her under slavery, only in noting that there were "no known heirs" interested in the claim.[5] In the gap between Blackburn's claim and the commissioners' decision lay both the promises and problems of postwar southern citizenship.

The Civil War and Reconstruction promised a second founding of the American nation. The war devastated the slave system that constituted the cornerstone of the nascent Confederacy and one of the pillars of the Union. Confederate surrender at Appomattox settled secession but not the war's ideological strife. On the ruins of a slave society, ex-Confederates and ex-Unionists struggled to lay a postwar foundation for the reunited American nation. Former enemies carried the battles of the war into the postwar years while constructing a new nation and a new people. Reconstruction determined which practices and principles would be buried under the postwar foundation and which would be salvaged as the building blocks of reunion.

The Civil War and Reconstruction especially upended traditions of citizenship. Federal authorities formalized a new entity – the American people – by creating, for the first time, a national citizenship that took precedence over state citizenship. The abolition of slavery through the Thirteenth Amendment in 1865, the establishment of birthright citizenship through the Fourteenth Amendment in 1868, and the introduction of manhood suffrage through the Fifteenth Amendment in 1870 dramatically expanded the confines of American citizenship. At the same time, federal officials imposed disabilities on former Confederates through the Military Reconstruction Acts of 1867 and the Fourteenth Amendment in 1868. *Claiming the Union* moves beyond the principles of citizenship as they were established in laws and amendments to examine the practices of citizenship as they were contested in dealings with the federal government.

Postwar considerations of the residents of the former Confederacy potentially demanded a thorough reconceptualization of citizenship that replaced exclusions by race and gender with inclusions according to loyalty. Former Confederate men, who had been enfranchised by virtue of their race and gender, had used their rights and privileges to tear the Union asunder. Black men and women, who had been considered least qualified to exercise self-government, had contributed to the Union cause in a variety of ways. White women, whose relationship to the state had been mediated through their fathers, husbands, and sons, had been called on to fulfill duties as loyal citizens, sometimes even in opposition to their male relatives. To what extent would the nation continue to adhere to limitations on the basis of race and gender? To what extent would loyalty replace ascriptive exclusions as the qualification for the full rights and privileges of citizenship?

After 1865, the United States was not simply a postbellum or postwar society, as it is often denoted. The reunited nation was a postemancipation society, a term used by scholars when referring to various societies as they shifted to free labor. Postwar reconfigurations of citizenship in the United States played out not only in the aftermath of a divisive civil war but also in the context of abolition.[6] The end of slavery prompted wide-ranging reconsiderations of the boundaries of citizenship: who qualified as good citizens and who did not, and who could be trusted with governance and who could not. Emancipation opened the omission of groups from the full rights and privileges of citizenship to unprecedented contestation. To the extent that racial hierarchies reinforced gender hierarchies, emancipation also raised the possibility of inclusions by gender. Postwar reconfigurations of citizenship, however, continued to be yoked by the logic of mastery, even amid abolition. Racial and gender hierarchy remained embedded in the foundation of the reunited nation.

After the war, former enemies debated the traits and qualities that comprised good citizenship and secured access to its rights and privileges, including suffrage, officeholding, jury service, rations, land restoration, pensions, and property claims. Loyalty emerged as a rival to white masculinity as the preeminent characteristic of good citizenship. On one end of the spectrum, Republicans, especially Radicals, emphasized wartime loyalty, condemning former Confederates as traitors and former Unionists as patriots. On the other end, Democrats and Conservatives promoted postwar loyalty, celebrating former Confederates as newly re-devoted citizens. Over the course of Reconstruction, former Confederates and their Democratic allies successfully decoupled postwar citizenship from wartime loyalty to secure the restoration of most rights and privileges. They succeeded not because they completely detached loyalty from citizenship, but because they successfully defined loyalty in the past tense. The extension of pardon, amnesty, and prosecutorial forbearance to alleged traitors signaled an official policy of forgetting.

The federal government could not unilaterally dictate loyal citizenship through law or amendment. Loyal citizenship was continually worked out in numerous exchanges between the people and their government. The people had their own ideas about what made a good citizen and what rights and privileges citizenship conferred. The Southern Claims Commission served as one venue for postwar contestations over loyal citizenship. After nearly a decade of debate, congressmen created the commission in 1871 to award compensation for property appropriated by the Union army to southerners residing in the former Confederate states. Republican congressmen rejected Democratic proposals to open the commission without reference to loyalties, explicitly limiting the claims process to loyal citizens. The characteristics of the loyal citizen became the primary source of contention. The commissioners of southern claims required claimants to prove their wartime loyalty as the prerequisite for the payment of these property claims. During its ten-year operation, the commission acted as the bulwark against the trajectory toward the acceptance of postwar loyalty for access to the rights and privileges of citizenship.

Representatives of the Southern Claims Commission acted as intermediaries between southerners and the federal government over the parameters of loyal citizenship. President U.S. Grant appointed three commissioners – all white northern Republicans – who decided the cases from their offices in Washington, DC. The commissioners required claimants to meet their standards of loyal citizenship to gain compensation for wartime losses.[7] They devised a questionnaire, termed interrogatories in official parlance, to uncover claimants' allegiances during the war. Local commissioners, called special commissioners, were stationed throughout the South and administered the interrogatories to claimants and their witnesses and then forwarded the transcripts to their superiors in Washington for judgment. If distrustful of a claimant's loyalty, the commissioners ordered an investigation by a roving special agent. Drawing on the evidence collected by their subordinates, the commissioners discussed each case until they reached a unanimous decision that they justified in their summary reports to Congress. At the end of every year, the commissioners submitted the decided claims for approval to the House of Representatives, which rarely overturned a decision.[8]

The records of the commission are filled with competing stories of loyal citizenship. In making sense of the war, participants constructed their perspectives and experiences into stories with beginnings and endings, conflicts and resolutions, and heroes and villains. The commissioners designed their interrogatories to elicit these narratives from claimants and witnesses. Because they responded to the commissioners' questions, southerners did not tell their stories with complete freedom. Because southerners often interjected testimony on additional topics they considered relevant, the commissioners never completely controlled the content and the trajectory of the exchange. Indeed, revisions of the interrogatories in 1872 and 1874 indicate the commissioners' attempts to refine their criteria to accommodate southern conceptions of loyal citizenship. Nevertheless, the commissioners possessed the authority to accept or reject southerners' narratives as official. They created their own narratives, recorded in their reports to Congress, which reconstructed southerners' stories according to a logic that made sense to them, excluding evidence they deemed irrelevant and including evidence they believed relevant. The claimants and commissioners shared joint but unequal authorship of their narratives of war.[9]

Claiming the Union uses the records of the Southern Claims Commission to examine reunion rather than disunion. Most historians employ the sources in accordance with the commissioners' original intentions to explore wartime loyalties.[10] This book places the records in their postwar context to examine postwar contestations over loyal citizenship between southerners and the federal government.[11] Southerners' impulses to petition the commission as loyal citizens emerged from their postwar perspectives, not just their wartime positions. Many southerners who historians would identify as conditional Unionists, neutral persons, disaffected Confederates, reluctant Confederates, and even former Confederates presented claims. These southerners did not meet the commissioners' criteria and do not fit historians' definitions, but they submitted their petitions, supposing they deserved recognition as loyal citizens as well as access to the rights and privileges it bestowed. Some claimants omitted damning facts, stretched the truth, and committed outright perjury in their testimony to win recompense for their property. Other self-professed loyal southerners refused to conciliate the commissioners, often telling the truth even when doing so damaged their prospects for compensation because they believed that they possessed the right to claim membership in the Union on their own terms. These lies or truths, as the case may be, reveal southerners' various understandings of the requirements for reconciliation with the federal government and their acceptance or rejection of those terms. The commissioners' decisions, then, do not simply reveal southerners as Unionists or Confederates. Instead, a decision of loyalty signaled a consensus, and a decision of disloyalty indicated a disparity between the claimants' and the commissioners' ideas about who qualified as loyal citizens.

The commissioners initially conceptualized loyal citizenship as implicitly white and masculine. They expected southern claimants to prove that they had possessed Union sympathies – what I term ideological citizenship – and that they had contributed to the Union cause – what I call active citizenship. Their solicitation of Union sympathies focused on political sympathies, specifically those in opposition to secession. Their conceptualization of Union contributions centered on political and military obligations such as voting and soldiering. The commissioners soon recognized that their understanding of loyal citizenship was, in many respects, untenable. They expected white male Unionists as claimants, but they also received thousands of petitions from white women, black men, and black women.

Southern claimants challenged the commissioners' presumption of the loyal citizen as an implicitly white masculine actor. White women, black men, and black women had not been able to meet the commissioners' standards of loyal citizens as voters and soldiers by virtue of their disfranchised position within southern society but nevertheless presented themselves as claimants.[12] Even some white men argued that Confederate persecution had prevented them from fulfilling their obligations to the Union. Some southerners rejected active citizenship, which required the fulfillment of obligations to the Union, and advanced a form of subject citizenship, which renounced obligations to the Union as impossible because of class-, gender-, or race-based oppression.[13]

Prompted by southerners' critiques, the commissioners revised their conceptualization of loyal citizenship in 1872 and 1874 but preserved many of their fundamental assumptions. They compensated for their initial focus on white men by devising a form of particularized citizenship, which acknowledged political obligations as race and gender specific. Recognizing that white women, black men, and black women, by virtue of their subordinate positions within southern society, could not meet the same standards for loyal citizenship as white men, they restructured their interrogatories into sections designated for "male," "female," and "colored" claimants. The commissioners retained their requirement for active citizenship by simply exempting white women, black men, and black women from proving that they had fulfilled various political obligations. In creating particularized citizenship instead of crafting universal citizenship, the commissioners included persecuted and disfranchised citizens without fundamentally rethinking their assumptions. They shifted from an exclusionary conception of citizenship, which favored white masculinity but presumed universality, to a particularized conception of citizenship, which recognized political obligations as race and gender specific.

Their understandings of loyal citizenship retained the assumptions of white male capability and female and black incapability. They accepted subordinated southerners as loyal citizens, primarily on the basis of their inability to perform the full obligations of citizenship – the very characteristics that had previously excluded them.

The process of claiming the Union involved disputes over citizenship, loyalty, and memory. Scholarship on American citizenship, especially the few sweeping histories, focuses on official citizenship, meaning the framework for membership in the nation as dictated by government authorities. Rogers Smith's *Civic Ideals* (1997), the most widely cited work, focuses on elites as they formulated official doctrine in legislation and legal opinion on the federal level. Scholars address the incorporation of blacks and women into citizenship during Reconstruction in the context of constitutional amendments, congressional legislation, and judicial opinion, most frequently the Fourteenth Amendment. These scholars examine the impulse to embrace or reject egalitarianism among congressional framers and constitutional interpreters.[14] Other scholars explore changes in federal policy concerning amnesty and pardon of former Confederates.[15]

The scholarship on official citizenship neglects what I call vernacular citizenship: the parameters for membership in the nation as advanced by recognized or prospective citizens. Smith justifies his focus on officials because "their actions have literally constituted the American civic community," further arguing that "it would be seriously misleading to write as if the views of those who were ineligible to hold political office shaped American citizenship laws as much as the views of those who did possess such prerogatives. Large portions of the population were for long stretches of time literally not seen or heard in the halls of power in America."[16] In debating citizenship during Reconstruction, however, these subordinated groups were seen and heard in the halls of power. Official citizenship in the postwar era did not emerge solely from legislation in statehouses and opinion in courthouses but in interactions at firesides and roadsides. People who did not hold political or judicial office had their own ideas about what constituted good citizenship and what benefits it bestowed. The postwar configuration of official citizenship developed in contestations between officials and the people. Membership in the postwar nation entailed more than an elite-driven restoration or extension of rights and privileges. *Claiming the Union* draws on and contributes to the scholarship on the constructed nature of citizenship by demonstrating the interplay between official and vernacular citizenship.[17]

Examinations of loyalty in the South during the Civil War primarily focus on loyalty to the Confederacy rather than the Union. Historians debate the extent to which the Confederacy retained the loyalties of its soldiers and civilians over the course of the war. Some argue that Confederates remained devoted to the Confederacy, only losing the war on the battlefield. Others contend that the Confederacy lost the support of soldiers and civilians and that these internal divisions contributed to Confederate defeat.[18] Historians increasingly explore not just Confederate but also Union loyalties in the South. These scholars investigate the origins of Unionism and the experiences of Unionists. These studies reveal loyalty to the Union as matters of not only principle but also expediency and circumstance. Southerners supported the Union not just because they believed in Union ideals, but also because they had always been distrusted as northern natives, because they found themselves under Union occupation, or because they anticipated a Union victory. These studies demonstrate that southern Unionists sustained their loyalties through the assistance of familial and communal networks and contributed significant services to the cause despite pervasive Confederate persecution.[19]

Few histories analyze how northerners, southerners, and westerners understood loyalty, and specifically southern loyalty, to the Union in the postwar years. Some local studies and microhistories follow the experiences of southern Unionists into the postwar years to explore continuing divisions within their communities. However, many studies of Civil War loyalties conclude with Appomattox as though that moment ended the story. Loyalty was not just relevant in the war years. Loyalty continued to matter in the postwar years. Congressmen limited the rights and privileges of citizenship according to specific definitions in their efforts to restore or reconstruct the South. For their part, southerners claimed the mantle of loyal citizenship in their attempts to exercise postwar political power.

Scholarship on the memory of the Civil War generally focuses on elites, mostly commemorators and sometimes politicians, who dominated the public discourse. Historians of Civil War memory in the South demonstrate that white southerners in organizations such as the Ladies' Memorial Societies, Southern Historical Society, United Confederate Veterans, and United Daughters of the Confederacy invented a "lost cause" narrative, which insisted that southern men had fought bravely on the battlefield and southern women had sacrificed at home, all in defense of the constitutional principle of state's rights.[20] Historians emphasize that the lost cause interpretation competed with the "union" and "emancipationist" narrative of the war. The union narrative celebrated the repudiation of secession and the preservation of the nation.[21] The emancipationist narrative focused on slavery as the cause of the war and abolition as its most significant legacy.[22] Historians of Civil War memory on the national level argue that white northerners and white southerners settled their differences by accepting a joint "reconciliationist" narrative that focused on the experiences of the war, particularly courage on the battlefield and sacrifice on the home front, rather than the divisive issues such as slavery that led the nation to war.[23] Historians particularly contend that the triumph of the lost cause narrative regionally and the reconciliationist narrative nationally came at the expense of the union and emancipationist narratives.[24] These studies recognize that historical memories morphed in content and form over time and that "official memory" or "collective memory" masked disputes among different groups for control of the dominant discourse.[25]

An examination of the claimants before the Southern Claims Commission shifts attention from devoted memorialists and politicians to reveal perspectives neglected in the historical scholarship. The commissioners and their subordinates recorded thousands of southerners whose voices on disunion and reunion would have otherwise remained silent. Compared to the former Confederates who ordinarily dominated the public discourse, former southern Unionists and disaffected Confederates left relatively few records.[26] This disparity can be attributed to a postwar hierarchy that reserved the public sphere for conservative white southern elites. The commission provided southerners, outside the ranks of commemorators and the halls of government, the opportunity to contest the meaning of the war and the qualifications for loyal citizenship with representatives of the federal government. Altogether, over 20,000 southerners submitted petitions.[27] These southerners did not simply mourn the loss of the Confederacy; they sought to claim the Union as their own.

Various configurations of citizenship, loyalty, and memory intertwined to enable southerners to claim different visions of the Union. Some believed that abolition represented the lasting legacy of the Civil War and argued that true freedom, and the prevention of future civil wars, required the exclusion of disloyal southerners from citizenship and the inclusion of loyal southerners. Others reasoned that the suppression of secession and the preservation of the Union mandated the restoration of all rights and privileges of citizenship to former Confederates. An interpretation of the war centered on slavery promised revolutionary change, but an interpretation of the war focused on secession negated the necessity for a reconstruction of the South. Former enemies embraced divergent memories of the war to secure leverage in its aftermath and thereby direct the fate of the reunited nation. Although the fighting on the battlefield had ended, the debate over the legacy of the war continued into the postwar era. As southerners reimagined membership in the national community, they reconceived the Union itself.

Reflecting the state's authority over matters of citizenship, the commissioners' formulation of particularized citizenship frames the organization for this book. The commissioners' interrogatories solicited various facts, but not complete stories. They filled the gaps in the testimony with what they would have considered "common sense" about how certain kinds of people thought and acted. Jews had "endeavored to manage so as to be able to prove their loyalty to whichever was the successful cause."[28] Germans had likewise "conducted themselves as to be able to prove loyalty to either the confederacy or the United States Government."[29] By contrast, Irishmen had taken firm stances because "an Irishman whose heart is in a cause where fighting is going on will have a hand in it, and show his sympathies by the hard blows he deals his adversary."[30] The commissioners considered race and gender differences, especially between whites and blacks and between men and women, most significant in their understandings of loyal citizenship. The bulk of the book is divided into chapters focusing on the commissioners' categories of citizens described as male, meaning white men; female, encompassing white women; and colored, comprising former slaves, free blacks, and other nonwhites. Gender and race, of course, intersected, but the commissioners imagined male and female citizens as implicitly white and categorized black citizens usually by their race and not their gender. Although the organization of the book adopts the commissioners' framework, the content of the chapters analyze how southerners challenged that framework.[31] Each section of the chapters examines a specific pattern in southerners' claims to loyal citizenship, both accepting and rejecting the commissioners' conceptualizations.

Chapter 1 situates the creation and operation of the Southern Claims Commission within congressional debates over the relationship between citizenship and loyalty. Despite the federal government's move to forgive wartime disloyalty, the commission retained its dedication to wartime loyalty as a prerequisite for the extension of the full rights and privileges of citizenship. As a result, the commission became a flash point for controversies over the role of wartime allegiances in determinations of postwar citizenship.

Chapter 2 examines white southern men's attempts to prove their loyal citizenship. Some convinced the commissioners that they had withstood the terrors of Confederate persecution and had sacrificed for the Union cause. Many other white southern men could not provide evidence that they had fulfilled their political obligations to the Union. Instead, they based their claims to postwar citizenship on their adherence to Union principles. Some former nonslaveholders and slaveholders pledged their devotion to a Union without slavery. Other former slaveholders vowed allegiance to the "Union as it was" or at least to a Union that preserved white supremacy. The commissioners, however, maintained active citizenship and rejected ideological citizenship as criteria for postwar citizenship. Chapter 2 suggests that the commissioners' standards of loyal citizenship eventually encouraged the celebration of devoted voters and soldiers on both sides.

Chapter 3 explores white southern women's attempts to reconcile the commissioners' expectation of national allegiances with the societal presumption of their apolitical and domestic character. Relatively few white southern women could prove to the commissioners' satisfaction that they had fulfilled political obligations to the Union on their own account. Some white southern women argued that their familial duties had preempted any loyalties to the Union or the Confederacy. Others derived their status as loyal citizens through their fathers, husbands, or sons. The commissioners melded white southern women's familial and patriotic duties, often granting them subject citizenship, usually through their male relatives. Chapter 3 demonstrates that postwar official citizenship failed to resolve the paradox of women's citizenship.

Chapters 4 and 5 focus on nonwhite southerners' negotiation of their previous status of subordination with their new status as citizens. Many nonwhite southerners asserted that the conditions of their oppression in southern society had prevented them from fully contributing to the Union cause. Instead, they insisted that they had sided with Union principles, which they identified as abolitionism and egalitarianism. The commissioners accepted most former slaves, free blacks, and Indians as postwar citizens by virtue of their subordinate status and presumed racial inferiority. Chapters 4 and 5 show that non-white southerners generally achieved recognition as loyal citizens on the basis of the very attributes that had previously disqualified them.

After the war, southerners fought to be accepted as loyal citizens and to claim the Union as their own. The commissioners insisted on an understanding of loyal citizenship that focused on actions over ideologies. Within this framework, southern blacks and white women especially fell short. Neutral men who had not taken a definitive stance during the war also failed to fulfill their political obligations to their nation. They had been, in southern parlance, not masters themselves, but mastered by others. The commissioners ultimately recognized many white women as well as black men and black women as loyal citizens, largely by applying their standards of loyalty to male relatives in the former case or by exempting them from their standards in the latter case. In this way, the commissioners accepted these southerners as loyal citizens without radically altering their underlying assumptions about good citizenship. White women, black men, and black women won inclusion, but generally not as independent citizens. Slavery and mastery had served as the foundation of antebellum southern citizenship to exclude the supposedly inferior race and inferior sex. *Claiming the Union* demonstrates that postbellum reconfigurations of southern citizenship continued to be yoked by the logic of slavery and mastery even amid formal abolition.

1

"We have Fought the First Skirmish"
Loyalty and Citizenship

Wendell Phillips, renowned abolitionist and women's rights advocate, declared in 1869 that "the war has just begun. We have fought the first skirmish."[1] After the official closing of the Civil War, former enemies waged new battles over reunion, most pressingly over membership in the reunited nation. Confederate and Unionist were wartime classifications that did not necessarily carry postwar implications. To what extent would distinctions according to loyalty limit or expand conceptualizations of citizenship? Insisting on the relevance of wartime loyalties, many Republicans argued that Confederates had abandoned the Union, incurring penalties, whereas Unionists had stood by the nation, earning rewards. Stressing the significance of postwar loyalties, many Democrats contended that Confederates deserved equality with Unionists because they had sincerely returned to their loyalties and had accordingly been pardoned and amnestied. All agreed on the centrality of loyalty to citizenship, but they disagreed over its definition with some fixing loyalty in the war years and others displacing loyalty to the postwar years.

The Civil War and Reconstruction inaugurated a national debate over the characteristics of national citizenship. The racial and gendered exclusions on citizenship, which had served as two of its most defining features, became less sacrosanct as white men betrayed the Union and black men, black women, and white women rallied to its cause. After the war, former enemies debated the extent to which loyalty should serve as a justification to include those formerly marginalized by race and gender and as a rationale to exclude those previously privileged by race and gender. Partisans agreed on the importance of loyalty, but they clashed over the definition of loyalty. This chapter places the Southern Claims Commission in the context of these debates over loyalty and its relationship to citizenship during the Civil War and Reconstruction. The creation of the commission and its subsequent operation were long-standing battles in this postwar conflict.

"Is He Who Was a Traitor Last Year, Necessarily a Traitor Now?"

All northern proposals for reconstruction assumed that loyalty would restrict the rights and privileges of citizenship in the postwar South. But what constituted loyalty? One congressman acknowledged that "no man who is a traitor" deserved a high political office, "but the question is, who is a traitor? Is he who was a traitor last year, necessarily a traitor now?"[2] At issue was whether wartime loyalty would be remembered as a qualification for citizenship or whether wartime disloyalty would be forgotten as a bygone relic. This shaped the extent to which former Confederates would be restored to their rights and privileges and the extent to which citizenship would be expanded to previously excluded groups. For a brief period during the Civil War and Reconstruction, radical Republicans succeeded in restricting many of the rights and privileges of citizenship according to wartime loyalties. These debates informed congressmen's understandings of loyalty and citizenship as they considered the payment of southern claims.

During the war, many congressional Republicans favored restricting access to the rights and privileges of citizenship to individuals who could swear oaths of past loyalty. In mid-1862, they created the so-called ironclad oath, which pledged loyalty in the past and the future. Individuals who subscribed to the ironclad oath certified that they had sided with the federal government since the beginning of the war and had voluntarily rendered no aid to the Confederate government. Radical Republicans especially favored the ironclad oath to past and future loyalty over oaths to only future loyalty. The latter oath, in which the taker promised to henceforth support, protect, and defend the Constitution and government of the United States, had been used in the first year of the war to restrict access to government positions and services. Starting in the second half of 1862, federal officials began broadly replacing oaths of future loyalty with oaths of past and future loyalty. Employees and officials of the federal government, except the president and vice president, pledged the ironclad oath. Veterans lost their pensions for their service in the War of 1812 and the Mexican-American War if they could not subscribe to the ironclad oath. Jurors and attorneys before federal courts and claimants against the federal government swore their ironclad loyalty. Government officials also extended the application of the ironclad oath to telegraph operators, newspaper correspondents, government contractors, and passport applicants. These restrictions gained wide support within the Republican ranks.[3]

Despite growing approval for ironclad oaths of past and future loyalty in his party, President Abraham Lincoln, in devising a plan to lure Confederates back into the Union, relied on oaths of future loyalty in his first formalized plan, issued in December 1863, for the "restoration," as he understood it, of former Confederates to the Union. Promising "malice toward none and charity for all," Lincoln offered "a full pardon" and the return of all property except slaves to all white southerners who swore an oath to "henceforth faithfully support, protect, and defend the Constitution" and to "abide by and faithfully support all proclamations ... having reference to slaves." His plan accepted "as sound whoever will make a sworn recantation of his former unsoundness." He excluded only high-ranking military and civil officials of the Confederacy, thereby welcoming a broad base of former Confederates into the Union.[4]

Lincoln's lenient plans of restoration signaled faith in southerners, even disloyal ones, as citizens. He publicly praised them as possessing "as much of moral sense, as much of devotion to law and order, and as much pride in, and reverence for, the history, and government, of their common country, as any other civilized, and patriotic people." He privately disapproved of an oath, such as the ironclad oath, "which requires a man to swear he has not done wrong" because "it rejects the Christian principle of forgiveness on terms of repentance." His requirement of future rather than past loyalty also fit with his contention that it was "enough if the man does no wrong *hereafter*." He deemed "repentance," as evidenced in the simple swearing of oaths to future loyalty, sufficient to welcome former Confederates as citizens.[5]

Lincoln could imagine former Confederates as loyal citizens on the basis of their future loyalty, but he could not envision that most former slaves could be incorporated on the same terms despite their past loyalty. For much of the war, Lincoln preferred that blacks make their way as citizens elsewhere and, for this reason, pursued colonization schemes. Far from providing a place for blacks as loyal citizens, he even proposed an apprenticeship system for former slaves. Toward the end of his presidency, Lincoln did shift away from colonization and gradualism with his recommendation of the enfranchisement of some black men: "the very intelligent, and especially those who have fought gallantly in our ranks." This departure, the first of its kind by an American president, acknowledged, albeit tentatively, that black men's loyal services to the Union earned them a claim to citizenship in the reunited nation, but he took little action on the federal level to extend suffrage to black men.[6]

Many radical Republicans, concerned about the shape of postwar society, rejected Lincoln's use of future loyalty in favor of past loyalty to access the rights and privileges of citizenship. They wanted to ensure that only truly loyal men could exercise power in the reunited nation. The Wade-Davis Bill of 1864, named after radical Republicans Benjamin Wade and Henry Winter Davis, required white southern men to pass various tests of loyalty to participate in the process of reunion: swearing an oath of future loyalty to call a constitutional convention, pledging an oath of past and future loyalty to vote for delegates to the convention, and proving that they had not held Confederate civil or military office under the Confederacy to stand as delegates to the convention. The bill also mandated that new constitutional conventions prohibit men who had held high Confederate civil or military office from voting for or serving as governor or legislator. The architects of the bill considered black male suffrage to reward loyal black men, but they ultimately abandoned it as too controversial. Passing easily in the House and just barely in the Senate, the bill died in the Executive Mansion through Lincoln's "pocket veto." Lincoln believed the greater leniency of his plan would encourage Confederates to return to their loyalties and, in this way, hasten Confederate surrender.[7]

Once the war officially closed, debates over the use of loyalty to restrict access to the rights and privileges of citizenship became less about encouraging Confederates to end the war and more about determining who could exercise political power in its aftermath. George B. Loring, an abolitionist and a radical, balked at reinvesting former Confederates with political power in the South. Arguing that "no oath of allegiance can purify them," Loring declared that "their return would be an eternal disgrace," which would "bring back all our controversy, paralyze all our efforts, overthrow all that we have accomplished, dishonor the white man, and enslave the black man." He rhetorically asked, "Shall we restore them to the fullness of their former rights? Never."[8] Distinctions based on wartime loyalties would preserve the fruits of Union victory. Democrats, in contrast, counseled forgiveness toward former Confederates through the acceptance of future loyalty for the restoration of citizenship. William E. Finck, an Ohio Democrat, reminded his fellow senators that "the North and the South are destined to live together as one people, in the same Union, and under a common Constitution." He called on former Unionists and former Confederates to "endeavor to live together as true friends and brothers."[9]

After assuming the presidency following Lincoln's assassination, Andrew Johnson, like his predecessor, accepted promises of future loyalty as sufficient for the restoration of citizenship to former Confederates. Johnson initially barred many classes of Confederates from general amnesty, but he subsequently granted thousands of individual pardons. His approval of sometimes hundreds of petitions in a single day demonstrated that the simple action of requesting a pardon was sufficient, in most cases, for its dispensation. As he explained to one White House visitor, "I intended that they should sue for pardon, and so realize the enormity of their crime." A pardon petition signified repentance from former disloyalty on the part of former Confederates – a demonstration of their willingness to return to the Union as faithful citizens. Johnson eventually expanded the terms of his general amnesty in 1868 to encompass "all and ... every person, who directly or indirectly, participated in the late insurrection or rebellion."[10]

Johnson's restoration policy employed postwar loyalty rather than wartime loyalty as the basis for postwar citizenship. Johnson, like many Democrats, contended that former Confederates could swear future loyalty and act as good citizens. Slavery had sent Confederates on their wayward course because it had allowed a minority of wealthy slaveholders "by means of forced and unpaid labor" to monopolize southern land and wealth. Without slavery, the South would revert to the natural laws of political economy, which would result in a social and economic revolution among white southerners and which would "give more good" – meaning white – "citizens to the commonwealth."[11]

Despite their demonstrated loyalty to the Union, Johnson could not imagine black southerners as good citizens. He positioned slaves as allies of their masters in oppressing nonslaveholding whites. "The colored man and his master combined kept [the poor white] in slavery." He also believed that black southerners possessed less "capacity for government than any other race of people" and that "wherever they have been left to their own devices they have shown a constant tendency to relapse into barbarism." He did not expand suffrage to include loyal black men or other disfranchised groups, insisting that "White men alone must manage the South."[12]

Johnson's plan for reunification on the basis of postwar loyalty restored many former Confederates to power throughout the South. The doctrine that "the people of the South, once rebels, are rebels no longer" prompted white southerners to disclaim their role in secessionism and claim the mantle of unionism.[13] Many reluctant Confederates revisited their initial opposition to secession and blamed the disaster of the war on rabble-rousing politicians. Johnson's plan led to the ascension to power of many former Confederates. Of the eighty senators and representatives that southern states sent to Washington, fifteen had served in the Confederate army, ten of them as generals. Another sixteen had served in civil and judicial posts in the Confederacy. Nine others had served in the Confederate Congress. One – Alexander Stephens – had been vice president of the Confederacy.[14]

The Supreme Court weighed in on the side of postwar over wartime loyalty as the requirement for access to the rights and privileges of citizenship through a series of decisions that involved Johnson's generous amnesty and pardon policies. Augustus H. Garland, a former Confederate congressman, contested the congressional requirement that lawyers before the Court of Claims swear their ironclad loyalty to the Union. Garland argued that his presidential pardon, bestowed by Johnson in 1865, released him from this requirement. A majority on the Supreme Court agreed, ruling in 1866 that a pardon "releases the punishment and blots out the existence of guilt, so that in the eye of the law the offender is as innocent as if he had never committed the offence."[15] This position was one of several that the court could have taken, including the view that the pardon erased neither conviction nor guilt and the view that the pardon erased conviction but guilt remained. The Supreme Court continued to apply the doctrine that pardon blotted out the existence of guilt in other cases to invalidate the congressional requirement that claimants before the Court of Claims seeking to recover property seized under the confiscation and abandoned property acts had to prove their ironclad loyalty.[16] In these ways, the Supreme Court strengthened the attempt to accept postwar loyalty rather than require wartime loyalty for access to the rights and privileges of citizenship. This was part of a larger movement in which the Supreme Court endorsed a Democratic interpretation of Reconstruction.[17]

With President Johnson and the Supreme Court bolstering oaths of postwar loyalty, Republican congressmen tried to overcome their differences and secure their authority to dictate the requirements for loyal citizenship. Radical Republicans proposed policies that limited former Confederates' voting and officeholding – one even revoking citizenship altogether – as well as policies that enabled black suffrage. Centrists and conservatives had been initially doubtful of the constitutionality and practicality of imposing permanent disabilities on former Confederates and of granting impartial suffrage to black men. These Republicans had turned to the Fourteenth Amendment, passed by Congress in 1866, as a reasonable plan for reunion. The amendment granted American citizenship to blacks, barred high-ranking former Confederates from holding state or federal office, and reduced congressional representation for states that disfranchised black men. Centrist and conservative Republicans had hoped to cooperate with President Johnson and former Confederates to devise a solution for the problem of reunion. However, intransigence by both Johnson and former Confederates, including the election of former Confederates to state and federal office, violence toward black and white former Unionists, and the rejection of the Fourteenth Amendment, convinced most Republicans to move toward more radical proposals.[18]

Republican congressmen, after much wrangling among themselves, created a process for reconstruction that temporarily restricted the exercise of full postwar citizenship to white southern men who could prove wartime loyalty. Congress approved the Military Reconstruction Act in 1867, repudiating the state governments organized under Johnson and dividing the South into military districts under the command of Union officers. Under military reconstruction, only former Unionists, including black men, who could swear oaths of past loyalty could vote or serve as delegates to new constitutional conventions. In addition to the Thirteenth and Fourteenth Amendments, Republicans secured the Fifteenth Amendment providing racially impartial, if not universal, suffrage. Congressional Reconstruction did not achieve the vision of its more radical architects, but it still constituted, at least momentarily, an unprecedented transformation of power in the South.[19]

Policies that limited access to the rights and privileges of citizenship according to wartime loyalties inaugurated a revolution in the South, ousting former Confederates and elevating black and white former Unionists. Registrars controlled access to the ballot in southern localities, excluding former Confederates who could not swear the ironclad oath and registering former Unionists, both black and white, who could. Federal officials encouraged registrars to require additional testimony to corroborate prospective voters' claims to loyalty. Military officials disfranchised perhaps 50,000 to 150,000 former Confederates.[20] Delegates to state conventions ratified constitutions that mandated varying levels of disfranchisement for former Confederates. Alabama, Arkansas, Mississippi, and Louisiana all disfranchised considerable numbers of former Confederates. Georgia, Florida, Texas, South Carolina, North Carolina, and Virginia, in contrast, adopted constitutions that provided for the disfranchisement of few or no former Confederates.[21]

A Republican commitment to the significance of wartime loyalty contributed to the extension of the vote to black men. Some Republicans favored citizenship, and its attendant rights and privileges, for black men as a reward for their fulfillment of political obligations to the Union, particularly through their military service. One centrist praised "the brave colored men who heroically bled in the defense of their country – a country from which thus far they have received injuries rather than blessings" and justified suffrage as the reward bestowed by a "grateful country."[22] The war convinced some Republican congressmen that loyal black men would make better citizens than disloyal white men. One radical asserted: "I do not believe ... that our Government rests on the complexion of its people, or the color of their hair. I believe that a patriot is a better citizen than a traitor."[23] Or, as one centrist put it, "Loyal men, of whatever color, have more right to the ballot than have disloyal men, however white they may be."[24] Even Republicans doubtful of the merits of black suffrage expressed this position: "I have not arrived at the point yet when I can believe that all men should be enfranchised." Nevertheless, the congressman concluded, "If I am asked which I would sooner trust, I would answer that I prefer to trust the meanest black man with a loyal heart who ever wore the chains of slavery to the most intelligent traitor who has waged war against my country." He judged that the "colored race" was "probably" not prepared for suffrage, but he was "sure" that "the rebels are unfit for it."[25] In these ways, Republican congressmen shifted the criteria for citizenship away from racial capabilities toward wartime loyalties.

Democratic opponents of black male enfranchisement dismissed Republicans' tributes to black loyalty. Some insisted that black men's loyalty and their contributions to the cause had been insignificant. One Democratic congressman asserted, "They did not win their freedom, and had but little agency in shaping the events which conferred it upon them. It came to them as one of the results and as incident to a great civil war in which white men contended for power, and in which colored men played but a subordinate part." This congressman attributed to "negroes" "but little agency" not because former Confederates tyrannized them but because they lacked "any of those high traits of character which indicate them as fit to become a governing race." The congressman could only envision one solution to the "defenseless condition of the negro race": "the highest impulses of humanity will impel the white people everywhere, I firmly believe, to provide what is necessary to their prosperity and comfort." Denying black men's (and women's) roles in emancipation and their contributions to Union victory provided this Democratic opponent a powerful justification for continued black disfranchisement.[26]

Black southerners' wartime loyalty opened space to consider their fitness for citizenship and its rights and privileges, and pragmatic calculations cinched many of their claims. Although hesitant about mass democracy and especially black democracy, many Republicans regarded black male enfranchisement as a necessary counterweight to former Confederate votes. They noted that the former Confederate states, once restored to the Union, would potentially exercise greater power than they had prior to secession. With emancipation, former slaves counted as full rather than three-fifths persons for the purposes of apportionment in Congress. Without enfranchisement, Republicans would have to ensure the continued disfranchisement of former Confederates to keep government in loyal hands. Doubtful about the longevity and propriety of policies that disfranchised former Confederates, Republicans instead supported black male enfranchisement.[27]

Women's rights activists unsuccessfully pushed for the simultaneous inclusion of female suffrage in Reconstruction measures. As in the antebellum years, they pressed for suffrage using both the language of republicanism and natural rights. However, they also hoped that they could capitalize on the importance of loyalty to further their agenda. Elizabeth Cady Stanton intended "to avail ourselves of the strong arm and the blue uniform of the black soldier to walk in by his side." Women had not, like black men, fought as soldiers for the Union cause, but they had offered other contributions to Union victory that they expected would be rewarded through the extension of the vote. One supporter observed, "The women did not go to the battle-field, with muskets and bayonets in their hands, ... but they did render services at home during the war equally as valuable as fighting." The movement for female suffrage ultimately failed because congressmen did not consider women's contributions sufficient to overcome presumptions of their domesticity, and moreover they could discern no pragmatic benefit to enfranchising women.[28]

In the first few years after the war, Republicans and Democrats disagreed between and among themselves over membership in the reunited nation. Radical Republicans distrusted the abilities of former Confederates to act as good citizens and therefore favored constraints on their exercise of political power. Moderate Republicans and most Democrats doubted the legitimacy of widespread disfranchising measures targeting former Confederates. Congressional Republicans ultimately reconciled their differences and limited access to the rights and privileges of citizenship to those who could prove their wartime loyalty to the Union. In this way, they shifted from restrictions on the basis of race, if not gender, to restrictions on the basis of wartime loyalty.

"An Invention of a Convenient and Just and Truthful Mode of Ascertaining the Claims of Loyal Citizens"

Congress created the Southern Claims Commission amid the ongoing debate over the use of wartime or postwar loyalty to determine access to the rights and privileges of citizenship. The disagreement over the definition of loyalty delayed congressional provision for the payment of southern claims. For "six long years," Senator Garrett Davis of Kentucky had worked to pass a law to compensate loyal citizens in the South for property appropriated by the Union army during the Civil War. Frustrated with the lengthy debate over southern loyalty, Davis in 1871 offered a reward for, as he put it, "an invention of a convenient and just and truthful mode of ascertaining the claims of these loyal citizens."[29] Ultimately, Congress was able to pass a law to provide for the settlement of southern claims but only by sidestepping the question of loyalty. As southern states returned to Congress, Republican and Democratic proponents mustered unity for the principle of paying southern claims through a body called the Southern Claims Commission but not enough to agree on the definition of loyalty. They left such questions to the commissioners to decide.

Southern claims for stores and supplies provided to the Union army originated as a result of the Union's foraging policies. Unreliable supply routes by railroad and water encouraged the practice in the western theater from the outset of the war. With slow progress in the eastern theater, foraging from the countryside became more common there after late 1862 as part of a general hardening of policy toward civilians, both Union and Confederate.[30] The Union army could clean out a family in a matter of days. As one claimant later recounted to the Southern Claims Commission:

Everything we had was swept out in one week, and we were left with very little to eat, and what little we had, we divided with some wounded Union soldiers left at a neighbor's house unprovided for.... After the battles were over and the troops were all gone, we walked over the cleared part of our farm, and there was scarcely a thing of any value remaining on the place but the buildings. All was desolation. We were nearly starved when the war closed, and have not been able to live on our place since.[31]

Union officers sometimes left receipts promising compensation to loyal southerners but more often left only empty storehouses and stripped fields. With or without promises of recompense, southerners believed that they deserved payment for their wartime losses. From the very beginning of the war, southerners complained to the federal government over the army's impressments of their crops and livestock, appropriation of their tools and their houses, and destruction of their fences, fields, and buildings.

During the war, citizens of the Union states but not the Confederate states succeeded in obtaining compensation for appropriated supplies. Southerners submitted claims to military officials and boards, the supply departments for quartermaster and commissary stores, the claims committees of both houses of Congress, and the Court of Claims.[32] William Reid, for example, requested compensation in 1862 from the federal government for wood, stock, and produce taken from his Fairfax County, Virginia, farm. His "confidence in the justice of his country" convinced Reid that the government would "promptly provide necessary means to remunerate him for the injuries he has suffered, by the acts of its army."[33] Reid misplaced his confidence. Congressmen passed a law in July 1864 allowing the supply departments to pay these claims only in the North and the West, thereby prohibiting the payment of claims, like Reid's, in the South. Because it limited the payment of claims to the loyal states, the act became known as the limiting act.[34] Border-state Republicans and Democrats supported the payment of claims for supplies appropriated in the South, but northern and western Republicans mounted stiff opposition. Republican senator Lyman Trumbull of Illinois complained of the "difficulty of arriving at the facts in that unsettled portion of the country" and argued that "to open the door for men to prove their loyalty" in the disloyal states would be "dangerous at this time."[35] Citing the impossibility of determining loyalty in the seceded states, even in the occupied regions, northern and western Republican congressmen thwarted border-state efforts to compensate loyal citizens of the seceded states during the war.

With the end of the war, supporters, mostly border-state Republicans, pushed for the payment of southern claims. Waitman Willey, a Republican from West Virginia who was one of the primary proponents, called on Congress to treat loyal men the same regardless of where they lived: "Are these Union men to be treated as rebels and no more? Is there any less justice in the claims which they present to Congress ... than in the claims ... in the loyal States?" Indeed, Willey discerned more justice in the claims of loyal men in the South because "for the nights of these long four years these men never laid their heads upon their pillows, except under terrible apprehensions of personal violence before they awoke in the morning."[36]

Border-state arguments about equal treatment for Union men once the war had ended were not sufficient to convince many northern and western Republicans of the propriety of paying southern claims. As Republicans sought to delay the restoration of former Confederate states to the Union, they also opposed efforts to recognize their residents' claims against the government. The House in January 1866 resolved to "reject all claims, referred to them for examination, by citizens of any of the States lately in rebellion, growing out of the destruction or appropriation of, or damage to, property by the Army or Navy while engaged in suppressing the rebellion." Although benevolence and humanity urged federal charity, no principle of law required compensation. With the fate of the defeated Confederate states undecided, northern and western Republicans refused to provide for the payment of southern claims.[37]

Much of the Republican opposition to the payment of southern claims from the end of the war in 1865 to the passage of a law in 1871 denigrated the nature of southern loyalty. Some northern and western Republicans dismissed true loyalty in the South as virtually nonexistent. Senator Jacob M. Howard, a Republican from Michigan, rhetorically asked, "If there were Unionists there of such undaunted pluck and of such dessert as represented, how did it happen they remained in the enemy's country during the whole war?" Howard assumed that any loyal man worthy of the name would have made himself so odious to his Confederate neighbors that he would have been driven out. By definition, then, southern residence proved disloyalty.[38]

Skeptical of the virtues of southern loyalty to the Union, opponents charged that the payment of southern claims would only reward former Confederates.

Northern and western Republican congressmen feared that those in charge of the claims process would not properly distinguish loyalty from disloyalty. A stalwart critic, Senator George F. Edmunds, a Republican of Vermont, complained that any southerner who "thought the rebellion was going to slunk" could deliver an "excellent speech" to "his uncle, to his aunt, to his cousin, that after all he thought the rebellion was a mistake." Even Confederate General Robert E. Lee would be able to claim status as a loyal citizen and secure payment for his wartime losses.[39] As a result, loyal northerners and westerners would end up paying millions of dollars to disloyal southerners. Senator Cornelius Cole, a Republican of California, argued that, because southerners would be able to offer false evidence of their loyalty, "the Government will in that way be imposed on by many persons who were really enemies to the Government during the war." The estimates for such fraudulent claims ran into the "fifty thousand millions."[40]

As southern states reentered the Union under Congressional Reconstruction, southern Republican congressmen became strong supporters of the payment of southern claims. They pointed out that many residents of the nonplantation and mountainous districts of Virginia, Tennessee, North Carolina, Alabama, and Georgia had supported the Union and that ordinances of secession had, in some cases, passed through fraudulent means or without popular support.[41] Southern Republican congressmen took offense at their northern and western colleagues' dismissal of southern Unionism. Senator Willard Warner, a Republican in Alabama, pledged, "I cannot, standing in the position that I do as in part the representative of southern loyalists, allow to go uncontradicted any doctrine which classes those men as enemies." Warner, a native Ohioan, acknowledged, "I was a Union man where it was easy to be for the Union." Southern Union men weathered "a storm of persecution and hate" that raised their loyalty "superior to mine," indeed to anyone in the loyal states.[42] After their states returned to the Union, southern Republican congressmen took the lead in the movement to pay southern claims, one by one proposing legislation for their respective states.[43]

Southern Republican congressmen found their Democratic colleagues to be ready allies in the movement to pay southern claims. Senator Thomas C. McCreery, a Democrat from Kentucky, advocated compensation to all southerners both former Unionists and former Confederates. He charged that "the word 'loyalty' ... now means an unfaltering devotion to the fortunes of the Radical party" rather than a devotion to the Union during the war. "It is time," he announced, "that the statesmen of this country were engaged in devising measures to promote the welfare and prosperity of the whole people." McCreery concluded that "hostilities ... have ceased; five years of peace have intervened; and it is time that some attention was paid to the rights of a common citizenship." Democratic supporters presented the payment of southern claims as an act of reconciliation that once more recognized former Confederates as loyal citizens.[44]

Some northern and western Republican opponents recognized that southern claims would not go away. Southerners continued to push the issue by appealing to their state representatives, their congressmen, the quartermaster and commissary generals, the secretary of war, the president, and any other official who could possibly influence the consideration of their claims. Republican congressmen complained that southerners made themselves a nuisance by "instituting appeals and constantly pressing claims." These claims dominated the legislative calendar, accounting for an estimated one-half to one-third of the legislation passed in the 1860s and 1870s.[45] Northern and western Republicans feared that they would not control Congress forever, and many discerned the necessity to formalize a process for the disposition of southern claims while they could still oversee policy. Republican Senator James W. Nye of Nevada stipulated, "I want to know whether" the parties deciding on southern claims "are in sympathy with those who carried on the war" because he warned that "those who hold the reins now will not hold them always."[46]

By the 1870s, then, potential southern claimants benefited from a convergence of interests. Promoting the payment of southern claims as a measure of justice to men who had courageously stood by the Union, Republicans in the border states and, once admitted, the South offered the strongest support. Hoping to erase distinctions between loyal and disloyal states and to facilitate the process of restoration, nearly all Democrats voted in favor of payment. With their predictions of fraudulent claims from disloyal southerners, northern and western Republicans offered the strongest opposition, but with a desire to provide a mechanism for adjudication while they still possessed the power to set the definition of loyalty, some opponents ultimately offered their backing. The return of every former Confederate state to Congress along with Democratic votes and Republican converts gave supporters the necessary support for the passage of a law.[47]

The majority agreed on the principle of paying southern claims, but they did not agree on the definition of loyalty that would guide payment. Some congressmen, both Republicans and Democrats, supported lenient definitions of loyalty. Some Republicans advocated rewarding southerners who had ultimately embraced the Union, such as men who had served in the Union army or navy even if they had initially backed secession. Some Democrats favored even more forgiving standards, insisting that the readmission of the former Confederate states had abolished distinctions between loyal and disloyal, that amnesty oaths and pardons had restored southerners to loyal citizenship, and that loyalty should be measured in the postwar and not wartime years. However, other congressmen, exclusively Republicans, favored a strict definition of loyalty, asserting that residence in a seceded state was evidence of disloyalty. These congressmen argued that southerners should be required to prove their loyalty during the entire war to gain status as a loyal citizen.[48]

Congressmen attempted to impose their definition of loyalty by stipulating specific bodies to adjudicate southern claims. Those who preferred a more lenient definition of loyalty supported opening the Quartermaster and Commissary departments, which already considered northern and western claims, or opening the Court of Claims, which adjudicated other types of property claims, to southern claims. Republicans objected to the supply department's indulgent standards of evidence in rendering their judgments of loyalty or disloyalty. Officials in the supply departments only required claimants to swear a loyalty oath and submit a statement from recognized Union men attesting to their loyalty.[49] Republicans balked at the Court of Claims because the federal government paid all its judgments without further approval by Congress. Moreover, claimants before the Court of Claims appealed decisions to the Supreme Court. Radical Republican congressmen knew from *Ex Parte Garland* in 1866 and subsequent cases that the Supreme Court's definitions of loyalty did not meet their stringent standards.[50]

A proposal for an independent commission of three commissioners won over the primary Republican opponents. Congress, in an act of March 3, 1871, created the Southern Claims Commission. The law limited the commission's jurisdiction in two main ways. First, the law restricted compensation to "those citizens who remained loyal adherents to the cause and the Government of the United States during the war." However, because congressional supporters could not agree on the definition of loyalty, the law left the parameters of loyalty unspecified. Second, the law restricted the commission to claims for "stores and supplies taken or furnished for the use of the [Union] army." This excluded claims for other types of property. Congressional Republicans attempted to ensure their party's oversight of the claims process by limiting the term for the commission as two years, stipulating that the president chose the commissioners, and subjecting the commissioners' decisions to congressional approval.[51]

President Grant chose three former Whigs who had cast their allegiance with the Republican Party. Grant nominated Asa Owen Aldis as president of the commission and Orange Ferriss (Figure 1.1) and James B. Howell (Figure 1.2) as commissioners. Aldis hailed from a prominent line of judges in Vermont. His father had served on both the Vermont Supreme Court and the U.S. Supreme Court. Following his schooling at the University of Vermont and Harvard Law School, Aldis went into private practice until 1857 when he left to serve on the Vermont Supreme Court. He served in this capacity through the Civil War until 1865 when he retired to accept a position as U.S. consul at Nice, in southeastern France. Returning from Nice in 1869, Aldis sought a judicial appointment. He received two offers: the chairmanship of the Southern Claims Commission or a seat on a commission for adjusting claims under the treaty with Mexico. Aldis chose to serve as chairman for the Southern Claims Commission. Aldis brought to the commission his experience with judicial procedure and his knowledge of the intricacies of the legal status of the South. Aldis's fellow commissioners had both served as members of Congress during Reconstruction. Ferriss studied law in his hometown of Glens Falls, New York, and later graduated from the University of Vermont. When Ferriss received his appointment to the

FIGURE 1.1. Orange Ferriss (c. 1860–1875), a Republican, served as a commissioner on the Southern Claims Commission from 1871 to 1880. Ferriss is most well known for his critique of President Andrew Johnson during his impeachment trial.
Source: Prints and Photographs Division, Library of Congress, Washington, DC.

commission, he had just finished two terms from 1867 to 1871 in Congress as a representative from New York where he had gained fame as a strong proponent of Johnson's impeachment. Howell, the third commissioner, was a lawyer, politician, and editor in Iowa, Ohio, and Illinois. He had filled a vacancy in the Senate in 1870 and 1871. While senator, Howell voted against the payment of southern claims four times, supporting an amendment to absolve the government of the responsibility but was absent on the final vote that created the commission.[52] Former Confederates criticized Grant's selections. As one newspaper noted, "The Southern men very generally express dissatisfaction at the Commissioners appointed to examine Southern Claims. They do not know Judge Alder; they prefer someone else to Mr. Ferriss, and they think that while Mr. Howell is an honest man, he is not a just or unprejudiced man."[53]

FIGURE 1.2. James B. Howell (c. 1860–1865), a Republican, served as a commissioner on the Southern Claims Commission from 1871 to 1880. While senator, Howell voted against the payment of southern claims four times, supporting an amendment to absolve the government of the responsibility.
Source: Photo no. 111-B-3200, National Archives, College Park, MD.

The commissioners' rules and regulations on collecting evidence demonstrate their determination to guard against former Confederates' attempts to defraud the government. The commissioners favored oral questioning, especially in large claims of more than $10,000, as it gave them greater control over the evidence by providing the advantage "of hearing the witness, or observing his appearance on the stand, of judging of his intelligence, fairness, and honesty, and by cross-examination of ascertaining his means of knowledge and testing his credibility." They created a set of interrogatories to be administered to all claimants and witnesses by local commissioners, called special commissioners, throughout the South in claims less than $10,000.[54] The commissioners attempted to corroborate claimants' and witnesses' testimony in a variety of ways. They printed lists of claimants, which their clerk distributed to southern post offices, to encourage information from knowledgeable individuals on the loyalty of claimants and to discourage former Confederates from petitioning for compensation.[55] They more frequently relied on the "rebel archives." The Union army had confiscated Confederate treasury and other records during the war and had transferred them to the corresponding federal departments. The rebel archives contained evidence of thousands of southerners who had participated in the rebellion by serving in the Confederate military or selling supplies and provisions to the Confederate government.[56] Finally, to facilitate investigations within southern communities, the commissioners secured the appointment in 1872 of three roving investigators, called special agents, to travel through the South and collect evidence in claims, especially in those exceeding $5,000.[57]

In their rulings on loyalty, the commissioners adopted stringent standards. As members of Congress during much of the recent debate, Ferriss and Howell knew and shared many of the fears that the payment of southern claims would only benefit former Confederates. With the various definitions available to them, the commissioners chose a strict definition of loyalty, one that mandated active devotion to the Union from secession to surrender. The commissioners regarded "voluntary residence in an insurrectionary State during the war" as "*prima facie* evidence of disloyalty." To overcome the presumption of their disloyalty, "the party claiming to be loyal must *prove* his loyalty. It is a fact to be established by proof, and is not to be presumed."[58] Republican proponents of a strict definition of loyalty found enthusiastic allies in the three commissioners of southern claims.

Over the course of their tenure, the commissioners' conceptualization of loyal citizens shifted from a standard implicitly white and masculine to one particularized by race and gender. Their initial interrogatories in 1871 presumed that only white men would petition their commission as loyal citizens. They included questions on voting in elections, serving in the military, and holding public office. The commissioners amended their interrogatories in 1872 to add questions for other claimants and ultimately revised their interrogatories in 1874 to include sections for all claimants, free claimants, male claimants, female claimants, and colored claimants. These categories of citizenship are discussed in separate chapters. Briefly stated as an overview, the creation of a particularized citizenship exempted female and black claimants from the commissioners' white masculine standards of loyal citizenship but did not create much in the way of new female or black standards.

Only if the claimant passed the first test of loyalty did the commissioners proceed to consider their second test of property. Understanding the prescribed "stores or supplies" stated in the 1871 act to include only certain types of property, the commissioners limited their jurisdiction to claims for medical, hospital, and engineer supplies as well as quartermaster and commissary stores. Following the practice of the Quartermaster Department, they placed rent and occupation of land, even by military officials, beyond the bounds of the stores or supplies specified in the act of Congress. They also denied compensation in claims for damaged property and "lawless depredation." With their rules and regulations, the commissioners adopted a narrow view of their jurisdiction, banning several types of property claims that could not withstand the objections expressed in the northern and western press and debates in Congress.[59]

That the federal government during Reconstruction provided for compensation for wartime property appropriations even though congressmen discerned no legal obligation to do so demonstrates the sanctity of property, at least for loyal citizens. American legal traditions linked property and citizenship. As property owners, white men possessed economic independence and therefore political independence and, for these reasons, could act as virtuous citizens. Married white women, generally, and slaves, absolutely, did not legally own property. They were, to different extents, the property of white men. In the early Republic, many states had restricted the privileges of citizenship, most notably voting and officeholding, to property holders. In the antebellum era, the elimination of restrictions on voting and officeholding related to property ownership had recognized that white men claimed property in themselves and their labor. During the Civil War and Reconstruction, the federal government acted on the understanding that freedom entailed the right to earn wages for one's labor. The commissioners doubted the ability of white women, black women, and black men to act as independent citizens and to accumulate significant propertyholdings. They understood white men as property owners. White women, black women, and black men faced greater hurdles in proving their claims because the commissioners found it hard to believe that they possessed the opportunities or even the capabilities to accumulate property in their own right. Most of the interrogatories directed specifically to female and black claimants concerned not their loyalty to the Union but rather the legitimacy of their property ownership. Therefore, much of the commissioners' conceptualization of particularized citizenship for women and blacks was dictated by their uncertain claims to property.[60]

Amid northern skepticism regarding southern allegiances, the commissioners devised guidelines sympathetic to the government. With their strict definition of loyalty and their high standards of evidence, the commissioners limited the possibility that former Confederates would defraud the government. Both Ferriss and Howell, perhaps radicalized by their time in Congress, exhibited greater severity toward southern claimants than the more sympathetic Aldis. Still, regardless of their individual proclivities, the commissioners investigated and discussed claims until they reached a unanimous decision. All three commissioners adhered to a strict definition of loyalty to the federal government, with some modifications, throughout their tenure.

"The Only Barrier Which Now Stands Between the Disloyal Claimants and the Treasury"

One year before its tenure was set to expire, one supporter pronounced that "the Southern Claims Commission is almost the only barrier which now stands between the disloyal claimants and the Treasury."[61] During its ten years in operation, the commission required southerners to prove their wartime loyalty to the Union to receive compensation for their wartime losses. The commission mandated wartime loyalty even as Congress abandoned it as a means to limit other rights and privileges of citizenship. Throughout the 1870s, wartime loyalty became embattled, so much so that many of its defenders no longer viewed it as a workable means of determining who constituted a good citizen. By the time the commission closed its doors in 1880, confidence in the usefulness of wartime loyalty as a condition for access to the rights and privileges of citizenship had waned. Although it was not the only barrier remaining for former Confederates, the commission was one of a dwindling number.

In the late 1860s and early 1870s, a spirit of reconciliation gained ground, resulting in a congressional shift away from requiring wartime loyalty to accepting postwar loyalty as the condition for access to the rights and privileges of citizenship. Congress, which had initially required newly elected congressmen to swear an oath of past loyalty, began accepting a modified oath of future loyalty from former Confederates.[62] A new party, the Liberal Republicans, which emerged in 1872, expressed many northerners' and westerners' weariness with Reconstruction policies, especially criticizing the effects of black enfranchisement and white disfranchisement in the South.[63] By the early 1870s, some of the last remaining restrictions on political participation in postwar public affairs based on wartime loyalties were the disabilities imposed by the Fourteenth Amendment. Petitions for the removal of these disabilities flooded Congress, and many found a receptive audience. Proposals for general congressional amnesty had failed in 1870 and 1871 but gained momentum in 1872 as a Liberal Republican policy.[64]

Arguments in favor of amnesty suggested that congressional policies that had promoted wartime loyalty had disempowered those best qualified and empowered those least equipped for postwar citizenship. Representative James G. Blair, a Liberal Republican of Missouri, depicted former Confederates as American patriots who, like their revolutionary forebears, had "simply raised their arms to strike down a Government which they thought failed to protect them." He argued that former Confederates "believing that they were right, were just as honest in their purposes and intentions, and their consciences just as free from wrong and crime, as the consciences of those who enlisted under the banner of the Union."[65] The misguided commitment to wartime loyalty banished the most qualified men from power and influence and left only the inept and corrupt in their place. Senator Frederick Sawyer, a Republican of South

Carolina, insisted that "it is due to those disabilities, and to those disabilities only, that we had not an ample field from which to select honest, capable men for our local public offices, men who would have made faithful officers." Sawyer particularly singled out black men as incapable of exercising political power. "Having been slaves, completely subject to the will of masters all their lives," he asked, "did you expect they could assume all at once the habits of thought and action of free, self-poised, unbiased intelligent legislators?"[66] Critics charged that allocating the franchise on the basis of wartime loyalties prevented former Confederates from reassuming their roles as loyal citizens and forced them to embrace vigilantism. Carl Schurz, a Liberal Republican of Missouri, blamed "Ku Klux outrages" on political disabilities, which "incite and sharpen their mischievous inclination by increasing their discontent with the condition they live in." Former Confederates were not poor citizens who needed to be disabled. Instead, they acted as poor citizens because they were disabled.[67]

Radical Republicans opposed amnesty and its removal of wartime loyalty as a means to limit access to the rights and privileges of citizenship. They rejected arguments that former Confederates could be remade into good citizens without the oversight of the federal government. Representative Isaac Parker of Missouri characterized former Confederates as "men who hated freedom and who loved bondage ... [and] sought to build up a government that should have in it an element of aristocracy, which should recognize the rights of the few, and leave unrecognized and unprotected and uncared for the rights of the many."[68] Radical Republicans believed that distinctions according to wartime loyalty preserved the Union's moral victory. Senator Oliver P. Morton of Indiana denounced amnesty because it implied that "there was nothing wrong in the rebellion, ... that it was simply an honest difference of opinion between parties in which there was no criminality on either side." He urged, "Let us not say to future generations that those ... who sought to build a new government whose foundationstone should be human slavery ... that these men did no wrong, that they were worthy of all acceptation, and of again being returned to the highest positions in the Government."[69] Radical Republicans only supported amnesty if they could be assured that former Confederates would act in good faith toward former slaves. Senator Charles Sumner of Massachusetts unsuccessfully proposed linking amnesty with civil rights to force former Confederates to act as good citizens, arguing that "rebels seeking amnesty must be just to colored fellow citizens seeking equal rights."[70]

A consensus among Liberal Republicans, moderate and conservative Republicans, and Democrats overcame radical Republican opposition to secure the passage of the Amnesty Act of 1872, which restored the right to hold office to all white southern men except congressmen of the 36th and 37th congresses, officers in the judiciary, military, and naval service, and heads of departments and foreign ministers of the United States who had supported the Confederacy. The Fourteenth Amendment had disabled approximately 20,000 southerners, and congressmen by special acts had removed disabilities from nearly 5,000 former Confederates. The Amnesty Act left only 300 to 700 former Confederates disqualified from office.[71] This measure was a blow to the doctrine that wartime loyalty best qualified a man for postwar citizenship.

The Southern Claims Commission operated within the growing opposition to wartime loyalty that characterized the movement for amnesty. The commissioners worked in relative peace for their first term, securing a four-year extension from 1873 to 1877. Starting in the mid-1870s, Democratic and northern and western Republican congressmen attacked the commission as they dismissed wartime loyalty as an adequate measure of who constituted a good citizen. Throughout their tenure, the commissioners withstood challenges by Democrats and Republicans who critiqued their conceptualization of and judgments on loyalty. Over the course of their tenure, the commissioners fended off numerous attempts to abolish their commission and force a redefinition of loyalty.

As the state and federal governments returned former Confederates to political power, southern Democrats tried to open the payment of southern claims to former Confederates by pushing for legislation to remove distinctions among citizens according to wartime loyalties. Critics charged that the Southern Claims Commission only rewarded southern traitors, those who "cannot honestly be called *southern people*."[72] William W. Wilshire, a Republican turned Democrat of Arkansas, offered a bill to abolish the Southern Claims Commission and allow local juries to decide on southern claims. W. M. Levy, a Democrat of Louisiana, proposed to open the Court of Claims without regard to loyalty to claims for stores and supplies taken by the Union army.[73] Southern Democrats also attempted to create an archival silence by defunding the upkeep on the rebel archives. The destruction of the archives would leave the Southern Claims Commission and other federal bodies without ready access to a means to corroborate southerners' claims that they had not contributed to the Confederate war effort.[74]

Republicans sounded dire warnings. After losing control of the House in 1874, southern claims became a source of alarm, especially during the campaigning for the presidential election of 1876. In one broadside, Republicans warned against "Rebel War Claims! Grand Raid on the Treasury. How Loyal Men are to be Taxed!! What Democratic Retrenchment Means." The broadside included a tally of 26 general bills and 350 private bills in the 1st Session of the 44th Congress alone to pay "rebel claims," amounting to over $2 billion, over five times the national debt.[75] One Republican complained that Democrats "do not love, but hate the Union with intense and undying hatred, and should they get possession of the Government they will throttle it."[76] These rebel claims by former Confederates would force the federal government to "pay the expense of both its own and the rebel Army."[77] Republicans regarded such bills as "a foretaste of the order of things that may be expected should the Confederate Democracy obtain control of the government."[78] Rebel raids would not stop at claims for quartermaster and commissary supplies or for captured and abandoned property. Former Confederates once in power intended to also secure compensation for emancipated slave property (Figure 1.3).[79]

FIGURE 1.3. Thomas Nast, "Rising of the Dead," 1874. In this cartoon, Republican cartoonist Thomas Nast conveyed the fear that Democrats would topple hard won Union victories. Headstones engraved with "slavery," "the pure white man that thought it was his own government," "inflation," "southern claims," and "repudiation" awaited resurrection under Democratic rule.
Source: Harper's Weekly, December 12, 1874.

Northern and western Democrats tried to shift the blame, condemning Republicans as the true proponents of rebel claims. "It may be well to remark that the only steps toward the payment of any rebels for anything were taken by the republican Congress of 1871. At that time a Southern Claims Commission was created." This Democratic critic conveniently omitted that the creation of the Southern Claims Commission had received overwhelming Democratic support. He then charged that the commission accepted "proof of loyalty, so called ... of a very attenuated character, or altogether fictitious" and therefore primarily rewarded former Confederates.[80] After providing for southern claims themselves, another critic accused, "Now they seek to create the impression that these claimants are a cause of the election of a Democratic Congress."[81]

Samuel J. Tilden, the Democratic candidate for president in 1876, attempted to diffuse the rebel claims controversy. Tilden penned a widely printed letter in which he pledged that no rebel claims would be paid. He insisted that the federal government could no longer continue to fight the Civil War through legislation, arguing that "the calamities to individuals which were inflicted by the late war are, for the most part, irreparable," especially "the million of our youth who went to untimely graves." As for war claims, he asserted that the federal government "cannot apportion anew among our citizens the damages or losses incident to military operations, or resulting in every variety of form from its measures for maintaining its own existence." Tilden foresaw only one safe course: "to let by-gones be by-gones, to turn from the dead past to a new and better future; and, on that basis, to assure peace, reconciliation, and fraternity between all sections, classes, and races of our people." Such a course would create a new prosperity "in which the evils of the past shall be forgotten."[82] Tilden's stance on southern claims suited his campaign's condemnation of political corruption and financial woes under Republican governance.

Republicans were, not surprisingly, unconvinced by Tilden's letter. They doubted that Tilden could stave off the "united mass of determined, hungry, and aggressive men" of the South. "Men trained in the school of slavery and accustomed to command, and as accustomed to obedience from their Northern allies, will find some means – it cannot be doubted from their past history – to indemnify themselves at our cost."[83] Republicans predicted that former Confederates would claim status as loyal citizens on the basis of Johnson's sweeping pardon and amnesty proclamations and then launch a rebel raid on the federal treasury.[84] The Republican campaign, in focusing on rebel claims, continued to "wave the bloody shirt" by calling on Republican voters to suppress yet another Confederate threat. Republicans won the disputed election and averted the evils of rebel claims, and the commissioners secured another extension of their term to 1880.

In the aftermath of the election, some southern Democrats accelerated their attacks on compensation to former Unionists and their efforts to reward former Confederates. The *Atlanta Daily Constitution* complained that claimants before the commission "confess that morally at least they were traitors to their section and their State." The *Constitution* advised eliminating the commission to "teach a lesson to those who, living in the South, yet desired to see their section dismantled and overrun, and their neighbors impoverished and preyed upon."[85] Toward this end, Representative Charles M. Shelley, a Democrat of Alabama, proposed the abolition of the commission, which adhered to strict standards of loyalty, and the removal of its jurisdiction to the Court of Claims, which accepted a pardon as proof of loyalty.[86]

The Democratic Party captured control of both houses of Congress in 1878, but dissension within the party between northern and western Democrats and southern Democrats prevented them from upsetting the southern claims process. Representative Edward S. Bragg, a Democrat from Wisconsin, complained that if the South was solid for the Democratic Party simply for the purpose of raiding the treasury, then southerners should just join the Republican Party. He feared that former Confederates defrauded the federal government through the Southern Claims Commission, charging that "every one of these claimants was an enemy." Southern Democrats objected to Bragg's definition of loyalty. Representative Ezekial J. Ellis, a Democrat from Louisiana, agreed with Bragg that the number of Unionists in the South had been miniscule, but he declared that "southern men" had been plentiful. "The southern man who was born there, reared there and who had been identified with the people, could only have been loyal when he entered the confederate army, and did his full duty as a soldier." He regarded these men as "the only loyal people in the south" and praised their devotion "to their country, to their God and to the noblest, highest and manliest emotion ever breathed by the human soul."[87]

Amid ongoing fears that a Democratic Congress would enable the payment of rebel claims and remove all legislative distinctions between loyal and disloyal, some northern and western Republicans withdrew support from southern claims. Thomas Nast, a Republican cartoonist, began referring to "$outhern claims" to stress former Confederate attempts to defraud the government (Figures 1.4 and 1.5).[88] Republican supporters of the Southern Claims Commission started to regard it, like Congressional Reconstruction as a whole, as a well-intentioned but misguided experiment. The *New York Times*, for example, which previously had praised the commission, now turned against it. The paper reported that Congress had established the commission in "good faith" to reward loyalists. The paper now believed "it must be confessed that the scheme has worked very badly." The commission had "no means sufficient" to accomplish its assigned task because "its investigations were necessarily partial and incomplete." The *Times* asserted that so-called loyal claims only rewarded "the skulkers and the sneaks" of the South.[89] These new critiques prompted Senator George F. Edmunds of Vermont to propose a constitutional amendment, which, if it had passed, would have prohibited the payment of all southern war claims.[90]

FIGURE 1.4. Thomas Nast, "Stand From Under!" 1878. In this cartoon, Republican cartoonist Thomas Nast depicted an ailing elephant, the symbol of the Republican Party (complete with bandage), about to be smothered under a landslide of economic woes by "$outhern claims," repudiation, and taxation as headless gentlemen pontificated oblivious to the danger. Nast often replaced the "s" in "south" and "southern" with a dollar sign to suggest a southern agenda to rob the federal government.
Source: *Harper's Weekly*, January 26, 1878.

FIGURE 1.5. Thomas Nast, "Probabilities," 1878. In this cartoon, Nast warned that "frequent southerly breezes, occasionally growing stronger, and at times threatening to become a perfect hurricane" battered northern shutters with proposals to pay "$outhern claims," "southern debt," and "lost property." The cartoon expressed Republican concerns about the possibility of rebel raids on the treasury.
Source: *Harper's Weekly*, May 4, 1878.

Before its enemies could close its doors, the commissioners of southern claims completed their work. Although hampered by Congress' refusal to appropriate funds for the salaries of the commission's investigators and clerks, they succeeded in deciding their final case before the expiration of their term in 1880. Over the course of its ten-year tenure, the commission received 22,298 claims totaling over $45 million, primarily from southerners in states that had been subjected to prolonged campaigning and occupation. They banned over 5,000 claims of southerners who had not submitted evidence. The commissioners disallowed 56 percent of the claims, primarily on the grounds of disloyalty, paying out only $5 million in claims.[91] Had the commissioners not finished their work in 1880, they almost certainly would have encountered opposition to any attempt to prolong the life of their commission.[92]

In the immediate aftermath of the war, supporters of limiting the rights and privileges of citizenship according to wartime loyalties argued that loyal southerners would make better citizens than disloyal southerners. In the 1870s, this argument lost ground. Congressmen restored political rights to former Confederates, allowing most to vote and run in state and national elections. They also moved against the payment of southern claims on the basis of wartime loyalty. Both were undergirded by a belief that wartime loyalty did not serve as a useful test for limiting postwar citizenship. Citizenship on the basis of wartime loyalty eventually faltered because its Republican supporters became wary of retaining distinctions on the basis of allegiances. Many came to believe that former Unionists (and those southerners who claimed Unionism's mantle) could not act as good citizens while former Confederates could. Republicans found loyalty unworkable and ultimately contradictory in advancing their postwar agenda of establishing republican governments in the South.

Over the course of the Civil War and Reconstruction, loyalty emerged as a pivotal characteristic of citizenship. A dedication to preserving the significance of wartime loyalty served to deprive former Confederates of some of the rights and privileges of citizenship and to bestow them on former slaves previously excluded. However, a growing spirit of reconciliation in the 1870s prompted many former Unionists to forgive former Confederates for their wartime transgressions. The restoration of former Confederates to most of the rights and privileges they had previously enjoyed signaled that wartime disloyalty did not nullify status as good citizens. At the same time, criticism of rule by black men who lacked the abilities to govern and white men who had sat out the war demonstrated the disenchantment with and rejection of wartime loyalty as an adequate qualification for access to the full rights and privileges of postwar citizenship.

The debates over the creation of the Southern Claims Commission and the hostility toward it demonstrate the importance of notions of loyalty in determining which southerners could claim the rights and privileges of citizenship in the reunited nation. Congressmen on both sides recognized the existence of loyal citizens in the South and supported compensation of their wartime losses through the creation of the commission. The commissioners of southern claims rejected postwar loyalty and embraced wartime loyalty to determine which southerners qualified as loyal citizens. They successfully defended this definition against attacks over the course of their tenure. As made clear in the chapters that follow, however, this definition of loyalty did not account for many southerners. Most of the claimants before the Southern Claims Commission did not meet the commissioners' standards of loyalty. Indeed, some claimants could only meet the Supreme Court's standard under which pardon or amnesty obliterated any treasonous offense. However tenuous the commissioners judged their justifications, southerners made specific claims to belonging in the Union on the basis of their perspectives, experiences, and circumstances. Examining this dialogue between claimants and commissioners over loyalty and disloyalty reveals much about the process of reunion in the aftermath of the Civil War.

2

Men's Union

Fixing the Standard of a Union Man

In his appearance as a witness before the Southern Claims Commission, J. Madison Wells, a prominent Louisiana politician, addressed the dilemmas facing southern Union men. Some Union men had been willing to sacrifice slavery to save the Union, even emancipating their slaves themselves. Most Union men, however, had protected their slave property during the war, even fleeing with them on the advance of Union troops. Wells conceded that these Union men had done so to "save [their] niggers," but he also explained that the Confederate army had detailed men to remove property, including slaves, beyond the reach of Union forces. Wells chastised the commissioners stating that "you gentlemen up here at the north, if you will permit me to say so, could not well fix the standard of a Union man in Louisiana," by which he meant a white Union man, "because he was compelled to do a great many things he didn't want to do unless at the risk of his life."[1]

Wells suggested that the northern commissioners could not appropriately fix the standard of a Union man in the South because they had been Union men where it had been easy to be Union men. The commissioners had not been called on to deal with the consequences of emancipation, and they had not been subject to intense persecution by civilians and authorities. Wells suggested that the commissioners were unrealistic in their expectation that white southern men prove they had wholeheartedly embraced and had publicly defended the Union cause. He contended that white Union men in the South had fulfilled different Union obligations and had possessed alternative Union ideals than white Union men in other sections. He specifically called on the commissioners to lay aside their regional presumptions to appreciate the position of white Union men who had benefited from slavery or who had been the victims of coercion.

Disputes over white men's loyalty to the Union before the commission followed several distinct patterns that centered on two related issues: the obligations that citizens owed to their nation and the ideals to which their nation aspired. The commissioners expected loyal citizens to prove that they had been active citizens to suppress secession, ideally, but not exclusively, by showing that they had voted for the Union at the ballot box and fought for the Union on the battlefield. "Bold outspoken uncompromising Union men" met the commissioners' standards of active citizenship by proving that they had publicly fulfilled their obligations to the Union. "At heart Union men" forced the commissioners to concede that Confederate persecution had limited white southern men's ability to publicly stand for the cause. "Independent Rebels and traitors" incurred the commissioners' opprobrium as southern men who had forsaken the Union by devoting themselves to the Confederacy. "Amiable, timid, and neutral characters" earned the commissioners' displeasure for concerning themselves with their families and their livelihoods rather than the fate of the Union. "Republicans since the war closed" tried to meet the standard of active citizenship, emphasizing that they had fulfilled their obligations to the Union through their postwar, if not wartime, actions. The commissioners expected that Union men had fulfilled their obligations not just to any Union cause but to a specific interpretation of the Union cause: the repudiation of secession. "Poor hardworking people" and "once slaveholders," however, offered alternative interpretations of Union ideals, ones devoted to the destruction or preservation of slavery rather than solely the suppression of secession. Ultimately, white southern men advanced their claims to the Union within a conceptualization of citizenship encumbered with racial and gendered assumptions that would ultimately favor active citizens on both sides of the Mason-Dixon line.

"A Bold Outspoken Uncompromising Union Man"

When he appeared before the commissioners, Robert S. Heflin of northern Alabama, an area of significant wartime Union strength, presented compelling evidence that he had sympathized with and contributed to the Union. He dismissed the legitimacy of secession and the "so called Confederate Government." He stressed that he had fulfilled his obligations to the Union by canvassing in the adjoining counties during the secession crisis in 1860 and 1861 and by helping more than 100 Union men escape to Union lines in nearby Rome, Georgia, in late 1864. Heflin asserted that he had become so notorious in his support of the Union that Confederate authorities had harassed him unceasingly so much so that his "whole life from the beginning of the war until I was forced to flee to the Union army for safety, was one continual scene of molestation and injury of every kind short of death, which I only escaped by fleeing from the county." He portrayed himself as a Union man who, in the face of repeated threats to his life, had refused to moderate his Union stance or to defer to Confederate authority. Heflin earned the commissioners' highest praise as "a bold outspoken uncompromising Union man." The commissioners rewarded white southern men who had regarded secession as unjust, impractical, and unconstitutional and had acted on those ideals to suppress secession, most especially as Union voters and soldiers. "Bold outspoken uncompromising Union men" proved that they had acted out their loyal citizenship in the public arena in defense of their country often at the expense of their personal interest.[2]

Fulfilling the commissioners' vision of "bold outspoken uncompromising Union men" was largely only possible for white southern men who had the opportunity to engage with the Union in public ways, generally those who had lived in areas that had experienced prolonged periods of Union occupation or in areas that had harbored a significant Union population. During the war, Union men in the mountainous and nonplantation districts of western Virginia, northern Alabama, northwestern Arkansas, western North Carolina, and eastern Tennessee, emboldened by communities of dissenters, could more openly express and act on Union sympathies. Union men in the Union-occupied South benefited from greater opportunities and protections in speaking out against the Confederacy and in aiding the Union. In contrast, Union men in the Confederate interior possessed fewer chances to assist the Union cause and, with fewer allies in their vicinity, confronted greater peril if they chose to do so.[3] After the war, the geography of loyalty benefited some white southern men over others in the claims process.

The white southern men who won the commissioners' praise as Union men evinced little ambivalence in their anti-secessionist sympathies. The commissioners asked white male claimants if they had sympathized with the Union cause, and they specifically linked Union sympathies with secession.[4] Joseph E. Segar, a politician from southeastern Virginia, fulfilled the commissioners' expectations for a Union man. He declared, "I never had a sentiment in my life time that was not Union, down to the bottom of my soul, and have not now." He swore that he had cherished his Union sympathies so near to his heart that: "I had determined to sacrifice my life." Keeping with the commissioners' interpretation of the war, he categorically rejected both "the policy and doctrine of secession." The commissioners accepted Segar as "a notoriously loyal man, devoted to the Union." Indeed, they considered his loyalty so "well known" that they suspended their standard practice of recounting the testimony in their report to Congress and "simply refer[red] to the evidence."[5]

But Segar had possessed sympathies that were not Union down to the bottom of his soul. In his antebellum speeches while a Virginia state legislator, he had expressed doubts about the Union and experimented with state sovereignty. During the debates over the Mexican cession, Segar offered support for some form of secession. He identified the states as "coequal sovereignties" and the federal government as "the general agent of these coequal sovereignties." If the Union ceased to guarantee his state "liberty and equal right," he vowed, "I would see even this Union dashed into fragments forever!"[6] By the secession crisis, however, Segar changed his mind. He renounced his earlier espousal of state sovereignty as folly: "This doctrine, so flattering to State pride, I confess I have not been altogether averse to falling into ... but it never had from me that assent which is founded in deliberate investigation, and honest conviction." Only with "this startling issue of the life or death of the government" did he finally fully consider, and ultimately repudiate, the doctrine of secession.[7] The commissioners, with a chronology starting in 1860, did not solicit testimony on claimants' stance during the sectional crises of the 1830s, 1840s, and 1850s. Segar opted to omit an explanation of his shifting positions to the commissioners and to instead present himself as continuously anti-secessionist.

Segar also chose to censor his antebellum defense of slavery. His views on slavery had determined his position on sovereignty and secession throughout his political career. In the 1830s and 1840s, Segar embraced state sovereignty because he believed that the federal government threatened slavery. He particularly resented continuing efforts to pass the Wilmot Proviso, which prohibited slavery in any territory gained in the Mexican-American War; he described such strategems "as an entering wedge to rive into fragments the whole institution of slavery."[8] During the secession crisis, Segar reassessed the Union as "the great bulwark of slavery."[9] He realized that the South had successfully dictated federal policy to ensure the return of fugitive slaves, equal treatment in the territories, and protection for slavery in the states. Secession, not the Union, threatened the "sure doom of the great southern institution of slavery."[10] His prewar political writings demonstrate that Segar, like many white southerners, accepted disunion when the Union threatened slavery and spurned disunion when the Union protected slavery.[11] After the war, Segar shifted his pronouncements on slavery, no longer celebrating it as "the great southern institution" and instead praising God for its abolition. In a political speech soon after the passage of the Reconstruction Act, he urged white southerners to accustom themselves to emancipation and support political and legal equality for freedmen.[12] By the time he appeared before the commission, Segar had reconciled himself to a Union without slavery. He recognized that the Union cause had transformed to encompass not just the suppression of secession but also the abolition of slavery. He accordingly supported emancipation and equality in his politicking, and he further demonstrated his acquiescence before the commission by refraining from remonstrating the federal government for its abolitionist policies. In keeping with their general practice, the commissioners did not ask Segar about slavery, and he did not volunteer his opinions. If a claimant kept slavery out of his testimony, the commissioners likewise neglected the issue. Under these circumstances, antebellum proslavery sympathies did not impede recognition of postwar loyal citizenship.

Bold, outspoken, uncompromising Union men not only declared Union sympathies, they put them into practice. Votes for the Union served as one way that a white southern man could emphasize that he had manfully fulfilled his obligations to the Union. The commissioners included interrogatories on votes, especially on secession, in all three versions of their interrogatories.[13] Over and over again, white southern men testified that they had voted for Union delegates to state constitutional conventions. They presented these votes as attempts to keep their states within the Union and thwart the movement toward secession.[14] White southern men also asserted that they had voted against secession in the states where the question had been submitted to the people. They depicted these votes less as political acts to preserve the Union and more as political statements to defy Confederate authority. For example, by the time secession had been put to the people in Virginia, the state had already been named the capital of the Confederacy and its citizens had already begun preparations for war. Aldridge James, a paralyzed Virginia planter, recounted his insistence that he be carried five miles to the polls – "I would have gone ten times five miles" – for the sole purpose of registering his "decided … union proclivities."[15]

Military service provided a key means through which white male claimants could prove that they had served their country and, moreover, had risked their lives in doing so. The commissioners included questions on Union military service in all three versions of their interrogatories.[16] In their appearance before the commission, white southern men related dramatic tales of their flight to Union lines to enlist in Union service. Melvin B. Carr testified that he had twice tried to escape from northern Alabama to Union lines in Georgia to serve the Union as a soldier. Confederates arrested him, foiling his first attempt. "But in less than half an hour, I got a chance to break from them and having a splendid horse, I outran them and escaped and came back to my father's." A family slave assisted him and his brothers in his second, successful, effort. The former slave recounted, "we traveled in the night fifteen miles" through hard rain. They needed to cross the Coosa River to approach Union lines and fortunately spotted a canoe on the opposite bank. Carr swam across, retrieved the canoe, and ferried his brothers to the other side. He then traveled to Indiana where he enlisted in the Indiana Cavalry, serving from October 1864 to July 1865.[17]

The commissioners expected that citizens owed obligations to the Union, and they regarded voting and especially military service as the most valuable contributions. With the expansion of the electorate in the antebellum era, white men assumed responsibilities as voters. The commissioners routinely commented on the vote that mattered most to them: on the ratification of the various ordinances of secession. They also cited votes for candidates for the presidency in 1860 and the state constitutional conventions in 1860 and 1861 in response to claimants' emphasis on these actions. The commissioners regarded military service as the ultimate sacrifice, focusing on it from the outset of their tenure. They informed Congress that "of the claimants found loyal, many … have actually served in the Union Army, many have aided our military operations as scouts and guides, and in other ways."[18] According to their counts, 10 percent of claimants relied on evidence that they had volunteered for Union military service.[19] They considered Union military service to be the only contribution significant enough to tally for reporting purposes to Congress. They did not bother to register any other contributions to the

Union cause (although they maintained statistics on various contributions to the Confederate cause). The commissioners regarded voting and soldiering as the quintessential acts, and the most unequivocal proof, of a loyal citizen. Such evidence, without any indication of disloyal sympathies or contributions, was generally sufficient for recognition as a Union man.

Public expressions of Union sympathy and public performance of Union obligations had earned white southern men notoriety as Union men and, consequently, had incurred Confederate persecution. In all three versions of their interrogatories, the commissioners queried witnesses on the public reputation of the claimant for loyalty or disloyalty, and they asked claimants if they had suffered any Confederate harassment.[20] William Mitchell could certify that his neighbor had been a Union man because Confederates had harassed him. Mitchell speculated, "I don't think there was another loyal man for miles, if there was they never showed their hands."[21] Outspoken Union men had shown their hands and, in the process, had endangered their necks. White male claimants emphasized that their political support of the Union during the secession crisis spurred retaliation and, in this way, demonstrated that they had promoted the public good over their private interest. John T. Bailey, a farmer in northern Alabama, recounted that he "was taken by the Rebel Soldiers from my home and hanged three times and left for dead" and "was also shot at three or four times during the war by the Rebel Soldiers."[22]

The commissioners considered evidence of Union reputation and Confederate persecution as key indications that a white Union man had sympathized with, contributed to, and sacrificed for his country in a courageous and principled manner. Over and over again, the commissioners noted in their reports to Congress that witnesses "testify to his loyal conversation and reputation" and that claimants had been the victims of Confederate oppression. The commissioners' attention to reputation and harassment highlights the public nature of their understanding of loyal citizenship: it had be performed in the public sphere and recognized by both friend and foe alike. Such men had not hidden their Union sympathies or refrained from assisting the Union cause out of fear of being marked and persecuted as a Union man. For the commissioners, the combination of proof of Union sympathies and contributions with indications of Union reputation and Confederate persecution transformed Union men into "bold outspoken uncompromising Union men."[23]

The commissioners sympathized with the "peril, hardship, sacrifice, and suffering" experienced by Unionists and praised them for their "steadfast courage and patriotic devotion to the Union, which do them honor and entitle them to the grateful consideration of the Government."[24] The federal government through the Southern Claims Commission rewarded "bold outspoken uncompromising Union men" who had served the public and not just private interest in a public and not just private manner with remuneration for their wartime sacrifices. These men had regarded secession as reckless and had favored the preservation of the Union. Even more, they had translated their sympathies into actions. Through their politicking, voting, and soldiering, these men contributed to the Union cause. In doing so, they had earned Confederate enmity and had placed themselves and their families at risk for their nation. The commissioners celebrated these southerners as uncompromising heroes who, by virtue of their manly bravery in the face of Confederate repression, deserved the full benefits of postwar citizenship.

"At Heart a Union Man"

In his appearance before the commission, David J. Garber of Virginia's Shenandoah Valley insisted, "I sympathized for the Union." Garber, however, had not publicly performed his obligations to the Union. He could not tell daring tales of his trials as a Union voter or his exploits as a Union soldier.[25] Garber had resided in an area well known to the commissioners for its intense level of Confederate persecution, so severe that they routinely excused claimants for failing to fulfill their obligations to the Union and even for acting in favor of the Confederacy.[26] Claimants like Garber convinced the commissioners that "bold outspoken uncompromising" loyalty to the Union had not always been possible. The commissioners were forced to acknowledge that Garber had been "at heart a Union man" who, as a result of Confederate persecution, had offered only covert assistance to the Union, but nevertheless deserved recompense. In doing so, they conceded that loyal citizenship could sometimes be secretly sustained but not publicly expressed.[27]

The relationship between private sympathies and public actions had been a source of contention among congressmen during debates over Reconstruction policies. As congressmen considered the reincorporation of white southerners into the Union after the war, they disputed the extent to which observers could fathom private sympathies from public actions and, more broadly, the extent to which private sympathies or public actions even mattered in determinations of loyalty. Some Republicans distrusted white southern men who claimed loyalty, and they argued that the federal government could only assess public action during the war, and not private sympathy.[28] Other Republicans argued that even if they accepted professed Union sympathies as sincere, they could not excuse Confederate conduct because, as one argued, the "morality" of the act did not change the "fact" of the act.[29] Most Republicans, however, accepted that Union sympathies combined with specific evidence of Confederate coercion could excuse the occasional performance of a Confederate service.[30] On the other side, some Democrats argued that determinations of loyalty, whether discerned from sympathies or actions, were really just Republican efforts to empower their party. In line with support for future loyalty as the condition for the restoration of citizenship, they regarded assertions of Union sympathies as evidence of loyal citizenship sufficient to excuse Confederate actions. One congressman suggested that only the man himself could know his own true sympathies in regard to loyalty and that the federal government should therefore accept a man's word.³¹ Debates over loyalty in the postwar context became debates over the "metaphysical," as the *Nation* ridiculed it, about whether or not loyalty was knowable by third parties.³²

At the beginning of their tenure, in formulating their standards for loyal citizenship, the commissioners insisted that they could indeed know southerners' loyalties. They required claimants to prove both private sympathies and, more stringently, public actions for the Union. Like most of their party, they discounted the level of coercion that southern Unionists had faced and therefore rejected a broad definition of duress. They did not even include an interrogatory in their first version that addressed any force or threat that may have compelled disloyal actions, probably to discourage claimants from offering excuses for their conduct. In response to claimants who insisted that "they were really loyal at heart, but acted under duress," the commissioners dismissed the pretext that white men "could not get away, and would have been taken by force if they had not gone without force, and therefore they yielded and went into the rebel service, apparently but not really of their free will." They defined duress as "actual force used against the claimant, or *imminent* danger of *immediate*, *forcible*, and *serious* injury."³³

Despite the commissioners' initially limited understanding of duress, claimants persisted in representing themselves as heartfelt Union men. They essentially suggested that their projected selves during the war had not aligned with their real selves. In making these arguments, white southern men spurned traditions of southern honor that ranked the external over the internal. An honorable man considered "giving the lie" – that is, charges that appearance and reality did not coincide – the worst insult. Indeed, a distinguishing feature that had separated white southern men from slaves was that slaves' projected and real selves never corresponded. To acknowledge that one's real and projected self did not match up was to dishonor oneself and to position oneself akin to a slave. White southern men who had secretly harbored Union sympathies but had publicly professed devotion to the Confederacy may have embraced an interpretation of lying more frequently associated with the North: one that prioritized practicalities, like profit and loss, rather than principles, like honor or dishonor.³⁴

After two years in operation, in response to claimants' stories of Confederate coercion, the commissioners reassessed their practice of strictly equating disloyal actions with disloyal sympathies by easing their definition of duress. They acknowledged that loyal citizens in the South had faced a level of coercion "not fully appreciated by us at first." Exposure to southerners' stories convinced them that the duress experienced by loyal citizens "is rarely of actual force, or of danger from the action of the constituted authorities," but instead that "the real imminent danger of injury" originated with the "terrorism and intimidation" of "constant and oppressive apprehension of lawless violence." As a result, they acknowledged that "men who were at heart true friends of the Union felt compelled to appear friendly to the confederate cause and to do disloyal acts."[35] The commissioners' more lenient definition of duress became standard. They devoted more attention to duress in their interrogatories, adding a question to their 1874 version on the "force, compulsion, or influence ... used to make you do anything against the Union cause."[36]

The "reign of terror" that had prevailed at the Mt. Crawford poll in Rockingham County, Virginia, during the vote on the ratification of the ordinance of secession provides the perfect example of duress that had not comprised "actual force" but rather "constant and oppressive apprehension of lawless violence." A military company surrounded the polls on Election Day. One man dared to vote against the ordinance of secession. Confederates pursued him for more than a mile before capturing him, carrying him back to the polls, and forcing him to rescind his vote. In their postwar testimony, several white male claimants recounted the scene at the Mt. Crawford poll and, even though some had not experienced actual force themselves, explained that they had not voted at all or had voted for the ordinance out of fear for their lives.[37] Claimants convinced the commissioners that Mt. Crawford had been a site of terrorist violence and lawlessness. In such cases, the commissioners attributed loyal inaction and disloyal action to defective southern communities rather than deficient citizens.

Claimants secured forgiveness when *"the whole tenor of the claimant's conduct before and after* shows him to have been really loyal" and "perhaps the sufferings and losses he was afterward subjected to by the rebels show that they regarded him as an enemy."[38] Typically, a claimant argued that he had actively opposed the Confederacy, often during the secession crisis, and thereby earned a public reputation for loyalty and provoked the wrath of his Confederate neighbors. As a result, the claimant was then only able to offer clandestine assistance to the Union cause and was often forced into some token show of support for the Confederate cause. Joseph Beery of the Shenandoah Valley in Virginia depicted himself as a heartfelt Union man who had only pretended Confederate allegiances. He offered both overt and covert contributions to the Union, voting against secession at his precinct and persuading and assisting Union men to escape to Union lines. He chose to privately, but not publicly, resist Confederate conscription. He furnished a substitute to fight for his son, but he encouraged the substitute to desert. When the plan backfired and the substitute reported him, he agreed to swear an oath of allegiance to the Confederacy to secure release from jail.[39] In their postwar claims, conscientious objectors received the most leniency in judgments involving duress. Dunkards, Mennonites, and Quakers in the Confederacy, as pacifists, had refused to bear arms against the Union. Jackson M. Jones of the North Carolina piedmont testified that he had secured an exemption from military service as a Quaker but that he had still been forced into the Confederate ranks because of his Union sympathies. "While there the roll was called and orders were given to fall into line, which I refused to do and was then knocked down with the breach of a musket. I was also pierced in the thigh and side with a bayonet and left without food or water for three days and nights," nearly dying from "cruel and brutal" treatment.[40]

The commissioners only excused disloyal action under conditions of violence. Martin Miligan of Alabama admitted that he had worked in a Confederate saltpeter cave but declared that he had accepted the employment to feed his starving family. The commissioners acknowledged that Miligan had found himself in "a hard position to be in, the pressure of poverty, but we think it cannot be regarded as the duress which in law excuses a disloyal act." They felt constrained to rule against Miligan, admitting that "we feel our sympathies moved for Mr. Miligan, but we do not see how we can legally excuse the disloyal act."[41] Less sympathetically, the commissioners ruled against another claimant who had been employed by the Confederate army, commenting that "the plea that he excuses the act upon, that he had a large family to support, would no more justify treason than a similar plea would have justified Judas Iscariot for selling his master for thirty pieces of silver. Most men need money for urgent reasons, but that is a miserable plea to justify treason."[42] American leaders had traditionally viewed economic dependence as a disqualification for virtuous citizenship. According to this logic, poor men made poor citizens precisely because they were economically beholden to an employer or a landlord and therefore could not render independent and principled political opinions. The commissioners expected loyal citizens to have sacrificed their private interest for the public good, and they therefore refused to accept economic need as a form of duress.

The more lenient definition of duress did not signal that the commissioners had abandoned their requirement for active citizenship. They recognized that loyal citizenship in the South could not just be assessed through public proclamations and performances, but they still required that white southern men offer some proof that they had performed their obligations to their nation. "A man must say enough or do enough to excite some such suspicions in the minds of some of his neighbors," the commissioners dictated, "in order to furnish the satisfactory evidence of his loyalty."[43] They assumed that a white southern man who had been persecuted must have performed some Union service to have gained a Union reputation and to have incurred such treatment.

The commissioners began their tenure with a relatively narrow set of ways that white southern men could prove their loyal citizenship. Within the first few years of their tenure, "at heart Union men" convinced the commissioners to ease their standards. They asserted that they had supported the Union but that Confederate persecution had prevented them from aligning their public actions with their private sympathies. At claimants' prompting, the commissioners accepted that Confederate terror had prevented some good Union men from contributing to the Union war effort and had compelled them to contribute to the Confederate war effort. They did so, however, generally when white male claimants could prove covert Union conduct and Confederate persecution. In this way, the commissioners modified, but retained, their requirement for active citizenship in opposition to secession.

"Independent Rebel and Traitor"

Reuben H. J. Garland, a Georgia farmer and "railroader," declared to the commissioners that, although he had been opposed to secession, his "sympathies were with the state and its cause" after the outbreak of war because "he did not want to see his state overthrown." He also admitted that he had supported the Confederate military by providing funds and provisions to friends and relatives in the Confederate army and raising money to outfit a company of Confederate soldiers and had sustained the Confederate economy by accepting Confederate bonds in trade and collecting taxes for the railroad. The commissioners marveled that "after swearing to all this, the independent rebel and traitor has the 'cheek' to ask the Government of the United States to treat him as a loyal adherent to the Union and the Government during the war."[44] To expose such "independent rebels and traitors," the commissioners directed their interrogatories to uncover the numerous ways in which white southern men had assisted the Confederacy. In response, white male claimants offered a variety of excuses for their disloyal actions, which the commissioners summarily rebuffed. The commissioners' condemnation of "independent rebels and traitors," like their praise of "bold outspoken uncompromising Union men," reinforced the active component of official citizenship.

Many Republicans in the North and West, the commissioners included, readily accepted that white southern men, even though they had laid down their weapons, continued to cherish Confederate allegiances, often disguised under a Union veneer. During the debates preceding the creation of the commission, Senator George H. Williams, a Republican of Oregon, posited that "a person in the South, considering this war on our part was wanton and wicked, and believing that all the calamities which were brought upon the South by its prosecution were the work of tyranny" would view himself justified in "resorting to any means to make himself even with the Government." Murders of black and white Unionists in the South during Reconstruction with the sanction of southern communities convinced Williams that former Confederates had not been "particularly scrupulous about the means which they have employed for the purpose of redressing their supposed grievances." Masked night riding during Reconstruction also demonstrated that former Confederates did not hesitate to conceal their identities to terrorize black and white Unionists. In this context, Williams argued that "it will be impossible … to distinguish between the friends and the enemies of the country if you undertake to pay these claims."[45]

To guard against rebels and traitors benefiting from their commission, the commissioners placed the burden of proof on claimants. Because they regarded voluntary residence in an insurrectionary state as evidence of disloyalty, claimants had to prove their loyalty.[46] The commissioners had little trouble imagining the various ways white southern men could assist the Confederacy, packing their interrogatories with references to disloyal deeds. Altogether, twenty-five of the thirty-four items in their first version covered claimants' participation in almost every aspect of Confederate services.[47] In the second and third versions, the commissioners drastically increased the list by adding disloyal actions they had somehow neglected in the first. These interrogatories built on a significant wartime and postwar inheritance of loyalty testing by encompassing many of the disloyal classes prohibited from amnesty, voting, and officeholding in state and federal policy.[48] The commissioners disallowed as many as 40 percent of all claimants on charges that they had offered aid and comfort to the enemy.[49] They considered Confederate military or civil service, a vote for secession, and an oath of allegiance to the Confederacy as the most unequivocal indications of disloyalty. Altogether, about 20 percent of rejected claimants fell in one or more of these categories.[50] Other justifications for denial included selling supplies to the Confederacy, purchasing Confederate bonds, receiving wages for Confederate services, and contributing to the outfitting of Confederate soldiers.[51] From the commissioners' perspective, these claimants, in performing these actions had acted as Confederate citizens.

White southern men before the commission attempted to recast disloyal acts as loyal acts usually with little success. Some argued that they had worked for the Union cause by encouraging desertion while serving as Confederate soldiers. Asa Daniel of Mississippi boasted that he had convinced 150 soldiers to return home during his one month in a Confederate camp.[52] Others insisted that they had accepted Confederate office to assist Union families. Thomas P. Lewis excused his term in the Alabama legislature in 1863 and 1864 because "the Union men of my county thought that I could be of more benefit to them in the Legislature, than out of it, and by so doing I could keep out of the rebel army and could support my family and help the Union men in my county."[53] Without additional evidence of loyalty, the commissioners dismissed stories of Union conspiracies to encourage desertion and "Union candidates" serving in Confederate office as "hardly credible" and "highly improbable."[54]

Former Confederates also unsuccessfully insisted that the commissioners' discriminations toward rebels and traitors were relics of the war. They rejected past loyalty in favor of future loyalty as the standard of citizenship and argued that their pardons and amnesty oaths restored their rights of citizenship, including their right to compensation for their wartime losses. John Hawk of Mississippi informed the commissioners, "I took the amnesty oath to the Union government in the year 1865 and claim that I am entitled to and received full pardon and amnesty for anything I might have done during the war."[55] Recipients presented their pardons and oaths as evidence of their status as loyal citizens of the reunited nation. The commissioners disapproved of the doctrine that pardon and amnesty obliterated treason. Orange Ferriss, one of the three commissioners, had served in the House of Representatives during President Johnson's impeachment trial. During the debate over the articles of impeachment, Ferriss had charged that "instead of punishing traitors, he [Johnson] has pardoned thousands." In doing so, Johnson had wronged the loyal people who had sacrificed their lives on the battlefields of the South to turn "vanquished rebels and their sympathizers" into his most "ardent admirers and earnest supporters."[56] Ferriss and the other commissioners refused to accept pardons as evidence of loyalty. Indeed, they considered an application for a pardon as evidence of disloyalty to the Union, noting that "pardons were granted ... to persons who had given aid and comfort to the rebellion" and that "Union men had no occasion to ask for pardon."[57]

"Independent rebels and traitors," like "bold outspoken uncompromising Union men," had fulfilled their political obligations to their nations, the former to the Confederacy and the latter to the Union. The commissioners condemned independent rebels and traitors for withdrawing their allegiances from the Union and bestowing them on the Confederacy. These white southern men could not meet the commissioners' standards of active citizenship in opposition to secession but could have met standards of active citizenship in defense of secession. Both good Union men and good Confederate men had voted in elections, served in the military, and accepted public office. They had supported opposing causes, but they had shared a similar conceptualization of the obligations of loyal citizens.

"An Amiable, Timid, Neutral Character"

From the commissioners' perspective, John N. Gatewood, a former Virginia slaveholder, presented little evidence in support of his contention that he had been "a Union man all the time." Gatewood could only offer that he had fed and nursed a sick Union officer and "never did anything to injure the Union cause." He had not voted against secession and had not enlisted in the Union army. From the commissioners' standpoint, Gatewood had not fulfilled his political obligations to the Union, a characteristic of a "bold outspoken uncompromising Union man." He also submitted no evidence of Confederate persecution to excuse what the commissioners regarded as his inaction, a commonalty of an "at heart Union man." At the same time, he had professed no sympathies and performed no services for the Confederacy, an attribute of an "independent rebel and traitor." Reviewing evidence that showed he had done little for the Union or the Confederacy, the commissioners denounced Gatewood as a "neutral," "timid," and "amiable" character. Such claims reveal a fundamental clash over the obligations loyal citizens owed to their nation and, more broadly, over the nature of politics as deferential or democratic.[58]

White male claimants who were vulnerable to charges of neutrality sometimes denied accountability for political affairs to embrace familial concerns. John T. Mitchell of Virginia admitted, "My feelings were not very strongly enlisted as I was too much occupied with taking care of my farm and managing my business to give much attention to the matter."[59] This orientation to private affairs might have been strengthened by wartime reassessments of masculine courage. Although many white male civilians and soldiers remained devoted to manly courage and its manifestation (acting on principle in defense of nation), many others learned that the vaunted courageous men often died or suffered first, whereas more pragmatic men survived to provide for their families. For these latter men, military service seemed to offer few rewards, as death and deprivation recognized no distinctions and conferred no immunities.[60] Many white male claimants regarded lying low as the wiser course for themselves and their families.

Condemnations of neutrality involved the commissioners' expectation that loyal citizens embrace public concerns, even at the expense of private affairs. The commissioners suspected that such claimants had not been conscientiously neutral but had been willing to sell their loyalties to the highest bidder. They charged that such claimants had "toted water on both shoulders," had "court[ed] the favor of the power in the ascendant," and had "serve[d] either side or anybody for a consideration."[61] They denounced them as "free and easy persons who without injury to their feelings or personal inconvenience can adapt themselves to any and all circumstances."[62] These men did not sacrifice self for nation but instead sacrificed nation for self. They did not stand for principles; indeed, they possessed no principles.

White male claimants susceptible to accusations of timidity rejected the commissioners' expectation of active citizenship. They offered a variety of excuses for their inability to support the Union. Some argued that their personal circumstances had prevented their service to the Union. Adam Fix of Virginia testified that he "did not vote either for or against the ordinance of secession, would have voted against it but I was sick."[63] Others contended that their isolation from the theaters of war had precluded them from offering their assistance to the Union war effort. Potential recruits who had resided in the Confederate interior had faced a dangerous journey to enlist in the Union army. Nicholas A. Carney in northwestern Arkansas insisted that "it was a good ways to the Union lines and a bad chance to get to them as the Rebels had the roads well guarded."[64] He did not mention that the Union army had fought several major battles nearby or that his county provided many soldiers to the Union cause. These claimants challenged the commissioners' understanding of citizenship in practice but not in theory. They did not identify an incapability to act as citizens, just an opportunity.

More challenging to the commissioners' requirement of active citizenship, other claimants who could be accused of timidity insisted that they had lacked not only the opportunity but the capability to assist the Union war effort. Over and over again, white male claimants repudiated public affairs, eschewing democratic in favor of deferential politics. They refused culpability for the war and placed the responsibility for politics strictly on politicians, repeatedly uttering statements such as "I was no politician" and so "I didn't take either side."[65] These claimants were often poor whites and yeomen who resided in plantation or high slaveholding districts where planter dominance was most assured rather than the nonplantation or low slaveholding districts where white male egalitarianism was more prevalent. The white men who disclaimed responsibility for politics explained their incapacity in various ways. Henry Ambos, a Georgia nonslaveholding farmer and fisherman, presented himself as politically powerless, contending that "when the State voted to secede I did not interfere one way or the other" as "it was-not-in-my-power to interfere against secession." John W. Edwards, a Virginia artisan, blamed his rudimentary education, noting that he "was confused and didn't know which was right" because he "had very little education."[66] These southerners rejected conceptualizations of white male citizenship rooted in political participation and political obligation, arguing that their ability to contribute to the Union war effort had been hindered by their marginal positions within southern society.

Condemnations of timidity highlight the commissioners' emphasis on white men's obligations to defend their nation in war. Assertions of Union sympathies, in their estimation, provided necessary, but not sufficient, evidence of qualification as loyal citizens. In weighing the testimony, "we invariably place more confidence in the conduct and acts of claimants" than in "their present professions of loyalty."[67] This is reflected in the overwhelming attention in the interrogatories to actions over sympathies. Over the years, as their interrogatories increased from thirty-four to fifty-three, the commissioners devised more and more questions on actions but retained only two questions on sympathies.[68] Arguing that "it is easier and more profitable to be loyal now than during the war," the commissioners often discounted words in favor of deeds in reaching their determinations.[69] The commissioners rejected one claimant because "he sat still, accepted the situation, and at the most simply sympathized."[70] They condemned another claimant as "a timid man who could not stand by his principles."[71] Although neither leaders nor followers, "timid" men, in the commissioners' accounting, shared culpability for the war. White men, they believed, owed their nation more than mere sympathy. Those who had remained undisturbed at home had not voted or fought to save their nation. They had not fulfilled their duties as citizens.[72] Angered that these white southern men had not done more to prevent rebellion and had not shown more independence, the commissioners condemned them as "distressingly quiet" and therefore complicit in secession.[73]

Most claimants who fell prey to dismissal for amiability had lived peacefully within their communities. They admitted that they had not suffered much persecution at the hands of their Confederate neighbors and had not been victimized by Confederate policies. Confederate hostility toward Unionists, although certainly pervasive, had not precluded cases of continuing friendships between southerners on opposite sides of the war. In certain instances, Confederates had shielded the property and the lives of their Union friends and had allowed known Unionists to live peaceably in their communities if they refrained from making themselves obnoxious to their neighbors.

The commissioners regarded amiable relations with Confederates as signs of Confederate allegiances. They rejected one claimant, in part, because "there are no indications that their confederate neighbors looked upon them as enemies of the confederate cause."[74] They assumed that Confederates had known the Union men in their midst, had not tolerated their presence, and had harassed them mercilessly. They condemned one claimant for "living quietly in a strong secession neighborhood," another for maintaining "a good social position" among his Confederate neighbors, and yet another for living "as happily and undisturbed in that Confederate community as his numerous Confederate neighbors."[75] Over and over again, the commissioners ruled against claimants who had not suffered the fate they imagined befell most Union men, unless they could demonstrate that they had been exempt from Confederate persecution as a result of some disability, such as mental or physical weakness, or circumstance, such as advanced age or prominent connections.[76]

The commissioners' rulings on neutral, timid, and amiable characters took place amid a momentous discussion over political authority in the postwar South. By the early 1870s, a growing consensus complained that limiting postwar political power in the South to those men who could prove wartime loyalties disqualified those best able to rule and empowered those least able to rule. To rectify these mistakes, the federal government granted amnesty to former Confederates and otherwise retreated from Reconstruction. The commissioners' banishment of neutral, timid, and amiable characters from the ranks of loyal citizens echoes a larger preoccupation with a certain brand of citizenship that facilitated the abandonment of the Reconstruction project. The imperatives of war had promoted military service on both sides as the quintessential act of loyal citizenship. The agreement on the importance of such forms of patriotic sacrifice contributed to the disempowerment of those dismissed as neutral, timid, and amiable men and the reempowerment of those once denigrated as rebels and traitors. The opposite of Union men were not Confederate men, but neutral, timid, and amiable men. Both Union men and Confederate men had supported their cause armed with courage, principles, and patriotism. Neutral, timid, and amiable men had shirked their duties. They had acted more as slaves and other dependents than free men.

"A Republican Since the War Closed"

James T. King, a Virginia physician, offered little evidence that he had fulfilled his obligations to the Union during the Civil War. He had voted for Union candidates to the secession convention when he had lived in Texas, but he had done little subsequently to contribute to the Union cause. He had not volunteered in the Union army, assisted Union men or Confederate deserters to escape to Union lines, or publicly praised the Union. He insisted that he "was cursed for my opinions all through the war and am so still" but did not offer harrowing tales of Confederate persecution. Despite the relatively sparse evidence in his favor, King declared himself "thoroughly loyal." He had held office during military reconstruction and had sworn the ironclad oath. Although the commissioners did not ask about postwar politics, he stressed, "I have been a Republican since the war closed." In response to King's emphasis on his postwar politics, the commissioners scoffed that "he and his witnesses say he is a republican now. So is Mosby."[77] Postwar Republican politics did not signal wartime Union allegiances, as the case of notorious rebel turned Republican John Singleton Mosby indicated. Claims by white southern men who identified themselves as "Republicans since the war closed" highlight the continuing postwar struggle for the fate of the Union.

Many claimants emphasized their postwar embrace of the Republican Party in explaining their loyal sympathies. Numerous claimants categorized themselves as postwar Republicans in their testimony before the commissioners. A few white male claimants even cited their support of radical Reconstruction, including the enfranchisement of black men, as proof of their status as loyal citizens. One claimant asserted, "I approve, so far as I understand, the amendments to the constitution of the United States, and the reconstruction acts passed by Congress."[78] In focusing on their Republican sympathies as proof of their status as loyal citizens, these claimants suggested that the issues of the war had not been settled at Appomattox and that the preservation of the Union was an ongoing process.

In recounting their loyal actions, many white male claimants cited their postwar Republican politics. Some equated anti-secessionist politics before and during the war with Republican politics after the war, identifying such actions as a continuing record of Union accomplishments. Reuben Matthews of North Carolina declared: "I never had a bit of sympathy for secession. I voted against it then, and now I vote the Republican ticket throughout. If I did not think the Republicans was for the Union I should not vote for them."[79] Others, especially those who had not been able to claim many wartime contributions to the Union, listed their postwar political offices. Thomas Nation of Alabama testified, "I held the election for our county under the Reconstruction act of Congress, and I am Deputy United States marshal for my county to take the late census."[80] In the ongoing struggle for the Union, these claimants cited their postwar Republican politics as evidence of their contributions to the cause.

White male claimants who identified themselves as postwar Republicans sometimes cited their persecution at the hands of vigilantes such as the Ku Klux Klan (KKK) as part of their claim to loyal citizenship. The commissioners asked about persecution by Confederates during the war, but these claimants cited their harassment by former Confederates after the war. Reuben Matthews of North Carolina interjected into his testimony, "I was never threatened during the war, but have been by the Ku Klux Klan since the war." He explained that he had been warned that he would have his head chopped off if he continued to vote the Republican ticket.[81] Similarly, Thomas Nation of Alabama informed the commissioners that he "was *Ku Kluxed* and it all originated on account of my Union sentiments." The KKK had dragged him from his bed one evening, made him "carry a negro girl a straddle of his neck," threatened to kill him, and dropped him in a ditch.[82] The claimants depicted KKK persecution as part of the continuing war between the friends and the enemies of the Union. Indeed, the KKK and similar movements served as efforts on the part of former Confederates to continue the Civil War in a guerrilla phase.[83]

Some postwar Republicans before the commission claimed loyal citizenship in what they hoped would be a new South. William A. Pattie, a Virginia merchant, had felt disfranchised in an antebellum southern society that had privileged slaveholders. He claimed that, during the secession vote, he had arrived at the polls, not to vote for secession but to inaugurate what he called a "revolution," one of nonslaveholders against slaveholders. A taxation measure passed by the Virginia Convention of 1861, the so-called Secession Convention, declared that "taxation shall be equal and uniform throughout the Commonwealth, and all property shall be taxed in proportion to its value." Prior to this measure, tax policy exempted slave property under the age of twelve and set a maximum valuation of only $300 on all other slave property.[84] Pattie carried his revolution into the postwar years through his Republican politics. Assistance from the federal government and affiliation with the Republican Party promised to mold the South in ways that would empower nonelites, white, and if necessary, black as well. He served as head of the Republican Party in his county and, in this capacity, secured the support of both white and black Unionists. In his postwar testimony, Pattie sought to claim a different South, one not associated with the Confederacy. He declared himself "a good southern man but not a southern sympathizer, nor a rebel."[85] In this new South, Pattie envisioned the Republican Party as a means of postwar empowerment for previously subordinated classes.

The commissioners dated the end of the war to the surrender of Confederate forces. In doing so, they rejected the positioning of Reconstruction as a second stage of the war and a continuing effort to secure Union victory. The commissioners usually ignored postwar sympathies, actions, and persecutions in their determinations of wartime loyalties. As they argued in one claim, "If the claimant has been at some time or is now as one of his witnesses intimates 'a black republican' it does not show that he remained during the war a loyal adherent to the Union Cause."[86] Democratic and Conservative opponents of the Southern Claims Commission charged that the commissioners would exploit their positions to reward southern Republicans. The rejection of claimants who relied on their Republican politics as their primary claim to loyal citizenship demonstrates that the commissioners did not use the claims process to secure political support for the national party by compensating southern Republicans.[87] Like the commissioners, many white Republicans in the North and West had little tolerance for white Republicans in the South, dismissing them as poor citizens who had been tardy and feeble in rallying to the cause. The commission reflected a larger trend in which northern and western Republicans marginalized southern Republicans within the party.[88]

Republican claimants who viewed postwar partisanship as a continuation of wartime disputes clashed with the commissioners who regarded the war as settled at Appomattox. Claimants who emphasized their Republican credentials reoriented the commissioners' interrogatories to embrace postwar contributions and address postwar persecution. Some southern Republicans viewed their embrace of the party as yet another stage in their struggle against the aristocratic slaveholders who had brought secession and ruin on the South. In response, the commissioners rejected the interpretation of the war as an ongoing partisan struggle. The debate over the role of postwar politics in determinations of loyal citizenship involved a larger dispute over whether the issues that had divided the nation were truly settled and whether victory had fully been achieved. The conceptualization of the war as a closed chapter of the American past contributed to a retreat from Reconstruction.

"Poor Hardworking People"

Simeon B. Shaw, a Virginia farmer, rooted his claim to loyal citizenship in his status as a "poor man." Shaw recounted his belief that Confederates waged war "in the interest of slavery." Without slave property to defend, he "regarded the war as altogether wrong and unnecessary." Moreover, he feared that "if the South had gained their independence, a poor man like [me] would stand no chance at all here."[89] Altogether, the evidence submitted in the claim labeled Simeon B. Shaw as, in the words of one witness, one of the "poor hard working people" who "had no sympathy with the slaveholders war on the union, or their attempt to break it up."[90] Claimants who identified themselves as some variation of "poor hardworking people" often presented the war as a contest waged for slavery in which they had possessed no stake. They devoted themselves to a specific iteration of the Union, one in line with their antislaveholder or antislavery proclivities. "Poor hardworking people" recognized the centrality of class, specifically the significance of a class-based disinterest in slavery, in determinations of loyal citizenship.

In their testimony before the commission, some yeomen and poor whites presented cases that emphasized they had little stake in defending slaveholders' property. Joseph Rozier, a South Carolina yeoman, insisted that "working white men here had no interest in the Slaveholders Rebellion."[91] For this reason, some former nonslaveholders had refused to fight on behalf of slavery. Thomas Staggs, a Tennessee farmer, explained, "I thought it was a war gotten up by the negro owners who wanted poor men like myself to do the fighting, but I thought this they themselves should do it, and I did not care what became of them."[92] Former nonslaveholders also argued that not only was a war to preserve slavery not to their advantage, but an independent Confederacy worked to their disadvantage. They represented themselves as an oppressed class and even compared themselves to slaves. Washington Holmes of Georgia reportedly believed that "if the rebels succeeded we would be ruined, would be no better than slaves."[93] A few former nonslaveholders, notably those from nonplantation districts, even claimed that they had supported the Union because they had opposed the institution of slavery. John J. Pass, a Georgia farmer, suggested that his nonslaveholding status had been a conscious decision rather than a pecuniary impossibility, declaring that he would never hold a slave in bondage even if he had "the wealth of the richest man in the world." Pass contended, "I was always opposed to holding human beings in bondage, was always opposed to the institution of slavery as it existed in this country." Former nonslaveholders who claimed antislavery sentiments frequently stressed that they had "always" opposed the institution, possibly to distinguish themselves from former slaveholders who, after the war, publicly proclaimed themselves pleased to be rid of their burdensome slave property.[94]

Yeomen and poor whites offered various reasons for their opposition to slavery. Pass asserted that he "thought it was a curse to the country," which could only be purged through emancipation and colonization.[95] Jacob Brunk of Virginia, a member of the Mennonite religious sect, affirmed himself as "conscientiously opposed to slavery."[96] Allen Ellis, a North Carolina farmer, carpenter, and minister, sounded little different from a northern abolitionist with his avowal that "bondage of man was unlawful and wrong."[97] George W. Joy, a native of Vermont transplanted to Virginia, traced his antislavery sentiments to his northern origins, swearing, "I was a Union man from the beginning – an abolitionist and anti-slavery man before the war, and I think I stand about that way today."[98]

Most nonslaveholders, however, had been interested in slavery. Before and during the war, nonslaveholders benefited from and contributed to the institution. Nonslaveholders relied on hired slaves for labor on their farms and businesses and on public hands for labor on public works such as roads and bridges. Additionally, the institution of slavery spurred the economic development of the South for all white southerners through slave trading and ancillary activities involving bankers, lawyers, factors, doctors, clothiers, farmers, blacksmiths, shippers, and insurers. In the plantation districts, yeomen and poor whites were embedded in the institution despite their small or nonexistent slaveholdings. Some coveted property in slaves before the war, and others were interested in the slavery either through patronage or kinship ties. White men, both slaveholders and nonslaveholders, could also find common cause as masters of dependents, both enslaved and free. In nonplantation districts of the mountains, the piney woods, and the hill country, yeomen and poor whites harbored a more ambivalent attitude toward slavery, disdaining abolitionism and embracing white supremacy but also resenting the political power that the institution afforded wealthy slaveholders. Few yeomen and poor whites, then, had been abolitionists. They may have harbored doubts about slavery and may have genuinely detested the institution and the privileges it bestowed on the slaveholding class, but they probably could not imagine solutions to all the problems that proslavery ideologues anticipated emancipation would entail.[99] However, this all changed with the abolition of slavery. Emancipation meant that former nonslaveholders no longer discerned any benefit from a slaveholders' republic and could more unanimously pronounce the institution and the war as antithetical to their interests.

In their testimony before the commission, some former nonslaveholders offered evidence that they had fulfilled their obligations to an antislavery Union. Henry Ambos, a Georgia farmer and fisherman, called a former slave as a witness in his claim. Joseph Brown, one of three black witnesses, reported that secessionists had suspected that Ambos had encouraged slaves to escape from their masters. Brown testified that he had fled from his master with Ambos's assistance.[100] William Drake of Virginia submitted evidence that he accorded former slaves at least a small measure of equality. John Hunt, a black neighbor, related: "When I go to his house I am treated just the same as though I was white." He concluded, "I honestly believe he was a loyal man to the Union and his treatment of our colored people before during and since the war bear me out in this opinion."[101]

Former nonslaveholders who emphasized their antislavery or antislaveholder sympathies or actions redrew the lines of division in the South. Before and during the war, slaveholders had fostered antipathy between yeomen and poor whites and slaves. Southern state legislators routinely passed laws cracking down on economic and social interactions between white and black southerners. Although the vast majority of white southerners supported the preservation of the institution of slavery, some nonslaveholders interacted with slaves and free blacks, even living and bearing children together.[102] Recounting sympathies with slaves or antipathies toward slaveholders as part of their postwar claims to loyal citizenship rejected slaveholders' identification of race as the preeminent division within southern society, thwarted slaveholders' dictates concerning slavery, and allied them with slaves against slaveholders in the slaveholders' war.

The commissioners generally considered claimants' status as former nonslaveholders, and any antislavery sympathies they may have possessed and antislavery actions they may have performed, as irrelevant. They did not include any interrogatories asking former nonslaveholders about their interest in slavery, their actions to protect or attack the institution, or their relationships with and opinions on slaves or slaveholders. When confronted with such testimony, the commissioners often ignored suggestions of a claimant's opposition to slavery, neglecting or dismissing such evidence in their reports to Congress. In one claim, they noted: "He may have been, as he says, opposed to slavery... But we fail to discover any evidences of Unionism."[103] The commissioners also rejected former nonslaveholders' redrawing of the South on class rather than race lines. They could not conceive that white southerners had been able to maintain meaningful interactions with black southerners. They disregarded one claimant's witnesses as "four colored persons, who had been slaves ... and whose means of information were slight, and whose statements are quite unsatisfactory," even though one black witness had known the claimant for twenty-two years.[104] The commissioners refused to accept that black witnesses could be in a position to know much about their white neighbors.

Many nonelite white southern men, both poor whites and yeomen, depicted themselves as a dispossessed underclass. "Poor hardworking people" argued that they had no interest or influence in the slaveholders' war. These claimants emphasized their antipathies toward slaveholders, sympathies toward slaves, and antislavery actions in their continuing fight to claim a stake in the emerging order of the postwar South. The commissioners, however, refused to recognize the relevance of such evidence to loyal citizenship. They adhered to a class-blind active citizenship based on white men's political obligations to suppress secession while nonelite white southern men advanced a class-conscious ideological citizenship rooted in antislaveholder or antislavery proclivities.

"Once a Slaveholder"

In his appearance before the commission, William L. Shackleford of Virginia claimed that he harbored "no sympathy with the rebellion nor with the rebel democracy who inaugurated the war." He insisted, "I adhered to the Union side all the time and do still." However, Shackleford doubted that other Union men would acknowledge that he had shared their cause. He explained that the Sherman brothers, two well-known Union men in his neighborhood, would probably refuse to recognize him as a Union man because "I was once a slaveholder and they didn't believe in slavery and may be prejudiced against me."[105] Many witnesses before the commission, like the Sherman brothers, linked slaveholding with allegiances during the war. Shackleford feared that his status as "once a slaveholder" impeded his claims to loyal citizenship. In the antebellum era, slaveholders' mastery over dependents, especially slave dependents, had constituted one of the crucial measures and facilitators of independence. With emancipation, former slaveholders had to recalibrate their understanding of their membership in the Union. Claims by white southern men who emphasized their status as former slaveholders highlight the continuing struggle over the meaning of the Union in the postwar years.

The commissioners did not query former slaveholders about the causes of the war, including opinions on controversies involving the constitutionality of slavery, the institution in the territories, the future of slavery in the slave states, fugitive slaves in the North, the status of slaves in the free states, or the Atlantic slave trade; their economic, political, or social interest in the institution; their relationships with slaves, free blacks, yeomen, or poor whites; or their positions on Reconstruction legislation, including emancipation, civil rights, and citizenship. In this manner, the commissioners ignored the most controversial issues that had motivated most white southerners from slaveholding families in the prewar, war, and postwar years. Former slaveholders who raised the issue of slavery in their testimony primarily did so at their own instigation.

A few former slaveholders before the commission represented themselves as reconstructed by insisting that they had possessed antislavery sympathies and that they had therefore supported the antislavery Union. Samuel Norris, a former North Carolina slaveholder who had owned five slaves at surrender, condemned "the war as the greatest evil, and slavery as it existed here as next to it."[106] Before and during the war, few slaveholders had actually favored the abolition of slavery. Some slaveholders harbored abstract reservations about the institution of slavery, but these doubts rarely translated into practical actions. They may have accepted emancipation for favored slaves, but few condoned general abolition, given the South's reliance on slaves as plantation labor and the predictions of race mixing and race war. At most, these slaveholders hoped that slavery would eventually die out through colonization of freed slaves to Africa or "diffusion" of the institution to the West. When expansion served to strengthen the institution, these slaveholders offered few other plans to eradicate the institution and effectively accepted it as a necessary evil. These sentiments grew more prevalent in the upper South as the result of republican ideals, evangelical Christianity, and economic diversity. Doubts hardly plagued slaveholders in the lower South, where the dominance and profitability of cotton and sugar cultivation strengthened the defense of the institution, shaping both republicanism and evangelicalism to its dictates.[107] Former slaveholders who cited their antislavery sympathies in their testimony before the commission may have genuinely disliked the institution in the tepid manner of upper South critics, they may have remembered earlier misgivings about the institution with more intensity and less ambivalence, or they may have perjured themselves in an attempt to gain compensation for their wartime losses. In any case, they hoped to endear themselves to the commissioners with their antislavery expressions.

In their testimony, former slaveholders more commonly portrayed themselves as reconstructed loyal citizens by asserting their postwar acceptance of Reconstruction policies. John H. Bowles of Virginia admitted, "I hated very much to lose my negroes," but conceded that "on the whole was satisfied with the way in which the war terminated."[108] Former slaveholders also, although far less frequently, indicated their reconstructed position by claiming to support racial equality. David Young, a former Georgia slaveholder, argued that "a black man was just as good as a white man, if he behaved as well."[109] Wishing to reconcile with the Union and possibly gain a little money, these former slaveholders presented themselves as good citizens who accepted the dictates of the federal government on emancipation and equality. In insisting that they had complied with emancipation, they met the minimum requirements for restoration of citizenship as stipulated by both Lincoln and Johnson. In asserting that they supported black enfranchisement, former slaveholders gave tacit acknowledgement to the radical Republican argument that black rights were an integral war goal without which victory would not be complete. Such concessions to the federal government were often disingenuous, as former Confederates advised one another to appease the conqueror and bide their time until the North lost interest in Reconstruction.[110] Whether sincere or not, these former slaveholders believed that an acceptance of emancipation or equality signaled their status as loyal citizens of the reunited nation.

In contrast to those who either avoided discussion of slavery or portrayed themselves as reconstructed on the issue, some former slaveholders refused to concede the illegitimacy of the institution and accept emancipation let alone equality. The proslavery argument was wide ranging. In the antebellum era, slaveholders had developed elaborate defenses of the institution. By the 1850s, many ideologues rejected the notion of slavery as a necessary evil and promoted slavery as a positive good. According to this argument, slavery benefited both slave and slaveholder. As a paternalistic system of reciprocal obligations, slaveholders treated their servants like dependent family members, and slaves rendered unto their masters their obedience and devotion.[111] Before the commission, the justness of the institution as a positive good to slaves did not figure prominently in former masters' explanations of their proslavery stances during the war.[112] Slaves' defection to the Union side en masse whenever the opportunity had arisen may have alienated former slaveholders from even their most favored "servants." In their testimony before the commission, unreconstructed former slaveholders defended their constitutional right to protect their economic investment in the institution. John Underwood Brown, an Alabama planter, as part of his assertion of his status as a loyal citizen, admitted, "I was in favor of secession" because "I had a great deal of property and considerable slave property, about a hundred and twenty negroes, and I wanted to save all this." Brown considered himself entitled to his slave property: "I thought that the property I had worked for and bought was mine and that I was guaranteed its possession and protection under the constitution."[113] While stressing their rights to slave property, these former slaveholders revealed the central role that slavery played in their allegiances during the war and that mastery played in their conceptualizations of their citizenship after the war.

Proslavery former slaveholders claimed and disclaimed different versions of the Union. Some unreconstructed former slaveholders represented the Union as proslavery and, on this basis, identified themselves as Unionists. William C. Lipscomb, a former Virginia slaveholder, presented the Union as the best means to preserve the institution. He remembered chiding secessionists that "if you had staid in your seats in Congress, why in the course of a year or two you would have had a majority there again." He concluded that "they ought never to have done it. They ought to have contended for their rights *in* the Union."[114] These former slaveholders' claimed a proslavery Union by addressing their sympathies during the secession crisis and the outbreak of war and omitting any discussion of their reaction to the federal government's policies toward slavery.

Other unreconstructed former slaveholders condemned the destruction of the proslavery Union and its degeneration into an antislavery Union. Wilson H. Dillon, a Mississippi planter, denounced the Emancipation Proclamation as "a most unjust measure," which punished thousands of innocent slaveholding Unionists for the crimes of secessionists "who brought the war upon us." After the proclamation, Dillon remembered that he "then did not care what the devil became of the country." Lincoln had betrayed the slaveholding Unionist who had stood by his nation. In response, Dillon had forsaken his country. He bristled, "It would have required more Christian forbearance than I possess to help a government that by its proclamation swept away a property that was constitutionally mine."[115] As the government had broken faith with them, former slaveholders felt justified in breaking faith with the Union by either turning toward the Confederacy or shifting toward neutrality.

Unreconstructed former slaveholders challenged the legitimacy of an antislavery Union. George Markham of Mississippi declared, "I wanted both slavery and the Union preserved." He rejected the commissioners' requirement for unconditional support of the Union with his clarification: "If you mean by continuously sympathizing with the course of the Union, that I sympathized with the destruction of slavery I say very plainly, that I do not think that Mr. Lincoln ought to have included the Union men's slaves in with those of the rebels." Markham conceded the impossibility "to have made the distinction while the war was going on." However, his qualification, "while the war was going on," exposed his hope that Union authorities would now compensate loyal former slaveholders for the "theft" of their slave property. His understanding of the Union, the entity to which he pledged devotion, did not involve the destruction of slavery and, indeed, would symbolically acknowledge his right to slave property through compensation.[116]

Some unreconstructed former slaveholders swore their devotion to a bygone proslavery Union. Robert Daniel, a Louisiana planter, felt justified in claiming compensation for his lost property because he "never desired the dissolution of the Union, and always considered the act of secession as a very unwise one." Daniel employed a particular definition of "the Union," however, carefully qualifying, "I sympathized with the efforts of the United States to restore the government as it was," but "I can not say as I could sympathize with the effort of the United States to restore the Union with the loss of the slaves."[117] The "government as it was," the "Union as formed by our fathers," and the "Union as it was" did not include the abolition of slavery or the civil rights agenda of Radical Republicans. Horatio Seymour, a prominent New York Democrat, coined "The Union as it was, and the Constitution as it is" after Lincoln issued the Preliminary Emancipation Proclamation, and it became the slogan for conservative Democrats for the remainder of the war.[118] In their

FIGURE 2.1. "The Union As It Was," 1874. As illustrated by a Thomas Nast cartoon in *Harper's Weekly*, a moderate Republican journal, in 1874, Republicans depicted southerners who supported "the Union as it was" as White Leaguers and Ku Klux Klan terrorists intent on imposing a white supremacist regime "worse than slavery," a system in which whites meted out violence to subjugate freedmen, women, and children.
Source: *Harper's Weekly*, October 24, 1874.

postwar testimony, these former slaveholders claimed a type of Unionism that had been perfectly acceptable to the federal government in 1861, but one that had been superceded by emancipationist policies. Former slaveholders who favored the "Union as it was" attempted to redeem a bygone Union, one that safeguarded white supremacy, if not slavery.

When claimants forced them to grapple with slavery, the commissioners recognized an antislavery Union but did not always reward its adherents. They looked favorably on reconstructed former slaveholders who expressed antislavery sympathies, accepted emancipation, and supported black rights, but they did not accept such evidence as sufficiently indicative of loyal citizenship. In one case, for example, they omitted from their report to Congress the claimant's evidence that he had supported the Union's emancipatory policies as irrelevant. On the other hand, the commissioners did reject claimants who professed proslavery sympathies. Holding slaves in bondage did not necessarily signal disloyalty, but criticizing emancipation did. They could not comprehend how claimants could repudiate Union policies of emancipation and still embrace the Union. In one case, they ruled that "the old gentleman goes on at great length to define his position, and it is extremely difficult to understand from his own statements how he could have been a Union man."[119] Republicans understood southerners who expressed support for slavery and devoted themselves to "the Union as it was" as White Leaguers and Ku Klux Klan terrorists intent on imposing a white supremacist regime "worse than slavery" (Figure 2.1).[120] At the very least, championing slavery lent a claim a tone of rebelliousness and defiance that the commissioners deemed unacceptable. The commissioners also disallowed claims if they discovered that claimants had acted to evade emancipation by removing their slaves from the reach of the Union army or by engaging in legal or economic transactions involving slave property after January 1, 1863. In one claim, they noted that "a Union man who had confidence in the Government of the United States and recognized its official acts as binding would hardly have bought a slave" after the Emancipation Proclamation.[121] Unreconstructed proslavery sympathies and actions constituted a repudiation of Union policy that invalidated loyal citizenship. The commissioners, like Andrew Johnson, considered acceptance of emancipation a minimum requirement for reunion.

The Civil War and Reconstruction forced a reassessment of the relationship between slaveholding and citizenship. Some former slaveholders depicted themselves as reconstructed, accepting the antislavery Union, whereas other former slaveholders emphasized themselves as unreconstructed, denouncing the antislavery Union. The commissioners were willing to ignore the issue of slavery but condemned unreconstructed slaveholders who were not. On one hand, they refused to accept antislavery sympathies and actions as sufficient evidence of loyalty. On the other hand, they regarded resistance to and protest of emancipation as evidence of disloyalty. Recognition as a loyal citizen did not require an explicit devotion to antislavery ideals, but it did require an implicit acceptance of abolition.

The commissioners envisioned ideal loyal citizens as independent white men acting on behalf of the common good. These men had publicly performed their political obligations to the Union, especially as Union voters or Union soldiers to combat secessionists. They could also prove that they had acted on behalf of the Union by providing evidence of secret contributions to the Union cause, public reputations for Union loyalties, or persecution by Confederates. Dependent white men, those who had perhaps sympathized with the Union cause but had failed to fulfill their obligations to it, were the antithesis of loyal citizens. The common good in the commissioners' conceptualization did not necessarily require the abolition of slavery or the establishment of racial equality. They did not consider antislavery sympathies or even actions as strong evidence of loyal citizenship, although they did expect claimants to refrain from harangues against emancipation. The commissioners' Union centered primarily on the suppression of secession.

White male claimants challenged the commissioners on the Union they were meant to defend and the means by which they were required to defend it. Some met the commissioners' standards by fulfilling their obligations as voters and soldiers to preserve the Union against the secessionists who sought to destroy it. Other white male claimants argued that Confederate persecution had prevented them from supporting the Union and, indeed, had forced them to contribute to the Confederacy. They insisted that they had not possessed the opportunity or capability to assist the Union cause. Still other white male claimants devoted themselves to an alternate Union, one dedicated to a set of antislavery or proslavery principles. Former nonslaveholders and even former slaveholders occasionally promoted an antislavery Union. Former slaveholders sometimes sought to resuscitate, at least symbolically, a proslavery Union. Though most white male claimants did not fit the commissioners' definition of loyal citizens or, for that matter, most historians', their efforts revealed their understandings of the Union and membership within it.

The claims process inadvertently facilitated a reconciliation that erased the significance of slavery. Former nonslaveholders did not secure an advantage by proving antislavery sympathies or antislavery actions. Former slaveholders who submitted claims to the commission could not escape the secession question, but could easily ignore the slavery issue. Most former slaveholders probably avoided dealing with slavery altogether by refraining from introducing the subject. Some former slaveholders made no effort to hide, and indeed felt compelled to declare, their resentment over what they regarded as the unjustifiable theft of their slave property. If slaveholders did not want the commissioners to hold their proslavery sympathies against them, however, they simply had to withhold their complaints about emancipation. When the commissioners condemned white southern men on the basis of their status as slaveholders, they usually did so because the claimants themselves raised the topic. White southern men were better off in the claims process – and, ultimately, in the reconciliation process – if they forgot the slavery controversy, as many white southerners by the turn of the century would do. Setting aside slavery as a source of division, northern and western Unionists ultimately shared more in terms of their conceptualization of citizenship with southern Confederates than with many self-professed southern Unionists. The commissioners' official citizenship eventually encouraged the celebration of devoted voters and soldiers on both sides.

3

Women's Union

Reckoning with the Female Union Man

Martha M. Wright of Mississippi testified before the Southern Claims Commission in 1876 that the Union was "good enough for us and I didn't believe we would ever get a better" one. However, she could offer little of what the commissioners considered strong evidence of loyal citizenship. She had not voted against secession or served as a soldier in the Union army. George W. Barrett, a witness, explained, "if she had been a man I couldn't say what she would have been," but, considering her gender, he judged that she had been opposed to the war. "As to her being what was called loyal in my view of what that was," he acknowledged, "I couldn't say whether she was or not."[1] A witness in another claim had so much trouble formulating a feminine or gender-neutral definition that he identified one woman as a "good Union man."[2]

Claimants and witnesses before the commission had so much trouble because loyalty and citizenship had traditionally been understood as the reserve of white men. According to the common law tradition of coverture, women possessed no individual relationship to the state unmediated by a father or a husband. Coverture came under attack in the antebellum era as courts held that married women could dissolve their allegiances independent of their husbands, but it remained influential as judges continued to rule that women's citizenship "naturally" followed their husbands'. According to the nineteenth-century ideology of "separate spheres," the cultural corollary to coverture, white women belonged in the private world of home and family, while white men belonged in the public world of business and politics. Although women's lives never matched gender ideology, especially in times of war, separate spheres nevertheless constituted a powerful metaphor for understanding women's place.[3] Together, coverture and separate spheres seemed to render a white woman's attempt to establish a direct relationship to the Union paradoxical.

The Southern Claims Commission forced a reckoning between contradictory impulses: the dictates of coverture and separate spheres and the necessity to prove loyal citizenship. The commissioners and the white female claimants who came before them handled these contradictory impulses with several patterns of representations of white southern women. "The rabidest kind of Union persons" rejected coverture and separate spheres and claimed independent politics. Wives and mothers with "nothing direct as to loyalty or disloyalty" preserved coverture by deriving citizenship through male relatives. White southern women who "took no part" affirmed separate spheres by claiming feminine domesticity and dismissing masculine politics. Disputes over what was considered "no more than natural" for white southern women exposed attempts to distinguish between women's domesticity and politics. Most white southern women achieved status as loyal citizens, not as independent actors who contributed to their nation, but as dependent subjects who suffered for their nation. Both official and vernacular citizenship attempted to resolve the paradox of women's citizenship in ways that preserved its basic dichotomies.

"The Rabidest Kind of a Union Person"

In her testimony before the commission, Lucretia C. Merry of Virginia swore that she "felt that the rebellion was very wrong, and did not want to see the government broken up." She had acted on her sympathies by speaking against the Confederacy and exerting her influence for the Union. In addition to feeding and nursing Union soldiers, she stated, "I always made it a point to convey all information to our troops that I thought might be of any benefit to them." In retaliation for her Unionism, she claimed, "The rebels threatened to arrest me, and also to shoot me." A Union spy corroborating her story declared, "I always considered her one of the strong Union persons" and indeed that "she had the reputation of being the rabidest kind of a Union person."[4] Merry confronted a set of interrogatories that imagined loyal citizens as white men, but she managed to prove that she had fulfilled her obligations to her nation. She was one of the minority of white female claimants who qualified as a loyal citizen without reference to the sympathies or contributions of a father, husband, or son. Claimants like Merry forced white men to reconsider the implicit masculinity of their standards. In acknowledging Merry as a "Union person," both the witness and the commissioners recognized that white men did not possess a monopoly on loyal citizenship.

In one respect, the commission's practices signaled a break with political coverture, which subsumed women's allegiances under their fathers' and husbands'. In the formal procedures laid out in the interrogatories, white female claimants who had owned the property at the time of its appropriation served as the primary actors in the claims process. The commissioners required these white southern women to testify to their own allegiances.[5] White female claimants who proved themselves loyal citizens independent of fathers or husbands met the challenge. In doing so, they addressed interrogatories originally conceived for men and answered them on their own account. Widowed, divorced, and other single women were best positioned to prove their loyal citizenship in this manner.

White female claimants who proved loyalty on their own account, like "bold outspoken uncompromising Union men," unhesitatingly embraced Union sympathies. Harriet J. Carey of Mississippi declared she had possessed "a most utter abhorrence" of secession and had considered it "a farce, and a very wicked thing." She further volunteered, despite her own status as a former slave mistress, that her "ideas of loyalty are not opposed to secession merely, but an approval of all the acts that established the freedom of the slaves." She did not associate herself with abolitionism – "you know we did not dare to call ourselves an abolitionist" – but she insisted, "Those were my sentiments always. I had an instinctive horror to the institution and looked upon it as going to be the bane of the country, if it was not checked." Indeed, she considered her support for "blotting slavery out of our government" and her identification of the institution as "evil" and "wicked" as the best test of her allegiances. Carey's political independence was likely nurtured by her economic independence. She operated a store that she had inherited from her husband on his death in 1849 and managed a plantation that she had purchased as an additional venture. Wives were bound by coverture, but widows were not. With both political and economic independence, Carey did not position herself as a woman who derived her allegiances from a father or a husband. Indeed, she made no reference to her male relatives or her gender in proving her loyal citizenship. Instead, she boldly claimed, not just opposition to secession, but also moral indictments condemning slavery and radical political positions securing freedom. Carey claimed opinions on the war, a matter traditionally reserved for men, without reference to men's opinions. Such testimony led the commissioners to praise evidence of her loyal citizenship as "unusually satisfactory."[6]

The most convincing white female claimants, like the most convincing white male claimants, also demonstrated that they had translated their sympathies into actions. Eliza Woodward of Virginia provided a compelling portrait of a woman who not only defied Confederate authority but patriarchal authority as well in her defense of her Union principles. Woodward, having married late in her forties, had arranged a marriage settlement that guaranteed her separate ownership and management of the considerable property she had accumulated after an inheritance from her father.[7] She therefore exercised control over her property and, when called upon, had refused to allow her holdings to support the Confederate cause. Woodward filled her testimony with accounts of her skirmishes with her husband and other Confederates. She had rebuffed her husband's order to feed several Confederate soldiers, declaring, "I would die before I would cook them a meal of victuals," and sending the soldiers off with the rebuke that "they were a set of rascals and I hoped they would get soundly thrashed. And they did. And wasn't I rejoiced?" Woodward described another occasion in which several Confederate marauders had stopped her and had attempted to steal poultry from her wagon. "I took the club in my hands and told them if they meddled with my stuff, I would break their necks." She boasted, "I shamed them for interfering with me and at last they let me pass on." Woodward seemed so independent of her Confederate husband that the commissioners were not even certain that she still cohabited with him at the time of her claim. She successfully presented herself as a woman who had refused to sacrifice the Union in deference to the judgment of men, even her own husband.[8]

White female claimants did not limit themselves to tongue lashing rascally Confederate men. Rachel R. Cole of northern Alabama presented evidence that she had collaborated with her neighbor, James R. Dorsey, to assist Union men and Confederate deserters in their flight to Union lines. Dorsey had sent Union men who wished to escape to Cole's house, and she had provided these men hiding places and directions. Cole also testified that she had engaged in espionage by monitoring a family of "bad and ambitious rebels" who "were keeping themselves posted up and were reporting on Union men" and by delivering notes and papers that she had concealed in her stockings. Cole had no Confederate husband to interfere with her Union activities during the war because she had separated and had obtained a divorce sometime prior to the war. A divorce signaled a public rejection of an institution that most white southerners regarded as one of the foundations of the social order. Cole had therefore likely already confronted and disregarded significant social ostracism before her embrace of the Union cause. Her freedom from male authority allowed her to offer tales of her own wartime exploits rather than to rely on those of a husband, son, or father. The commissioners were sufficiently convinced, commending her as "an active Union woman" who discharged her "duties" to the Union "fearlessly."[9]

Those white female claimants who proved their loyalty on their own account also sometimes provided evidence that they had been the targets of Confederate persecution. White women, especially elites, had typically benefited from the dictates of gentlemanly behavior and prohibitions against violence toward their sex. White women who had ventured so far outside their sphere in favor of the enemy cause were less likely to benefit from this immunity. Women who had acted on behalf of the Confederacy in untraditional ways by entering the political realm could root their behavior in traditional motivations, specifically that they had ultimately supported their menfolk. Women who had supported the Union, in contrast, more unequivocally challenged the gender hierarchy.[10] Caroline H. Atkisson, "a single woman" as she called herself or "a maiden lady" as the commissioners termed her, was well known in her Alabama community as "outspoken," "defiant," and even "demented" in her devotion to the Union. Unmarried white women could find a place for themselves in the South by embracing "single blessedness," a state of purity and disinterest devoted to the care of family members.[11] Atkisson rejected single blessedness in favor of speaking out in defense of the Union cause. She stressed that her stance had incurred the wrath of Confederates. An officer had asked her if she was in favor the Union. "On my reply that I was," she recounted, "he ordered me to shut up or he would knock my damned brains out, with a board he had in his hand." The officer had also threatened to burn down her house if she did not stop speaking in support of the Union. She asserted that she "staid in the woods two days because of said threats." This was the reversal of the more typical testimony by white female claimants: they had fed their husbands who had fled to the woods to hide from the conscript officer. With this evidence of her own persecution and flight, Atkisson demonstrated that she had become marked for Confederate persecution – not as retaliation for the sympathies or actions of a husband or other male relative. Instead, Atkisson suggested that she had become a target as a result of her own reputation for loyalty and support of the Union cause. Such evidence persuaded the commissioners that "contrary to the great many of the southern ladies, she sympathized with the Union cause."[12]

"Union persons" compelled the commissioners to evaluate them as citizens, if not totally on their own terms, at least in their own right. White women needed all, or most, of these components – Union sympathies, Union actions, and Confederate persecution – to prove their loyalty on their own account. Without all of these components, they found establishing themselves as loyal citizens on the same criteria as their white male counterparts impossible. These women secured recognition as loyal citizens independent of husbands, fathers, and other male relatives. They did so by proving their capabilities, and not their incapabilities, to articulate their sympathies and fulfill their obligations to the Union. Moreover, they continued to declare their defiance of former Confederates through their testimony before the commission. In doing all this, however, these white southern women challenged white middle-class notions of feminine domesticity, decorum, and subordination. The further identification of Lucretia Merry as not just a "Union person" but "the rabidest kind of Union person" implied that white women who claimed loyal citizenship in so independent a manner acted outside accepted gender conventions as though somehow seized with an infection that caused them to act contrary to nature. Most women were not so "rabid." The commissioners evaluated most white female claimants' allegiances not directly as independent women but indirectly as household dependents.

"As She Was a Woman, Nothing Direct as to Loyalty or Disloyalty Can Be Expected"

From her perspective, Lucy A. Weaver of Georgia presented sufficient evidence of her loyal citizenship. She advanced a political position, testifying, "My sympathies were constantly with the Union cause. I felt that we ought not to go out of the Union." She matched her actions to her sympathies by "talk[ing] all I could against secession." From the commissioners' perspective, Weaver offered only feeble indications of her allegiances. Given the "nature of the case," meaning a case prosecuted by a white woman, they realized that Weaver could present "little proof of loyal or disloyal acts." They concluded, "As she was a woman, nothing direct as to loyalty or disloyalty can be expected." The commissioners relied on the assumptions of coverture to subsume white women's loyalties under those of their male relatives. They noted that Weaver's two brothers had served as Confederate soldiers and that she had lent one of them forty dollars, which constituted "indirect aid to the rebellion, helping a recruit to enter their army, and seems to us a clear indication of her sympathies." They considered the loan weak evidence of disloyalty but nevertheless ruled against Weaver. In many ways, coverture remained a dominant force in determinations of loyal citizenship.[13]

The commissioners considered the majority of white female claimants in concert with their male relatives. Under coverture, women's property as well as their labor and future earnings became their husbands' on marriage.[14] The commissioners therefore assumed that married and widowed women had not owned property in their own names and that whatever stores and supplies the Union army had appropriated had been the property of their husbands. Indeed, most white female claimants inherited the claims from their husbands and therefore had not owned the property when the Union army arrived in their vicinity. In their procedures, the commissioners required proof of loyalty from the original owner of the property as well as his or her heirs. As a result, white female claimants had to prove both the loyalty of themselves and the loyalty of their husbands in these cases. For example, if a husband lost property to the Union army, died after losing the property, and left his property to his widow, the commissioners required that the widow demonstrate both her own loyalty and her deceased husband's loyalty to win compensation.[15] Most white southern women before the commission, then, qualified as claimants jointly with their deceased husbands and had their loyalty assessed in concert with their deceased husbands and other heirs.[16]

The commissioners also judged white female claimants by their husbands, sons, fathers, brothers, and uncles even when their male relatives' loyalties were not, according to their own rules, at issue. If women submitted wills or deeds that verified that they had owned the property when the Union army took it, the commissioners did not mandate that husbands be deposed to swear to their own loyalties.[17] In theory, this required white southern women who had owned the claimed property at the time of its appropriation to prove themselves as independent political actors. In practice, however, because of the implicit masculinity of their standards of loyal citizenship, the commissioners could not imagine how wives, mothers, and daughters could do so.[18] They exempted white female claimants from answering questions about loyal obligations outside women's purview, such as voting and soldiering, but they did not add any additional interrogatories about loyal contributions within women's domain. At the same time, the commissioners collected quite a bit of information about white female claimants' male relatives. They asked white female claimants about "near relatives" in the Confederate military and then again specifically about husbands and sons in the Confederate military, and they also asked white female claimants if their husbands had been in the Confederate civil service and if their husbands had been loyal to the Union.[19] As a result, in many cases, even when white female claimants had owned the property in their own right, the commissioners had not elicited much evidence about white women's sympathies and contributions but had instead compiled significant evidence about their male relatives' sympathies and contributions.

With the commissioners' focus on the loyalties of male relatives and with few fixed prompts to solicit testimony on their own loyalties, white southern women in Union families attempted to capitalize on coverture by linking their loyal citizenship not to their own sympathies but to those of their male relatives. Some contended that their husbands' allegiances had prevailed over their own, claiming sympathies but subordinating them to their husbands. Mary L. White of Virginia testified, "I was sometimes for the North and sometimes for the South," but "my husband desired peace and he being at the head of the family I think that might stand."[20] Others suggested their husbands' allegiances had been their own, implying that their sympathies derived solely from their husbands. Agnes Withers of Virginia explained, "being a married woman my sympathies went with my husband," the female equivalent of white men's explanation that they "went with the state."[21] These white southern women explained their own sympathies through reference to their husbands' sympathies with varying levels of personal responsibility.

Coverture allowed white southern women to claim political sympathies while preserving their feminine domesticity. In response to the question on her sympathies during the war, Mary Elizabeth Finnall of Virginia pondered the "hard question," cautiously explaining, "I am conscientious in this matter, and dont want to say anything wrong or that will condemn me hereafter." After a pause, she responded: "When the war first began I had not given the matter much consideration. I was living somewhat isolated and did not hear so much about our national difficulties as I did after we moved to Locust Grove where my father resided." She had been living with her husband on another property, but they had been forced to relocate when Confederate soldiers occupied their farm. Her sympathies aligned "wholly with the union cause" after her move to the "old homestead" where she "became better acquainted with the objects of the rebellion," presumably through her father Meredith Eskridge. Finnall aligned herself with her father who she described as a "determined opposer of secession" and a "very staunch union" man who "could not bear the idea of secession or the severing of the union." She identified her father as a "natural Union man" on account of his Whig politics and asserted, "It was natural that I should feel as he did about these things." Just as a man "naturally" understood himself politically, a woman "naturally" aligned herself with her family. By linking herself with her father's strong Union sentiments, she was able to speak less emphatically of her own. She insisted that she "never had any desire to see the union destroyed" and had "always been glad the war terminated as it did."

Finnall struck a delicate balance between patriotic declarations and womanly deference. By narrating her acquiescence in her father's opinions, she infused her otherwise tepid statements with her father's uncompromising stance and thereby claimed a vigorous Unionism without resorting to unladylike political harangues.[22]

White female claimants frequently relied on coverture to meet the commissioners' requirement that loyal citizens demonstrate contributions to the Union cause. The strongest evidence of loyalty – voting and soldiering for the Union – was only available to white men. White southern women claimed these loyal deeds through their husbands and other male relatives. The commissioners wanted to know how claimants had voted in relevant elections, and white women offered their husband's votes. Anna Dixon of Virginia emphasized that her husband had been the only man to vote for Abraham Lincoln in their county.[23] The commissioners inquired whether claimants had enlisted in the Union military, and white women discussed their husband's service. Martha A. F. Terrett of Virginia testified that her husband had died in the Union army.[24] Although identification as a "wife" did not necessarily imply a relationship with the state, identification as a voter's wife and, especially, a soldier's wife did bestow rights and privileges and convey a claim on the nation.[25]

Confederate persecution of their Union husbands provided white female claimants with indirect evidence of their own loyal citizenship. Henrietta S. Bowden explained that she had been ousted from her position as matron of the Eastern Lunatic Asylum in Williamsburg, Virginia, in 1861 as a punishment for her husband's politics.[26] White southern women also presented the deaths of their husbands and other male relatives as evidence of Confederate persecution. Mary Jane Clem described the armed Confederates who had dragged her husband from their Virginia home in June 1862 and had murdered him in retaliation for his Union sentiments.[27] These women had suffered Confederate persecution as a result of their husbands' loyalties. They had not been targeted on their own as a result of their own allegiances. Persecution in these women's claims, then, did not constitute evidence of their actions as citizens but of their sufferings as wives.

The commissioners were receptive to white women's use of coverture to link their loyalties to those of their Union husbands and fathers. They often determined white women's loyalty on the basis of their male relatives' loyalties, sometimes barely mentioning the former while fully detailing the latter. They noted that one white female claimant had owned the property in her own right, so "the question of his [the husband's] loyalty is not of much importance." Even though they acknowledged that the husband's loyalty was not at issue in the case, they nevertheless provided a lengthy explanation to prove that "her husband was unquestionably a loyal man" in which they listed his votes and other contributions to the Union. Their entire summary on the question of loyalty centered on the claimant's husband, so much so that the commissioners forgot themselves and mistakenly referred to the husband as the claimant.

After detailing the husband's qualifications, the commissioners simply deemed the loyalty of "his widow" to be "fully proved." They granted the claimant loyal citizenship by evaluating her husband's allegiances and extending those allegiances to her as his wife.[28]

White female claimants with Confederate relatives found that coverture worked to their disadvantage. In their deliberations after the war, the commissioners suspected that a Confederate relative tainted a person with disloyalty, and they regarded white women as especially susceptible. With these suspicions, the commissioners continued wartime policies. Union partisans and officials during the war had believed that familial loyalties affected national loyalties. Union policy operated under the assumption that Confederate relatives could possibly compromise the loyalties of Union men and women. Union authorities regarded families with conflicting loyalties as a public problem as evidenced by their regulation of visits and correspondence across the lines. They preferred what one Union official called an "impassable barrier" between Union men and women and their Confederate relatives. Even "expressions of personal sympathy and encouragement" constituted comfort to the enemy, having "a very great effect in inducing them to persevere in their disloyal and traitorous purposes."[29]

In their postwar claims before the commission, women with Confederate relatives sometimes attempted to distance themselves from the taint of disloyalty. Most did not assert their political independence, like "the rabidest kind of Union person" detailed in the previous section, and instead they usually left patriarchal authority intact. Some claimants presented evidence that they had disagreed with their Confederate husbands often in line with the teachings of Union fathers or other male relatives. Stephanie Chotard of Louisiana repudiated the disloyalty of her husband, Henry Chotard, Jr., and embraced the loyalty of her uncle, Robert J. Walker. Chotard suggested that her husband, a Confederate veteran who hailed from a prominent secessionist family, had failed to uphold the marriage contract. The logic of coverture presumed male competence and female incompetence, but Chotard presented evidence that upended this equation. One witness condemned Henry as a "dissipated," "worthless," and "trifling" wastrel who "never was worth a cent" himself but spent all Chotard's money and "even sacrificed her family silver." The witness emphasized the reversal of gender roles in likening Chotard to "a good many of our Southern girls who marry husbands and support them." In offering these stories of Henry's profligate ways, Chotard suggested that a husband who had so failed in his duties to his wife would never wield enough influence to affect her political sentiments. Henry had broken the reciprocal pledge of the marriage contract to protect and support his wife, freeing Chotard from her obligations to serve and obey her husband. In the breach, Chotard suggested that she reverted to the teachings of her natal family. She had been raised by her Uncle Robert John Walker, a notorious Union man, on the death of her parents. Chotard freed herself from political dependence on her husband by proving political dependence on another male relative. She depicted herself as under the cover of her Union uncle rather than her Confederate husband. In this way, she asserted an identity as a loyal citizen that challenged Confederate but preserved male authority.[30]

Attempts to distance themselves from Confederate relatives led some white female claimants into apparently unwomanly declarations. Ellen E. Evans of Virginia asserted that she had differed with her husband over the war. She complained that he had been "a rebel of the deepest dye." His Confederate sympathies had been "the principle cause of the unhappiness" that compelled her to seek a divorce. Lawmakers, however, did not conceive of political difference as legitimate cause to warrant the dissolution of the sacred ties of marriage. Legally, she had been granted her request on the basis of her husband's habitual drunkenness. In her claim before the commission, Evans presented evidence that she had "wished her husband and all her male relatives who went out to fight against the Union would be killed." Evans presented a kind of politics that contradicted a woman's presumed instinct to care for her family.[31]

The commissioners readily believed that white female claimants with Confederate male relatives had been Confederates themselves. They rejected most of these white southern women, in part, as a consequence of their Confederate male relatives. Their conceptualization of loyal citizenship, focusing on political obligations primarily the province of white men, left little room for white southern women to prove their loyalty independently of male relatives. In white women's claims, even when male relatives' loyalty was technically not at issue, they frequently referred to Confederate husbands and sons in their reports to Congress, regarding them as circumstantial evidence of disloyalty, which tipped their judgments toward denial. Often, the mere fact of having male relatives in Confederate service, even without an admission that white female claimants had provided aid and comfort to them, was the most damning piece of evidence. They assumed that white women's concern for their relatives in the Confederate army had interfered with whatever political allegiances they may have possessed.[32] The commissioners also routinely noted that white male claimants had sons and sometimes brothers in Confederate service as strikes against them, but they did not cite the great variety of male relatives that recurred in their summary reports in white female claims.[33] In addition, because the commissioners recognized so many more obligations for white men, the fact of having a son in Confederate service was not generally the most damning piece of evidence against them. They regarded voting against secession as a loyal act within the purview of all white men and considered failure to do as particularly worthy of censure.[34]

Some white female claimants did manage to convince the commissioners that they had not shared their husband's Confederate loyalties. Women like Chotard successfully divorced their loyalties from their husbands by associating themselves with the loyalties of other male relatives.[35] However, asserting a political difference from a husband represented a hard case to convincingly present. The commissioners ruled against Evans, finding her brand of politics highly suspect. In their report to Congress, they dismissed Evans' contention that she had divorced her husband for his Confederate loyalties and rejected the testimony that she had wished death on her Confederate relatives as "improbable." White women could disassociate themselves from their husbands' disloyalty but needed to do so in a persuasive – that is, suitably feminine – manner.[36]

The commissioners concluded that "the instances are undoubtedly rare where family sympathies, particularly the husband's and wife's did not coincide on the question of secession."[37] Nevertheless, they presumed marital unity for wives but not for husbands. In one claim, the commissioners noted that they had "no doubt" of the wife's loyalty but had suspicions about the husband's loyalty and therefore rejected the claim.[38] White men could not capitalize on the loyalties of their wives or other female relatives and, indeed, hardly ever even attempted, let alone conceived, such a strategy. The commissioners did not assess the loyalties and disloyalties of wives and daughters in judging white male claimants as frequently as they considered the loyalties and disloyalties of husbands and sons in deciding on white female claimants. The commissioners' assumption of marital unity was not gender neutral. They subsumed white women's allegiances under their husbands but not white men's loyalties under their wives. They accepted subject citizenship for white women, but they demanded independent citizenship for white men.

The positioning of wives as dependents of their husbands in claims before the commission mirrored a postwar push in southern law to bolster husbands as the public face of the household. Jurists reaffirmed husbands' authority over their household dependents, setting aside the private sphere as a sacred space shielded from public scrutiny. With the abolition of slavery, marriage assumed greater importance as an institution structuring the social order and determining private obligations and public power. The dissolution of one domestic relationship, indeed the very fact that such relationships could be dissolved, made it all the more imperative to protect the others.[39]

In cases with "nothing direct as to loyalty or disloyalty," both claimants and the commissioners drew on coverture by adopting a form of dependent citizenship derived through male relatives. Many white southern women expressed their loyalties to the state by citing the loyalties of their fathers, husbands, and sons, sometimes strategically choosing to align themselves with Union rather than Confederate relatives in pursuit of federal compensation. In making these claims, they emphasized their dependence rather than independence and their passivity rather than activity. The commissioners could envision few ways that white women could directly prove their own loyal citizenship, so they often subsumed white women's allegiances under those of their male relatives. They ruled in favor of white southern women with male relatives who had supported the Union and against those with male relatives who had favored the Confederacy. In doing so, they perpetuated coverture by granting women political personas through their fathers, husbands, and sons. Many claimants and the commissioners resolved the problem of women's relationship with the state by citing their men's relationship with the state. In its simplest incarnation, good Union women were the faithful wives, mothers, and daughters of good Union men.

"As a Woman I Took No Part"

Eliza A. Clarke of Virginia expressed Union sympathies by stressing her opposition to secession and support for the preservation of the Union. However, "As a woman," Clarke explained, "I took no part whatever in the war." She explained that she "never did anything to help the Confederate cause or hurt the Union," but she insisted that she "would have been willing to contribute to the success of the Union so far as my means and circumstances would permit." In accordance with traditional gender ideology, white female claimants often repudiated the public world of politics as beyond the private realm of domesticity. The commissioners dismissed Clarke's claims to loyal citizenship and ruled that "if the lady had been really for the Union she could or should have produced better proof." Many white southern women identified themselves as loyal citizens according to traditional notions of women's domesticity, but the commissioners judged them as disloyal citizens according to an expectation for feminine patriotism.[40]

White female claimants balanced their political with the domestic sympathies in different ways. Some staked a position in the male world of politics but prioritized the female world of domesticity. Mary Jane Gordon of Mississippi insisted, "Of course my desires were with the Union cause," but she emphasized, "Having a very afflicted husband to watch over, care for, did not suffer my feelings to be carried away from him even in matters of importance to myself and country," and admitted, "My feelings were enlisted and fixed on the well being of my family's good." Gordon tacitly accepted that white women should possess political sympathies, but she explained that she had sacrificed "myself and country" in service to her family.[41] Others rebuffed the male world of politics altogether and claimed only an interest in the female world of domesticity. Eliza A. Lively of Virginia admitted, "I did not think or feel anything" about the Union or the Confederacy. Instead, she only cared about the war as it concerned her son: "I thought if I could get my son I did not care any thing about it" and "didn't care which side conquered so [long as] I got my son again."[42]

Although many women may have attempted to obfuscate their loyalties by distancing themselves from politics, some women sincerely could not understand why the commissioners insisted that they claim a position on the war. White female claimants sometimes voiced surprise that the commissioners would even broach the topic of their politics. When asked about her sympathies, Mary E. Jennings, a Virginia widow, exclaimed: "Mine! Well I am no politician and never had anything to do with it." In response to Commissioner

Aldis's instructions that she choose one side or the other, Jennings replied, "Well, indeed I do not know." Such expressions of seemingly sincere astonishment on being queried on their politics suggests that some white women understood themselves as apolitical, even as they acted in ways historians identify as political.[43]

Just as white southern women disputed the necessity that they prove their Union sympathies, they challenged the requirement that they prove their Union contributions. Some claimants stressed their limited ability to act on behalf of the Union. "Being a woman," Mary Jane Gordon of Mississippi explained, she "could do nothing more than express my sentiments occasionally in favour of my country."[44] Others dismissed speaking out against the Confederacy and in favor of the Union as futile, contending that white women had possessed no power to alter the course of events. Margaret Johnson of Mississippi suggested that even if she had done all a woman could and had expressed her Unionist sentiments, "I don't know that I had any influence" in the decision to secede because "of course I could not prevent it."[45] This placed women as subjects of the state to which they owed obedience rather than participants in the state to which they owed obligations. Tabitha Courter of Georgia concluded: "I had nothing to do with either party. I couldn't make war and I couldn't break it. I had nothing to do with it." Courter linked the power to "make war" with the power to "break" war. Without either, she had "nothing" to do with the war.[46] Indeed, discounting the possibility of women's active citizenship altogether, Harriet Lunceford of Virginia could only contemplate supporting the Union by imagining a sex change: "I told people if I was a man I would oppose secession."[47] Some stressed that meddling with men's affairs would not have been appropriate. Mary J. Ellison of Georgia declared, "It was the duty of the men to take charge of Govt and attend to such things." Ellison, as a "lady" with "no politics," had "never thought of any interference."[48] These claimants articulated the feelings of powerlessness and purposelessness that had struck white women at the beginning of the war when both Union and Confederate leaders had exalted the masculine virtues of honor and courage on the battlefield. Both sides had ultimately developed ideologies of feminine patriotism, but these claimants did not draw on them in their testimony.[49] These female claimants based their inability to act on behalf of the Union on the disabilities of their sex. Assertions that white women could not contribute to the Union cause promoted a form of subject citizenship rooted in political incapacity.

White southern women who "took no part" sometimes depicted themselves as obedient to a higher authority. Some white female claimants stressed their submission to divine authority. These women identified God as the preeminent actor: "We didn't make this war, Providence sent it upon us," "I thought the good Lord would bring all things out right," "I felt that which ever way the war turned would be the result of an over ruling providence," and "God would end the war in his own time." Such commentary reflected the pervasive providential interpretation of the war that had positioned divine will as the primary determinant of the war's outcome. A belief in providence did not necessarily negate the role of human action in securing God's beneficence, but it could degenerate into a form of fatalism that rendered human action irrelevant. Women before the commission who subjected themselves to a higher authority suggested that they had possessed no role in preventing the onset of the war or deciding its result. Like those who distanced themselves from "men's affairs," these women suggested that they had left the matter in more capable hands.[50]

In most cases, the commissioners insisted that white southern women had possessed obligations to the state. They generally refused to accept arguments that the politics of war had been beyond the female sphere. As they ruled in one claim, "We cannot believe this woman was so ignorant as not to know that secession was a separation and dissolution of the Union and that the war on the part of the south from the first was to maintain that separation."[51] The commissioners dismissed white southern women's attempts to place their responsibilities as wives and mothers over their responsibilities as patriots. In another claim, they considered a woman's emphasis on her "family's good" as "plainly evasive" and charged that "it is idle for her to say, that for 3½ years of the war her husband's ill health so engrossed all her thoughts that she had no decided interest in or sympathies with either side in the war."[52] Deeming the issues of the war so simple and so consuming that even white women had been able to understand its implications, the commissioners considered such responses to be "such as no sincere Union woman would have given."[53] They suspected these white southern women of dishonesty, supposing that they attempted to manipulate gender ideology to hide their disloyalty to the Union.

This disconnect between the commissioners and the claimants may possibly be traced to gendered experiences of the war that diverged by region. Before the war, mass politicization had drawn elite white women into electioneering as symbols and as partisans. During the war, this politicization had accelerated and broadened as both sides sought to fully mobilize the populace for war. White women in all regions experienced this politicization, but these shifts were more marked in the Union than the Confederacy. Northern white women were more organized and politicized during the war through groups such as the U.S. Sanitary Commission than their southern counterparts. After the war, this regional divergence had deepened. As northern and western white women formed an independent women's rights movement, many white southern women retreated to traditional gender hierarchies and conventions. White southern women may have acquired a new understanding of their capabilities, but their work lost its public component as the ideal of patriotic womanhood waned in influence with the end of the war. Defeated Confederate men also attempted to retrench patriarchy over white and black dependents.[54] Despite regional differences, the commissioners expected most white southern women to claim the political womanhood necessitated by the exigencies of war.

The commissioners did exempt a small number of white women from proving their loyal sympathies and contributions. They returned the claim of Martha W. Dunbar for further evidence because she had presented only her former slaves and family members – those "interested for money or affection" – as her witnesses. Martha D. Claiborne, Dunbar's married daughter, criticized the commissioners' focus on citizens' obligations to the state and instead stressed the state's obligations to its subjects. She dismissed the commissioners' requirement for additional testimony as "scarcely tenable." Claiborne insisted her mother had been "too old, too reticent and retired, too near the grave, too oppressed with care and anxiety, to run about through the country and gossip about her *loyalty*." She explained that Dunbar had interacted with only family and slaves during the war because her infirmities had confined her to the plantation. She complained that the Union army had offered them little protection and had in fact "despoiled" them of their property "when the household consisted exclusively of females." She charged that "the U.S. gave no protection to its loyal subjects" and reasoned that "loyalty cannot be demonstrative without protection." She concluded, "To expect two infirm women, living alone, outside the lines, in a district swarming with regular and irregular cavalry, bushwhackers and jayhawkers, to fling out a Union flag, and thus invite the robber and incendiary is, I submit, rather unreasonable." Claiborne drew on notions of reciprocal obligations, insisting that the state owed its "subjects" protection before "subjects" could be expected to contribute to its defense. Even the part she imagined that white women like her mother could contribute seemed relatively insignificant. She portrayed the commissioners' expectation that claimants demonstrate that they had spoken out in favor of the Union as, in the mouths of women, frivolous acts of gossip. Claiborne effectively dismissed the notion that her mother be forced to offer additional proof of her loyal citizenship.[55]

Chastened, the commissioners accepted Claiborne's arguments and approved the claim without further evidence. Although they allowed Dunbar's claim, the commissioners did not apply Claiborne's argument that "loyalty cannot be demonstrative without protection" more generally in other claims. Claiborne's logic demanded that the commissioners modify their requirements for active citizenship, abandoning it under Confederate control and only applying it under Union occupation. The commissioners could have argued that white men had abandoned their obligations first by not acting against secession, thus breaking the contract and relieving the government from fulfilling its obligations. They could also have reasoned that white men chose to stay under Confederate protection by remaining in their homes rather than escaping to Union protection across the lines. White women, however, could not have as decisively acted against secession or moved without their families and could have therefore contended that they still deserved the government's protection. The commissioners' failure to accept Dunbar's logic more generally for white women suggests the degree to which their conceptualization of loyal citizenship continued to presume white masculinity.

The commissioners generally only lowered their standards for loyal citizenship when white women convincingly demonstrated that, not just their sex, but their "sex and condition," precluded the submission of definitive evidence. In one claim, the commissioners noted "the proof of claimant's loyalty is feeble and yet as strong as could reasonably be expected of one of her sex and condition."[56] The conditions that the commissioners accepted included "poor," "ignorant," "harmless," "obscure," "simple," "old," and "infirm" – not words that described a white man's qualifications for loyal citizenship.[57] They accepted weak evidence of loyalty if white female claimants otherwise testified to their Union sympathies, if their neighbors also corroborated their Union reputations, if they were not related to Confederate soldiers, and if an investigation revealed no disloyal acts. Mary E. Davis of Virginia scored a trifecta as a "poor, ignorant, harmless" widow. The commissioners accepted that Davis had possessed little capacity to accurately choose her allegiances during the war, noting that "the claimant can not read or write" and even "didn't know what secession meant." They concluded, "Of so poor and ignorant and obscure a person and a female, but little proof can be expected."[58] The commissioners' exemption of select women on the basis of "sex and condition" incorporated them into loyal citizenship without recognizing their abilities to ever meet the political obligations of loyal citizenship.

The commissioners and white female claimants clashed over white southern women's relationships with and obligations to the state. Faced with the challenge of proving a political stance given their presumed apolitical nature, many white southern women resolved the contradiction by denying a relationship to the state and embracing domestic concerns. By defining politics as men's affairs and depicting themselves as powerless, these white women attempted to divorce themselves from the war. With these arguments, they distanced themselves both from a strict understanding of politics as voting, in which they stressed they could not participate, as well as a broader notion of politics as public affairs, in which they emphasized they had not been interested either by circumstances or capabilities. In doing so, they rejected the commissioners' expectation of active citizenship and instead proposed subject citizenship. They rooted their sympathies and behaviors in the private sphere of the family and the household. The commissioners, however, demanded that most white southern women prove their loyal citizenship. In keeping with the increased politicization of the Civil War era, they expected most southerners, even white women, to have possessed political sympathies and to have fulfilled political obligations.

"No More than Natural"

Perhaps Martha W. Taylor of Tennessee felt justified in claiming status as a loyal citizen because she "was opposed to the breaking up of the Union" and "felt I was out by force." Or perhaps she thought she would be recognized as a loyal citizen because, as a woman, "of course, I did not vote." Despite her expectations, the commissioners refused her claim. They focused on damning statements Taylor uttered in justifying her loyal citizenship. She freely admitted that she "sympathized with the South," explaining that "most of my relations and interests were here and it was no more than natural." The commissioners accepted that it was "no more than natural" for Taylor to have sympathized with her friends and her neighbors and that this sympathy outweighed, even determined, any political sympathies she may have possessed.[59] Women's citizenship merged personal issues with political ones. Their wartime patriotic duties included raising virtuous citizens to fight on the battlefield and drawing on their domestic natures to care for their nation's soldiers. Such configurations of patriotism created contradictions. On the one hand, their sympathies and services supported the public cause. On the other hand, their actions merely fulfilled their private duty. "Personal" and "political" are ideological, and not fixed, categories, and the identification of white women's sympathies and actions as "personal" or "political" depended on what was considered "natural" to their sex.

"Sympathy" had specific gendered meanings. In the Revolutionary era, Patriot leaders focused on masculine sympathy as a powerful idiom for justifying the Patriot cause. The king demonstrated unjust and tyrannical "unfeeling" through his inattention to colonial grievances. Americans united in "fellow feeling" in response to the betrayal. Sympathy functioned as a political principle to create an imagined national community. In the antebellum era, a new definition of sympathy arose alongside the old. American reformers associated sympathy with white women as a natural trait of the feminine sphere of home and family. Some reformers recognized the concept of sympathy as inherently domestic but also appreciated its potentially political implications. They connected private sympathy with public policy by suggesting that "feeling right" should influence law and politics. By the Civil War, sympathy referred to both the male realm of politics and the female realm of domesticity.[60]

The commissioners' use of "sympathy" in the interrogatories generally, although not exclusively, encompassed the male realm of politics. They initially asked claimants in their interrogatories, "Did you sympathize with the Union cause, or with the rebellion?" They followed the question with additional questions that oriented claimants toward formal politics as evidenced by their repeated references to votes. In this way, the commissioners encouraged claimants to explain how they had translated their sympathies into political acts of loyalty or disloyalty. In the last version of their interrogatories, the commissioners removed the phrasing that signaled formal politics, asking "On which side were your sympathies during the war, and were they on the same side from beginning to end?" This change effectively broadened the question from the realm of politics, tacitly acknowledging a broader pool of petitioners, but did not explicitly encompass the realm of domesticity.[61]

Both white southern women and white southern men experienced the Civil War as a clash of sympathies, but they often responded to the interrogatory on sympathies in divergent ways. Many white southern women discussed their concern for the safety and well-being of relatives and friends rather than their assessment of secession. As one white female claimant defined it, sympathy "mean[t] that one should feel sorry and troubled for those who *suffer*."[62] With this definition of sympathy, white women often admitted, as did Adele Currin of Tennessee, that "my sympathies were with the southern people as I had been raised among them."[63] White southern men made similar admissions, but when they did so, they more frequently dismissed their "personal" sympathies, which they distinguished from their "political" sympathies. James Freeman of North Carolina, for example, insisted that "his sympathy for the South during the war was from personal, and not from political considerations, that he was always opposed to secession and the war."[64] White men, however, usually associated the question with politics and automatically discussed their "political," and not their "personal," sympathies. White southern men undoubtedly had sympathies for Confederate relatives, friends, and neighbors but often did not acknowledge them in their testimony, likely deeming them irrelevant to discussions of their loyalties and of course detrimental to their claims. The comparison between these female and male claimants' responses to the interrogatory on sympathy highlights that white southern women were often accustomed to thinking in terms of their personal relationships and unaccustomed to advancing an abstract tie to the nation in the ways the commissioners expected. Lacking the vocabulary regularly used by white men placed them at a disadvantage in prosecuting their claims.

The commissioners attempted to categorize claimants as either strictly for the Union or for the Confederacy and expected white southern women to choose one side or the other. They believed that "true Union adherents knew where their sympathies were," meaning that they did not suffer the clash of feelings that many white southern women narrated.[65] From the commissioners' perspective, with their presumption that all southerners had been rebels unless proven otherwise, admissions of sympathy with the South, even ones "personal" rather than "political" in character, undermined a white woman's claim to loyal citizenship. Indeed, in acknowledging these sympathies before a commission restricted to loyal citizens, these women seemingly swore their Confederate leanings in utter defiance of the commission's stated objectives. In some cases, as the commissioners suspected, the testimony signaled a white woman's deliberate attempts to obscure her disloyalty. In other cases, however, white southern women's sympathies were conflicted because notions of women's relationship to the state were conflicted.

The ambiguity between personal and political that characterized assessments of white southern women's sympathies also typified evaluations of their actions. In petitioning for compensation for their wartime losses, white female claimants depicted similar actions as personal or political depending on whether they had performed them for either the Union or the Confederacy. Drawing on ideas about feminine patriotism, some presented seemingly loyal acts as contributions to the Union cause. Relying on ideas about feminine domesticity, others dismissed apparently disloyal acts as apolitical. Nineteenth-century definitions of women's nature provided space for divergent interpretations of white women's wartime conduct.

Opposing Confederate enlistment was one loyal act that white female claimants could cite that coincided with their responsibility to nurture and influence their husbands and sons. Nancy H. Fair of Arkansas had refused to heed the call of Confederate leaders to sacrifice her loved ones to the cause. She declared that she had objected to the conscription of her sons: "I felt like I could kill the Confederates who made them go."[66] In presenting such stories as evidence in their claims, white female claimants suggested that their actions as wives and mothers contained a political dimension that should be recognized by the government. The commissioners, however, refused to accept white southern women's protest of their husbands' and sons' service in the Confederate military as evidence of loyal citizenship. They noted that one white woman's opposition to Confederate enlistment indicated her "personal affection and desire" for her male relative and that such feelings "would be quite natural" but, in their estimation, had "no bearings whatever upon the question of loyalty."[67] The commissioners, then, understood these acts as inherent in women's natural impulse to care for their menfolk and therefore regarded them as personally and not politically motivated. White women presented their opposition to Confederate enlistment as an act appropriately within their sphere of influence, but the commissioners regarded such acts as only ambiguous evidence of loyal citizenship precisely because of their positioning within the domestic domain.

Services to Union soldiers, such as feeding and nursing them, also constituted a means by which white female claimants could claim loyal contributions compatible with their presumed domestic natures. The commissioners considered white men's enlistment as Union soldiers as unmistakable evidence of loyal citizenship in keeping with their public obligations. Unable to claim status as Union soldiers themselves, many white women instead cited assistance to Union soldiers. Elizabeth A. Anderson of Georgia secured the testimony of Robert Ayres, a Union veteran, to praise "the very many little acts of kindness bestowed on me by yourself" while he had been imprisoned in her husband's jail.[68] The commissioners dismissed actions such as cooking and nursing for Union soldiers as only circumstantial evidence of loyalty. They charged that white southern women may have performed such services from "humane motives" rather than from Union sympathies.[69] They considered women particularly susceptible to such "humane motives" because of their maternal sympathies, musing that "feelings of humanity and the recollections that her own son was in the hands of the Union men might well have prompted her conduct in the matter."[70] The commissioners regarded services to Union soldiers as only equivocal proof of loyal citizenship, partially because of the domestic character of such services. As with opposition to Confederate enlistment, what made these contributions appropriate actions for white women was precisely what rendered them meager evidence of loyal citizenship.

While white southern women emphasized the public component of seemingly loyal contributions, they stressed the personal component of apparently disloyal contributions. They excused acts such as caring for their male relatives in Confederate service, providing supplies to Confederate soldiers, or performing work for the Confederate government by linking them with feminine and therefore apolitical sensibilities. These white southern women discussed such acts within the language of sentiment and suffering rather than the language of politics and nationalism. They suggested that they had only done what seemed natural to them and that, as a result, they could not be held responsible. In doing so, these white southern women distanced themselves from the principles underlying the Confederate war effort. They expected the commissioners to apply the idealized separation between public and private and between political and domestic to their claims.

Over and over again, white southern women attested that they had fed their husbands and sons in Confederate service. Annie Horton of North Carolina counted fifteen grandsons in the Confederate army to whom she had sent "victuals and clothes whenever I got a chance for they were suffering for something to eat and wear."[71] White southern women, whose main duty had been the care of their families, scarcely bothered to disguise what they regarded as their understandable and appropriate support of their male relatives in Confederate service. Martha A. E. Rice of Georgia admitted: "I furnished my youngest with some clothing and something to eat when he would send to me for it. Who would not for a child?"[72] These women did not acknowledge their actions as aid and comfort to the enemy. They considered assistance to their male relatives in Confederate service as natural acts of wives and mothers, and they expected that the commissioners would not hold them accountable for fulfilling their familial duties. The commissioners, however, usually considered supplying husbands, sons, and brothers in the Confederate army as acts of disloyalty that constituted "indirect aid to the rebellion" and, even more, "a clear indication" of Confederate sympathies.[73]

Some white female claimants admitted that they had performed various labors for the Confederacy but denied the political character of these contributions. Louisa Gooch acknowledged that she had sewn clothing for soldiers for the Confederate Commissary in Raleigh, North Carolina, but identified these acts as merely work necessitated by her personal circumstances and unassociated with any political principles. Gooch explained, "I did it because I needed the money... I did not do it for any love for the Rebels, but simply to make money to help live on." She contended that her wage labor did not represent an attempt to politically contribute to the Confederacy but an attempt to economically care for her family.[74] Another white southern woman excused her labor for the Confederacy as a social obligation without political implications. Mary

S. Darden explained that her participation in a Confederate sewing society in her Mississippi neighborhood "was not voluntary on my part, only done for policy, and not to willingly assist the Confederacy." She argued that "a female in this county at that time would have been discountenanced by her neighbors who would have refused when solicited" and that "my neighbor ladies would have thought very strange if I had refused when asked to help them on such occasions and I did not wish to be unfriendly with my neighbors." Darden's phrasing presents her familiarity with matters of etiquette and unfamiliarity with the language of politics. The "duress" – to apply the commissioners' phrasing – that Darden presented to explain her disloyal deed as "not voluntary" was of social ostracism or "discountenance" rather than physical force. Darden considered a reputation for "unfriendliness" and "strangeness" sufficient excuse for outfitting Confederate soldiers.[75] The commissioners regarded white women's labors, even sewing and cooking, as aid and comfort to the enemy. In fact, the only interrogatory that targeted feminine disloyal acts, indeed the only interrogatory that addressed specifically feminine allegiances at all, concerned these kinds of domestic labors.[76] The commissioners ruled that such actions were "as much as a woman of her circumstances had opportunity to do in aid of the rebellion."[77]

The commissioners labeled actions as personal or political generally in favor of disloyalty, particularly in cases with little available evidence. Their treatment of white southern women's marital decisions highlights this tendency. Mary Abercrombie of Arkansas suggested that her engagement and subsequent marriage to a Union officer constituted evidence of her loyal, and specifically "political," conduct. Abercrombie had married Clifford Sims in the aftermath of the war. She informed the commissioners that "the fact of her receiving the attentions of an United States officer and subsequently marrying him was considered in the States in Rebellion to be a marked exhibition of preference, of a political character, and no one sympathising with the States in Rebellion held any intercourse or acquaintance with United States officers."[78] The commissioners dismissed Abercrombie's argument, remarking that "experience has shown so many instances where confederate hostility has been softened and changed into affection through the mysterious power of love that we cannot presume that that was not the case with Miss Abercombie." They suggested that the couple had been "attracted and captivated by each other in the usual and natural and honest way of falling in love without the least regard to political considerations."[79] The commissioners' identification of marital choices as apolitical in the Abercombie case contrasts with their identification of marital choices as political in another claim. Amelia B. Taylor of South Carolina claimed an identity as a Union woman in her own right, without reference to either of her two husbands. Even though she had sympathized with "the southern people," she had favored the "old government as it was before the war" and had condemned secession as "a great mistake." In the commissioners' eyes, Taylor's choice in 1872 of a former Confederate colonel, Alexander

R. Taylor, as her second husband cast doubt on her Union sympathies. Even though they generally dismissed testimony regarding postwar actions, the commissioners considered this fact significant enough to underline in her deposition and important enough to cite in their report to Congress as one of their justifications for their ruling of wartime disloyalty.[80] The ambiguity within feminine domesticity and patriotism allowed the commissioners to interpret martial choices as both personal and political.

White female claimants were caught within dichotomies between men and women, public and personal, political and domestic. White southern women claimed sympathies and actions considered natural for their gender. They had sympathized with the sufferings of others. They had discouraged their male relatives from enlisting in the Confederate army. They had nursed and fed soldiers on both sides. White southern women considered these sympathies and actions as not only appropriate for their gender but also compatible with and even indicative of their loyal citizenship. The commissioners rejected their attempts to lend a political character to services that were domestic in nature. The attributes that rendered these actions natural for women were the very characteristics that impaired them in the commissioners' eyes as useful tests to determine loyalties. At the same time, the commissioners refused to accept that women's presumed apolitical nature erased the political meaning of their services to Confederate soldiers and their labors for the Confederate cause. This means that the commissioners often regarded white women's contributions to the Union as personal and their contributions, sometimes even the same very contributions, to the Confederacy as political. The slippage between the personal and political dimensions of feminine loyalty demonstrates a failure to resolve the paradox of white southern women's citizenship.

As they drew on their wartime memories to prove their postwar citizenship, white southern women faced the challenge of defining a relationship with the state that did not conflict with their status as daughters, wives, mothers, and, more generally, as women. White southern women who desired the entitlements of loyal citizenship had to craft a convincing portrait of feminine loyalty and overcome the apparent contradiction of claiming feminine politics. Some claimed loyal citizenship on their own account on the basis of their own sympathies and contributions to the Union, and others did so through their fathers, husbands, and sons. Some argued that choosing a side in the war would have violated their women's place, and others attempted to redefine women's domains. These women grappled, some successfully and others unsuccessfully, with the necessity to present themselves as loyal citizens of the Union without implicating themselves in sympathies and behaviors inappropriate to their sex.

The commissioners understood female citizenship as subordinate to male citizenship. They accepted many white southern women as loyal citizens through an examination of their male relations. They believed that status as wives and mothers often predominated over any supposed political sympathies and contributions. Although the commissioners recognized female citizens as different from male citizens by creating a separate section for them in their interrogatories, they subtracted from rather than added to their conceptualization of loyal citizenship. They exempted white women from interrogatories on obligations outside their purview, but they did not add interrogatories on contributions within their domain. While they recognized actions within the province of white men, such as voting and soldiering, as political obligations, they marginalized actions within the province of women, such as nurturing soldiers and opposing enlistment, as personal undertakings. In endorsing a form of subject citizenship for white southern women, the commissioners perpetuated the gender hierarchies of the household on the national stage.

The Civil War brought a new recognition of white southern women as patriots, but not a full extension of rights and privileges as citizens. The war presented opportunities for white women to serve their nation in untraditional ways. Despite the responsibilities assumed by white women during the war, the participation recognized and celebrated by both sides reinforced white women's dependent and domestic character. Both praised women for their sacrifices during the war, not only their sacrifices of dresses and foods, but also their sacrifices of husbands and sons on the battlefield. The Union government rewarded female citizens with privileges such as property claims and widows' pensions. Their rewards, however, did not include suffrage, despite the efforts of women's rights activists. Full citizenship remained associated with white masculinity, which rendered female citizenship contradictory and subordinate. In the eyes of the federal government, women accessed the vote, just as they accessed national allegiances, through their husbands and sons. The postwar reassessment of citizenship did not resolve the paradox of female citizenship.

4

Former Slaves' Union

Bestowing Charity or Rewarding Loyalty

C. W. Dudley, a South Carolina claims attorney, wrote to the commissioners of southern claims at the beginning of their tenure urging them to extend "charity" to black claimants. He feared that the commissioners would exclude black southerners because "strictly speaking, the negro was not a 'citizen,' according to Southern doctrine." He argued that "it is not to be presumed that Congress intended to provide for the white man only, & used the word 'citizen' for that purpose." The commissioners must not bar the door against the "needy coloured man." At the same time, he added, in the manner of one relating a startling development, "the coloured people actually did the most, in act of the government." Dudley simultaneously depicted former slaves as both dependent and independent people, deserving the privileges of citizenship as an act of benevolence to an unfortunate race and as a reward for their patriotic contributions.[1]

Whether former slaves would be incorporated as citizens as an act of benevolence or as a reward for loyalty partially depended on assessments of their role in the war. On the one hand, slaves had been property, not citizens, and they had owed their loyalty to their masters and mistresses, not to any government. In fact, slaves, as property, had constituted a primary component of slaveholders' perceived citizenship rights. On the other hand, slaves had sympathized with and contributed to the Union cause. They had withdrawn their labor from their masters and mistresses and offered it to the Union army. Historians have assigned different weights to slaves' status as property under the dominion of their masters and mistresses and to slaves' power as people to oppose the coercions of slavery. Stanley Elkins argued in 1959 that slavery in the United States created a closed system in which slaves became infantilized and internalized their masters' values. Since then, scholars emphasize the various ways that slaves resisted their enslavement. Disputes over agency remain contentious among Civil War historians who disagree over the origins of emancipation, with some emphasizing the authority of politicians like Abraham Lincoln, and others stressing the actions of slaves themselves.[2] Former slaves' appearances before the Southern Claims Commission shift attention away from the determination of whether or not slaves possessed agency in the war years to an exploration of how such questions mattered in the postwar years. The incorporation as citizens of a people who had been considered the antithesis of citizens carried potential contractions that obstructed former slaves' efforts to claim the Union as their own.

Claimants and commissioners before the Southern Claims Commission grappled with the challenge of former slaves – the antithesis of citizens – claiming the rights and privileges of citizens. Black southerners who explained their wartime loyalties as "always Union men although slaves" emphasized that they had sympathized with and contributed to the Union cause despite, and indeed because of, their enslavement. "Hard down slaves" blamed their inability to act as loyal citizens in the ways the commissioners expected on their enslaved status. "Friends to the old government" presented themselves as postwar citizens and called on the federal government to help secure their postwar freedoms. The commissioners exempted many former slaves from their standards for loyalty on the assumption that they had been unable to act as good citizens. However, they suspected that some former slaves, those who seemed too independent of or too dependent on their masters and mistresses, had been "slaves disloyal." Recognition or dismissal of slaves' participation in the Union war effort was a powerful argument justifying their inclusion or exclusion from postwar citizenship. Divergent interpretations of wartime slave agency had political uses in the postwar struggle over citizenship. For the most part, the conditions on which the commissioners accepted former slaves as loyal citizens did not provide black southerners a secure foundation for postwar citizenship.[3]

"Always A Union Man Although a Slave"

Johnson Gary of Virginia had been born a slave. As such, during the war, he had not been able to vote, hold office, own property, testify against whites, or legally marry. In all these ways, he had been the antithesis of the ideal citizen. Still, in his appearance before the commission, he explained, "I was always a Union man although a slave." He knew that "by the laws of god I ought to be free and that if the U.S. troops succeeded they would see justice done." Gary further asserted that, although he had been enslaved, he had not served the will of his masters. Claiming the curses of his owners as badges of pride, he boasted to the commissioners, "I was a bad Nigger." His refusal to comply with his enslavement had caused his sale from master to master until he had been owned by "most of the men" in his community. The formulation "always a Union man although a slave" alluded to the incongruity of a former slave claiming allegiances to the nation. Many former slaves, like Gary, resolved the contradiction by fixing their status as Union people in the very conditions that had previously disqualified them from citizenship: their enslavement.[4]

In the congressional debate over the payment of southern claims, congressmen rarely counted former slaves among the loyal citizens who deserved recompense for their sacrifices for the Union. In debates over southern claims, congressmen generally conflated "southerners" with white men and less frequently with white women. Even congressmen sympathetic to the plight of black southerners conceptualized "freedmen" as distinct from "southerners." On the few occasions that congressmen mentioned black southerners in the debate over southern claims, they usually did so merely to denounce former slaveholders' attempts to finagle compensation for their slave property. Congressmen, then, generally considered black southerners as property to be claimed by others rather than as citizens claiming property themselves.[5]

When they began their work in 1871, the commissioners in DC, like the congressional framers of their commission, did not imagine former slaves as loyal citizens. Their original printed interrogatories did not refer to slavery at all. They did not contemplate and then dismiss former slaves as potential claimants before their commission; they probably had not pondered them at all. The story of former slaves' participation in the war was not one they initially considered as relevant to their task of identifying loyal citizens and rewarding them for their losses. As a result, in the first months of operation, former slaves confounded and frustrated the commission's representatives when they submitted numerous claims for compensation. In response to an inundation of petitions by black southerners, W. B. Figures, a special commissioner in Huntsville, Alabama, asked his superiors, "Is it required of colored citizens that they should prove their loyalty the same as of white claimants?" Figures felt uncertain of his course in recording testimony because, although black southerners had been invested with citizenship after the war, they had possessed "no such status" during the war.[6] Unwilling to exclude blacks from their commission but equally unprepared to account for them, the commissioners in DC initially ordered special commissioners to treat black claimants just like white claimants.

Following the printed interrogatories, special commissioners asked former slaves questions geared toward white southern men. Under the first two versions of the interrogatories issued in 1871 and 1872, special commissioners asked former slaves numerous irrelevant questions: How did you vote on the ordinance of secession? Were you in any branch of the Confederate army, navy, militia, or home guard? Have you ever held any office in the Union army or navy or been educated at Military Academy at West Point or at the U.S. Naval Academy? Did you ever hold any office under the Confederate government? Were you a member of a vigilance committee or otherwise involved in the imprisonment, expulsion, or execution of Union soldiers or Union sympathizers? – and on and on in like manner.[7] Even special commissioners, who received compensation by the page, tired of recording "N/A" or other negative responses in the testimony. Operating from Natchez, Mississippi, an area with a significant number of black claimants, E. H. Stiles objected to the "needless" questions "not applicable to the circumstances of the party."[8]

The inundation of claims from former slaves eventually forced the commissioners to provide for them in their procedures. They revised, albeit in a limited manner, their interrogatories. In the 1872 version, they simply added a colored claimant section but continued to require former slaves to answer the loyalty questions, which presumed white masculinity. In the 1874 version, they finally exempted former slaves from answering many irrelevant questions applicable primarily to white men. In the process, commissioners neglected to query some former slaves on their loyalties at all. The interrogatories for free claimants, which exempted former slaves, comprised the main section addressing the loyalty question. On one extreme, black claimants answering questions before 1874 responded to a variety of irrelevant questions. On the other extreme, black claimants after 1874 might not testify to their loyalty at all.[9] The commissioners, then, did not devise any provisions to uncover the loyalties of black southerners. In their interrogatories, they did not solicit information about former slaves' experiences of slavery or their understandings of the Union and the Confederate causes. Consequently, the commissioners did not reconceptualize loyal citizenship to incorporate former slaves but instead largely exempted them from their standards. This meant that former slaves who proved their Union sympathies and actions did so on their own initiative and innovation. Although the commissioners' interrogatories barely mentioned slavery in any substantial manner relating to loyal citizenship, almost every former slave interjected commentary on the institution in explaining their sympathies and actions during the war.

Former slaves identified their loyal sympathies as a self-evident consequence of their enslavement. Most former slaves before the commission centered their interpretations of the war not on the preservation of the Union but on the abolition of slavery. Most white Unionists, especially those in the North and the West, condemned the war for destroying the Union, but former slaves before the commission celebrated the war for eradicating slavery. Major Middleton of Georgia declared that he had "sympathised with the Union cause" and "was not exactly opposed to the rebellion."[10] These assertions would have been a contradiction for a white Unionist, but not for a former slave who equated the "Union cause" with the extension of freedom and not with the suppression of rebellion. James Burwell of Virginia explained that "the Rebels were fighting for slavery and the others were fighting for freedom."[11] Identifying the Union cause as freedom and the Confederate cause as slavery, former slaves represented their allegiances during the war as straightforward and obvious. As one former slave remarked, "I was a slave and could not be anything else" but a "Union Man."[12]

Some former slaves met the commissioners' standard expectation for claimants to prove their contributions to the Union cause by showing that, despite their enslavement, they had defied their masters and mistresses and assisted the Union army. Slaves' rebellion during the Civil War built on a long-standing opposition to white authority. Slaves plotted or executed several slave revolts in localities across the South, including Richmond, Virginia, in 1800; German Coast, Louisiana, in 1811; Charleston, South Carolina, in 1822; and Southampton, Virginia, in 1831. Slaves also sided with the enemies of their masters and mistresses in nearly every conflict in North America. They joined the Spanish militia in Florida in combating the British in the colonial period, they fought with the British during the American Revolution and the War of 1812, they allied with Indians in the southeast in the colonial through early national eras, and they escaped across the Rio Grande in the Mexican-American War. Slaves continued this tradition in the Civil War with approximately 200,000 serving in the Union army and navy. Many more slaves worked as military or civilian laborers or as informants and guides.[13]

Formerly enslaved men before the commission presented their services to the Union army, especially as soldiers and support staff, as evidence of their loyal citizenship. John Cuthbert, a former Georgia slave, remembered that when the war first broke out, "I didn't know what war was then." He recounted learning that the Union soldiers were fighting for their freedom and hearing that "some had got killed in freeing us and I said I would be glad if freedom did get through here." When the Union army arrived in Savannah, he had offered his own contribution to the cause of freedom, enlisting as a soldier and seeing action in South Carolina, Florida, and Georgia during his year and a half in service.[14] Former slaves described joining the Union army as contributions to the Union cause that inspired a transformation in their sense of themselves. Edward Harper had served as a guide to General William T. Sherman's army on its arrival in his Georgia neighborhood in January 1864. He boasted, "All I did was to conduct the Union army on to the Rebels and they captured two or three thousand of them and made them prisoners, my old master was among them." His master had heard of his exploits with the Union army and had threatened to kill him. Harper admitted, "I was guilty of the charge and rather than be killed I went with the Yankee army." After choreographing the capture of his master, Harper remembered, "I felt like a new man as if I had been converted."[15]

Despite their failure to account for former slaves' sympathies with and contributions to the Union cause, the commissioners believed that most had been loyal to the Union. They had not solicited such stories of loyal citizenship, but they nevertheless gave former slaves a hearing. The commissioners were not particularly struck by former slaves' equation of the Union cause with freedom and the Confederate cause with slavery. They did not often bother to mention former slaves' embrace of freedom or critique of slavery in their reports to Congress. Instead, in cases in which they considered loyalty incontestable, the commissioners focused on actions rather than sympathies. They generally granted special approbation to formerly enslaved men who had offered long-term service to the Union army as soldiers, teamsters, and laborers. Testimony by these black male claimants forced them to acknowledge black men's contributions to the Union cause and, by extension, their role in Union victory. They noted in one claim, for example: "There is no doubt of his loyalty. He worked for the Govt, gave information to our officers, and was decidedly on the Union side."[16] The commissioners considered this kind of service, available only to black men, as the strongest evidence that former slaves submitted. When formerly enslaved men could provide such evidence of lengthy assistance to the Union army, the commissioners praised their claims as "well proved."[17] Among black claimants as among white claimants, the commissioners regarded actions within the purview of men as more significant contributions to the Union cause than actions within the purview of women.

The commissioners had written former slaves out of the story of loyal citizenship in the wartime South, not considering them relevant enough to incorporate into their interrogatories. Nevertheless, former slaves forced the federal government to account for them as loyal citizens. They redirected interrogatories that assumed white masculinity into answers that highlighted their enslaved experience. Former slaves identified the Union cause as freedom instead of merely reunion. They told the commissioners that they had reclaimed their labor from their Confederate masters and mistresses and had devoted it to the Union. In siding with the Union over the Confederacy, these former slaves suggested that they had maintained their independence despite the dehumanizing compulsions of the institution of slavery. In this manner, former slaves successfully reconciled the contradiction between citizen and slave and, indeed, based their status as loyal citizens in their perspectives and experiences as slaves. Former slaves claimed a place for themselves in the story of the war and, moreover, forced the federal government to acknowledge that place.

"A Hard Down Slave"

Jerry Brown of Georgia had hoped that "we should have some better times" if the Union won the war, but he had been unable to contribute to the cause in the manner the commissioners expected of loyal citizens. He had not voted against secession or joined the Union army. He had not even, as many former slaves asserted, offered his services to Union soldiers. In fact, he had served his "young master" in the Confederate army as a cook for nearly two and a half years. In excusing what the commissioners regarded as his inaction for the Union war effort and his support of the Confederate war effort, he explained, "I was a hard down slave." With this statement, he suggested that his actions had been under the control of his master. Nevertheless, Brown offered an alternative form of resistance as his contribution to the Union cause: he had prayed to God for Union victory. The commissioners ultimately accounted for these former slaves' wartime enslaved status by exempting them from their standards of loyal citizenship.[18]

In their testimony before the commission, former slaves described the abuse threatened and inflicted on them under slavery: "They would pin us up pretty close," "Rebels threatened to send me to jail," "They would whip me severely & put me in the stocks," and "He would put us in the barn & burn us all up."[19] Black claimants in the Natchez vicinity described a systematic campaign of terror that had started in the early days of the war. Fearing a slave insurrection in the summer of 1861, whites in Natchez convened trials at the local racetrack and eventually hanged many of the alleged conspirators. The executions continued through the war with victims numbering between ten and sixty. A vigilance committee charged James Carter with reading news of the battles to other blacks. Whites questioned him at the racetrack every day for three weeks. In their attempt to extract a confession, "they whipped me terribly," stopping only when he fainted and resuming again as soon as he gained consciousness. The committee had already hanged eight slaves in his presence and decided to hang Carter as well. Only the interference of a white deacon in the Baptist Church saved Carter from death.[20] In their postwar testimony, former slaves who had not witnessed the racetrack trials, beatings, and hangings recounted hearing about them and keeping quiet out of fear for their lives. James K. Hyman warned a fellow slave during the dark days of the war against talking in favor of the Union: "There was people always watching and listening and if any thing would got out that the gallows at the race track would get him."[21]

The watchfulness of their masters and mistresses, former slaves asserted, had restricted them from speaking, let alone acting, in favor of the Union. Under slavery, Jerry Myres of Georgia remembered, "we couldn't do any thing" except "mind how we talked over matters" because whites "would whip us half to death if they heard us talking on the side of the Yankees or if we were caught doing anything for them."[22] Many former slaves recounted that what services they had been able to perform for the Union had been necessarily secretive in nature. "We could not do anything except at the risk of our lives," one former slave observed. "It had to be concealed with yourself, if you did anything."[23] Some former slaves reported that they had fed Union prisoners, had helped them escape, and had hidden Confederate deserters, all surreptitiously. Judy Rose testified that she had given food to Union prisoners in Savannah. Confederates arrested her, but she then tricked her Confederate captors and gained her release by claiming, "I did not know any better." Despite her assertions of ignorance, Rose confided to the commissioners: "I helped them after that, but I had to keep it concealed."[24]

Many former slaves before the commission offered contributions to the Union cause that emerged from the enslaved experience. In the prewar and war years, slaves participated in "everyday" resistance, such as escape, disobedience, malingering, sabotage, and dissembling. In their testimony before the commission, former slaves drew on such forms of resistance to argue that they had supported the Union cause. Former slaves commonly highlighted their conversations among themselves as their contributions to the Union cause: "I used to talk to a few of my own color about our chances for freedom," "We always conversed on these subjects alone, and never in the presence of others," and "When we did talk to one another ... it used to be in whispers."[25] State laws had prohibited slaves from congregating among themselves, and so such acts had constituted resistance to white authority. Former slaves stressed that the severe punishments that slaveholders threatened and inflicted had prevented them from meeting the commissioners' expectation of public speech in favor of the Union. George Corprew of Virginia defied boasts by his white neighbors that he "should be shot" and that "the rope was made to hang me as soon as the rebel soldiers got back" by continuing to talk to the "colored people" about the war.[26] Former slaves had not been able to vote for the Union during the war, but they had been able to talk in its favor. Spreading rumors that the Union cause would bring freedom, Union soldiers would whip the Confederacy, and the Union army was approaching had been one means by which former slaves had been able to support the Union cause.[27]

Operating within their experiences of enslavement to meet the commissioners' requirements, former slaves presented praying and thinking as acts against the Confederacy and in favor of the Union. Over and over again, former slaves related that they had devoted their prayers to the Union cause: "I prayed that God would help us & be on the U.S. side," "We all went to singing and praying & we kept it up all night," and "I prayed myself every day for the Yankees to come."[28] Former slaves also offered their ability to think independently from their masters as a significant means by which they resisted their enslaved status and contributed to the Union. John Ford of Alabama admitted that his labor had been under the control of his master whom he had accompanied as a personal servant in the Confederate army. He had sacrificed his body to the Confederacy, but he emphasized that his mind had remained his own: "I had always to think one thing and speak another."[29] Former slaves counted such efforts as "work" in and of themselves. Joseph Bacon of Georgia explained that "the cords were drawn pretty tight on the slave; we had to walk straight & do all our work by thinking."[30] The commissioners expected loyal citizens to prove independence of action; former slaves often instead demonstrated independence of mind.

In addition to having been unable to publicly support the Union cause as a result of their owners' terror, some former slaves before the commission argued that they had been forced to support the Confederate cause. During the war, slaves had provided indispensable services to the Confederate war effort as military laborers, constructing the fortifications and manufacturing the munitions necessary to wage war, and as civilian laborers, growing the food essential to sustain the army.[31] Before the commission, former slaves emphasized that their contributions to the Confederate war effort had been coerced. Benjamin Sterling Turner of Alabama likened his labor for the Confederacy to his labor for his master. He explained: "Being a slave I was necessarily compelled to serve the Confederates in the trenches or otherwise. But I never did anything for them voluntarily. I never was a slave voluntarily, but was such in obedience to the laws of the nation."[32] Work for their masters had not signified acceptance of the master-slave relation as legitimate. Similarly, labors for the Confederacy had not denoted a dedication to the Confederate cause.

Some former slaves even argued that their enslaved status had rendered both their sympathies and their actions altogether meaningless and irrelevant. Adrien Croizet of Louisiana cited his status as a slave during the war to explain his position, or more accurately, lack of a position. He told the commissioners: "I was a slave and could not take any side," "I was a slave and did not know hardly what was going on," and "I was a slave and did not know who the Union were."[33] By repeatedly prefacing his statements with his excuse that he had been a slave, Croizet implied that slaves could not be expected to have taken a side in the war. He took refuge in his wartime enslaved status to excuse his inaction for the Union government. As one former slave explained, loyalty to the state was not permissible in a slave society: "I don't know much about what you call loyalty cause we black people and our masters did not talk about such things. 'twas not allowed."[34]

The commissioners exempted most former slaves who convincingly seemed like "hard down slaves" from their standards of loyal citizenship. They required white claimants, even white women, to prove that they had sympathized with and contributed to the Union cause. In contrast, they routinely absolved former slaves for their inaction for the Union and action for the Confederacy. As one special commissioner noted, "Any aid or comfort they may have given the *Rebellion* must necessarily have been done under compulsion they at the time being under the control of and subject to the orders of their master."[35] Quite frequently, the commissioners determined former slaves' loyalty on the basis of asserted sympathies alone, sometimes considering the question so self-evident that they ignored it altogether or simply noted that loyalty had been "established" by the evidence.[36] They almost never omitted a discussion of the question of loyalty in claims submitted by white southerners. In general, the commissioners believed that a "strong presumption" existed that former slaves had been loyal to the Union by virtue of their legal status.[37] This logic accepted that former slaves had possessed little ability to affect the course of the war, effectively miring former slaves in the master-slave relation and adopting their former masters' views of them as property under white control.

Their acceptance of former slaves as "hard down slaves" reinforced the commissioners' preconceptions about black incapability. Over and over again, they dismissed former slaves as "ignorant," "unintelligent," "slow," "easily misled," and "helpless."[38] R. B. Avery, one of the commission's special agents, reported to his superiors that "many of the colored people were mere blocks, without the capacity to reason as to the effect Union victories would have upon this race."[39] The commissioners treated many former slaves as members of a dependent race, deserving compassion and leniency. Charles Benjamin, the clerk of the commission, encouraged one former slave's attorney to resubmit a disallowed claim for reconsideration. "As we are all tender towards colored claimants, who are more ignorant, slow and helpless than their white colleagues," Benjamin had "no doubt" that the case would be approved for reexamination.[40]

Former slaves testified to the coercive and oppressive character of the institution of slavery. They portrayed themselves as "hard down slaves" who had been exploited and abused by their former owners and had therefore sympathized with the Union cause of freedom. As a result of their enslavement, these former slaves argued that they had often been unable to engage in the kinds of actions the commissioners expected of loyal citizens and, indeed, had sometimes been forced to behave as commissioners expected of disloyal citizens. Nevertheless, they highlighted talking, praying, thinking, and other secretive contributions as alternative forms of resistance. As long as former slaves mentioned their gratitude for freedom and condemned their abuse and harassment by white southerners, the commissioners sympathized with their plight as slaves. As long as they could classify black claimants as slaves too oppressed to help themselves or too ignorant to know better, the commissioners excused acts of disloyalty. In these ways, they included "hard down slaves" on the basis of the qualities that had justified their exclusion from citizenship. Representatives of the commission accepted former slaves as loyal citizens within the jurisdiction of their commission even though they had not been invested with citizenship under slavery. Even so, the commissioners did not accept many of these former slaves as loyal citizens on par with white southerners.

"Friend to the Old Government"

Henry Beedles, a Georgia former slave, swore to the commissioners, "I was always a friend to the old government." He had talked in favor of the Union cause, specifically relating: "We expected the old government was our friend but we did not expect anything from the rebels. We had tried them long enough & they still kept us in slavery." Beedles appeared before the commission to secure some kind of recompense from his "friend," the federal government. He and his wife Polly, despite the oppressions of slavery, had managed to secure a competence for themselves, a house and some stables. All this they had sacrificed to the Union cause – a life's work gone in a matter of days. Polly Beedles mourned, "We did all we could for the Yankees and it made me feel badly to see them take my property after we had been such good friends to them & had done all we could for them." The Beedleses had managed to replace their destroyed house with a "shanty," but they had "a hard time & have a hard time yet." Stressing their friendship with the Union, former slaves called on the federal government not only for compensation for their Union contributions during the war but also, more broadly, for assistance in securing their economic livelihood after the war.[41]

Friendship provided black southerners a useful metaphor for their relationships with representatives of the federal government. The language of friendship generally served as a means through which previously apathetic, disfranchised, or subordinate groups entered discussions of political life. Friendship implied affinity, equality, and reciprocity.[42] Former slaves' use of friendship transcended differences of race and region to assert a political community based on devotion to Union principles. Former slaves identified these Union principles as not merely reunion, but ultimately freedom. Members of this community of friends – former slaves and the federal government – owed mutual obligations to promote freedom as part of a wartime as well as a postwar relationship.

The process by which the Union had become the friends of the "colored people" had been a circuitous one. In the early national era, the federal government protected and expanded the institution of slavery by waging war to establish sovereignty over the territories, converting Indian lands into marketable real estate, establishing a land policy amenable to the formation of plantation estates, building infrastructure to enable the sale of slave-grown cash crops, and providing military assistance to suppress slave rebellions. At the beginning of the Civil War, the Union government renounced any intentions to interfere with the institution of slavery and instead cited the preservation of the Union as the motivation for war. Despite presidential pronouncements and congressional resolutions, slaves inserted slavery into the wartime agenda. With slaves daily entering Union lines and seeking their freedom, commanders decided to take advantage of slave labor. The use of slave labor and eventually the grant of freedom soon became legally established through various so-called confiscation acts, the Emancipation Proclamation, and the Thirteenth Amendment. The Union government shifted policy to embrace emancipation as a wartime exigency necessary to save the Union.[43]

In his postwar testimony, one former slave recounted the transformation from a war for Union to a war for freedom. Benjamin Sterling Turner of Alabama had paid close attention to the policies of the Union government and the Union army. He recalled that when the war first broke out "of course my sympathies were for freedom," but he had not been able to determine which side shared his goals. When General George B. McClellan returned several "captured" slaves who had entered his lines, Turner agonized that he "did not know how to decide" where to stand in the war. He remembered wavering in his loyalties, "waiting to see which side would give me my freedom." Lincoln's issuance of the Emancipation Proclamation finally settled his loyalties. From that moment on, he reported, "I was with the federals." As a newly inaugurated congressman at the time of his claim, Turner likely recognized the importance of the federal government and its policies in the shift toward emancipation and, moreover, in the extension of voting and officeholding to former slaves (Figures 4.1 and 4.2).[44]

Turner, in his discernment of a definite shift in the Union government's policy on emancipation, was exceptional. Most former slaves before the commission presented a mythical Union, one that had always embraced abolition.[45] They simply identified the Union cause as freedom with very little commentary

FIGURE 4.1. Benjamin Sterling Turner (c. 1875–1894) was born a slave before the Civil War and was elected a U.S. congressman during Reconstruction. In this portrait, likely taken after his service as a congressmen, Turner represented himself as a man of learning and stature.
Source: Brady-Handy Collection, Library of Congress, Washington, DC.

on the gradual and reluctant shift in policy. What they explained in their testimony was not when the Union turned to embrace emancipation, but why they had not immediately understood that the Union represented freedom. These former slaves narrated a story of discovery, not one of changing Union policies. Thomas Williams of Alabama confessed that slaves in his neighborhood had been "to a considerable extent ignorant" about the war.[46] Former slaves often blamed their obliviousness on their former masters and mistresses, who

FIGURE 4.2. Gaylord Watson, "From the Plantation to the Senate," 1884. This composite of plantation scenes and portraits highlighted the transformation of former slaves to senators during the Civil War and Reconstruction. The portraits include Benjamin Sterling Turner (top left) as well as Rev. Richard Allen, H. R. Revels, Frederick Douglass, Josiah T. Walls, Joseph H. Rainy, and William Wells Brown, not all of whom served in the Senate.

Source: Prints and Photographs Division, Library of Congress, Washington, DC.

had "kept us in the dark & where we could not hear."[47] Other former slaves accused their former owners of lying: "If the North was victorious in the end, we colored ones were to be sent to Cuba & sold" and "The Yankees had horns, and would drive the darkies in teams to pull wagons like mules."[48] These former slaves did not acknowledge a moment when the Union government had not been their "friends," representing their causes and their interests.

Many former slaves before the commission acknowledged the role of federal authority in securing their freedom. Levi Allain, a former slave in Louisiana, in a typical formulation, focused on the importance of the president: "I was freed by President Lincolns proclamation."[49] Other former slaves recognized the importance of the Union army in giving force to the Emancipation Proclamation. They routinely identified the arrival of Union troops and the consequent withdrawal of their owners' authority as significant events. Joseph Proctor, a former slave in Savannah, recounted: "Our old master run away. We had to laugh to seen them running away. I never saw such a site in my life.... They came in on one side and the rebels went out the other." Witnessing white southerners, who had once claimed mastery over their slaves' lives, suddenly reduced to ignominious flight was a sight that Proctor still relished nearly ten years later.[50] Former slaves highlighted these moments – the issuance of the Emancipation Proclamation, the withdrawal of their masters' and mistresses' authority, and the arrival of Union troops – as pivotal events in their chronology of the war.[51]

Historians disagree over the parties responsible for emancipation. Some argue that the credit belongs to Abraham Lincoln or military commanders, who set official Union policy, or emphasize the role of Union soldiers, who accepted escaped slaves into their ranks. Federal officials and Union officers and soldiers deserve acknowledgment for refusing to hold stubbornly to a war strictly for the preservation of the Union. Other historians attribute emancipation to the slaves themselves. These scholars appropriately contend that slaves first placed emancipation on the agenda. By escaping to Union lines, by making freedom an issue, slaves prompted a broadening of the war to suppress secession to a war for freedom. By refusing to work for their masters, slaves undermined the institution of slavery and obstructed the South's ability to wage war.[52]

Before the commission, former slaves, even those who had taken the initiative by escaping to Union lines, rarely credited themselves with their own emancipation. Slaves had long favored abolition but had lacked the resources to overthrow the institution on their own. Former slaves recognized the role of the Union in securing, and maintaining, their freedom. Moreover, it was in former slaves' political interest not to argue that they had forced the issue of emancipation on a reluctant nation. In devaluing their own role, freedpeople effectively promoted emancipation as a triumph of Union authority rather than a realization of a personal agenda. Doing so potentially placed the Union government under obligation to help former slaves establish the foundations of their freedom. Former slaves claimed the war as a victory over slavery, a victory incomplete without the eradication of the last vestiges of the institution.[53]

Many formerly enslaved men emphasized that they repaid their Union friends by casting their votes for the Union after the war. They extended their stories of their loyal citizenship into the postwar years to highlight their support of the Republican Party. David Combs of Mississippi compared the war years, "I could not vote then," with the postwar years, "I vote now for the Union."[54] Former slaves provided evidence of their postwar backing of the Republican Party despite the fact that none of the commissioners' interrogatories addressed postwar political affiliations. Although the commissioners generally viewed postwar votes as irrelevant in determinations of loyalty, former slaves, judging by the frequency of such assertions, considered their votes "for the Union" as proof of their continuing dedication to the Union cause. Loyalty, for many former slaves, was not just a matter of the past during the Civil War but also a matter of the present and future during Reconstruction.

Many former slaves had anticipated that Union victory would secure them a better chance in life, but they discovered that Union appropriations could reverse many of their gains. The former slaves who appeared before the commission had managed to secure some property in the prewar and wartime South but then lost much of it to the Union army. Former slaves who had exercised some control over their own time, especially those who had worked on their own account after finishing their allotted tasks or those who had arranged to hire their own time from their masters and mistresses, could potentially accumulate significant propertyholdings. The war had brought additional money-making opportunities provided by both the Union and the Confederacy, as both sides sought to mobilize all laborers for their cause.[55] For many former slaves, this had all vanished, almost in an instant, with the arrival of Union troops. Nancy Jones of Alabama reported that Union troops had cleaned her out in a matter of hours. She mourned the loss of her cows, hogs, oxen, and mare: "I tell you we were a long time making that little money."[56] Many former slaves found it difficult, almost impossible, to recover from these losses. Over and over again, they related that the Union soldiers had taken all of their worldly goods, leaving them with nothing, not even, in the words of one former slave, "a blanket to throw on my shoulders."[57]

Some former slaves critiqued their treatment at the hands of their so-called friends. James Miller remembered that he had initially thought the war was "too good to be true." Knowing his freedom was at stake, "I prayed that they might come through." When the Union soldiers did come to Savannah, however, Miller recounted that they were not the liberators he had expected. Immediately on their arrival, the Union soldiers began killing Miller's hogs. In protest, "my wife came out and commenced crying," but the soldiers "told her to get a way from them or they would lick her." Two of the soldiers stormed into the house and demanded Miller's two new pairs of shoes. When Miller gave one of his pairs but refused to sacrifice the other, a soldier drew his revolver and shot him. Miller complained to the officer in command to no avail. The officer "said he did not care" and that "he was going to take all he could get." In his testimony, Miller remembered, "I said nothing more and he went in and took everything I had." The Union soldiers had left one reminder, the ball still residing halfway between his knee and hip, which Miller exhibited to the special commissioner as evidence in his claim.[58]

As claimants before the commission, former slaves called on the federal government to meet their obligations by rewarding them for their loyalty and compensating them for their sacrifices. Prince Ponder of Georgia viewed his claim as just recompense for his contributions, suggesting, "I think if the Government knew how much service I did for them they would pay me without a word."[59] One special commissioner called on his superiors to rectify the injustices inflicted on black southerners. He reported:

There is no class of Southern Claimants who suffered so much in proportion to their means, by the Union army as the colored people. Through their toil and many other hardships they had got together some of comforts of life. They had been led, almost instinctually, to believe the Union army for which they had been so long praying were and would be their best friends, under such circumstances, to be made the first to contribute to the wants of their *"best friends"* seemed to them to be hard and they felt humiliated before their old masters who had been "damning" the Yankees from the commencement of the war.[60]

The special commissioner condemned the irony of the Union imposing so severely on its "best friends."

Petitions before the commission were part of a larger effort by former slaves to call on the federal government for assistance in securing an economic livelihood for themselves and their families. After the war, many former slaves hoped that the federal government would confiscate land from former slaveholders and redistribute it to former slaves. Especially in rural areas, many former slaves regarded independent land ownership as a key foundation for their freedom. Radical Republicans proposed measures for confiscation and redistribution, but ultimately the federal government rejected such legislation. President Johnson even dispossessed former slaves of land that they had already cultivated under earlier federal confiscation and redistribution efforts. White northerners and westerners were reluctant to infringe on former Confederates' rights to their property, and they also were fearful that black southerners lacked the skills to be productive farmers if granted economic independence. As a result, most former slaves remained landless and financially insecure.[61]

The commissioners were skeptical that many former slaves had the work ethic to accumulate significant propertyholdings. The colored section of the interrogatories almost exclusively dealt with the property rather than the loyalty issue, including several questions to establish property ownership.[62] The commissioners included these questions because they suspected that in many cases the crops or livestock had actually been owned by the slaveholder and not the slave. When confronted with black southerners who claimed that they had been propertyholders, the commissioners often expressed skepticism. They disallowed the claim of one former slave because "there is nothing to show that this slave was more industrious, thrifty, or money getting than usual, or even that he had any such character for industry and economy."[63] Indeed, the commissioners sometimes dismissed examples of black productivity as simply another one of slavery's coercions. In some areas, slaveholders had provided slaves provision grounds. Slaves had fed themselves from these provision grounds and sold the excess and, in this way, could accumulate money to buy stock, wagons, or other property. With little understanding of the slave economy, the commissioners refused to recognize slaves' property as the proceeds of independent labor – examples of their industriousness – and instead viewed their property as rations – indications of their masters' largesse.[64] The commissioners acknowledged some former slaves as "industrious," but they often identified them as exceptions. They praised one former Arkansas slave as "industrious beyond his class."[65] Like many government agents and civilian reformers in the postwar South, the commissioners thought that slaves, either as a consequence of their racial inferiority or as vestige of their degradation, had not labored on their own account without coercion.[66] The former slaves who received compensation proved to the commissioners' satisfaction that they had been unusually "industrious." Those who could not found the federal government unreceptive to their claims.

Former slaves used the language of friendship to chart a new postwar relationship to replace the institution of slavery. They identified the Union as their friend in effecting their emancipation, and they presented themselves as the friend of the Union in the continuing effort to secure freedom. In doing so, they emphasized the mutual obligations of friendship in not just the wartime but also the postwar years. Most immediately, former slaves called on the federal government to act as their friends in approving their claims. Although most former slaves secured compensation as loyal citizens, many were hampered by an assumption that they were not productive workers. In this way, former slaves before the commission, like former slaves more generally, found the federal government an unreliable friend in helping them secure the economic foundation of freedom.

"A Slave Disloyal"

June R. Gordon of Georgia insisted, "I sympathized with the Union cause." However, he had done little to support the Union cause beyond cooking for a few Union soldiers and supplying them conveyances. Instead, he had hoped "God would bring them through" and had continued to work at his trade for the Confederate army. In his testimony before the commission, he explained: "The way I came to be in the army with the rebels was that my master hired me out.... I tried to stay at home & work at my trade but he told me that he couldn't get the right boys that he wanted & he would keep me there only 2 or 3 weeks, but he kept me there 2 years." His narrative of his Confederate service attributed responsibility to his master: his master had hired him out, his master had selected him, and his master had kept him in service. The commissioners suspected that Gordon had been disloyal, citing only the fact that "the claimant was for two years a servant in the confederate army." They denied the claim, noting "if we can believe a colored man and a slave disloyal, we would require further proof of loyalty in this case."[67] June R. Gordon was one of fourteen former slaves who the commissioners rejected at least partially on the loyalty question.[68] They suspected that some favorite slaves, mostly personal servants, drivers, and artisans, who seemed too dependent on or independent from their masters and mistresses had sympathized with and contributed to their owners' cause.

Asa Owen Aldis, the president of the commission, needed to look no further than his own family history for an example of a devoted relationship between slave and slaveholder. In an account of his family written for his children, Aldis told the story of a loyal family slave. Chloe had been a "favorite" with Aldis's grandmother. "Chloe was treated with the greatest tenderness by my grandmother." Indeed, her commitment to her slave cost her life. Grandmother Aldis caught measles from Chloe while supervising her care. Aldis depicted the dedication between slave and slaveholder as mutual, describing Chloe as "much attached" to his father, with whom she remained even after she legally gained her freedom in 1773. In his will, Aldis's grandfather left Chloe a bequest in recognition of her services to the family.[69] The commissioner's memory of Chloe paralleled devoted slave stories of the prewar and wartime South that were popular in the postwar years.[70] Such stories likely primed Aldis and the other commissioners to interpret some former slaves not as loyal citizens of the Union but instead as loyal slaves of their masters and mistresses.

Former slaves who did not express unequivocal gratification with emancipation in their testimony raised the commissioners' suspicions. Joseph Jefferson of Mississippi testified: "At the beginning of the rebellion I did not know anything about it, had no feelings or sympathy about the matter one way or the other. From the beginning of the war to the close I dont know that I had any sympathy on either side." He further explained that as a young man he had offered his master $1,200 dollars for his freedom, but his master had refused. "I wanted to be free," but by the time of the Civil War, he noted, "I had got to be so old that my freedom wouldn't do me much good." Proslavery ideology had promoted one of the benefits of slavery as masters' and mistresses' care of elderly dependents. Jefferson received his freedom in his old age after he had lost his most productive years to slavery. The commissioners ruled against

Jefferson. They omitted his discussion of freedom and merely noted, "He says distinctly that he had no feeling or sympathy for either side."[71] In suspecting that former slaves could favor slavery over freedom, the commissioners drew on popular romanticizations of slavery. Whites imagined that former slaves, faced with the hardship of supporting themselves, longed for, in the words of one song, "dem good ole times" of life under slavery.[72]

Most of the fourteen claimants that the commissioners singled out as possibly disloyal had not expressed satisfaction with enslavement but instead had performed some service to the Confederacy on what seemed to be voluntary terms. In line with predominant Western traditions, the commissioners understood slavery as coercion and freedom as autonomy.[73] They tried to fit former slaves' stories of slavery into these categories. However, the day-to-day operations of slavery had not easily conformed to such a dichotomy. Most former slaves attempted to tell their stories of their enslavement within the commissioners' framework, but a few – those suspected by the commissioners of having voluntarily performed some service for the Confederacy – failed to engage the concepts, either not perceiving the necessity to do so or not choosing to make their claims on those grounds.

Former slaves who seemed autonomous enough from their masters and mistresses to be able to choose their labors raised the commissioners' skepticism. One former slave, Israel Smith of South Carolina, admitted to having voluntarily served the Confederacy during the war. He testified that he had played in a band for a Confederate rifle company: "I went with this company ... of my own accord; I was not compelled to do so, and only went for the pay I received." What made Smith different from the numerous other former slaves excused for contributing to the Confederate cause? The commissioners refused to overlook labors for the Confederacy when claimants did not fit their conception of a coerced slave. In their report to Congress, they listed various factors that set Smith apart from other slaves and justified their refusal to excuse his disloyal act. Before the war, Smith, a carpenter by trade, had hired his time from his master for $25 a month. "Otherwise," the commissioners concluded, "he controlled his own time and actions." In particular, they noted that Smith had made contracts for himself, had acquired some property, and had owned a carpentry shop. They further emphasized that "he was an unusually intelligent man" in that he could read and write and even remarked on his proficiency in noting that "his signature is well written." Given Smith's autonomy, privilege, and intelligence, the commissioners deemed his actions on behalf of the Confederacy as little different from a white man's. Consequently, they ruled that his services constituted "direct material aid to the confederate cause." The commissioners held former slaves responsible for labors for the Confederacy when they sounded too autonomous, too privileged, and too intelligent to fit their notion of the typical former slave.[74]

The ability of a slave to have secured wages for his or her services also triggered the commissioners' suspicions that the claimant had not been treated as a slave. George Gardner had worked as a butcher for the Confederacy from the beginning of the war until the arrival of General William. T. Sherman in Savannah in December 1864. Gardner explained, "I never was in any such [Confederate] department except as a slave." He insisted: "I had to do it. I was hired to the head boss W. H. Davis, for twenty dollars a month. My mistress, Mrs. Harmon, hired me to Davis." In this way, he disavowed personal responsibility for his actions. R. B. Avery, special agent for the commission, rejected Gardner's attempt to liken himself to a mere object and expected him to function as an actor in his own right. He believed that Gardner should have refused work for the Confederate butcher and should have tried to find employment with one of the "citizen butchers." The commissioners accepted Avery's logic in their report to Congress.[75]

Apparently devoted slaves seemed, in the commissioners' estimation, likely to have performed voluntary services to the Confederacy. Edmund Boone, a former Arkansas slave, reported that his master "took" him as a cook and waiter for two years while he served in the Confederate army. Boone insisted, "I object[ed] to going & told my master that I did not want to have anything to do with war, but I had no choice for I had to do what I was ordered." He did not consider his work inconsistent with his loyal citizenship: "I went but never shot a gun or carried a weapon. I was just cook & waiter for my master and that was all." Lafayette Boone, Edmund's former master, reinforced his testimony, depicting him as as a "loyal Subject," a "very reliable servant, honest faithful and moral," and a "good" and "inoffensive old Darkey." He agreed that Edmund had been loyal during the war, but by loyal, he meant loyal to his master. The closest Lafayette came to addressing loyalty as the commissioners understood it was his assertion that Edmund "certainly had no inducements to be disloyal." He dismissed the idea of arguing over loyalties with his slave. "I did not hold any political discussions with him," he disparaged, because "he was my slave and under my controll until the end of the war." Lafayette based his conclusion that Edmund had been a "loyal Subject" on the "general principles" of the master-slave relation. He cited no evidence of Edmund's thoughts, expressions, or actions, relying solely on the fact that Edmund had been his slave and therefore subject to his will. Edmund's decision to stay with his master in the Confederate army had probably been less about his obedience to his master and more about his devotion to his wife. Two witnesses, both former slaves, revealed that Lafayette had promised Edmund his wife's freedom. Faced with the difficulty of articulating his complex reasons for remaining with his master, Edmund probably favored a simpler story, one that he likely expected would be compelling to the commissioners, and chose to present himself as controlled by his master, which was certainly how his former master preferred to remember his slave. If this was his strategy, Edmund miscalculated. The commissioners ruled that "had he been loyal, he would have gone off with the Union soldiers rather than staid with his master who was in the rebel army." They may have concluded that Boone's service in the Confederate army indicated that his loyalties to his master took precedence over any supposed loyalties to the Union government.[76]

Formers slaves rejected partially on the grounds that they had performed labors for the Confederacy were hampered by an inability to explain the more subtle manifestations of coercion in their lives. Whereas coercion appeared as distinct moments of menace or violence in the testimony of white southerners, coercion had characterized the lives of slaves. Signs that they could not fully control their own destinies abounded. Their labor for their owners, their sale at the auction block, their forced migration to distant plantations, their punishment for insubordination or rebellion, and their rape and concubinage bore witness to the fact that coercion had invaded nearly every aspect of their lives. As a force so self-evident and so pervasive, coercion had been almost impossible to articulate in its full proportions. James S. Dean, a Virginia blacksmith, made some efforts to convey the involuntary nature of his labor for the Confederacy. He admitted that he had known that he had aided the enemy, but "I could not help it, they made me do it." He asserted that his labor had been coerced, but he did not bother to explain all the considerations that may have figured in his decision to stay in Confederate service. There is plenty of other evidence in the claim to suggest Dean's limited ability to act on behalf of the Union or in opposition to the Confederacy, but neither he nor his witnesses emphasized this information as a source of coercion in their lives. Had Dean run off to the Union army, he would have left his wife and children at the mercy of a possibly vengeful mistress. His brother had attempted to escape, prompting the mistress to send his brother's wife and her children south in retaliation. In denying the claim, the commissioners mentioned that Dean had served as a blacksmith with the Confederate army, but they did not mention that his mistress had retained control of his wife in bondage. Dean's failure to impress on the commissioners the coercive nature of the institution of slavery led them to reject him, in part, on the loyalty issue.[77]

The elite, favorite, and nominal slaves who failed the test of loyal citizenship did not match the commissioners' vision of ignorant or abused slaves. The commissioners judged a few former slaves as possibly disloyal if they had seemed too dependent on or too independent from their masters and mistresses and if they had seemingly expressed disloyal sympathies or performed disloyal acts. They held these former slaves to the same standards as white southerners, expecting them to demonstrate that they had not only sympathized with but contributed to the Union cause. Although they acknowledged that most former slaves had undoubtedly favored the Union as a result of their wartime enslaved status, they believed that a few former slaves had been leniently treated and had therefore possibly sympathized with and contributed to the Confederacy. The commissioners rendered their judgments concerning the loyalties of former slaves within a bifurcated conception of the institution as either harsh and exploitative or lenient and benevolent. They forced these claimants' stories to fit into their preconceptions of slavery. Their decisions in these cases reveal the extent to which former slaves' acceptance as loyal citizens depended on their inability to meet the qualifications of loyal citizens.

Former slaves before the Southern Claims Commission faced the challenge of claiming status as loyal citizens when they had previously been the antithesis of citizens. Nearly universally, they insisted on an ideological citizenship that promoted a mythical Union, one that had always represented freedom. They depicted slavery as an oppressive institution in which their masters and mistresses, to different extents, had controlled their time and their labor. Yet at the same time, former slaves insisted on defining themselves as separate from their former owners. They advanced positions that measured the distance between slavery and freedom, variously emphasizing their Union sympathies, stressing their Union contributions, and dismissing their Confederate services. Many former slaves claimed active citizenship, managing to meet the commissioners' standards, but many others claimed subject citizenship, seeking exemption from the commissioners' standards. Collectively, former slaves offered alternative understandings of the ways in which loyal citizens could claim membership in the nation.

The commissioners generally held former slaves to a lesser standard of loyal citizenship than they required of white men and women. They recognized that some former slaves, primarily formerly enslaved men who had offered their services as soldiers, teamsters, and laborers to the Union army, had met their standards of loyal citizenship. In many other cases, however, they accepted that slaveholders' oppression had prevented former slaves from supporting the Union cause and had even forced them into contributing to the Confederate cause. They viewed many of these former slaves, those who had not fulfilled their obligations to the Union, as helpless, simpleminded, and indolent – not typical characteristics of good citizens. The commissioners accepted as loyal citizens most former slaves, especially those who seemed abused and exploited, but disallowed a few former slaves, those who seemed autonomous, privileged, and intelligent. They held these latter claimants to the same standards they held their former masters and mistresses.

The contest over the representation of slaves and slavery had pressing urgency in the postwar years as northerners, westerners, and southerners considered new definitions of citizenship. In requesting recognition of themselves as loyal citizens, a necessity of the claims process, former slaves attempted to explain their qualifications for acceptance in the reunited nation. They staked this claim publicly in defiance of a hostile white population. Although the commissioners accepted them as loyal citizens, they did not consider former slaves as full and equal citizens on par with whites. In fact, the commissioners' admission of former slaves as loyal citizens partially depended on their resemblance to the commissioners' idea of an ignorant and abused slave and not on their resemblance to a worthy citizen. The conditions on which they accepted many former slaves as loyal citizens – their inability to meet their standards of good citizenship – did not provide black southerners a firm foundation for postwar citizenship. Most former slaves may have successfully won status as loyal citizens to the Union government during the Civil War for the purposes of the commission, but they found their attempts to gain status as full citizens of the reunited nation more difficult to achieve.

5

The Colored Union

Being All Things to All Men

The witnesses in the claim of Carroll Jones of Louisiana depicted two different men: one who had been loyal to the Confederacy and one who had been loyal to the Union. Jones was recognized as free born but was actually the son of a slave woman and her white master. He was alternatively described as "colored," "negro," "mulatto," and "half breed," and his wife as "colored," "negress," and "Choctaw."[1] Several white witnesses, former Confederates, asserted that Jones had supported the Confederacy. He had assisted in raising a Confederate company during the war and had campaigned for office on the Democratic ticket after the war. Several black witnesses, former Unionists, insisted that Jones had favored the Union. He had kept slaves informed about the progress of the Union army during the war and had stood for office on the Republican ticket after the war. Jones's attorney suggested that as a "free man of color," Jones had been "compelled ... to be all things to all men."[2]

The necessity "to be all things to all men" indicates the anomalous and contradictory position of people in the South who did not fit the model of free whites and enslaved blacks. They were free but lacked the rights of most free persons. They were not white but not enslaved like most nonwhite persons. Free nonwhite southerners had not always been anomalous and contradictory. They became so through the concerted efforts of many white southerners to bifurcate the racial hierarchy to privilege all whites as free, subordinate all blacks as enslaved, and remove all Indians as savages. Southerners like Jones had to contend with the compulsion to "be all things to all men" because they were positioned on the shifting ground between white and black and between free and slave. They understood themselves and were understood by others in relation to the black and white racial hierarchy.

Before the Southern Claims Commission, nonwhite southerners who had been free before the war negotiated the necessity to "be all things to all men" in ways that both reinforced and contested black and white categories of loyal citizenship. Many free blacks, with assertions that "all the colored people were for the Union," understood themselves or represented themselves as little different from former slaves in their sympathy with and support for abolition as the Union cause. Some free blacks, denoting themselves as "called free" and emphasizing their freedom as merely nominal, championed equal rights as the Union cause. The commissioners applied their practices for former slaves to most free black claimants, accepting them as equivalent to former slaves in their abilities to prove their loyal citizenship. However, they held some claimants merely "called colored" to their standards for white southerners, suspecting that these claimants had not understood themselves or comported themselves akin to former slaves and free blacks. Similar to southerners "called colored," Indians did not fit into black and white conceptualizations of loyal citizenship. Claimants who issued declarations such as "the Indians were all Union people" presented claims on the basis of an Indian identity that distinguished their loyal citizenship from both white and black southerners. Free nonwhite southerners challenged the formulation of loyal citizenship as a binary between free whites and enslaved blacks. The commissioners' decisions in these claims reveal a conceptualization of racialized citizenship that marked colored as inferior and white as superior.

"All the Colored People Were for the Union"

Harriet Dallas of the Georgia low country identified herself as a free black woman to the commissioners because her husband had purchased her freedom, along with her daughter's, six months before the arrival of the Union army in Savannah. Still, her distinctions from slaves were not otherwise immediately evident. She had probably remained legally enslaved because state legislators had severely restricted manumission after 1801. Moreover, in her postwar testimony on her wartime loyalties, she sounded almost identical to a former slave: "I was for the Union all the time when the State went out I thought freedom would come and I was glad she went out." She had not been able to contribute to the Union cause, and indeed an investigation revealed that her husband, a river boat pilot, had assisted Confederates in their attempts to capture a Union gunboat. Dallas and her witnesses did not differentiate between the loyalties of free blacks and former slaves, asserting that "all the colored people were for the Union." The commissioners accepted this formulation, treating Dallas like a former slave and exempting her from their requirement for evidence of both loyal sympathies and contributions. The classification of free blacks with former slaves reflected a postwar assertion of black southerners as a community of loyal citizens.[3]

In the prewar and war years, free blacks had faced numerous restrictions that rendered them akin to "slaves without masters." Indeed, a legal presumption marked black southerners as slaves unless proven otherwise. To emphasize their dependent status, every southern state denied black men the right to vote. On the assumption that blacks could not serve as competent witnesses, free blacks were prohibited from testifying in court against both white and black defendants. To guard against insurrection, free blacks were prevented from keeping weapons or holding meetings. In an attempt to subordinate blacks to white oversight, many free blacks were forced to secure white guardians. Proponents of restrictive laws intended to push free blacks into positions as closely approximating slaves as possible. Legislators restricted, even prohibited, manumission. Periodic enslavement campaigns further threatened free blacks' minimal freedoms.[4] After the war, these restrictions provided free blacks before the commission with many reasons to equate their wartime status with slaves.

In their appearance before the commission, many free blacks, like former slaves, based their loyal sympathies on their opposition to slavery. Free blacks who had been born slaves but had secured their freedom through purchase or manumission had especially empathized with the plight of slaves. Green Puckett, a nominally free black in the Georgia upcountry who had bought his freedom before the war, declared: "I was a Union man Strong because I believed the Union men favored my freedom and the freedom of my people and because I said that I wanted my people free.... I said I wanted to know and see that my people was free if I only lived one minute afterwards."[5] Free blacks who had never been personally enslaved under southern law sometimes asserted that they had sympathized with the Union cause for the sake of their enslaved relatives and friends. "I liked the Union best," Abraham Johnston of the Georgia low country explained, "because I thought that was the side for freedom, and my wife was a slave."[6]

Many free blacks, like former slaves, reported contributions to the Union cause. Phil Sewell and his son Phil Jr., two nominally free blacks who had purchased themselves from their master, formed a "partnership" during the war to help white and black Union people escape to Union lines. Sewell Jr. traveled at night with a wagon to Petersburg, Virginia, and met his father at prearranged destinations to pick up Union men and women to ferry them to Union lines.[7] Like former slaves, many free blacks in their testimony before the commission recounted various other contributions to the Union cause, including acting as soldiers, laborers, informants, guides, nurses, cooks, and laundresses.

Like former slaves, many free blacks also complained that Confederate terror had prevented them from fully translating their Union sympathies into Union contributions and even forced them into assisting the Confederate cause. Over and over again, free black men admitted that they had been compelled to work on Confederate fortifications. This type of coercion had been common because slaveholders had been reluctant to lend their enslaved property to the cause and so authorities had turned to the free black population.[8] Some free blacks recounted their attempts to resist Confederate efforts to appropriate their labor for the Confederate cause. Benjamin Summers of southeastern Virginia explained that he had unsuccessfully tried to escape his impressment to work on coastal fortifications. He charged that he had been "given five hundred lashes and then rubbed down with salt brine" as a punishment. Summers lacked the evidence that the commissioners favored: voting and soldiering for the Union. He presented what evidence he did possess: his scarred body. The special commissioner flinched at the sight of Summers's "fearful looking body," which seemed "as though large pieces of flesh had been dug out."[9]

Most free blacks who referred to the "colored people" in ways that included both former slaves and free blacks and that drew no distinctions between them did not attempt to prove to the commissioners that they were identical in perspectives and experiences to former slaves. They regarded such commonalties as self-evident. James Dennison of Savannah revealed his understanding of himself as part of a wartime community of both free and enslaved colored people in a variety of ways. First, when he discussed "we" and "us," he included both free blacks and slaves. As he had told his "colored friends," he knew that the war would "free us all" and specifically that "we the colored people would be free" once the Union army arrived. Second, Dennison, although he had accounted himself as free, had only gained his freedom at the end of the war, and this freedom was likely only nominal. He had bought himself about ten years before the war: "But I failed to get my paper and they sold me right back into slavery a second time and then I went to work and bought myself again." Georgia's restrictions on manumission meant that Dennison's second purchase of himself, like his first, had probably not been legal. Third, although Dennison had arranged his nominal freedom, his wife had remained enslaved under an abusive master, one who had "almost killed her" for talking in favor of the Yankees. Finally, Dennison demonstrated his connections with the slave population by calling two former slaves as witnesses to corroborate his testimony. In these ways, referring to both slaves and free blacks as a unit, possessing only an insecure nominal freedom, having enslaved relatives, or associating with colored friends, many free blacks revealed their embeddedness in a colored community of both free blacks and slaves.[10]

Although many free blacks understood themselves as part of an enslaved and free colored people, such representations were sometimes a postwar rather than a prewar or wartime sensibility or strategy. In the prewar and war years, Georgiana Kelley of Savannah had benefited from her distinctions from slaves and other free blacks and, indeed, likely understood herself as different. She maintained close relationships with prominent whites who oversaw her interests. Her guardian, Richard D. Arnold, the mayor of Savannah for the last two years of the war, likely regarded Kelley as superior to other people of African descent. He believed that "mulattoes," as a result of their "Caucasian blood," were superior to "negroes." During the war, when the Union army appropriated her property, she turned to Mayor Arnold to (unsuccessfully) lobby Union authorities for the return of her property. Kelley also distinguished herself as a member of a group of free women of color, many of them elite, who sewed Confederate uniforms. The advertisement of this service in the local paper secured her a reputation as a free woman of color who supported the Confederate cause.[11] In contrast, in the postwar years, Kelley portrayed herself as a member of an oppressed race, little different from former slaves. In her testimony before the commission, she informed the commissioners that "you must know that all of my color sympathised with the Union Cause, because we were oppressed and who don't want to get from under oppression." She declared, "If you are oppressed you know that every time you draw your breath, you want the side that doesn't oppress you to gain in the battle." In excusing her services to the Confederacy, she asserted that "We were in slavish times then & if I had not done it, I don't know what they would have done to me, I was a seamstress." Kelley also minimized her relations with prominent Confederates – including her guardian Mayor Arnold who possessed relevant knowledge about her propertyholdings – by failing to call her white patrons as witnesses. She emphasized her connections with the enslaved population by calling former slaves as witnesses on her behalf. She had turned to her white guardian during the war in her failed attempt to secure the return of her property, but she relied on former slaves after the war to successfully gain compensation from the commission. The wartime and postwar reversals of power enabled Kelley to proclaim herself a member of the colored people and provided incentives for doing so in ways that she would not have dared in the prewar or war years.[12]

The records of the commission reveal the postwar affinities and alliances between free blacks and former slaves who participated in the creation of a new racial community. They understood and represented themselves as similar to one another, especially in their dealings with the government. Emancipation eliminated the legal distinction between former slaves and free blacks, and enfranchisement elevated the two groups to the same political level. Reconstruction empowered black southerners and disempowered many white southerners, making black allies in many ways more valuable than white allies. Many free blacks discerned the benefits of publicly standing with the formerly enslaved population. By themselves, free blacks did not represent a significant power within postwar politics. In combination with former slaves, however, they constituted a compelling force.

The commissioners, for the most part, found the contention that "all the colored people were for the Union" persuasive. They were willing to believe that most former slaves had been loyal to the Union by virtue of their subordinate status, and they routinely extended this presumption to free blacks. They generally considered free blacks as members of the same community as former slaves.[13] Despite their practice of listing all evidence in favor of loyalty – a practice necessitated by congressional oversight – the commissioners sometimes simply stated that a free black had been loyal to the Union, even if the claimant offered very little evidence.[14] Free blacks, like Georgiana Kelley, who had benefited from their distinctions from slaves in the prewar and war years capitalized on their similarities with former slaves in the postwar years.

The commissioners had no reason to doubt Kelley's contention that she had suffered the same oppressions as slaves and approved her claim.[15] In practice, despite theoretical distinctions, the commissioners usually considered the differences between slave and free members of the colored community as barely meaningful.

Free blacks who asserted that "all the colored people were for the Union" understood and represented themselves as similar to former slaves in their oppression within the slave South, their interpretation of the Union cause as abolition, and their constrained opportunities to assist the Union army. These free blacks identified themselves as free but otherwise drew few distinctions between themselves and enslaved southerners. They claimed loyal citizenship collectively as an oppressed racial group. They did so even if they had not always represented themselves in this manner in the prewar and war years. The commissioners accepted this unity of identity among most colored people, exempting most free blacks from their requirements for active citizenship and accepting most free blacks as loyal citizens, often on the basis of their inability to fulfill wartime political obligations. Assertions of and acceptance that "all the colored were for the Union" demonstrate the strength of a shared postwar identity that transcended differences in antebellum status.

"We Were Called Free"

Joseph Brown of Virginia was not a typical black southerner. He had never been enslaved, having been born to a free mother, and had never lived with a master or mistress, having owned a farm of about 132 acres. Brown understood himself as both similar to, as well as different from, former slaves. He emphasized: "Of course I was a Union Man always. I was born free & so was my wife, but we had no liberty." As his neighbor attested, "We were both free born and were called free but we were denied the rights of a citizen." Unlike free blacks who made no distinctions between themselves and enslaved southerners in accounting for their allegiances, Brown exhibited a consciousness of himself as a "born free" person. At the same time, he also stressed that white southerners prevented free blacks from enjoying the benefits of their free status, particularly complaining that "we had no chance for education & hardly any rights at all." He anticipated that the Union would bestow full citizenship: "I always believed the Yankees would give me my rights." Free people of color who represented themselves as distinct from former slaves and who critiqued the nominal nature of their freedom presented different claims to loyal citizenship: ones rooted in the denial of their rights under the Confederacy and the expectation of their rights under the Union.[16]

Free people of color before the commission who specifically distinguished themselves from the enslaved population often did so on the basis of their status as freeborn men and women of color with some percentage of white racial ancestry. Samuel Hord, a freeborn man of color in Virginia, identified himself as seven-eighths white and one-eighth colored. He informed the commissioners, "I sued and got the rights by law of a white man" during the war. When asked if the "result of the war gave you that right," he responded, "O, if I had got them by the war I would have been no more than any other but I got them since the war as a white man." In correcting that he had gained his rights as a "white man," Hord differentiated himself from the masses of former slaves and free blacks who received their rights as a result of Republican policies.[17] James C. Muschett of Virginia took similar pride in his whiteness. When asked "what proportion of colored blood you have in your veins," Muschett responded by calculating his white blood: "well I think they supposed I had about – some said I was fifteen sixteenths white." Muschett's attorney summarized his racial status as "one seventh colored." Even though one-seventh was only eight-hundredths off, Muschett felt the necessity to correct his attorney. Muschett objected, "O no, not one seventh. My mother was three fourths white while she was a slave. Her father was a white man. My father was a white man. That would make me about fifteen-sixteenths." Finally, Muschett insisted, "a great many people would consider me white." Though the attorney noted his fraction of blackness, Muschett himself emphasized the predominance of his white racial heritage.[18] Other free people of color revealed their distinct identity through their associations, primarily socializing with and living among other free people of color.[19]

Free people of color who cherished a sense of themselves as distinct from slaves tended to focus on the denial of their rights as their main indictment of the Confederacy. Beverly Matteur of Virginia, "a free born man with fair skin," argued that "a free person whose blood was tinctured at all, had no more rights than a slave."[20] Free people of color listed many rights denied in the South, including "we had to get a pass to go around, we could not leave town without a pass, we could not own property in our own names, and we were looked upon with more suspicion because we were free."[21] And, of course, free people of color criticized the denial of the right of suffrage. Milton Copeland, a freeborn man of color in Virginia, complained: "I had no vote. No colored people had a vote then."[22] Some free people of color speculated that their oppression under Confederate rule would have ultimately culminated in their enslavement. William James, a freeborn man of color in Virginia, charged that "if the Rebels gained their independence they would make slaves of all of us free colored people."[23] The restrictions governing their lives led free people of color to conclude over and over again that they had been "called free" by name but had not been free in actual fact.

Some free people of color had secured privileges for themselves but had witnessed the erosion of those privileges in the prewar and war years, and consequently they also came to critique the South for its treatment. During peaceful times, free people of color could hope to escape notice or rely on a white patron to protect their interests, but the war had brought them to the attention of hostile white southerners. In the shock of war, their white allies had constituted meager defense against the enmity of Confederates intent on the subjugation of people of African descent and the entrenchment of white supremacy. Such transformations had been most marked in the lower South among long-standing communities of elite free people of color. One claimant before the commission, Cornelius Donato of Louisiana, had shared many commonalities with his white neighbors: appearance, wealth, and slave ownership. Donato explained to the commissioners that among "colored creoles" and white southerners "to a certain extent they agreed." However, Donato's testimony revealed that white southerners' tolerance for elite free people of color had evaporated during the war. He charged, "The white men always consider[ed] the colored element an enemy to the country at that time." According to white southerners, Donato seethed, "we were nothing else but God-damned niggers, and we had no business to stay in the country, and that they ought to take every one of us and drive us out of the country." He was particularly aggrieved that he could not spare his mother from such indignities, remembering that "she was greatly humiliated about all these things. We were insulted by the Confederates and such a thing as that." These elite, freeborn claimants – those who had enjoyed status and privilege before the war – revealed that they came to support the Union rather than the Confederacy as the best means to defend their interests.[24]

Free people of color who disputed their free status and dismissed its meager benefits emphasized their conviction that the Union would grant them their rights of citizenship. Donato declared, "I was very glad of course to see the war because we all thought the war would enfranchise us and give us our rights as citizens and abolish slavery and all that and putt every man on an equal footing as citizens."[25] This rights talk extended to black women as well as black men. Sarah Carter, a member of a prominent "family of free persons of color" in Georgia, reported, "We thought under the old Government we would be free and have our rights."[26] Free women of color, unlike white women who often eschewed politics, entered into these discussions of rights without apology or excuse for intruding on a supposedly male domain.

The commissioners were convinced that some free people of color had been merely "called free" and therefore had been loyal citizens by virtue of their oppression in the South. In some cases, they recognized these freeborn people of color as different from former slaves, identifying them as "a free man of color" or a "free woman of color."[27] In other cases, they simply categorized them with other colored claimants.[28] In most cases, however, the commissioners accepted that free people of color had suffered under similar oppressions as former slaves. They sympathized with one claimant's plight as a "free born" man without the "rights of citizenship because of the colored blood in his veins." As their investigation uncovered no disloyal acts, the commissioners invoked "the legal presumption, which arises from his status as a colored man" and assumed his loyalty by virtue of his race.[29] For these reasons, the commissioners – as in cases with former slaves – frequently exempted free people of color from proving that they had not only sympathized with but also

The Colored Union

contributed to the Union cause. To the commissioners, these free people of color were more similar to former slaves than white southerners.

Free people of color who criticized the nominal nature of their freedom possessed specific ideas about the meaning of freedom. They fixed their citizenship in rights: the denial of rights in the Confederacy and the expectation of rights in the Union. The commissioners accepted most free people of color, even those who distinguished themselves from slaves, as similar in their oppressions and therefore in their loyalties. So, in their most immediate goal, that of securing compensation for their wartime losses, southerners "called free" were successful. However, these free people of color highlighted freedom as not just the mere absence of enslavement but also the bestowal of the rights and privileges of citizenship. These free people of color claimed a specific kind of Union, one based on racial equality and one that ultimately remained unfulfilled.

"Called a Colored Person ... but ... Not a Slave"

François Bouligny, a Louisiana sugar planter, told a typical tale of his wartime experiences in his testimony before the commission. Confederates, desperate for manpower, had attempted to conscript him two years into the war. Under the cover of darkness, he had escaped to Union lines where he had remained for the rest of the war.[30] A common tale for many claimants before the commission, but an uncommon one for a claimant identified as "colored" in the commission's records. Bouligny presented relatively little of what the commissioners regarded as strong evidence. The commissioners rejected his claim on the grounds that he had not sufficiently proven his loyal citizenship. Noting that Bouligny had accumulated a significant amount of wealth and that he had been conscripted into the Confederate army, they concluded, "It is plain that such a person could not be treated as slaves are, even if he had African blood in his veins; and that such a person should be required to prove loyalty." The commissioners contended, "This claimant is called a colored person; but he was not a slave." The appearance before them of free people of color like Bouligny challenged the commissioners' routine conflation of colored and slave. The commissioners realized that Bouligny had been "called a colored person," but he had not been treated as a "colored person" – that is, as a slave. The commissioners refused to extend the exemptions usually granted to claimants who were "colored" to claimants merely "called colored."[31] They withheld a presumption of loyalty from thirty-eight free people of color who seemed autonomous like white southerners and not subordinated like black southerners, holding them to their standards for white southerners and deeming them deficient in their support of the Union.[32] The cases of southerners "called colored" highlight the degree to which official citizenship remained black and white.

About a dozen free people of color struck the commissioners as possibly disloyal because of some service they had provided to the Confederacy. By emphasizing their subordinate status within southern society, most free people of color succeeded in convincing the commissioners to overlook their actions in support of the Confederacy. A few free people of color could not fit, or would not fit, their experiences into this standard story of white oppression and black subordination. These rejected claimants admitted to a variety of services to the Confederacy in both a civilian and military capacity, including playing drums in the Confederate army, coopering for Confederate authorities, butchering for the Confederate commissary, working on Confederate gunboats, hauling munitions for the Confederacy, working on Confederate fortifications, and acting as servants to Confederate soldiers.[33] Many of these claimants testified in a similar manner as many free blacks in relating their sympathies. In expressing their position within southern society and their sympathies in favor of the Union, these free people of color could sound like free blacks who likened their status to slaves. Emmanuel Sheftall, although "born free," dismissed his status as "just as much a slave as any other colored person."[34] Although their accounts of their sympathies could seem identical to free blacks, they often described their services to the Confederacy in very different ways, and this roused the commissioners' suspicion.

A few free people of color seemed to the commissioners to prioritize their personal affairs over public affairs. James Goin of Alabama had acted as a servant to Confederate officers. The special commissioner considered it self-evident that a man with Union sympathies and a "freeman" would not "of his own accord" perform such services for the Confederacy. Goin responded: "*Why I went for money*. They paid me forty dollars a month." He considered his motivations obvious. He had simply earned money in the same way that enterprising free people of color and free blacks had long accumulated money in the antebellum years. This course of action was eminently pragmatic. He had taken advantage of lucrative opportunities even if he had to labor for white southerners who had regarded him as racially inferior and who had favored the enslavement of his race. He had not had the luxury of standing on principle and refusing to work for white southerners.[35]

Free people of color ruled potentially disloyal also fell victim to contrasting meanings of coercion. Archibald Jackson of South Carolina had acted as a cook and a laborer in the Confederate army for about a year. In excusing his service, Jackson could have argued that he had been little more than a slave and had not been able to help himself. This was the tactic that his lawyer chose, arguing that "surrounded by his hereditary superiors, and masters … there was no road of escape" for free blacks except compliance.[36] Jackson offered a contrasting explanation of his labor, one that emphasized his subordination as a free man of color, but one that did not excuse his behavior as the result of his supposed inherited inferiority. He agreed with the special agent's phrasing that he had "the privilege of doing as you pleased," but he meant something very different than the special agent intended. He explained, "I meant I could go or refuse as I pleased but I knew if I went it would be better for me and my family but if preferred I might be arrested and sent to Gillisonville Jail or Charleston

Jail." He had the privilege of doing as he pleased in that he "had the privilege by taking what comes," meaning "the risk." He had not been "shot tied up and whipped or sent to jail," so in that sense he had not been coerced.[37]

Free people of color and free blacks did not operate within a world in which choice and coercion possessed unequivocal meaning or even a world in which choice and coercion were the most important distinctions. In the claims process, free people of color confronted the challenge of fitting their experiences during the war into the vocabulary of the commissioners. Most white men, with their freedom less encumbered than free people of color, demonstrated little hesitation in identifying such choices as coercion by Confederate officials. Most free people of color showed no reluctance in identifying their labor as coerced, but some free people of color took every opportunity to claim freedoms wherever they could, even under coercive circumstances. Jackson in effect transformed a potentially unilateral relationship into a reciprocal relationship by choosing to accept wages for his labor rather than be forced to labor through compulsion. In doing so, he negotiated a careful line between autonomy and oppression – a line primarily drawn up by the commissioners and not by free people of color.

The commissioners rejected free people of color who had offered their services to the Confederacy if they had seemed autonomous like white southerners and not coerced like black southerners. Despite Archibald Jackson's explanations regarding the hazards of refusing to labor for Confederates, the commissioners ruled that "he voluntarily aided the confederacy and did not adhere to the Union cause."[38] The commissioners might have excused labor for the Confederacy if free blacks appeared ignorant. They disallowed one free man of color because he had labored for the Confederacy "with full knowledge that it was in aid of the confederate cause." Because "he is said to be very intelligent," "he did it after he was free," and "no force, compulsion, or duress is shown here," they deemed his services "aid and comfort to the enemy."[39] In these decisions, the commissioners considered free blacks' work for the Confederacy as little different from white southerners' work for the Confederacy. They did not consider these free people of color as subject to the will of others like slaves but responsible for their actions like white southerners. Indeed, they regarded these free people of color as "nearly white," as they noted repeatedly in their summary reports.[40] For these reasons, the commissioners expected these southerners to meet the same standards of loyal citizenship as white southerners.

Another set of eleven claimants appeared to the commissioners to have adopted neutral stances during the war. The commissioners could find few indications of disloyalty: little evidence of the expression of disloyal sympathies and little proof of the performance of disloyal acts. At the same time, however, these free people of color had not done much for the Union. Moreover, they did not seem to have been subordinated within southern society, which would have excused such seeming neutrality. Indeed, some seemed to have even prospered under southern society. Former slaveholders of color faced the greatest difficulties positioning themselves as victims of an oppressive society. Like most free blacks, they attempted to portray southern society as repressive, yet at the same time, unlike most free blacks, they had most clearly benefited under its auspices. To the commissioners, these free people of color who had embraced the South's most peculiar institution, seemed to more closely resemble white southerners than black southerners.[41]

Some former slaveholders of color, like free blacks who complained of the nominal nature of their freedom, stressed their rights in their discussions of their loyal citizenship. Alfred Anderson of Virginia identified himself as "a Union man" who "could not be anything else." He rejected the terms of his exclusion under antebellum society. Highlighting the irrationality of his subjugation, Anderson offered his two main qualifications: "I was born free, and had a great deal of property." Despite possessing what he considered sufficient credentials, he protested, "I had not the rights of a free man." Anderson reported expectations similar to many free blacks: "I would get all my rights if the Union triumphed, and so I always desired its success." Although he emphasized freedom, Anderson ignored slavery. He omitted the topic of slavery from his discussions of the war, and the commissioners did not initially ask. Anderson did not identify the Union cause as the cause of abolition, and he did not express any sympathy with such a cause. His notation that he had owned "a great deal of property" only obliquely referred to his status as a slaveholder.[42]

One former slaveholder of color discounted his commitment to the institution. Heluter Taunoir had owned fifty-seven slaves on his sugar plantation in Louisiana. He excused his slaveholding because "it was the habit to have slaves to work for you, but my slaves were treated like my children." It would certainly have been untenable for a free man of color to have employed free labor rather than slave labor on such a large scale. Taunoir further insisted, "I was perfectly willing to see them set free so that I could be freed myself," and "I would rather be as I am now, poor as I am, than as I was then before the war with my riches." However severe the economic blow, he suggested that the promise of full citizenship and rights outweighed his investment in slavery. In articulating such arguments, Taunoir rejected his ownership of slaves as oppressive and evaded his own complicity in the institution of slavery.[43]

The commissioners ruled against free people of color who did not fulfill their obligations to the Union if they seemed to more closely resemble white southerners than black southerners. These claimants had not expressed disloyal sympathies or committed disloyal deeds, but they appeared to the commissioners as too autonomous and too privileged to be categorized with former slaves and free blacks. The commissioners identified Alfred Anderson as a "mulatto" who owned a large amount of property, including "a Plantation well stocked with Slaves and other live Stock." They ruled that Anderson's "apparent interests opinions and sympathies were the same as those of other slaveholders, and like most of those of the white race his sympathies were with the Confederacy and the South and against the Government." They did not classify Anderson as "live Stock" along with his former slaves nor did they recognize him as a white man, but they did charge him with having white men's interests, opinions, and sympathies.⁴⁴ The commissioners identified Heluter Taunoir as "a colored man … born free." Counting Taunoir's wealth in both land and slaves, they also regarded him as "a free person [who] should not be held as a slave and have loyalty presumed." They considered it "quite plain" that "he should be required to prove loyalty." Because "no proof of loyalty is adduced, except his own statement," they ruled against him.⁴⁵ The commissioners condemned these slaveholders on this basis despite recognizing that slaveholding, at least among white southerners, did not automatically indicate disloyalty to the Union.

In their decisions on free people of color, the commissioners exhibited apparent inconsistencies. They denied James Goin and Archibald Jackson for their labors for the Confederate cause, but they found little objectionable with the numerous other free blacks who had performed similar work. They deemed Alfred Anderson and Heluter Taunoir suspicious on the basis of their significant wartime slaveholdings, but they evinced little wariness toward other former slaveholders of color who presented similar claims.⁴⁶ The commissioners' reasoning appears arbitrary because their rulings hinged on their sense of whether or not free people of color seemed more akin to black or white southerners. They attempted to categorize these claimants with either "colored" claimants or "every" (that is, white) claimants to determine whether or not they should be exempted from their standards of loyal citizenship. The commissioners weighed, not so much loyal act and disloyal act, but proximity to blackness or whiteness.

The free people of color rejected on the loyalty test for either offering their services to the Confederacy or failing to fulfill their obligations to the Union appeared to the commissioners to have possessed the freedom to choose to support the Union or the Confederacy. They did not strike the commissioners as similar to other black southerners in their inability to control their time or their oppression under southern society. Instead, they seemed to the commissioners to have exercised considerable autonomy and to have benefited from substantial privileges. They were merely "called colored" but not treated as "colored." Experience with the claims taught the commissioners that some southerners did not fit easily into the racial categories of "black" and "white," but they still conceived of citizenship in black and white terms.

"The Indians Were All Union People"

The commissioners initially imagined loyal citizenship for whites, but they were ultimately forced to assess loyal citizenship for nonwhites as well. When they created a category for colored claimants, they understood such southerners in opposition to their implicitly white standard, and they primarily envisioned them as black southerners, as slaves or the descendants of slaves. The commissioners likely had not expected to encounter Indians petitioning as loyal citizens. When claimants like Adelphia Miles of Virginia declared "the Indians were all Union people," the commissioners were suddenly confronted with the necessity to consider Indians. Such claims to loyal citizenship were shaped by Indians' negotiation of the southern racial hierarchy, particularly Indians' responses to white efforts to categorize them as "negroes" and "mulattoes." Indians did not fit within the commissioners' black and white conceptualization of race. Sometimes the commissioners recognized Indianness, as with the Pamunkeys of Virginia, but other times they did not, as with the Lumbees of North Carolina. In either case, they ultimately retained a conceptualization of standard citizenship as implicitly white and colored citizenship as implicitly black. The commissioners revised their conceptualization of loyal citizenship for white women, former slaves, and free blacks, but not Indians.[47]

In the antebellum era, state and federal governments had worked to eradicate the southern Indian presence. Whites forced the removal of thousands of Indians in the South to reservations in the West. Despite these efforts, remnants of the Cherokees, Chickasaws, Choctaws, Creeks, and Seminoles managed to stay in the vicinity of their ancestral lands after the federal government relocated their nations west of the Mississippi. Moreover, the federal government only targeted Indian nations for removal and not the thousands of Indians who resided on reservations, owned their land individually, or lived on marginal tracts. Indians who remained in the South faced increased pressures as whites attempted to erase their presence, often by refusing to recognize them as indigenous peoples and instead redefining them as free blacks.[48]

During the Civil War, native peoples split, with some siding with the Union and some with the Confederacy. Prior to the war, neither Lincoln nor Davis had much use for Indians. Lincoln had envisioned the spread of white progress across the continent, and Davis had advocated the removal of Indians from his state of Mississippi. Once the conflict began, however, both presidents lobbied for Indian support, negotiating treaties with various Indian nations. Most southern Indians offered their services to the Confederacy. The Pamunkeys in Virginia along with the Lumbees in North Carolina were among the few Union supporters, and later both presented themselves as claimants before the commission.[49]

After the war, as congressional Republicans worked to incorporate blacks as citizens, Indians remained largely outside the confines of American citizenship. During debates over Reconstruction, some congressmen objected to citizenship measures, fearing that they would encompass Indians as well. In an attempt to assuage such fears, Reconstruction measures explicitly excluded "tribal Indians" and "Indians not taxed" and, in this way, excepted members of Indian nations from their provisions. The focus of such debates revealed that congressmen primarily considered Indians as members of Indian nations out West and not as potential citizens in the North or South.[50]

The Pamunkeys' claims before the commission reminded representatives of the federal government of their existence as an indigenous people in the South. In their testimony, they explicitly identified themselves as Pamunkeys. They did not denote themselves as members of the colored people or liken their status to the enslaved or free black populations. Instead, they rooted a Pamunkey identity in their reservation on the Pamunkey River in King William County, Virginia. As one claimant noted, "I am a Pamunkey Indian and live at Indian Town King William Co where I was born and raised and have lived all my life." Those on the reservation, who had been born there, raised there, or lived there, understood themselves as "belong[ing] to the Pamunkey tribe of Indians."[51]

In their appearances before the commission, Pamunkeys did not devote much of their testimony to an explanation of their sympathies. They did not link their sympathies with an expectation that the Union would abolish slavery or grant equal rights as former slaves and free blacks frequently asserted. The only clue in their testimony to the origins of their sympathies emerges from their complaints about Confederate impressments.[52] During the war, Virginia had passed legislation that forced free blacks to work on fortifications, under which Confederates had apparently also rounded up Pamunkey men.[53] The Pamunkeys had probably found conditions laboring on Confederate fortifications alongside slaves and free blacks as an imposition and degradation.

In any case, the Pamunkeys provided ample evidence of what mattered most to the commissioners: their services to the Union. The Pamunkeys did not, like many former slaves and free blacks, contend that Confederate repression had prevented them from assisting the Union cause. Instead, they emphasized their contributions as Union guides, pilots, and spies. Lambert C. Page, for example, testified, "I was a pilot for Genl. McClellan's boats on the Pamunkey River and piloted the boats down that and the York River and around to James River to Harrison's Landing to where Gen McClellan retreated after the 7 days fight."[54] Page numbered one among ten to fourteen men in Union service with "not one in the rebel service" out of a village of about twenty-five households.[55] The Pamunkey claimants and witnesses suggested that not only these men but also the whole village had assisted the Union. For example, Edward Bradby had infiltrated Confederate lines and passed along intelligence to Pamunkeys in Union service to convey to Union authorities. Those in the service had relied on their relatives and friends not only to collect information on the enemy, but also to cook for them and to conceal them from Confederates.[56]

Status as Pamunkey sometimes rested uneasily with assertions as "Union people." Terrill Bradby, one Pamunkey claimant, felt the necessity to make his case to the commissioners: "I considered that my volunteering in the Union service made me a citizen, and I have voted the Republican ticket twice since the war. I regularly registered, and registered now as a voter and have never been challenged. I pay taxes." Bradby linked his citizenship to his military service, his voting, and his taxpaying – all political obligations that the commissioners venerated (Figure 5.1).[57] Still, there were potential contradictions in claiming the privileges of Union people and identifying as Indian people. Thomas Cook, the Pamunkey headman, petitioned the commission as a loyal citizen, but he also asserted, "I have never voted because I did not think I had a right to do so."

FIGURE 5.1. Terrill Bradby, 1899. As the federal government abandoned its attempt to reconstruct the South, the value of the label "Union people" diminished. After former Confederates successfully displaced former Unionists – black, white, and Indian – and redeemed their state in 1870, the Pamunkeys publicly presented themselves in ways more compatible with the sensibilities of the white southerners who surrounded them. Terrill Bradby became what scholars call a "show Indian." He and other Pamunkeys reenacted Pocahontas's saving of Captain John Smith at events such as the Yorktown Centennial in 1881 and the Jamestown Exposition in 1907. The Pamunkeys retained a memory of their Union service, which they shared with anthropologists who visited them in the late 1880s and early 1890s, but they did not reenact their wartime support of the Union in their public performances.

Source: BAE GN 00893 06197600, National Anthropological Archives, Smithsonian Institution, Suitland, Maryland.

Cook presented abstaining from the vote as an act of Indianness, noting that another claimant had never voted, even after the war, because "He prefers, I believe, to be thought an Indian."[58] State and federal governments in the antebellum era had extended citizenship to Indians in an attempt to dissolve their tribal sovereignty and dispossess them of their lands. In this way, claims to loyal citizenship conflicted with claims to Indian sovereignty.

The Pamunkeys' assertion of their Pamunkey identity before the commission emerged in defiance of long-standing governmental attempts to deny their status as sovereign peoples and relegate them to marginal positions. During the colonial era, the Virginia governor had established the Pamunkeys as subordinate to white authority, requiring them to pay a yearly tribute. Although an infringement of their sovereignty, this status ironically helped them retain part of their ancestral lands. In the antebellum era, white Virginians had successfully dispossessed other Indians by claiming that they were not Indians and were actually blacks.[59] Just before the outbreak of the Civil War, white Virginians had deployed this tactic against the Pamunkeys, arguing that they had "so largely mingled with the negro race as to have obliterated all striking features of Indian extraction." The governor required the Pamunkeys to prove that they were less than one-fourth "negro" or face subordination as "free negroes or mulattoes." In this way, the state laid the groundwork to terminate Pamunkey existence and appropriate their reservation if they did not maintain a state-dictated level of racial purity.[60]

The commissioners accepted the Pamunkeys' presentation of themselves as Indians, but they did not expand their conceptualization of loyal citizenship to account for them as Indians. They did not create a separate series of interrogatories for Indian claimants as they did for female claimants and colored claimants. Instead, the commissioners exempted many Indians from their standards of loyal citizenship for white men, sometimes not bothering to justify their findings of loyalty. They simply noted that the claimants were Indians without devoting much attention to evidence of their Union sympathies and services. In this manner, the commissioners labeled Pamunkeys as Indians in their reports to Congress, but they applied the same criteria to these Indians that they applied to former slaves and free blacks.

The Pamunkeys challenged the commissioners' black and white bifurcation of the South, but other Indians fit with the commissioners' conceptualization. Indians in Robeson County, North Carolina, or the Lumbees as they are known today, identified themselves as "free" and "colored" before the commission.[61] Nancy Sampson remarked on the nominal nature of their freedom, noting, "We were always free but had no privileges."[62] These assertions, strikingly similar to many free blacks, reflected their legal status in the state. The Robeson Indians had been legally erased from the state's population by the antebellum era. Like many other natives in the South, these Indians coalesced as a people through hundreds of years of migration and cultural exchange among indigenous communities and blacks and whites in North Carolina, South Carolina, and Virginia. Like many other Indians in the South, their presence as indigenous peoples had been officially eradicated. White North Carolinians used the state's 1835 constitution to disfranchise Indians by classifying them as "free Negroes, free mulattoes, and free persons of mixed blood descended from negro ancestors to the fourth generation." Legally defined as free blacks, Indians had also not been able to testify against whites, serve in the militia, or legally bear arms without a license. In these ways, white North Carolinians categorized Indians, those in Robeson among them, with free blacks in the antebellum years to limit their freedoms. In dealing with government officials, the commissioners of southern claims included, Indians identified themselves as "free people of color" in accordance with their official classification.[63] Nevertheless, Robeson Indians retained an identity as Indians within their community. They understood themselves as an indigenous people who had been robbed of their ancestral lands and unfairly treated as "negroes."[64] The Robeson Indians refrained from such assertions in their testimony before the special commissioner. As a result, the commissioners, when they received the forwarded testimony, had no reason to consider the Robeson Indians claimants as any different from any other free black claimants.

In their testimony, the Robeson Indians appeared similar to many former slaves and free blacks. Like many former slaves and free blacks, they admitted that they had contributed to the Confederate cause, and they offered little evidence that they had contributed to the Union cause. Much of the testimony in the Robeson claims read like a rote recitation of negative answers to the interrogatories: "I never knew him to contribute any money or property to aid the Union cause or its army. I never knew him to be molested or threatened with injury on account of his Union sentiments. I never knew him to contribute anything to aid the Confederate Government or its officers or soldiers."[65]

Despite the sparseness of their testimony, Robeson Indian claimants likely had been active participants against Confederates, but perhaps not in ways the commissioners would have condoned. The Robeson Indian claimants did not mention any involvement with the Lowry band as evidence of their contribution to the Union cause. During and after the war, Henry Berry Lowry had led a group of multiracial dissidents who resisted the domination of Confederates during the war and Conservatives after the war. Indian and black men, evading conscription, along with escaped Union prisoners, hid in the swamps and launched raids against slaveholders and even the county courthouse. The Home Guard retaliated, killing several Lowry relatives. The Lowry band subsequently exacted vengeance with the toll numbering approximately two dozen whites, including former Confederate officials, the sheriff, state militia officers, and a Ku Klux Klan leader.[66] The Robeson Indians who submitted their claims to the commission after the war likely had some involvement in the Lowry band because several of the Robeson Indian claimants were related to members.[67] Evidence that the Robeson Indian claimants had attacked the Confederate Home Guard and raided their houses would seem natural evidence to bolster their claims, especially because they otherwise provided so little proof of their contributions to the Union. The Robeson Indian claimants likely omitted these stories because white Republicans had repudiated the Lowry band, favoring law and order under white control rather than extra legal raids under black and Indian control in their attempts to counteract conservative vigilantism.[68]

The commissioners and their subordinates easily fit the Robeson Indian claimants into their conceptualization of white and black loyal citizenship. They treated the Robeson Indian claimants like other free blacks. They administered interrogatories for colored claimants and labeled them as freeborn colored people, and they exempted the handful of claimants from Robeson County from their standards of active citizenship. As they noted in one claim, they declined to require further proof of loyalty because "being a negro," the claimant "has the presumption of loyalty in his favor."[69]

The fate of the Pamunkey and the Robeson Indians before the commission reflect the place of indigenous peoples in the postwar Union. Indigenous claimants identified themselves in a variety of ways that emphasized or de-emphasized their status as indigenous peoples. The Pamunkey Indians, with historic recognition by Virginia as Indians, asserted themselves before the commission as Indians. The Robeson Indians, with their state officially categorizing them with free blacks, identified themselves as colored persons. Both groups were caught within a black and white world. The commissioners recognized the Pamunkeys as Indians, but they did not detect the Robeson Indian identity. In either case, they did not account for a special category of Indian citizenship, and the cases of Indians did not cause the commissioners to rethink their conceptualization of loyal citizenship. In the postwar years, both the Pamunkey Indians and the Robeson Indians would ultimately seek recognition as loyal Indian citizens as the federal government moved to more aggressively subordinate Indians as dependent peoples by revoking their treaty status and eventually terminating their reservations and requiring individual allotments of land. Within this process, the bestowal of American citizenship and assimilation as loyal Americans was used as a means to dispossess Indians of their lands. In this way, being both Indian people and Union people was contradictory.

Free nonwhite southerners who had not suffered the injustices of enslavement but also had not experienced the privileges of freedom occupied a precarious position. Many free blacks asserted that they had supported the Union side in the war in solidarity with their enslaved brethren. Like former slaves, they based their claims to loyal citizenship in an antislavery interpretation of the war. Some free blacks also anticipated a genuine rather than nominal extension of freedom, one based on black equality and rights. They discerned a broader meaning in the war – broader than a war over secession, broader even than a war for abolition. Like free blacks, Indians sought status as loyal citizens, but such claims rested uneasily with status as sovereign peoples. In the aggregate, free blacks and Indians claimed the Union as their own in ways that challenged the simple division between black and white and in ways that demanded a thorough reconstruction of the southern racial hierarchy.

The commissioners interpreted the loyal citizenship of free blacks and other nonwhites within a black and white framework. They imagined black southerners as subordinate and dependent and white southerners as autonomous and independent. They accepted most free blacks as similar to former slaves in their oppressed position within southern society and therefore exempted them from their standards of loyal citizenship. They even fit Indians into their black and white conceptualization of citizenship, often judging them as akin to "negroes" in their loyalties to the Union. They did hold some free people of color – those who seemed too autonomous, too privileged, and too intelligent to be classed with other black southerners – to their standards for white southerners, requiring that they had not only sympathized with but also contributed to the Union cause. As with former slaves, many free blacks and Indians won recognition as loyal citizens based on characteristics that had previously marked them as the antithesis of loyal citizens.

The federal government attempted to incorporate former slaves and free blacks as citizens. To effect this transformation, the commissioners created categories of citizens. Their standard category remained implicitly white and masculine, but they created another category for colored claimants. They imagined these colored southerners as primarily former slaves or the descendants of slaves. They exempted most colored southerners from their standards of loyal citizenship on the basis of their subordination in southern society. The commissioners encountered numerous southerners who did not fit their conceptualization of loyal citizens as free white men and enslaved blacks. These free blacks, some who had been manumitted and some who had never been enslaved, and Indians, some who identified as Indians and some who claimed Indian ancestry, demonstrated that race in the South could not be simply encapsulated within the notation "col'd" and, consequently, that loyal citizenship also could not be simply divided into white and black varieties.

Conclusion

The commissioners looked forward to the day when "the bitter sectional feelings engendered by the war and the causes which produced it ... pass away" and when "the citizens of the United States ... become a homogeneous people, united in their support of the General Government and devotedly attached to all its free institutions." They lamented the continuing acrimony that marred reunion, particularly regretting that some white southerners "speak imperiously and contemptuously of 'your Government,' like one owing allegiance to some other sovereignty of power."[1] The commissioners urged southerners to once again claim the Union as their own instead of viewing reunion as a punishment imposed on them. They would live to witness the reconciliation between former enemies and even, unwittingly, contribute to its development. However, the terms of this reconciliation were not ones that the commissioners would have envisioned when they first began their commission in 1871.

The Southern Claims Commission in its creation and operation was a forum through which federal officials and southerners debated, and attempted to resolve, the divisive issues of the war. The congressmen who established it, the commissioners and other agents who directed it, and the claimants who petitioned it contested the nature of the Union cause and the obligations and privileges of citizenship. Who counted as loyal citizens? What ideals did the Union represent? What did citizens owe to their nation? Southerners presented their stories to stake a claim in the postwar nation. The commissioners evaluated southerners' depictions of the war and their role within it to assess their worthiness to be recognized as loyal citizens of the Union and partake of its benefits. They sometimes praised southerners as patriots but more often condemned them as shirkers, cowards, and traitors. In the process, the commissioners and claimants disputed how the Union had been preserved and also the nature of the Union preserved.

The suppression of secession formed the core of the commissioners' understanding of the Union cause. They regarded the act of secession as the inaugural moment of the rebellion. They generally only addressed slavery when claimants themselves raised the issue. As Republicans, they certainly understood the slavery controversy as the ultimate cause of the war. Before he became a commissioner of claims, Orange Ferriss had denounced the "bloody conflict" inaugurated by the "worshippers" of slavery to "extend its area and perpetuate its existence."[2] As commissioners, however, they recognized that the act of secession, not the desire to preserve slavery, had constituted the crime against the Union. The commissioners, then, singled out secession as the most relevant issue of the war and of loyal citizenship.

The commissioners expected southerners not only to have sympathized with the Union cause but also to have fulfilled implicitly white masculine obligations to the Union. They considered votes in opposition to secession and military service to defeat secessionists as the most unequivocal means by which southerners could have acted as loyal citizens. The commissioners eventually attempted to compensate for their initial focus on political obligations largely restricted to white men. They shifted to a particularized conception of citizenship, creating separate categories for men, women, and blacks, but not for Indians. They recognized that many white women and black men and women, by virtue of their subordinate positions within southern society, could not meet their standards for loyal citizens. They retained their requirement that southerners prove that they had supported and not just sympathized with the Union. They simply exempted white women and black men and women from answering interrogatories about acts not within their purview. This accepted women and blacks as loyal citizens but often by positioning them as dependents incapable of truly acting as loyal citizens. A white male voter and soldier remained the quintessential loyal citizen.

Southerners before the commission revealed more expansive interpretations of the war and, thus, the Union preserved by the war. Many followed the commissioners' lead, testifying about their sympathies regarding secession. Of the claimants who commented on the issues that motivated secession, most pinpointed slavery. Black southerners, both newly freed slaves and free blacks, readily identified the institution as the impetus for the war. They imagined a reunited nation that advanced the cause of freedom, not just through abolition but also through equality. White southerners also recognized the significance of the slavery question both in bringing about the war and in determining their allegiances. Some white southerners placed responsibility for the rebellion on slaveholders whose machinations foolishly forced their states from the Union to protect their slave property. They planned on a reunited nation that broke the power of the slaveocracy and brought nonelites to power. Other white southerners blamed the war on northern abolitionists whose unrelenting assault on slavery necessitated secession as a defensive measure to preserve the institution. They envisioned a reunited nation that resuscitated proslavery ideals, if not the institution itself. Through the commission, these various southerners contested the meaning of the war to shape the contours of postwar politics and the direction of the reunited nation.

Obligations to the Union matched interpretations of the cause. Many white southern men met the commissioners' standards of active citizenship in suppressing secession by politicking and soldiering. Numerous others presented contributions to different Union causes – ones unrecognized by the commissioners. Many black southerners described the ways they had advanced the Union cause of abolition by resisting their enslavement. Some white southerners recounted that they had kept slaves informed of Union progress and helped slaves escape to Union lines. Other white southerners explained that they had protected their slave property in accordance with a proslavery Union cause. In addition, southerners before the commission often insisted that they had met their obligations to the Union after hostilities had officially ceased. Postwar Republicans emphasized their postwar votes for the Union and their support of Reconstruction. Former Confederates insisted that they had faithfully returned to the Union as loyal citizens by laying down their arms and swearing amnesty oaths. Finally, some southerners before the commission insisted that they could not fulfill obligations to the Union at all. Most reasoned that the pervasiveness of Confederate persecution rendered the expectation of active citizenship unreasonable. Some suggested that their positions in southern society by virtue of their race, gender, or class had prevented them from supporting the Union cause and had even forced them into contributing to the Confederate cause.

The proceedings of the Southern Claims Commission contributed to two main postwar movements. First, the commissioners inadvertently facilitated an official reconciliation between former Unionists and former Confederates that evaded the issues of the war. The commissioners ignored the role of slavery within the war to focus narrowly on conduct in response to secession. They weighed disloyal acts and even inaction more heavily than even the strongest assertions of Union sympathies. During their tenure, the commissioners' attention to wartime allegiances in determinations of loyal citizenship only served to inflame former Confederates against the federal government. In the long run, the commissioners' promotion of wartime actions over ideologies promoted an understanding of citizenship that would forgive former Confederates as patriots fighting for a cause they believed just and would marginalize many former Unionists, both white and black, as cowards shirking their obligations to their nation.

Second, the commissioners moved from an exclusionary conception of citizenship, which favored white masculinity but presumed universality, to a particularized conception of citizenship, which recognized political obligations as race and gender specific but still marked white women and black men and women as lesser citizens. In exempting these groups from answering interrogatories on obligations outside their purview, the commissioners highlighted that subordinated southerners could not meet their standards of loyal citizenship. They commenced operations with an implicitly white and masculine understanding of loyal citizens and simply subtracted all obligations that white women and black men and women could not fulfill. The commissioners further reinforced their dependent positions by sometimes requiring black claimants to submit reliable – that is, white – witnesses to prove their property ownership and often determining the loyalties of white female claimants by assessing the loyalties of their male relatives. The commissioners recognized these southerners as loyal citizens but only on the basis of their dependence and subordination – in essence, their inability to perform the full obligations of citizenship, the very characteristics that had previously excluded them. Attempting to craft criteria for loyal citizenship, applicable to all, would have required a radical rethinking of their assumptions.

These two movements combined to leave many southerners in marginalized positions. White women and black men and women may have been able to gain compensation from the commission as loyal citizens within the commissioners' formulation of particularized citizenship, but ultimately representations of them as dependents reinforced their subordination after the war. Status as loyal citizens had brought substantive gains. Black men especially had been enfranchised partially on the argument that they had served as loyal citizens during the war and would (at the very least) constitute better citizens than traitors. However, with the causes of the war forgotten and former Confederates celebrated as devoted (if mistaken) patriots, efforts to protect and promote the rights and privileges of white women and black men and women who had not acted as patriots lost favor. The racial and gendered ideologies relied on by the commissioners helped maintain hierarchies of power by justifying women's and blacks' exclusion from participatory democracy and hindering their ability to claim the Union on their own terms.

The federal government gradually abandoned the project of Reconstruction. Congress had restored most former Confederates to their antebellum rights through the Amnesty Act of 1872, allowing them to vote and hold office and otherwise participate in state and national affairs. After the contentious election of 1876, Republican President Rutherford B. Hayes withdrew the protection of the federal army from former Unionists and Republicans in the South as a conciliatory measure. This "compromise of 1877" returned the last Confederate states to "home rule." Although black southerners had secured enormous achievements in the aftermath of the war, the Supreme Court eventually limited the extent of these gains. Through a series of cases in the 1870s and 1880s, the Court restricted Congress' authority to prohibit racial discrimination by private individuals and severely limited the "privileges and immunities" protected by the Fourteenth Amendment. By the turn of the century, white southern legislators succeeded in disfranchising black southerners by requiring various poll taxes and poll tests. At the same time, Congress removed the last disabilities on a few hundred former Confederates through the Amnesty Act

Conclusion

of 1898. Disfranchisement of black former Unionists and amnesty of white former Confederates occurred as lynching spread throughout the South.[3]

By the turn of the century, distinctions according to wartime loyalties had all but vanished. One congressman regretted that restrictions on former Confederates had ever been imposed. In his words, "Years have rolled by since that great struggle closed, and the American people look at public matters growing out of the war ... in calmer moments when their judgment can be trusted." Freed from their former spirit of vengeance, Americans now counseled the restoration of the "equality of all men" through the removal of "discriminations" against former Confederates. Americans now celebrated both Union and Confederate soldiers, who both "gave to the cause of their country their lives, their fortunes, and their sacred honor." White women only entered this story as mothers. The war was a family squabble between white Americans: "a contest of a mother's children – one dying for his home, the other for his country." Black southerners made a cameo appearance as devoted "mammies" who had comforted crying white babies during the war. Many white Americans had written slavery as a cause of the war out of the story of the war. White northerners, westerners, and southerners depicted masters and mistresses as kind and caring and slaves as faithful and devoted. Congressmen had once considered the war a mighty contest between slavery and freedom, but within a generation they remembered the war as a great blessing, which in settling the secession question, advanced a unified nationalism, a patriotic people, and a more perfect union.[4]

Public discourse at the turn of the century praised the courage and sacrifice of both Confederates and Unionists. The fight for equality became one between whites in the former Union and former Confederacy over sectional discriminations imposed after the war rather than race and sex discriminations across the nation. For the sake of reconciliation, white Americans focused on the joint experience of the war and ignored the divisive issue of slavery. They remembered slavery less as a cause of the war and more as a benign, even virtuous, institution. In 1868, at the height of Radical Republican strength, Orange Ferriss, one of the commissioners of southern claims, predicted that the spirit of slavery would soon recede and that "the day is not far distant when none will be found so poor as to do honor to its memory."[5] Just thirty years later, Ferriss had been proven shortsighted. Southerners who attempted to preserve a meaning of the war that recognized the role of slavery and the culpability of slaveholders lost the fight on the national level.

Appendix A

TABLE A1. *Senatorial Votes in the 41st Congress on Southern Claims Divided by Region*

Senator	State	Party	1	2	3	4	5	6	7
Bayard, Thomas F.	DE	Democrat	A	A	U	F	A	F	F
Saulsbury, Willard	DE	Democrat	F	F	A	A	F	A	A
Davis, Garrett	KY	Democrat	F	F	F	F	F	F	F
McCreery, Thomas C.	KY	Democrat	F	F	U	F	F	A	U
Hamilton, William T.	MD	Democrat	F	F	A	F	F	F	F
Vickers, George	MD	Democrat	F	F	A	F	F	F	F
Blair, Francis P.	MO	Democrat	-	-	-	F	F	F	F
Drake, Charles D.	MO	Republican	F	A	U	-	-	-	-
Schurz, Carl	MO	Republican	F	F	A	A	A	F	F
Boreman, Arthur I.	WV	Republican	F	F	U	F	F	F	A
Willey, Waitman T.	WV	Republican	F	F	A	F	A	F	A
Spencer, George E	AL	Republican	F	F	F	F	F	F	F
Warner, Willard	AL	Republican	F	F	F	F	F	F	F
McDonald, Alexander	AR	Republican	F	F	F	F	F	F	A
Rice, Benjamin F	AR	Republican	F	F	F	F	F	F	F
Gilbert, Abijah	FL	Republican	F	F	A	A	A	A	U
Osborn, Thomas W.	FL	Republican	F	F	U	U	U	U	F
Hill, Joshua	GA	Union Republican	F	F	F	F	F	F	F
Miller, Homer	GA	Democrat	A	A	A	F	F	F	
Harris, John S.	LA	Republican	F	F	F	F	F	F	A
Kellogg, William P.	LA	Republican	F	F	A	F	F	F	A
Ames, Adelbert	MS	Republican	A	A	A	F	U	U	A
Revels, Hiram R.	MS	Republican	A	A	A	F	F	F	A
Abbott, Joseph C.	NC	Republican	A	A	F	A	F	F	A

(*continued*)

TABLE A1. (continued)

Senator	State	Party	1	2	3	4	5	6	7
Pool, John	NC	Republican	A	A	F	A	A	A	A
Robertson, Thomas J.	SC	Republican	F	F	F	F	F	F	F
Sawyer, Frederick A.	SC	Republican	A	A	A	A	F	F	A
Brownlow, William G.	TN	Republican	A	A	A	A	A	F	U
Fowler, Joseph S.	TN	Union Republican	F	F	F	F	F	F	A
Flanagan, J. W.	TX	Republican	A	A	A	F	F	F	F
Hamilton, Morgan C.	TX	Republican	U	U	A	U	U	U	A
Johnston, John W.	VA	Conservative	A	A	A	F	F	F	F
Lewis, John F.	VA	Republican	A	A	F	A	F	F	A
Buckingham, William A.	CT	Republican	A	A	A	U	U	U	U
Ferry, Orris S.	CT	Republican	U	U	A	A	A	A	A
Hamlin, Hannibal	ME	Republican	F	F	A	U	U	U	U
Morrill, Lot M.	ME	Republican	A	A	A	A	A	A	A
Sumner, Charles	MA	Republican	U	U	U	A	A	A	A
Wilson, Henry	MA	Republican	A	A	F	U	U	U	F
Cragin, Aaron N.	NH	Republican	A	A	A	A	U	U	U
Patterson, James W.	NH	Republican	F	A	A	A	A	A	A
Anthony, Henry B.	RI	Republican	F	U	A	U	U	U	U
Sprague, William	RI	Republican	A	A	F	A	U	A	F
Edmunds, George F.	VT	Republican	U	U	A	A	A	U	U
Morrill, Justin S.	VT	Union Republican	A	A	A	U	U	U	U
Trumbull, Lyman	IL	Republican	U	U	A	U	A	U	U
Yates, Richard	IL	Union Republican	A	A	U	A	A	U	F
Pratt, Daniel D.	IN	Republican	F	F	F	F	F	F	F
Morton, O. H. P.	IN	Union Republican	A	A	U	F	F	F	U
Harlan, James	IA	Republican	U	U	U	A	U	A	U
Howell, James B.	IA	Republican	U	U	A	A	U	U	A
Pomeroy, Samuel C.	KS	Republican	F	A	F	F	U	U	U
Ross, Edmund G.	KS	Republican	F	F	F	A	F	F	A
Chandler, Zachariah	MI	Republican	U	U	A	A	U	U	U
Howard, Jacob M.	MI	Republican	U	U	U	U	A	U	A
Norton, Daniel S.	MN	Union Conservative	A	A	A	-	-	-	-
Ramsey, Alexander	MN	Republican	F	A	F	F	U	A	U
Stearns, Ozora P.	MN	Republican	-	-	-	A	A	U	U
Thayer, John M.	NE	Republican	A	A	F	F	U	A	F
Tipton, Thomas W.	NE	Democrat	F	F	A	F	F	F	F
Cattell, Alexander	NJ	Republican	A	A	A	A	U	A	A

Appendix A

Senator	State	Party	1	2	3	4	5	6	7
Stockton, John P.	NJ	Democrat	F	F	U	A	F	F	A
Conkling, Roscoe	NY	Republican	A	A	A	A	U	U	U
Fenton, Reuben Z.	NY	Republican	A	A	A	F	A	F	A
Sherman, John	OH	Republican	U	U	A	U	U	U	F
Thurman, Allen G.	OH	Democrat	F	F	A	F	A	A	A
Cameron, Simon	PA	Republican	A	A	A	A	A	A	U
Scott, John	PA	Republican	F	F	U	F	F	F	U
Carpenter, Matthew	WI	Republican	F	U	U	A	A	A	A
Howe, Timothy	WI	Union	F	F	F	A	A	F	F
Casserly, Eugene	CA	Democrat	F	F	A	F	F	A	A
Cole, Cornelius	CA	Republican	U	U	A	U	U	U	F
Nye, James W.	NV	Republican	F	A	U	A	U	U	F
Stewart, William M.	NV	Republican	A	A	U	U	U	U	F
Corbett, Henry W.	OR	Union Republican	A	A	U	U	U	F	U
Williams, George	OR	Union Republican	U	U	U	A	A	A	U

Note: A indicates absent, F indicates favorable vote, and U indicates unfavorable vote by senators in the 41st Congress. Italicized senators voted favorably on all their recorded votes.

Sources:

1. Motion to pass over a bill granting jurisdiction of southern claims to the quartermaster and commissary departments (S. No. 249) in *Congressional Globe*, 41st Congress, 2nd Session (June 6, 1870), 4147.
2. Amendment absolving the government of responsibility to pay southern claims in *Congressional Globe*, 41st Congress, 2nd Session (June 6, 1870), 4148.
3. Vote to adjourn to avoid consideration of S 249 to pay southern claims in *Congressional Globe*, 41st Congress, 2nd Session (June 13, 1870), 4412–4413.
4. Motion to table the McDonald amendment to the Army Appropriations Bill (H. R. No. 2816) allowing the payment of southern claims in *Congressional Globe*, 41st Congress, 3rd Session (February 28, 1871), 1788.
5. Motion to table the McDonald amendment to the Army Appropriations Bill (H. R. No. 2816) allowing the payment of southern claims in *Congressional Globe*, 41st Congress, 3rd Session (February 29, 1871), 1794.
6. Vote on the McDonald amendment to the Army Appropriations Bill (H. R. No. 2816) in *Congressional Globe*, 41st Congress, 3rd Session (March 1, 1871), 1821.
7. Motion to agree on the conference report amendment establishing the Southern Claims Commission in *Congressional Globe*, 41st Congress, 3rd Session (March 3, 1871), 1973.

TABLE A2. *Total Votes in the Senate in the 41st Congress by Region*

Region	Favorable	Unfavorable
Border states[a]	45	5
Southern states[b]	85	13
New England states[c]	8	33
Mid-Atlantic, Northwestern, & Mid-Western states[d]	52	51
Western states[e]	9	20

[a] Delaware, Kentucky, Maryland, Missouri, and West Virginia.
[b] Alabama, Arkansas, Florida, Georgia, Louisiana, Mississippi, North Carolina, South Carolina, Tennessee, Texas, and Virginia.
[c] Connecticut, Maine, Massachusetts, New Hampshire, Rhode Island, and Vermont.
[d] New Jersey, New York, Pennsylvania, Illinois, Indiana, Iowa, Kansas, Michigan, Minnesota, Nebraska, Ohio, and Wisconsin.
[e] California, Nevada, and Oregon.
Source: The votes totaled in Table A2 are taken from the seven roll calls in Table A1.

TABLE A3. *Votes in the Senate in the 41st Congress by Political Affiliation*

Political Affiliation	Favorable	Unfavorable
Republican	126	102
Democrat	51	4
Union Republican	15	16
Union	5	0
Conservative	4	0

Source: The votes totaled in Table A3 are taken from the roll calls in Table A1.

Appendix A

TABLE A4. *Number of Claims Reported by State and by Year*

State	1871	1872	1873	1874	1875	1876	1877	1878	1879	1880	Total	%
TN	116	397	409	554	242	489	275	275	445	85	3,287	19.34
VA	262	545	427	475	318	303	292	241	288	46	3,197	18.81
GA	83	174	262	210	209	211	270	381	402	37	2,239	13.17
AL	31	345	206	299	205	238	232	186	214	33	1,989	11.70
AR	65	184	307	277	187	164	144	114	302	59	1,803	10.61
MS	12	213	357	180	151	197	166	102	196	65	1,639	9.64
NC	9	272	420	273	128	112	111	147	169	15	1,656	9.74
LA	0	27	28	59	57	60	80	36	138	32	517	3.04
SC	0	41	30	34	44	59	47	43	74	5	377	2.22
WV	0	0	19	32	12	7	26	11	32	1	140	0.82
FL	1	3	8	7	8	17	9	16	19	1	89	0.52
TX	1	8	5	7	0	10	7	7	14	3	62	0.36
Total	580	2,209	2,478	2,407	1,561	1,867	1,659	1,559	2,293	382	16,995	100

Sources: First General Report, 9–16; Second General Report, 2; Third General Report, 5–36; Fourth General Report, 2; Fifth General Report, 5; Sixth General Report, 1; Seventh General Report, 3; Eighth General Report, 3; Ninth General Report, 3; and Tenth General Report, 1.

TABLE A5. *Number of Cases Reported Allowed and Disallowed by Year*

Year	Reported	Rejected	Allowed
1871	580	256 (44%)	324 (56%)
1872	2,209	1,148 (52%)	1,061 (48%)
1873	2,478	1,386 (56%)	1,092 (44%)
1874	2,407	1,244 (52%)	1,163 (48%)
1875	1,561	786 (50%)	775 (50%)
1876	1,867	891 (48%)	976 (52%)
1877	1,659	945 (57%)	714 (43%)
1878	1,559	902 (58%)	657 (42%)
1879	2,293	1,740 (76%)	553 (24%)
1880	382	291 (76%)	91 (24%)
Total	16,995	9,589 (56%)	7,406 (44%)

Sources: First General Report, 9–16; Second General Report, 2; Third General Report, 5–36; Fourth General Report, 2; Fifth General Report, 5; Sixth General Report, 1; Seventh General Report, 3; Eighth General Report, 3; Ninth General Report, 3; and Tenth General Report, 1.

TABLE A6. *Amount of Claims Reported Allowed and Disallowed by Year*

Year	Claimed	Allowed	Disallowed
1871	$1,656,357.98	$344,168.20	$1,312,189.78
1872	$3,850,241.05	$806,699.31	$3,043,541.74
1873	$4,717,887.29	$643,713.04	$4,074,174.25
1874	$5,242,706.46	$770,711.37	$4,471,995.09
1875	$4,557,762.42	$532,510.50	$4,025,251.92
1876	$4,264,877.74	$474,632.45	$3,790,245.29
1877	$5,761,106.27	$434,638.48	$5,326,467.79
1878	$2,791,036.66	$287,628.44	$2,503,408.22
1879	$8,698,460.56	$241,611.22	$8,456,849.34
1880	$3,696,566.34	$100,607.68	$3,595,958.66
Total	$45,237,002.77	$4,636,920.69	$40,600,082.08

Sources: First General Report, 9–16; Second General Report, 2; Third General Report, 5–36; Fourth General Report, 2; Fifth General Report, 5; Sixth General Report, 1; Seventh General Report, 3; Eighth General Report, 3; Ninth General Report, 3; and Tenth General Report, 1.

TABLE A7. *Allowed Claimants in Union Military Service*

Year	Military	Percent
1871	40	12%
1872	122[a]	11%
1873	164	15%
1874	120	10%
1875	66	9%
1876	66	7%
1877	37	5%
1878	47	7%
1879	58[b]	10%
Total	717	10%

[a] In addition to Union soldiers, this figure includes "persons who ... had been otherwise employed in the military service of the United States."

[b] In contrast to the other figures, which include only counts for claimants in the Union army, this figure includes claimants who had served in the Union army (55) and Union navy (3).

Notes: The commissioners recorded counts of claimants in Union military service only in nine of their ten years in operation. They did not tally the number of Union soldiers in cases decided in 1880.

Sources: First General Report, 8; Second General Report, 2; Third General Report, 2; Fourth General Report, 3; Fifth General Report, 5; Sixth General Report, 1; Seventh General Report, 3; Eighth General Report, 3; and Ninth General Report, 4.

Appendix A

TABLE A8. *"Aid and Comfort to the Enemy" in the Disallowed Claims*

Year	Military Service	Civil Service	Secession	Oath	Total Aid and Comfort	Total Disallowed Claims	%
1871	40	Not Tallied	Not Tallied	Not Tallied	40	256	16
1872[a]	227	Not Tallied	121	33	381	1,148	33
1873[b]	249	34	Not Tallied	22	305	1,386	22
1874[c]	150	26	63	Not Tallied	239	1,244	19
1875[d]	110	13	33	Not Tallied	156	786	20
1876[e]	104	13	30	8	155	891	17
1877[f]	82	Not Tallied	24	6	112	945	12
1878[g]	115	Not Tallied	34	9	158	902	18
1879	238	29	70	19	357	1,740	21
Total	1,315	115	375	97	1,902	9,298	20

[a] The commissioners did not tally voting for secession and swearing an oath of allegiance to the Confederacy separately. The separate figures for 1872 are estimated by distributing the total figure of 154 according to the ratio between the two acts tallied for 1879.

[b] The commissioners did not tally claimants who were in the Confederate civil service or who swore an oath of allegiance to the Confederacy separately. The separate figures for 1873 are estimated by distributing the total figure of 56 according to the ratio between the two acts tallied for 1879.

[c] 1874. The commissioners did not tally claimants who were in the Confederate civil service and who voted for secession separately. The separate figures for 1874 are estimated by distributing the total figure of 89 according to the ratio between the two acts tallied for 1879.

[d] The commissioners did not tally claimants who were in the Confederate military, who were in the civil service, and who voted for secession separately. The separate figures for 1875 are estimated by distributing the total figure of 156 according to the ratio between the three acts tallied for 1879.

[e] The commissioners did not tally claimants who were in the Confederate military, who were in the civil service, who voted for secession, and who swore an oath of allegiance to the Confederacy separately. The separate figures for 1876 are estimated by distributing the total figure of 155 according to the ratio between the four acts tallied for 1879.

[f] The commissioners did not tally claimants who were in the Confederate military, who voted for secession, and who swore an oath of allegiance to the Confederacy separately. The separate figures for 1877 are estimated by distributing the total figure of 112 according to the ratio between the three acts tallied for 1879.

[g] The commissioners did not tally claimants who were in the Confederate military, who voted for secession, and who swore an oath of allegiance to the Confederacy separately. The separate figures for 1878 are estimated by distributing the total figure of 158 according to the ratio between the three acts tallied for 1879.

Notes: The commissioners did not include any count of aid and comfort to the enemy in disallowed claims in their final report to Congress in 1880.

Sources: First General Report, 8; Second General Report, 2; Third General Report, 2; Fourth General Report, 3; Fifth General Report, 5; Sixth General Report, 1; Seventh General Report, 3; Eighth General Report, 3; Ninth General Report, 4.

Appendix B

The commissioners issued three versions of their "standing interrogatories" for claimants and their witnesses in 1871, 1872, and, finally, in 1874. Over the course of their three versions, the commissioners expanded and refined their questions. Their revisions demonstrate their increasing attention to disloyal acts. In addition, their revisions indicate greater attention to unanticipated claimants like women and blacks. In their first and second versions, the commissioners recommended questions for witnesses on the loyalty question. In their third version, the commissioners standardized these questions.

Standing Interrogatories of 1871

I. Questions to be answered by claimants under oath.

1. Where did you reside for six months prior to the 1st of April, 1861? Where were you in person during the said six months? What was your business or occupation during that period?
2. Where did you reside from the 1st of April, 1861, to the 1st of June, 1865? Where were you personally during that period? What was your business or occupation during that time? Did you change your residence during that time? If so, when, and where was your new residence?
3. Did you ever pass beyond the military or naval lines of the United States and enter the rebel lines? If so, how often, when, where, and for what purpose, and how long did you stay within the confederate lines on each occasion?
4. Did you ever take any oath or affirmation to bear allegiance to the so-called Confederate States, or to aid or support them in any way, or to "bear true faith" or "yield obedience" to them? If so, when and where? State fully in regard to the same.

Appendix B   147

5. Have you ever taken any amnesty oath? If so, when, where, and under what condition? Have you been pardoned by the President? If so, when and where, and upon what conditions?
6. Where you ever, directly or indirectly, or in any manner connected with the civil service of the so-called Confederate States? If so, how, when, and where, in what capacity, and for what periods? Was any oath required of you for such service; and if so, what?
7. Did you ever hold any office or place of trust, honor, or profit under the confederate government, or under any of the States or Territories subordinate thereto? If so, state the nature and character of the office, the place at which and the period for which you held it?
8. Did you hold any clerkship or have any agency or employment of any kind for, or under, or for the benefit of the so-called Confederate States? If so, state fully in regard to the same.
9. Were you ever, in any capacity, in the military or naval service of the so-called Confederate States, or of any State or Territory subordinate thereto?
10. Were you ever an officer or soldier, or sailor or marine, of the confederate army or navy, or did you ever furnish a substitute for the confederate army or navy, or were you, directly or indirectly, in any way connected with, or employed by or under, or for either the commissary department, quartermaster's department, the medical department, the engineer's department, the ordnance department, the impressments service, the provost marshal's department, or any other bureau, branch, or department of the confederate service? Did you, at any time, have charge of any stores or supplies for the use of the confederate army, navy, or government, or the charge or care of trains, team or teams, wagon or wagons, vessels, boats, or other craft, or munitions of war for the use of the confederate army or navy? If so, state fully in regard to the same.
11. Were you ever in any service, employment, or business of any kind whatsoever for the confederate government, or its army or navy? Did you ever furnish any aid, or any supplies or stores, or property of any kind, to or for the so-called Confederate States, or any State in rebellion, or to the army, navy, militia, home-guards, armed forces, or military organizations thereof, or for any officer, soldier, or sailor thereof? If so, state fully in regard to the same. Did you ever give any information to any officer, soldier, or sailor of the confederate army or navy, or to any person employed by or for the so-called Confederate States, or acting on their behalf, or for their benefit, which might aid in any way any military or naval operations carried on against the United States? State fully in regard to the same.
12. Were you in any manner employed in the manufacture of munitions of war, of clothing, of boots, shoes, saddles, harness, or leather, of equipment for soldiers, or of any stores or supplies for the use of the

confederate army or navy, or were you in any way employed by or did you aid or assist others engaged in such manufacture? If so, state when and where, and by or for whom you were so employed, and for what period of time.

13. Were you ever, directly or indirectly, employed in the collection, impressment, or purchase, or the sale of stores, supplies, or any property for the use or benefit of the confederate government, or any State in rebellion, or the army, navy, or other forces thereof? Did you have any interest or share in contracts with, or purchases for, the confederate government, or its army or navy, or any State in rebellion, or its forces? If so, state fully all particulars.
14. Were you ever engaged in blockade-running or illicit traffic, or intercourse between the lines, or were you ever in any way interested therein? Did you ever have any interest or share in any goods, wares, merchandise, stores, or supplies brought into or exported from the so-called Confederate States during the war? If so, state fully all particulars.
15. Did you leave the so-called Confederate States between 19th of April, 1861, and 19th of April, 1865? If so, when and how did you leave; where did you go; for what purpose; how long were you absent; in what business were you engaged while absent, and when and to what place did you return in the so-called Confederate States?
16. Were you the owner, or part owner, or in any way interested, in any vessel used in navigating the ocean to or from any port in the confederacy, or upon any waters in the confederacy. If so, what vessels, when and where employed, and in what business?
17. Were you ever arrested by the confederate government, or by any officer, soldier, or other person professing to act therefor, or for any State in rebellion; if so, when, where, by whom, and how long were you kept under arrest; how did you get released? Did you, for the sake of being released, or upon release take any oath of any kind to the confederate government. If so, what? [Put the same questions as to arrest by the United States Government, &c.]
18. Was any of your property ever taken by the confederate authorities, or by any officer, soldier, or other person acting or assuming to act on their behalf, or in behalf of any State in rebellion. If so, what property, when and for what use, and have you received pay therefor?
19. Were you ever threatened with damage or injury to person, family, or property on account of your Union sentiments? If so, state when, by whom, and what the threats were.
20. Were you ever molested or in any way injured on account of your Union sentiments? If so, state fully all the particulars.
21. Did you ever contribute anything – any money or property – in aid of the United State Government, or in aid of the Union army or cause? If so, state fully as to the same.

Appendix B

22. Did you ever do anything for the United States Government or its Army, or for the Union cause during the war? If so, state fully what you did.
23. Had you any near relatives in either the Union or confederate armies? If so, state who and how related to you. Did you contribute anything to supply them with military equipments or with money? State fully as to the same.
24. Have you owned any confederate bonds, or any interest or share therein, or had any share or interest in any loans to the confederate government; or did you in any way contribute to support the credit of the so-called Confederate States during the late rebellion?
25. Have you ever given aid and comfort to the rebellion? If so, state fully all the circumstances.
26. Were you ever engaged in making raids into the United States from Canada, or engaged in destroying the commerce of the United States in the lakes or rivers adjoining Canada?
27. Were you ever engaged in holding in custody, directly or indirectly, any persons taken by the rebel government as prisoners of war, or any persons imprisoned or confined by the confederate government, or the authorities of any State in rebellion, for political causes. If so, when, where, and under what circumstances; in what capacity were you engaged, and what was the name, rank and command of your principal?
28. Were you ever a member of any society or association for the imprisonment, expulsion, execution, or other persecution of any persons on account of their loyalty to the United States, or did you ever assist in such acts?
29. Were you ever a paroled prisoner of the United States. If so, when and where, and by whom paroled?
30. Have you ever held any office in the Army or Navy of the United States? Were you educated by the United States at the Military Academy at West Point, or at the United States Naval Academy?
31. Did you ever receive any pass from any officer of the confederate government, or from any person having or assuming to have authority to issue the same. If so, who gave you the pass; for what purpose; for what period of time; did you sign or swear to any promise or obligation in order to get it, or swear or promise to "bear true faith and yield obedience to the Confederate States;" did you use the pass, and for what purpose?
32. Are you or were you under the disabilities imposed by the fourteenth article of the amendments to the Constitution of the United States? Have you held any office under the United States Government since the war; If so, what office; and did you take the (so-called) "ironclad" oath?
33. At the beginning of the rebellion did you sympathize with the Union cause, or with the rebellion? What were your feelings and what your

language on the subject? On which side did you exert your influence and cast your vote? What did you do, and how did you vote? How did you vote on ratifying the ordinance of secession? After the ordinance of secession was adopted in your State, did you adhere to the Union cause, or did you "go with the State?

34. In conclusion, do you solemnly declare that, from the beginning of hostilities against the United States to the end thereof, your sympathies were constantly with the cause of the United States; that you never, of your own free will and accord, did anything, or offered, or sought, or attempted to do anything, by word or deed, to injure said cause or retard its success, and that you were at all times ready and willing, when called upon, or if called upon, to aid and assist the cause of the Union, or its supporters, so far as your means and power, and the circumstances of the case permitted?

No questions have been prepared to be put to witnesses called by the claimant to prove his loyalty, but the commissioners expect that you will put such questions as each case may require. In all cases the witness should be asked his age, residence, and occupation, when his acquaintance with the claimant began, and especially whether the acquaintance was intimate throughout the war; whether he lived near the claimant, and how far from him; whether he saw him often, how often; whether he conversed often with the claimant about the war its causes and progress; whether the witness was an adherent of the Union cause, and whether the claimant so regarded him; what the claimant said as to the war, the cause of it, the Union cause, and of his (the claimant's) sympathy with and adherence to the cause and the Government of the United States; whether the witness knew, and if so, how he knew, the sympathies and opinions of the claimant, and what they were, and whether the claimant conversed on these subjects with the witness alone, or in the presence of others; whether the witness knew the public reputation of the claimant as to loyalty, and if so, what it was; and especially how the claimant was regarded during the war by his loyal neighbors; whether he (the claimant) ever contributed any money or property to aid the Union cause or the Union Army, or ever gave information to officers or soldiers of the Union Army in aid of their movements and cause; whether the claimant was ever molested or threatened with injury to himself, his family, or his property, on account of his Union sentiments; and whether the claimant ever contributed anything in any way to aid the confederate government, or its officers or soldiers, or ever owned any confederate bonds, or did anything to sustain the credit of the Confederate States.

If you have been informed of any facts to impeach the loyalty of the claimant, you should put such questions as will elicit the facts. You are required to be very thorough in putting questions as to the loyalty of the claimants, especially in cases where there is any doubt as to its genuineness.

Appendix B

In concluding the examination of each witness to the loyalty of claimant, you will put the following question:

"Do you know of any act done, or language used by the claimant, which would have prevented him from establishing his loyalty to the confederacy if it had been maintained as a separate government? If so, state the same particularly."

II. Questions as to the taking or furnishing of the property, to be answered by the claimant and his witnesses, under oath

1. Were you present when any of the articles of property specified in the claimant's petition were taken?
2. Did you see any of them taken? If so, specify the articles you saw taken.
3. Did you see any of the articles named in the petition taken, other than those you have specified?
4. When and where and by whom were the articles taken, which you say you saw taken?
5. Who was present when you saw them taken?
6. Was any United States officer, either commissioned or non-commissioned, present at the taking? If so, state his name, rank, regiment, and the command to which he belonged. Did he order the property to be taken? Did he say anything about the taking?
7. Describe how the property was taken, and give a full account of all you saw done, or heard said, upon the occasion of the taking.
8. How was the property removed – by soldiers, or in wagons, or in what manner? State fully as to each article taken and removed.
9. To what place was it removed? Did you follow it to such place, or see it, or any portion of it, at any such place, or on its way to such place? How do you know the place to which it was removed?
10. Do you know the use for which the property was taken? What was the use, and how do you know it? Did you see the property so taken used by the United States Army? Did you see any part of the property so used? State fully all you know as to the property or any of it having been used by the Army; and distinguish between what you saw and know, and what you may have heard from others, or may think, or suppose, or infer to be true.
11. Was any complaint made to any officer on account of such taking? If so, state the name, rank, and regiment of the officer. What did he say about it? State fully all that he said.
12. Was any voucher or receipt for the property asked for? If so, of whom asked? State name, rank, and regiment. Was any receipt or paper given? If so, produce it, or state where it is and why it is not produced. If no voucher or receipt was given, state why none was given, and if refused, why it was refused; state all that was said about it. State fully all the

conversation between any officer or other person taking the property, and the claimant, or any one acting for him.

13. Was the property or any of it taken in the night-time? At what hour of the day (as near as you can tell) was it taken? Was any of the property taken secretly, or so that you did not know of it when taken?
14. When the property was taken was any part of the Army encamped in that vicinity? If so, state how far from the place where the property was taken, and what was the company, regiment, or brigade there encamped. How long had it been encamped there? How long did it stay there, and when did it leave? Had there been any battle or skirmish near there, just before the property was taken? Did you know the quartermasters, or any of them, or any other officers of the Army for whose use the property is supposed to have been taken?
15. Describe clearly the condition of the property when taken, and all that tends to show its value at the time and place of taking. Thus, if corn, was it green or ripe; had it been harvested; was it in the shock or husked, or shelled; where was it? If grain, was it standing; had it been cut; was it in shocks, or in the barn or in stacks; had it been thrashed? If horses, mules, or cattle, state when they were taken, how taken, and fully their condition, age, and value. Have you talked with claimant about their value?
16. What means have you of knowing quantity taken? How much did you see taken and removed? What quantity was taken in your presence? As to quantity, distinguish carefully as to what you saw and know, and what you may think or believe from what you have heard from others?
17. If you have testified as to the taking of wood, how do you know it was taken? How do you know the quantity? Was it measured? By whom? What was the kind, quality, and value of the wood? Was it taken in the tree, standing, or had it been cut? Where was it taken?
18. If rails were taken, did you see them taken. How taken – in wagons, or by soldiers? To what place taken? How do you know, and what do you know, as to the quantity taken? Were the rails new or old? Did officers try to prevent their being taken? Was any complaint made to officers on account of the taking?
19. Do you know, suppose, or believe that the property described in each item was taken for the actual use of the Army, and not for the mere gratification of individual officers or soldiers already provided by the Government with such articles as were necessary or proper for them to have?
20. Do you know, suppose, or believe it was taken in consequence of the failure of the troops of the United States to receive from the Government in the customary manner, or to have in their possession at the time, the articles and supplies necessary for them, or which they were entitled to receive and have?

Appendix B

21. Do you know, suppose, or believe that it was taken in consequence of some necessity for the articles taken, or similar articles, which necessity justified the officers or soldiers taking them?
22. Do you know, suppose, or believe it was taken for some purpose so necessary, useful, beneficial, or justifiable as to warrant or require the Government to pay for it?
23. Do you know, suppose, or believe that it was taken by, or under the order or authority of some officer, or other person connected with the Army, whose rank, situation, duties, or other circumstances at the time authorized, empowered, or justified him in taking it or ordering it to be taken?

NOTE – The witness must be caused, in answering the five preceding questions, to state fully, clearly, and carefully his or her various reasons for the knowledge, supposition, or belief entertained with respect to each question.

Standing Interrogatories of 1872

Revised Questions to be Answered by Claimants

1. What is your name, age, residence, and occupation?
2. Where did you reside from the 1st of April, 1861, to the 1st of June, 1865? If on your own land, what is the size of your farm? How much of your farm was cultivated, and how much was woodland? Where is it situated? What was your occupation during that time? Did you change your residence or business during that time; if so, where was your new residence, and what your new business?
3. Did you ever pass beyond the military or naval lines of the United States and enter the rebel lines; if so, how often, when, where, and for what purpose, and how long did you stay within the confederate lines on each occasion?
4. Did you ever take any oath or affirmation to bear allegiance to the so-called Confederate States, or to aid or support them in any way, or to "bear true faith" or "yield obedience" to them; if so, when and where? State fully in regard to same.
5. Have you ever taken any amnesty oath; if so, when, where, and under what condition? Have you been pardoned by the President; if so, when and where, and upon what conditions?
6. Were you ever, directly or indirectly, or in any manner, connected with the civil service of the so-called Confederate States; if so, how, when, and where, and upon what conditions?
7. Did you ever hold any office or place of trust, honor, or profit under the confederate government, or under any of the States or Territories subordinate thereto; if so, state the nature and character of the office, the place at which, and the period for which you held it?

8. Did you hold any clerkship, or have any agency or employment of any kind for, or under, or for the benefit of the so-called Confederate States? If so, state fully in regard to the same.
9. Were you ever, in any capacity, in the military or naval service of the so-called Confederate States, or of any State or Territory subordinate thereto?
10. Were you ever an officer or soldier in the confederate army; if yea, when, where, how long, and when did you leave such service? [Each one of these questions must be fully answered.]
11. Were you ever in the State militia of any State while subordinate to the confederacy? If yea, state when, where, how long, and when you left the service.
12. Were you ever in the home guard, or upon any vigilance committee, or committee of safety, while subject to the confederacy? If yea, state when, where, and how long.
13. If you claim that you were conscripted into the rebel service, state fully all circumstances.
14. Did you ever furnish a substitute for the rebel army? If yea, state fully all circumstances.
15. Were you directly or indirectly, or in any way, connected with or employed in the quartermaster's department of the confederate service, or the commissary's department, or the medical department, the engineers' department, the ordnance department, the impressment service, the provost-marshal's department, or any other branch of the confederate service?
16. Were you employed on any railroad in the service of the confederate government? Did you aid in the transportation of soldiers, munitions of war, or supplies for the confederate government? If yea, state fully all circumstances. If you claim that what you did was not "giving aid or comfort" to the rebel cause, state fully all the facts and reasons for such your claim.
17. Did you at any time have charge of any stores or supplies for the use of the confederate army, navy, or government, or the charge or care of trains, team or teams, wagon or wagons, vessels, boats, or other craft, or munitions of war, for the use of the confederate army or navy? If so, state fully in regard to the same.
18. Were you ever in any service, employment, or business of any kind whatsoever for the confederate government, or its army or navy? Did you ever furnish any aid, or any supplies or stores, or property of any kind, to or for the so-called Confederate States, or any State in rebellion, or to the army, navy, militia, home guards, armed forces, or military organizations thereof, or for any officer, soldier, or sailor thereof? If so, state fully in regard to the same. Did you ever give any information to any officer, soldier, or sailor of the confederate army or navy, or to any person

Appendix B

employed by or for the so-called Confederate States, or acting on their behalf, or for their benefit, which might aid in any way any military or naval operations carried on against the United States? State fully in regard to the same.

19. Were you in any manner employed in the manufacture of munitions of war, of clothing, of boots, shoes, saddles, harness, or leather; of equipment for soldiers, or of any stores or supplies for the use of the confederate army or navy; or were you in any way employed by, or did you aid or assist others engaged in such manufacture? If so, state when and where, and by or for whom you were so employed, and for what period of time.

20. Were you ever, directly or indirectly, employed in the collection, impressment, or purchase, or the sale of stores, supplies, or any property for the use or benefit of the confederate government, or any Sate in rebellion, or the army, navy, or other forces thereof? Did you have any interest or share in contracts with, or purchases for, the confederate government, or its army or navy, or any State in rebellion, or its forces? If so, state fully all particulars.

21. Were you ever engaged in blockade-running, or illicit traffic or intercourse between the lines, or were you ever in any way interested therein? Did you ever have any interest or share in any goods, wares, merchandise, stores, or supplies brought into or exported from the so-called Confederate States during the war? If so, state fully all particulars.

22. Did you leave the so-called Confederate States between the 19th of April, 1861, and the 19th of April, 1865? If so, when and how did you leave; where did you go; for what purpose; how long were you absent; in what business were you engaged while absent, and when and to what place did you return in the so-called Confederate States?

23. Were you the owner, or part owner, or in any way interested in any vessel used in navigating the ocean to or from any port in the confederacy, or upon any waters in the confederacy? If so, what vessels, when and where employed, and in what business?

24. Were you ever arrested by the confederate government, or by any officer, soldier, or other person professing to act therefor, or for any State in rebellion? If so, when, where, by whom, and how long were you kept under arrest? How did you get released? Did you, for the sake of being released, or upon release, take any oath of any kind to the confederate government? If so, what? [Put the same questions as to arrest by the United States Government, &c.]

25. Was any of your property ever taken by the confederate authorities, or by any officer, soldier, or other person acting or assuming to act on their behalf, or in behalf of any State in rebellion? If so, what property, when and for what use, and have you received pay therefor?

26. Were you ever threatened with damage or injury to your person, family, or property on account of your Union sentiments? If so, state when, by whom, and what the threats were.
27. Were you ever molested or in any way injured on account of your Union sentiments? If so, state fully all the particulars.
28. Did you ever contribute anything – any money or property – in aid of the United States Government, or in aid of the Union Army or cause? If so, state fully as to the same.
29. Did you ever *do* anything for the United States Government, or its Army, or for the Union cause, during the war? If so, state fully what you did.
30. Had you any near relatives – any *husband, son, brother, or nephew* – in the confederate army? If yea, state *his name*, whether *he is now living*, and where he resides. Did you furnish him with any military equipments, any clothing, or any money? Did you contribute in any way to aid or support him while in the rebel service? [*Each* of these questions under No. 30 must be fully answered.]
31. Have you owned any confederate bonds or any interest or share therein; or had any share or interest in any loans to the confederate government; or did you in any way contribute to *support the credit* of the so-called Confederate States during the rebellion?
32. Have you ever given any aid and comfort to the rebellion? If so, state fully all the circumstances.
33. Were you ever engaged in making raids into the United States from Canada, or engaged in destroying the commerce of the United States in the lakes and rivers adjoining Canada?
34. Were you ever engaged in holding in custody, directly or indirectly, any persons taken by the rebel government as prisoners of war, or any persons imprisoned or confined by the confederate government, or the authorities of any State in rebellion, for political causes? If so, when, where, and under what circumstances? In what capacity were you engaged, and what was the name, rank, and command of your principal?
35. Were you ever a member of any society or association for the imprisonment, expulsion, execution, or other persecution of any persons on account of their loyalty to the United States, or did you ever assist in such acts?
36. Were you ever a paroled prisoner of the United States? If so, when and where, and by whom paroled?
37. Have you ever held any office in the Army or Navy of the United States? Were you educated by the United States at the Military Academy at West Point, or at the United States Naval Academy?
38. Did you ever receive any pass from any officer of the confederate government, or from any person having or assuming to have authority to issue the same? If so, who gave you the pass; for what purpose; for what period of time; did you sign or swear to any promise or obligation in

Appendix B

order to get it, or swear or promise to "bear true faith and yield obedience to the Confederate States;" did you use the pass, and for what purpose?

39. Are you or were you under the disabilities imposed by the fourteenth article of the amendments to the Constitution of the United States? Have you held any office under the United States Government since the war? If so, what office; and did you take the (so-called) "iron-clad" oath?

40. At the beginning of the rebellion did you sympathize with the Union cause, or with the rebellion? What were your feelings and what your language on the subject? On which side did you exert your influence and cast your vote? What did you do, and how did you vote? How did you vote on ratifying the ordinance of secession? After the ordinance of secession was adopted in your State did you adhere to the Union cause, or did you "go with the State?"

41. [Original question 34.] In conclusion, do you solemnly declare that, from the beginning of hostilities against the United States to the end thereof, your sympathies were constantly with the cause of the United States; that you never, of your own free will and accord, did anything, or offered, or sought, or attempted to do anything, by word or deed, to injure said cause or retard its success, and that you were at all times ready and willing, when called upon, or if called upon, to aid and assist the cause of the Union, or its supporters, so far as your means and power and the circumstances of the case permitted?

If the claimant be a female, ask the following questions:

42. Are you single or married? If married, when were you married? Was your husband loyal to the cause and Government of the United States throughout the war? Where does he now reside, and why is he not joined with you in the petition? How many children have you? Give their names and ages. Were any of them in the confederate service during the war? If you claim that property named in your petition is your sole and separate property, state how you came to own it separately from your husband; how your title was derived; when your ownership of it began? Did it ever belong to your husband? If the property for which you ask pay is wood, timber, rails, or the products of a farm, how did you get title to the farm? If by deed, can you file copies of the deeds? If single, have you been married? If a widow, when did your husband die? Was he in the confederate army? Was he in the civil service of the confederacy? Was he loyal to the United States Government throughout the war? Did he leave any children? How many? Are any now living? Give their names and ages. Are they not interested in this claim? If they are not joined in this petition, why not? State fully how your title to the property specified in the petition was obtained.

If the claimant be a colored person, ask the following questions:

43. Were you a slave or free at the beginning of the war? When did you become free? What was your business after you became free? How and when did you come to own the property named in your petition? How did you get the means to pay for it? Who was your former master? Are you now in his employment? Do you live on his land? Do you live on land purchased of him? Are you indebted to your former master for land or property, and how much? Has anybody any interest in this claim besides yourself? State fully all the facts in your answers to these questions.

In all cases a witness called to prove loyalty should be asked his age, residence, and occupation; when his acquaintance with the claimant began, and especially whether the acquaintance was intimate throughout the war; whether he lived near the claimant, and how far from him; whether he saw him often, and how often; whether he conversed often with the claimant about the war, its causes and progress; whether the witness was an adherent of the Union cause, and whether the claimant so regarded him; what the claimant said as to the war, the causes of it, the Union cause, of his own sympathy with and adherence to the cause and Government of the United States; whether the witness knew, and if so, how he knew, the sympathies and opinions of the claimant, and what they were, and whether the claimant conversed on these subjects with the witness alone, or in the presence of others; whether the witness knew the public reputation of the claimant as to loyalty, and if so, what it was; and especially how the claimant was regarded during the war by his loyal neighbors; whether the claimant ever contributed any money or property to aid the Union cause, or the Union Army, or ever gave information to officers or soldiers of the Union Army in aid of their movements and cause; whether the claimant was ever molested or threatened with injury to himself, his family, or his property, on account of his Union sentiments; whether the claimant ever contributed anything in any way to aid the confederate government, or its officers or soldiers, or ever owned any confederate bonds, or did anything to sustain the credit of the Confederate States; and whether the claimant ever did any act or used any language which might have prevented him from establishing his loyalty to the confederacy if it had been maintained as a separate government.

Revised questions as to the taking or furnishing of property, to be answered by claimants and witnesses.

1. Were you present when any of the articles of property specified in claimant's petition were taken?
2. Did you *see* any of them taken? If so, specify the articles you saw taken.

Appendix B 159

3. Begin with the first article (item No. –) which you have specified that you saw taken, and give a full account of all you saw and heard in connection with the taking of that article?

[The special commissioner should require the witness to state all the *circumstances*: for it is only by a knowledge of *all* of them that the commissioners of claims can judge whether the taking was such a one as the Government is bound to pay for. The common phrase, "I saw the property taken by the United States soldiers," is not enough, for there was much lawless taking.

The witness should be required to detail the facts as to *each* item, when the items were taken at different times; but if all, or more than one, were taken at the same time, that fact should appear, and then a repetition of the circumstances is needless.

The special commissioner must be careful to elicit *all* the facts, as well those against as for the claim, especially as to those articles of property which were the special objects of pillage and theft, such as horses, mules, cattle, hogs, &c.

Claimants must bear in mind that a neglect to observe these directions *works to the prejudice of the claimant*, and may defeat the claim.]

4. Where were the articles taken? When were they taken? Give the day, month, and year, if you can. By whom were they taken? Did you see more than *one* soldier engaged in the taking? How many soldiers were present? State the number as near as you can. How many helped take the property? How long were they engaged in taking the property?
5. Who were present other than soldiers when you saw them taken? Give the names of all you know.
6. Was any United States officer, either commissioned or non-commissioned, present at the taking? If so, state his name, rank, regiment, and the command to which he belonged. Did he order the property to be taken? Did he say anything about the taking?
7. Describe how the property was taken, and give a full account of all you saw done, or heard said, upon the occasion of the taking.
8. How was the property removed, by soldiers or in wagons, or in what manner? State fully as to each article taken and removed.
9. To what place was it removed? Did you follow it to such place, or see it or any portion of it at any such place, or on its way to such place? How do you know the place to which it was removed?
10. Do you know the use for which the property was taken? What was the use, and how do you know it? Did you see the property so taken used by the United States Army? Did you see any *part* of the property so used? State fully all you know as to the property or any of it having been used by the Army; and distinguish between what you saw and know, and what you may have heard from others, or may think, or suppose, or infer to be true.

11. Was any complaint made to any officer on account of such taking? If so, state the name, rank, and regiment of the officer. What did he say about it? State fully *all* that he said.
12. Was any voucher or receipt for the property asked for? If so, of whom asked? State name, rank, and regiment. Was any receipt or paper given? If so, produce it, or state where it is, and why it is not produced. If no voucher or receipt was given, state why none was given, and if refused, why it was refused; state *all* that was said about it. State fully all the conversation between any officer or other person taking the property, and the claimant, or any one acting for him.
13. Was the property, or any of it, taken in the night-time? At what hour of the day (as near as you can tell) was it taken? Was any of the property taken secretly, or so that you did not know of it when taken?
14. When the property was taken, was any part of the Army *encamped* in that vicinity? If so, state how far from the place where the property was taken, and what was the company, regiment, or brigade there encamped. How long had it been encamped there? How long did it stay there, and when did it leave? Had there been any battle or skirmish near there, just before the property was taken? Did you know the quartermasters, or any of them, or any other officer of the command for whose use the property is supposed to have been taken?
15. Describe clearly the *condition* of the property when taken, and all that tends to show its value at the time and place of taking. Thus, if corn, was it green or ripe? Had it been harvested? Was it in the shock, or husked, or shelled? Where was it? If grain, was it standing; had it been cut; was it in shocks, or in the barn, or in stacks; had it been thrashed? If horses, mules, or cattle, state when they were taken, how taken, and fully their condition, age, and value. Have you talked with claimant about their value?
16. What means have you of knowing the *quantity* taken? State *particularly* how you estimate the quantity. Did you count or weigh the articles? Give us all your *data*. How much did you see taken and removed? What quantity was taken in your *presence*? As to quantity, distinguish carefully as to what you saw and know, and what you may *think or believe from what you have heard from others*.
17. If you have testified to the taking of *wood*, how do you know it was taken? How do you know the quantity? Was it measured? By whom? What was the kind, quality, and value of the wood? Was it taken *in the tree*, standing, or had it been cut? *Where* was it taken?
18. If rails were taken, did you *see* them taken; how taken; in wagons, or by soldiers? To what place taken? How do you know, and what do you know, as to the quantity taken? Were the rails new or old? Did officers try to prevent their being taken? Was any complaint made to officers on account of the taking?

19. Has any part of this claim been paid? Has any payment been made, in whole or in part, for any property taken at the same times as the property now under consideration? Were any such payments understood or claimed by the paying officer to be in full settlement of the accounts? Give all the circumstances.

Standing Interrogatories of 1874

The following questions will be put to every person who gives testimony:

1. What is your name, your age, your residence, and how long has it been such, and your occupation?
2. If you are not the claimant; in what manner, if any, are you related to the claimant or interested in the success of the claim?

The following questions will be put to every claimant, except claimants who were slaves at the beginning of the war:

[NOTE – If the original claimant be dead, these questions are to be answered by each of the heirs or legatees who were not less than sixteen years of age when the war closed.]

3. Where were you born? If not born in the United States, when and where were you naturalized? Produce your naturalization papers, if you can.
4. Where were you residing and what was your business for six months before the outbreak of the rebellion, and where did you reside and what was your business from the beginning to the end of the war? And if you changed your residence or business, state how many times, and why such changes were made.
5. On which side were your sympathies during the war, and were they on the same side from beginning to end?
6. Did you ever do anything or say anything against the Union cause; and if so, what did you do and say, and why?
7. Were you at all times during the war willing and ready to do whatever you could in aid of the Union cause?
8. Did you ever do anything for the Union cause or its advocates or defenders? If so, state what you did, giving times, places, names of persons aided, and particulars. Were the persons aided your relations?
9. Had you any near relatives in the Union Army or Navy; if so, in what company and regiment, or on what vessel, when and where did each one enter service, and when and how did he leave service? If he was a son, produce his discharge-paper, in order that its contents may be noted in this deposition, or state why it cannot be produced.

10. Were you in the service or employment of the United States Government at any time during the war; if so, in what service, when, where, or how long, under what officers, and when and how did you leave such service or employment?
11. Did you ever voluntarily contribute money, property, or services to the Union cause; and if so, when, where, to whom, and what did you contribute?
12. Which side did you take while the insurgent States were seceding from the Union in 1860 and 1861, and what did you do to show on which side you stood?
13. Did you adhere to the Union cause after the States had passed into rebellion, or did you go with your State?
14. What were your feelings concerning the battle of Bull Run or Manassas, the capture of New Orleans, the fall of Vicksburgh, and the final surrender of the confederate forces?
15. What favors, privileges, or protections were ever granted you in recognition of your loyalty during the war, and when and by whom granted?
16. Have you ever taken the so-called "iron-clad oath" since the war, and when and on what occasion?
17. Who were the leading and best-known Unionists of your vicinity during the war? Are any of them called to testify to your loyalty; and if not, why not?
18. Were you ever threatened with damage or injury to your person, family, or property on account of your Union sentiments, or were you actually molested or injured on account of your Union sentiments? If so, when, where, by whom, and in what particular way were you injured or threatened with injury?
19. Were you ever arrested by any confederate officer, soldier, sailor, or other person professing to act for the confederate government, or for any State in rebellion? If so, when, where, by whom, for what cause; how long were you kept under arrest; how did you obtain your release; did you take any oath or give any bond to effect your release; and if so, what was the nature of the oath or bond?
20. Was any of your property taken by confederate officers or soldiers, or any rebel authority? If so, what property, when, where, by whom; were you ever paid therefor, and did you ever present an account therefor to the confederate government, or any rebel officer?
21. Was any of your property ever confiscated by rebel authority, on the ground that you were an enemy to the rebel cause? If so, give all the particulars, and state if the property was subsequently released or compensation made therefor.
22. Did you ever do anything for the confederate cause, or render any aid or comfort to the rebellion? If so, give the times, places, persons, and other particulars connected with each transaction.

23. What force, compulsion, or influence was used to make you do anything against the Union cause? If any, give all the particulars demanded in the last question.
24. Were you in any service, business, or employment, for the confederacy, or for any rebel authority? If so give the same particulars as before required.
25. Were you in the civil, military, or naval service of the confederacy, or any rebel State, in any capacity whatsoever? If so, state fully in respect to each occasion and service.
26. Did you ever take any oath to the so-called Confederate States while in any rebel service or employment?
27. Did you ever have charge of any stores, or other property, for the confederacy, or did you ever sell or furnish any supplies to the so-called Confederate States, or any State in rebellion; or did you have any share or interest in contracts or manufactures in aid of the rebellion?
28. Were you engaged in blockade-running, or running through the lines, or interested in the risks or profits of such ventures?
29. Were you in any way interested in any vessel navigating the waters of the confederacy, or entering or leaving any confederate port? If so, what vessel, when and where employed, in what business, and had any rebel authority any direct or indirect interest in vessel or cargo?
30. Did you ever subscribe to any loan of the so-called Confederate States, or of any rebel State; or own confederate bonds or securities, or the bonds or securities of any rebel State issued between 1861 and 1865? Did you sell, or agree to sell, cotton or produce to the confederate government; or to any rebel State, or to any rebel officer or agent, and if so, did you receive or agree to receive confederate or State bonds or securities in payment; and if so, to what amount, and for what kind and amount of property?
31. Did you contribute to the raising, equipment, or support of troops, or the building of gunboats in aid of the rebellion; or to military hospitals or invalids, or to relief-funds or subscriptions for the families or persons serving against the United States?
32. Did you ever give information to any person in aid of military or naval operations against the United States?
33. Were you at any time a member of any society or organization for equipping volunteers or conscripts, or for aiding the rebellion in any other manner?
34. Did you ever take an oath of allegiance to the so-called Confederate States? If so, state how often, when, where, for what purpose, and the nature of the oath or affirmation.
35. Did you ever receive a pass from rebel authority? If so, state when, where, for what purpose, on what conditions, and how the pass was used.
36. Had you any near relatives in the confederate army, or in any military or naval service hostile to the United States? If so, give names, ages on entering service, present residence, if living, what influence you exerted,

if any, against their entering the service, and in what way you contributed to their outfit and support.
37. Have you been under the disabilities imposed by the fourteenth amendment to the Constitution? Have your disabilities been removed by Congress?
38. Have you been specially pardoned by the President for participation in the rebellion?"
39. Did you take any amnesty oath during the war, or after its close? If so, when, where, and why did you take it?
40. Were you ever a prisoner to the United States authorities, or on parole, or under bonds to do nothing against the Union cause? If so, state all the particulars.
41. Were you ever arrested by the authorities of the United States during the war? If so, when, where, by whom, on what grounds, and when and how did you obtain your release?
42. Were any fines or assessments levied upon you by the authorities of the United States because of your supposed sympathy for the rebellion? If so, state all the facts.
43. Was any of your property taken into possession or sold by the United States under the laws relating to confiscation, or to captured and abandoned property?

The following questions will be put to all male claimants or beneficiaries who were not less than sixteen years of age when the war closed:

44. After the presidential election of 1860, if of age, did you vote for any candidate or on any questions, during the war, and how did you vote? Did you vote for or against the candidates favoring secession?: did you vote for or against the ratification of the ordinance of secession, or for or against separation in your State?
45. Did you belong to any vigilance committee, or committee of safety, home-guard, or any other form of organization or combination designed to suppress Union sentiment in your vicinity?
46. Were you in the confederate army, State militia, or any military or naval organization hostile to the United States? If so, state when, where, in what organizations, how and why you entered, how long you remained each time, and when and how you left. If you claim that you were conscripted, when and where was it, how did you receive notice, and from whom, and what was the precise manner in which the conscription was enforced against you? If you were never in the rebel army or other hostile organization, explain how you escaped service. If you furnished a substitute, when and why did you furnish one, and what is his name, and his present address, if living?
47. Were you in any way connected with or employed in the confederate quartermaster, commissary, ordnance, engineer, or medical

Appendix B

department, or any other department, or employed on any railroad transporting troops or supplies for the confederacy, or otherwise engaged in transportation of men and supplies for the confederacy? If so, state how employed, when, where, for how long, under whose direction, and why such employment was not giving "aid and comfort" to the rebellion.

48. Did you at any time have charge of trains, teams, wagons, vessels, boats, or military supplies or property of any kind for the confederate government? If so, give all the facts as in previous questions.
49. Were you employed in saltpeter-works, in tanning or milling for the confederate government, or making clothing, boots, shoes, saddles, harness, arms, ammunition, accouterments, or any other kind of munitions of war for the confederacy? If so, give all the particulars of time, place, and nature of services or supplies.
50. Were you ever engaged in holding in custody, directly or indirectly, any persons taken by the rebel government as prisoners of war, or any person imprisoned or confined by the confederate government, or the authorities of any rebel State, for political causes? If so, when, where, under what circumstances, in what capacity were you engaged, and what was the name and rank of your principal?
51. Were you ever in the Union Army or Navy, or in any service connected therewith? If so, when, where, in what capacity, under whose command or authority, for what period of time, and when and how did you leave service? Produce your discharge-papers, so that their contents may be noted herein.

The following questions will be put to every person testifying to the loyalty of claimants or beneficiaries:

52. In whose favor are you here to testify?
53. How long have you known that person altogether, and what part of that time have you intimately known him?
54. Did you live near him during the war, and how far away?
55. Did you meet him often, and about how often, during the war?
56. Did you converse with the claimant about the war, its causes, its progress, and its results? If so, try to remember the more important occasions on which you so conversed, beginning with the first occasion, and state with respect to each, when it was, where it was, who were present, what caused the conversation, and what the claimant said, in substance, if you cannot remember his words.
57. Do you know of anything done by the claimant that showed him to be loyal to the Union cause during the war? If you do, state what he did, when, where, and what was the particular cause or occasion of his doing it. Give the same information about each thing he did that showed him to be loyal.

58. Do you know of anything said or done by the claimant that was against the Union cause? If so, please state, with respect to each thing said or done, what it was, when it was, where it was, and what particular compulsion or influence caused him to say or do it.
59. If you have heard of anything said or done by the claimant, either for the Union cause or against it, state from whom you heard it, when you heard it, and what you heard.
60. What was the public reputation of the claimant for loyalty or disloyalty to the United States during the war? If you profess to know his public reputation, explain fully how you know it, whom you heard speak of it, and give the names of other persons who were neighbors during the war that could testify to his public reputation.
61. Who were the known and prominent Union people of the neighborhood during the war, and do you know that such persons could testify to the claimant's loyalty?
62. Were you, yourself, and adherent of the Union cause during the war? If so, did the claimant know you to be such, and how did he know it?
63. Do you know of any threats, molestations, or injury inflicted upon the claimant or his family, or his property, on account of his adherence to the Union cause? If so, give all the particulars.
64. Do you know of any act done or language used by the claimant that would have prevented him from establishing his loyalty to the confederacy? If so, what act or what language?
65. Can you state any other fact within your own knowledge in proof of the claimant's loyalty during the war? If so, state all the facts and give all the particulars.

The following questions concerning the ownership of property charged in claims will be put to all claimants, or the representatives of deceased claimants:

66. Who was the owner of the property charged in this claim when it was taken and how did such persons become owner?
67. If any of the property was taken from a farm or plantation, where was such farm or plantation situated, what was its size, how much was cultivated, how much was woodland, and how much was waste-land?
68. Has the person who owned the property when taken since filed a petition in bankruptcy, or been declared a bankrupt?

The following questions will be put to female claimants:

69. Are you married or single? If married, when were you married? Was your husband loyal to the cause and Government of the United States throughout the war? Where does he now reside, and why is he not joined with you in the petition? How many children have you? Give their names and ages. Were any of them in the confederate service during the war?

Appendix B

If you claim that the property named in your petition is your sole and separate property, state how you came to own it separately from your husband; how your title was derived; when your ownership of it began. Did it ever belong to your husband? If the property for which you ask pay is wood, timber, rails, or the products of a farm, how did you get title to the farm? If by deed, can you file copies of the deeds? If single, have you been married? If a widow, when did your husband die? Was he in the confederate army? Was he in the civil service of the confederacy? Was he loyal to the United States Government throughout the war? Did he leave any children? How many? Are any now living? Give their names and ages. Are they not interested in this claim? If they are not joined in this petition, why not? State fully how your title to the property specified in the petition was obtained. Did you ever belong to any sewing-society organized to make clothing for confederate soldiers or their families, or did you assist in making any such clothing, or making flags or other military equipments, or preparing or furnishing delicacies or supplies for confederate hospitals or soldiers?

The following questions will be put to colored claimants:

70. Were you a slave or free at the beginning of the war? If ever a slave, when did you become free? What business did you follow after obtaining your freedom? Did you own this property before or after you became free? When did you get it? How did you become owner, and from whom did you obtain it? Where did you get the means to pay for it? What was the name and residence of your master, and is he still living? Is he a witness for you; and if not, why not? Are you in his employ now, or do you live on his land or on land bought from him? Are you in his debt? What other person besides yourself has any interest in this claim?

The following questions will be put to all colored witnesses in behalf of white claimants:

71. Were you formerly the slave of the claimant? Are you now in his service or employment? Do you live on his land? Are you in his debt? Are you in any way to share in this claim, if allowed?

The following questions will be put to claimants and witnesses who testify to the taking of property, omitting in the case of each claimant or witness any questions that are clearly unnecessary:

72. Were you present when any of the property charged in this claim was taken? Did you actually see any taken? If so, specify what you saw taken? Did you actually see any taken? If so, specify what you saw taken.
73. Was any of the property taken in the night-time, or was any taken secretly, so that you did not know of it at the time?

74. Was any complaint made to any officer of the taking of any of the property? If so, give the name, rank, and regiment of the officer, and state who made the complaint to him; what he said and did in consequence; and what was the result of the complaint.
75. Were any vouchers or receipts asked for or given? If given, where are the vouchers or receipts? If lost, state fully how lost. If asked and not given, by whom were they asked; who was asked to give them, and why were they refused or not given? State very fully in regard to the failure to ask or obtain receipts.
76. Has any payment ever been made for any property charged in this claim? Has any payment been made for any property taken at the same times as the property charged in this claim? Has any payment been made for any property taken from the same claimant during the war; and if so, when, by whom, for what property and to what amount? Has this property, or any part of it, been included in any claim heretofore presented to Congress, or any court, Department, or officer of the United States, or to any board of survey, military commission, State commission or officer, or any other authority? If so, when and to what tribunal or officers was the claim presented? Was it larger or smaller in amount than this claim; and how is the difference explained; and what was the decision, if any, of the tribunal to which it was presented?
77. Was the property charged in this claim taken by troops encamped in the vicinity, or were they on the march; or were they on a raid or expedition; or had there been any recent battle or skirmish?
78. You will please listen attentively while the list of items, but not the quantities, is read to you, and as each kind of property is called off, say whether you saw any such property taken.
79. Begin now with the first item of property you have just said you saw taken, and give the following information about it: First. Describe its exact condition – as, for instance, if corn, whether green or ripe, standing or harvested, in shuck or husked, or shelled; if lumber, whether new or old, in buildings or piled; if grain, whether growing or cut, &c. Second. State where it was. Third. What was the quantity? Explain fully how you know the quantity; and if estimated, describe your method of making the estimate. Fourth. Describe the quality, to your best judgment. Fifth. State as nearly as you can the market-value of such property, and the names of any officers belonging to the command. Eighth. Describe the precise manner in which the property was taken into possession by the troops, and the manner in which it was removed. Ninth. State as closely as you can how many men, animals, wagons, or other means of transport, were engaged in the removal; how long they were occupied, and to what place they removed the property. Tenth. State if any officers were present; how you knew them to be officers; what they said or did in relation to the property, and give the names of any, if you can. Eleventh.

Appendix B

> Give any reasons that you may have for believing that the property was authorized by the proper officers, or that it was for the necessary use of the Army.
> 80. Now take the next item of property you saw taken, and give the same information, and so proceed to the end of the list of items.

Source: The commissioners printed their interrogatories to claimants and witnesses in their general reports to Congress. See First General Report, 24, 27–30; Second General Report, 51–59; and Fourth General Report, 38–42.

Notes

Introduction

1. Mary Blackburn Testimony, September 11, 1874, Mary Blackburn Allowed Claim, Augusta County, Virginia, Southern Claims Commission, Allowed Claims, 1871–1880, Records of the Land, Files, and Miscellaneous Division, Records of the Accounting Officers of the Department of the Treasury, 1775–1927, Record Group 217, National Archives, Washington, DC (hereafter cited as Allowed Claim). On special commissioners' fees, see Frank W. Klingberg, *The Southern Claims Commission* (Berkeley: University of California Press, 1955), 79.
2. Mary Blackburn Testimony, September 11, 1874, Mary Blackburn Allowed Claim, Augusta County, Virginia.
3. On the inegalitarian traditions of American citizenship, see James H. Kettner, *The Development of American Citizenship, 1608–1870* (Chapel Hill: University of North Carolina Press, 1978); Judith N. Shklar, *American Citizenship: The Quest for Inclusion* (Cambridge, MA: Harvard University Press, 1991); Rogers M. Smith, *Civic Ideals: Conflicting Visions of Citizenship in U.S. History* (New Haven, CT: Yale University Press, 1997); Evelyn Nakano Glenn, *Unequal Freedom: How Race and Gender Shaped American Citizenship and Labor* (Cambridge, MA: Harvard University Press, 2002); Mae M. Ngai, *Impossible Subjects: Illegal Aliens and the Making of Modern America* (Princeton, NJ: Princeton University Press, 2004).

   On southern citizenship, see Edmund S. Morgan, *American Slavery, American Freedom: The Ordeal of Colonial Virginia* (New York: Norton, 1975); Eric Foner, *Reconstruction: America's Unfinished Revolution, 1863–1877* (New York: Harper & Row, 1988); Stephanie McCurry, *Masters of Small Worlds: Yeoman Households, Gender Relations, and the Political Culture of the Antebellum South Carolina Low Country* (New York: Oxford University Press, 1995); Kathleen M. Brown, *Good Wives, Nasty Wenches, and Anxious Patriarchs: Gender, Race, and Power in Colonial Virginia* (Chapel Hill: University of North Carolina Press, 1996); Saidiya V. Hartman, *Scenes of Subjection: Terror, Slavery, and Self-Making in Nineteenth-Century America* (New York: Oxford University Press, 1997); Michael Vorenberg,

Final Freedom: The Civil War, the Abolition of Slavery, and the Thirteenth Amendment (Cambridge and New York: Cambridge University Press, 2001).

For nineteenth-century analyses of women's analogous position to slaves, see Ellen Carol DuBois, *Feminism and Suffrage: The Emergence of an Independent Women's Movement in America, 1848–1869* (Ithaca: Cornell University Press, 1978), 31–40; Blanche Glassman Hersh, *The Slavery of Sex: Feminist-Abolitionists in America* (Urbana: University of Illinois Press, 1978), 189–200; Jean Fagan Yellin, *Women and Sisters: The Antislavery Feminists in American Culture* (New Haven, CT: Yale University Press, 1989), 3–52; Sylvia D. Hoffert, *When Hens Crow: The Woman's Rights Movement in Antebellum America* (Bloomington: Indiana University Press, 1995), 55–57; Amy Dru Stanley, "Instead of Waiting for the Thirteenth Amendment: The War Power, Slave Marriage, and Inviolate Human Rights," *American Historical Review* 115, no. 3 (June 2010): 732–765.

4 Mary Blackburn Testimony, September 11, 1874, Mary Blackburn Allowed Claim, Augusta County, Virginia.
5 Summary Report, 1875, Mary Blackburn Allowed Claim, Augusta County, Virginia.
6 For an introduction to the scholarship on postemancipation societies, see Rebecca J. Scott, Thomas C. Holt, and Frederick Cooper, eds., *Societies After Slavery: A Select Annotated Bibliography of Printed Sources on Cuba, Brazil, British Colonial Africa, South Africa, and the British West Indies* (Pittsburgh: University of Pittsburgh Press, 2002). Uses of "postemancipation" are scattered in the historiography of the American South. See Richard P. Fuke, *Imperfect Equality: African Americans and the Confines of White Racial Attitudes in Post-Emancipation Maryland* (New York: Fordham University Press, 1999); Jane Elizabeth Dailey, *Before Jim Crow: The Politics of Race in Postemancipation Virginia* (Chapel Hill: University of North Carolina Press, 2000); Hannah R. Rosen, *Terror in the Heart of Freedom: Citizenship, Sexual Violence, and the Meaning of Race in the Postemancipation South* (Chapel Hill: University of North Carolina Press, 2009).
7 The commissioners also required claimants to prove that they had owned the property for which they sought compensation and that it had been appropriated by the authority of the Union army during the war.
8 Klingberg, *The Southern Claims Commission*, 73–88.
9 On narrative, see Clifford Geertz, "Thick Description: Toward an Interpretive Theory of Culture," in *The Interpretation of Cultures* (New York: Basic Books, 1973), 6–20; Frederic Jameson, *The Political Unconscious: Narrative as a Socially Symbolic Act* (Ithaca, NY: Cornell University Press, 1981); Edward L. Ayers, "Narrating the New South," *Journal of Southern History* 61, no. 3 (August 1995): 555–566; Karen Halttunen, "'Domestic Differences': Competing Narratives of Womanhood in the Murder Trial of Lucretia Chapman," in *The Culture of Sentiment: Race, Gender and Sentimentality in Nineteenth-Century America*, ed. Shirley Samuels (New York: Oxford University Press, 1992); Priscilla Wald, *Constituting Americans: Cultural Anxiety and Narrative Form* (Durham: Duke University Press, 1995); Cara W. Robertson, "Representing 'Miss Lizzie': Cultural Convictions in the Trial of Lizzie Borden," *Yale Journal of Law and the Humanities* 8 (1996): 351–416; Hendrik Hartog, "Lawyering, Husbands' Rights, and the Unwritten Law in Nineteenth-Century America," *Journal of American History* 84 (June 1997): 67–96. For examples of scholarship that engage with narrative in innovative ways, see Edward L. Ayers,

The Promise of the New South: Life After Reconstruction (New York: Oxford University Press, 1992); James E. Goodman, *Stories of Scottsboro* (New York: Pantheon Books, 1994).

10 Klingberg, *The Southern Claims Commission*; Sarah Larson, "Records of the Southern Claims Commission," *Prologue* 12, no. 4 (1980): 207–218; John Hammond Moore, "Getting Uncle Sam's Dollars: South Carolinians and the Southern Claims Commission, 1871–1880," *South Carolina Historical Magazine* 82, no. 3 (1981): 248–262; John Hammond Moore, "Richmond Area Residents and the Southern Claims Commission, 1871–1880," *Virginia Magazine of History & Biography* 91, no. 3 (1983): 285–295; John Hammond Moore, "Sherman's 'Fifth Column': A Guide to Unionist Activity in Georgia," *Georgia Historical Quarterly* 68, no. 3 (1984): 382–409; Eugene A. Hatfield, "Stephen Green Dorsey and the Southern Claims Commission: A Question of Loyalty," *Atlanta Historical Journal* 29, no. 2 (1985): 19–29; John Hammond Moore, "In Sherman's Wake: Atlanta and the Southern Claims Commission, 1871–1880," *Atlanta Historical Journal* 29, no. 2 (1985): 5–18; Michael K. Honey, "The War Within the Confederacy: White Unionists of North Carolina," *Prologue* 18, no. 2 (1986): 75–93; Kenneth W. Noe, "Red String Scare: Civil War Southwest Virginia and the Heroes of America," *North Carolina Historical Review* 69, no. 3 (1992): 301–322; Edna Greene Medford, "'I Was Always a Union Man': The Dilemma of Free Blacks in Confederate Virginia," *Slavery & Abolition* 15, no. 3 (1994): 1–16; Reginald Washington, "The Southern Claims Commission: A Source for African-American Roots," *Prologue* 27, no. 4 (1995): 374–382; Stephen S. Michot, "'War Is Still Raging in this Part of the Country': Oath-Taking, Conscription, and Guerrilla War in Louisiana's Lafourche Region," *Louisiana History* 38, no. 2 (1997): 157–184; Noel G. Harrison, "Atop an Anvil: The Civilians' War in Fairfax and Alexandria Counties, April 1861-April 1862," *Virginia Magazine of History & Biography* 106, no. 2 (1998): 133–164; Rebecca M. Dresser, "Kate and John Minor: Confederate Unionists of Natchez," *Journal of Mississippi History* 64, no. 3 (2002): 188–216; Anthony E. Kaye, "Slaves, Emancipation, and the Powers of War: Views from the Natchez District of Mississippi," in *The War Was You and Me: Civilians in the American Civil War*, ed. Joan E. Cashin (Princeton, NJ: Princeton University Press, 2002), 60–84; Margaret M. Storey, "Civil War Unionists and the Political Culture of Loyalty in Alabama, 1860–1861," *Journal of Southern History* 69, no. 1 (2003): 71–106; Margaret M. Storey, *Loyalty and Loss: Alabama's Unionists in the Civil War and Reconstruction* (Baton Rouge: Louisiana State University Press, 2004).

11 Only a few historians examine the commission in its postbellum context and none explore loyalty in any depth. Benjamin E. Bowie focuses on the congressional debates surrounding the payment of southern claims but provides little attention to the testimony from southerners. Frank W. Klingberg addresses the congressional debates as well the claims themselves, but he only analyzes claims for amounts over $10,000, neglecting poorer southerners. Frank W. Klingberg, "The Southern Claims Commission: A Postwar Agency in Operation," *Mississippi Valley Historical Review* 32, no. 2 (1945): 195–214; Benjamin E. Bowie, *"The Southern Claims Commission"* (Master's Thesis, University of Mississippi, 1949); Benjamin E. Bowie, "The Southern Claims Commission, 1871–1880," *Journal of Mississippi History* 12 (April 1950): 105–115; Klingberg, *The Southern Claims Commission*.

12 Stephanie McCurry refers to this as the "problem of political obligation." Stephanie McCurry, "Citizens, Soldiers' Wives and 'Hiley Hope Up' Slaves: The Problem of Political Obligation in the Civil War South," in *Gender and the Southern Body Politic*, ed. Nancy Bercaw (Jackson: University Press of Mississippi, 2000), 95–124.
13 I have borrowed the term subject citizenship from Judith Shklar. See Shklar, *American Citizenship*, 32–34, 39.
14 Smith, *Civic Ideals*; Herman Belz, *Reconstructing the Union: Theory and Policy During the Civil War* (Ithaca, NY: Cornell University Press, 1969); Harold Melvin Hyman, *A More Perfect Union: The Impact of the Civil War and Reconstruction on the Constitution* (New York: Knopf, 1973); Michael Les Benedict, *A Compromise of Principle: Congressional Republicans and Reconstruction, 1863–1869* (New York: Norton, 1974); Phillip Shaw Paludan, *A Covenant with Death: The Constitution, Law, and Equality in the Civil War Era* (Urbana: University of Illinois Press, 1975); Herman Belz, *Emancipation and Equal Rights: Politics and Constitutionalism in the Civil War Era* (New York: Norton, 1978); Harold Melvin Hyman and William M. Wiecek, *Equal Justice Under Law: Constitutional Development, 1835–1875* (New York: Harper & Row, 1982); Robert J. Kaczorowski, *The Politics of Judicial Interpretation: The Federal Courts, Department of Justice and Civil Rights, 1866–1876* (New York: Oceana, 1985); William E. Nelson, *The Fourteenth Amendment: From Political Principle to Judicial Doctrine* (Cambridge, MA: Harvard University Press, 1988); Earl M. Maltz, *Civil Rights, the Constitution, and Congress, 1863–1869* (Lawrence: University Press of Kansas, 1990); David A. J. Richards, *Conscience and the Constitution: History, Theory, and Law of the Reconstruction Amendments* (Princeton, NJ: Princeton University Press, 1993); Earl M. Maltz, *The Fourteenth Amendment and the Law of the Constitution* (Durham, NC: Carolina Academic Press, 2003); Deak Nabers, *Victory of Law: The Fourteenth Amendment, the Civil War, and American Literature, 1852–1867* (Baltimore: Johns Hopkins University Press, 2006).
15 Jonathan T. Dorris, *Pardon and Amnesty Under Lincoln and Johnson: The Restoration of the Confederates to Their Rights and Privileges, 1861–1898* (Chapel Hill: University of North Carolina Press, 1953); Harold M. Hyman, *Era of the Oath: Northern Loyalty Tests During the Civil War and Reconstruction* (Philadelphia: University of Pennsylvania Press, 1954); William C. Harris, *With Charity for All: Lincoln and the Restoration of the Union* (Lexington: University Press of Kentucky, 1997); Kathleen Rosa Zebley, "Rebel Salvation: The Story of Confederate Pardons" (PhD Dissertation, University of Tennessee, 1999).
16 Smith, *Civic Ideals*, 7.
17 My approach to official and vernacular citizenship has been influenced by Aihwa Ong's identification of "cultural citizenship" as a dual process of self-making and being made. See Aihwa Ong, "Cultural Citizenship as Subject-Making: Immigrants Negotiate Racial and Cultural Boundaries in the United States," *Current Anthropology* 37, no. 5 (1996): 737–762; Aihwa Ong, *Buddha Is Hiding: Refugees, Citizenship, the New America* (Berkeley: University of California Press, 2003). "Vernacular citizenship," as I define it, differs from "cultural citizenship." Scholars often use the term cultural citizenship to refer to a sense of belonging or an expression of national identity mediated through a real or imagined community

in the absence of, even unrelated to, full rights and privileges. Renato Rosaldo defines cultural citizenship as "the right to be different (in terms of race, ethnicity, or native language) with respect to the norms of the dominant national community, without compromising one's right to belong, in the sense of participating in the nation-state's democratic processes." Vernacular citizenship in my usage draws on cultural citizenship, especially in its emphasis on a cultural sense of belonging, but also incorporates citizens' claims on the government for rights and privileges. See Renato Rosaldo, "Cultural Citizenship in San Jose, Califomia," *Polar* 17 (2008): 57.

18 On loyalty in the Confederacy, see Richard E. Beringer et al., *Why the South Lost the Civil War* (Athens: University of Georgia Press, 1986); Drew Gilpin Faust, "Altars of Sacrifice: Confederate Women and the Narratives of War," *Journal of American History* 76, no. 4 (1990): 1200–1228; James M McPherson, *What They Fought For, 1861–1865* (Baton Rouge: Louisiana State University Press, 1995); Gary W. Gallagher, *The Confederate War* (Cambridge, MA: Harvard University Press, 1997); James M. McPherson, *For Cause and Comrades: Why Men Fought in the Civil War* (New York: Oxford University Press, 1997); Chandra Manning, *What This Cruel War Was Over: Soldiers, Slavery, and the Civil War* (New York: Alfred A. Knopf, 2007).

19 On loyalty to the Union, see Phillip Shaw Paludan, *Victims: A True Story of the Civil War* (Knoxville: University of Tennessee Press, 1981); Durwood Dunn, *Cades Cove: The Life and Death of a Southern Appalachian Community, 1818–1937* (Knoxville: University of Tennessee Press, 1988); Daniel W. Crofts, *Reluctant Confederates: Upper South Unionists in the Secession Crisis* (Chapel Hill: University of North Carolina Press, 1989); Michael Fellman, *Inside War: The Guerrilla Conflict in Missouri During the American Civil War* (New York: Oxford University Press, 1989); Wayne K. Durrill, *War of Another Kind: A Southern Community in the Great Rebellion* (New York: Oxford University Press, 1990); Daniel E. Sutherland, *Seasons of War: The Ordeal of a Confederate Community, 1861–1865* (New York: Simon & Schuster, 1995); Steven Tripp, *Yankee Town, Southern City: Race and Class Relations in Civil War Lynchburg* (New York: New York University Press, 1997); Thomas G. Dyer, *Secret Yankees: The Union Circle in Confederate Atlanta* (Baltimore: Johns Hopkins University Press, 1999); Daniel E. Sutherland, *Guerrillas, Unionists, and Violence on the Confederate Home Front* (Fayetteville: University of Arkansas Press, 1999); John C. Inscoe and Gordon B. McKinney, *The Heart of Confederate Appalachia: Western North Carolina in the Civil War* (Chapel Hill: University of North Carolina Press, 2000); Victoria E. Bynum, *The Free State of Jones: Mississippi's Longest Civil War* (Chapel Hill: University of North Carolina Press, 2001); John C. Inscoe and Robert C. Kenzer, eds., *Enemies of the Country: New Perspectives on Unionists in the Civil War South* (Athens: University of Georgia Press, 2001); Storey, *Loyalty and Loss*; Gordon B. McKinney, "Layers of Loyalty: Confederate Nationalism and Amnesty Letters from Western North Carolina," *Civil War History* 51, no. 1 (2005): 5–22; Jonathan Dean Sarris, *A Separate Civil War: Communities in Conflict in the Mountain South* (Charlottesville: University of Virginia Press, 2006).

20 Rollin G. Osterweis, *The Myth of the Lost Cause, 1865–1900* (Hamden: Archon Books, 1973); Thomas Lawrence Connelly, *The Marble Man: Robert E. Lee*

and His Image in American Society (New York: Knopf, 1977); Charles Reagan Wilson, *Baptized in Blood: The Religion of the Lost Cause, 1865–1920* (Athens: University of Georgia Press, 1980); Thomas L. Connelly and Barbara L. Bellows, *God and General Longstreet: The Lost Cause and the Southern Mind* (Baton Rouge: Louisiana State University Press, 1982); Gaines M. Foster, *Ghosts of the Confederacy: Defeat, the Lost Cause, and the Emergence of the New South, 1865 to 1913* (New York: Oxford University Press, 1987); Alan T. Nolan, *Lee Considered: General Robert E. Lee and Civil War History* (Chapel Hill: University of North Carolina Press, 1991); John A. Simpson, *S. A. Cunningham and the Confederate Heritage* (Athens: University of Georgia Press, 1994); Gary W. Gallagher, *Jubal A. Early, the Lost Cause, and Civil War History: A Persistent Legacy* (Milwaukee, WI: Marquette University Press, 1995); Kirk Savage, *Standing Soldiers, Kneeling Slaves: Race, War, and Monument in Nineteenth-Century America* (Princeton, NJ: Princeton University Press, 1997); Gary W. Gallagher, *Lee and His Generals in War and Memory* (Baton Rouge: Louisiana State University Press, 1998); Gary W. Gallagher and Alan T. Nolan, *The Myth of the Lost Cause and Civil War History* (Bloomington: Indiana University Press, 2000); David W. Blight, *Race and Reunion: The Civil War in American Memory* (Cambridge, MA: Harvard University Press, 2001); David R. Goldfield, *Still Fighting the Civil War: The American South and Southern History* (Baton Rouge: Louisiana State University Press, 2002); Karen L. Cox, *Dixie's Daughters: The United Daughters of the Confederacy and the Preservation of Confederate Culture* (Gainesville: University Press of Florida, 2003); Alice Fahs and Joan Waugh, eds., *The Memory of the Civil War in American Culture* (Chapel Hill: University of North Carolina Press, 2004); James M. McPherson, "Long-Legged Yankee Lies: The Southern Textbook Crusade," in *The Memory of the Civil War in American Culture*, ed. Alice Fahs and Joan Waugh (Chapel Hill: University of North Carolina Press, 2004), 64–78; Gary W. Gallagher, *Causes Won, Lost, and Forgotten: How Hollywood and Popular Art Shape What We Know About the Civil War* (Chapel Hill: University of North Carolina Press, 2008); Caroline E. Janney, *Burying the Dead but Not the Past: Ladies' Memorial Associations and the Lost Cause* (Chapel Hill: University of North Carolina Press, 2008).

21 On the union memory of the war, see Bynum, *The Free State of Jones*; John R. Neff, *Honoring the Civil War Dead: Commemoration and the Problem of Reconciliation* (Lawrence: University Press of Kansas, 2005); Gallagher, *Causes Won, Lost, and Forgotten*; Gary W. Gallagher, *The Union War* (Cambridge, MA: Harvard University Press, 2011). The so-called union narrative is more precisely an anti-secession narrative. Champions of both the so-called union narrative and the emancipationist narrative envisioned specific iterations of the Union and its ideals.

22 On the emancipationist memory of the war, see William L. VanDeburg, "The Battleground of Historical Memory: Creating Alternative Culture Heroes in Postbellum America," *Journal of Popular Culture* 20, no. 1 (1986): 49–62; David W. Blight, "'For Something Beyond the Battlefield': Frederick Douglass and the Struggle for the Memory of the Civil War," *Journal of American History* 75, no. 4 (1989): 1156–1178; David W. Blight, "'What Will Peace Among the Whites Bring?': Reunion and Race in the Struggle Over the Memory of the Civil War in American Culture," *Massachusetts Review* 34, no. 3 (1993): 393–410; David W. Blight, "The Meaning or the Fight: Frederick Douglass and the Memory of the Fifty Fourth

Massachusetts," *Massachusetts Review* 36, no. 1 (1995): 141–153; Savage, *Standing Soldiers, Kneeling Slaves*; David W. Blight, "Fifty Years of Freedom: The Memory of Emancipation at the Civil War Semi-Centennial, 1911–15," *Slavery & Abolition* 21, no. 2 (2000): 117–134; Kathleen Clark, "Celebrating Freedom: Emancipation Day Celebrations and African American Memory in the Early Reconstruction South," in *Where These Memories Grow: History, Memory, and Southern Identity*, ed. W. Fitzhugh Brundage (Chapel Hill: University of North Carolina Press, 2000), 107–132; Martin Henry Blatt, Thomas J. Brown, and Donald Yacovone, eds., *Hope & Glory: Essays on the Legacy of the Fifty-Fourth Massachusetts Regiment* (Amherst: University of Massachusetts Press, 2001); Blight, *Race and Reunion*; Court Carney, "The Contested Image of Nathan Bedford Forrest," *Journal of Southern History* 67, no. 3 (2001): 601–630; Mitchell A. Kachun, *Festivals of Freedom: Memory and Meaning in African American Emancipation Celebrations, 1808–1915* (Amherst: University of Massachusetts Press, 2003); James P. Weeks, "A Different View of Gettysburg: Play, Memory, and Race at the Civil War's Greatest Shrine," *Civil War History* 50, no. 2 (2004): 175–191; John Cimprich, *Fort Pillow, a Civil War Massacre, and Public Memory* (Baton Rouge: Louisiana State University Press, 2005); Dennis Fisher, "'We Have Our Memories and Our Present Grievances': African-Memory During the Great War, 1917–1919," *Journal of the American Studies Association of Texas* 36 (2005): 23–44; Andre Fleche, "'Shoulder to Shoulder as Comrades Tried': Black Men and White Union Veterans and Civil War Memory," *Civil War History* 51, no. 2 (2005): 175–201.

23 Paul H. Buck, *The Road to Reunion, 1865–1900* (Boston: Little, Brown, 1937); Stuart Charles McConnell, *Glorious Contentment: The Grand Army of the Republic, 1865–1900* (Chapel Hill: University of North Carolina Press, 1992); Nina Silber, *The Romance of Reunion: Northerners and the South, 1865–1900* (Chapel Hill: University of North Carolina Press, 1993); James A. Kaser, *At the Bivouac of Memory: History, Politics, and the Battle of Chickamauga* (New York: P. Lang, 1996); Carol Reardon, *Pickett's Charge in History and Memory* (Chapel Hill: University of North Carolina Press, 1997); Blight, *Race and Reunion*; Gallagher, *Causes Won, Lost, and Forgotten*.

24 Blight, *Race and Reunion*.

25 For a conceptual overview of memory studies, see Jeffrey K. Olick and Joyce Robbins, "Social Memory Studies: From 'Collective Memory' to the Historical Sociology of Mnemonic Practices," *Annual Review of Sociology* 24 (1998): 105–140.

26 For examples of this genre, see William Gannaway Brownlow, *Sketches of the Rise, Progress, and Decline of Secession: With a Narrative of Personal Adventures Among the Rebels* (Philadelphia: Applegate & Co., 1862); Levi H. Naron, *Chickasaw, a Mississippi Scout for the Union: The Civil War Memoir of Levi H. Naron*, ed. Michael B. Ballard, Thomas D. Cockrell, and R. W. Surby (Baton Rouge: Louisiana State University Press, 2005); Dennis E. Haynes, *A Thrilling Narrative: The Memoir of a Southern Unionist*, ed. Arthur W. Bergeron (Fayetteville: University of Arkansas Press, 2006).

27 These claimants do not match the numbers of white southerners involved in the United Daughters of the Confederacy (UDC) and the United Confederate Veterans (UCV), but they do compare favorably. Gaines Foster cites estimates of UCV membership ranging from 35,000 to 160,000, and Karen Cox identifies 100,000 as the

peak membership of the UDC. See Foster, *Ghosts of the Confederacy*, 107; Cox, *Dixie's Daughters*, 50.

28 Summary Report, 1873, Aaron Lippman Disallowed Claim, Duplin County, North Carolina, Summary Reports of the Commissioners of Claims in All Cases Reported to Congress as Disallowed Under the Act of March 3, 1871, Southern Claims Commission, 1871–1880, Records of the United States House of Representatives, 1789–1990, Microfilm Publication P2257, Record Group 233, National Archives, Washington, DC (hereafter cited as P2257).

29 Summary Report, 1874, William F. Meyrer Disallowed Claim, Pulaski County, Arkansas, in P2257.

30 Summary Report, 1871, Patrick Sheehan Disallowed Claim, Warren County, Mississippi, in P2257.

31 This study draws on scholarship that views gender and race as socially constructed categories. See Joan Wallach Scott, *Gender and the Politics of History* (New York: Columbia University Press, 1988); Thomas Walter Laqueur, *Making Sex: Body and Gender from the Greeks to Freud* (Cambridge, MA: Harvard University Press, 1990); David R. Roediger, *The Wages of Whiteness: Race and the Making of the American Working Class* (London: Verso, 1991); Theodore W. Allen, *The Invention of the White Race* (London: Verso, 1994); Grace Elizabeth Hale, *Making Whiteness: The Culture of Segregation in the South, 1890–1940* (New York: Pantheon Books, 1998); Mark M. Smith, *How Race Is Made: Slavery, Segregation, and the Senses* (Chapel Hill: University of North Carolina Press, 2006).

Chapter 1 "We have Fought the First Skirmish"

1 Harold M. Hyman, *The Radical Republicans and Reconstruction, 1861–1870* (Indianapolis: Bobbs-Merrill, 1967), 480.

2 *Congressional Globe*, 37th Congress, Special Session (March 9, 1863), 1562.

3 Constitutional framers specified the oath for the executive, so Republican congressmen could not impose the ironclad oath on the president or vice president even though some would have preferred to do so. Hyman, *Era of the Oath*, 25; Jeffrey E. Vogel, "Redefining Reconciliation: Confederate Veterans and the Southern Responses to Federal Civil War Pensions," *Civil War History* 51, no. 1 (2005): 71.

4 Benedict, *A Compromise of Principle*, 71–77; Foner, *Reconstruction*, 49, 74; Harris, *With Charity for All*, 131–134.

5 Harris, *With Charity for All*, 19, 141.

6 Paul D. Escott, *"What Shall We Do with the Negro?": Lincoln, White Racism, and Civil War America* (Charlottesville: University of Virginia Press, 2009), 53–54, 96–97, 100–101, 106–107; Eric Foner, *The Fiery Trial: Abraham Lincoln and American Slavery* (New York: W.W. Norton, 2010), 127–129, 184–186, 221–226, 231–236, 239–240, 282–283, 330–332.

7 William R. Brock, *An American Crisis: Congress and Reconstruction, 1865–1867* (New York: St. Martin's Press, 1963), 24–26, quotation at 26; Belz, *Reconstructing the Union*, 198–243; Benedict, *A Compromise of Principle*, 70–83; Harris, *With Charity for All*, 186–190; Robert W. Burg, "Amnesty, Civil Rights, and the Meaning of Liberal Republicanism, 1862–1872," *American Nineteenth Century History* 4, no. 3 (Fall 2003): 33.

8 George B. Loring, *The Present Crisis: A Speech ... at Lyceum Hall, Salem ... April 26, 1865, on the Assassination of Abraham Lincoln* (South Danvers, MA: Howard, 1865), reprinted in Hyman, *The Radical Republicans and Reconstruction, 1861–1870*, 234–236.
9 *Congressional Globe*, 39th Congress, 1st Session (May 8, 1866), 2462.
10 Eric L. McKitrick, *Andrew Johnson and Reconstruction* (Chicago: University of Chicago Press, 1960), 48–51, 142–150; Foner, *Reconstruction*, 183–184, 190.
11 Dan T. Carter, *When the War Was Over: The Failure of Self-Reconstruction in the South, 1865–1867* (Baton Rouge: Louisiana State University Press, 1985), 29–30.
12 Foner, *Reconstruction*, 179–181.
13 *Congressional Globe*, 39th Congress, 1st Session (May 8, 1866), 2468.
14 Carter, *When the War Was Over*, 61–95.
15 See *Ex Parte Garland* (1866), 71 U.S. 380.
16 See *United States v. Padelford* (1869), 76 U.S. 539; *Pargoud v. United States* (1871), 80 U.S. 156; *United States v. Klein* (1871), 80 U.S. 147; *Armstrong v. United States* (1871), 80 U.S. 154. For further analyses of the Supreme Court's decisions concerning pardon and amnesty in the Civil War era, Dorris, *Pardon and Amnesty Under Lincoln and Johnson*, 393–422; Ashley M. Steiner, "Remission of Guilt or Removal of Punishment? The Effects of a Presidential Pardon," *Emory Law Journal* **46** (Spring 1997): 959–960, 968–970; Wayne A. Logan, "The Ex Post Facto Clause and the Jurisprudence of Punishment," *American Criminal Law Review* **35** (Summer 1998): 1275–1280; Elizabeth Lee Thompson, "Reconstructing the Practice: The Effects of Expanded Federal Judicial Power on Postbellum Lawyers," *American Journal of Legal History* **43**, no. 3 (July 1999): 306–330; Norman W. Spaulding, "The Discourse of Law in Time of War: Politics and Professionalism During the Civil War and Reconstruction," *William & Mary Law Review* **46** (April 2005): 2001–2019; Daniel W. Hamilton, "A New Right to Property: Civil War Confiscation in the Reconstruction Supreme Court," *Journal of Supreme Court History* **29**, no. 3 (November 2004): 254–285; Anthony Dick, "The Substance of Punishment Under the Bill of Attainder Clause," *Stanford Law Review* **63** (May 2011): 1183–1183, 1191, 1206.
17 Pamela Brandwein, *Reconstructing Reconstruction: The Supreme Court and the Production of Historical Truth* (Durham: Duke University Press, 1999), 61–95.
18 Brock, *An American Crisis*, 95–211; Benedict, *A Compromise of Principle*, 134–222; Foner, *Reconstruction*, 134–222.
19 Brock, *An American Crisis*, 95–211; Benedict, *A Compromise of Principle*, 223–243, 327–335.
20 Burg, "Amnesty, Civil Rights, and the Meaning of Liberal Republicanism, 1862–1872," 35.
21 Foner, *Reconstruction*, 323–324; Steven Hahn, *A Nation Under Our Feet: Black Political Struggles in the Rural South from Slavery to the Great Migration* (Cambridge, MA: Harvard University Press, 2005), 189–198.
22 *Congressional Globe*, 39th Congress, 1st Session (May 9, 1866), 2513.
23 *Congressional Globe*, 39th Congress, 1st Session (May 8, 1866), 2469.
24 *Congressional Globe*, 39th Congress, 1st Session (June 4, 1866), 2948.
25 *Congressional Globe*, 39th Congress, 1st Session (May 9, 1866), 2505.
26 Alfred Avins, ed., *The Reconstruction Amendments' Debates: The Legislative History and Contemporary Debates in Congress on the 13th, 14th, and 15th*

Amendments (Richmond: Virginia Commission on Constitutional Government, 1967), 243–245, 210–211.

27 Brock, *An American Crisis*, 295; James M. McPherson, *The Struggle for Equality: Abolitionists and the Negro in the Civil War and Reconstruction* (Princeton: Princeton University Press, 1964), 294, 430; LaWanda Cox and John H. Cox, "Negro Suffrage and Republican Politics: The Problem of Motivation in Reconstruction Historiography," *Journal of Southern History* 33, no. 3 (August 1967): 303–330; Benedict, *A Compromise of Principle*, 325–336.

28 DuBois, *Feminism and Suffrage*, 42, 57, 62–63, quotation at 63; Hoffert, *When Hens Crow*, 32–72; Alexander Keyssar, *The Right to Vote: The Contested History of Democracy in the United States* (New York: Basic Books, 2000), 173–180, quotation at 177; Faye E. Dudden, *Fighting Chance: The Struggle over Woman Suffrage and Black Suffrage in Reconstruction America* (New York: Oxford University Press, 2011), 72, 173.

29 *Congressional Globe*, 41st Congress, 3rd Session (March 3, 1871), 1971.

30 On the evolving Union policy toward southern civilians, see Mark Grimsley, *The Hard Wand of War: Union Military Policy Toward Southern Civilians, 1861–1865* (Cambridge: Cambridge University Press, 1995).

31 Kate H. Couse Testimony, March 19, 1873, Peter Couse Allowed Claim, Spotsylvania County, Virginia.

32 Klingberg, *The Southern Claims Commission*, 21–24.

33 William S. Reid Petition, Fairfax County, Virginia, c. May 23, 1862, Petitions and Memorials Referred to the Committee on Claims, 37th through 39th Congresses, Records of Committees Relating to Claims, 1794–1946, Records of the United States House of Representatives, 1789–1990, Record Group 233, National Archives, Washington, DC.

34 *Congressional Globe*, 38th Congress, 1st Session (July 2, 1864), 3499; Bowie, "The Southern Claims Commission," 10–11; Klingberg, *The Southern Claims Commission*, 24–26.

35 *Congressional Globe*, 38th Congress, 1st Session (July 2, 1864), 3499–3500.

36 *Congressional Globe*, 39th Congress, 1st Session (February 6, 1866), 671.

37 *Congressional Globe*, 39th Congress, 1st Session, (January 18, 1866), 302.

38 *Congressional Globe*, 40th Congress, 3rd Session (January 13, 1869), 328.

39 *Congressional Globe*, 41st Congress, 2nd Session (June 6, 1870), 4149.

40 *Congressional Globe*, 41st Congress, 2nd Session (March 4, 1870), 1681–1682.

41 *Congressional Globe*, 41st Congress, 2nd Session (April 27, 1870), 3018.

42 *Congressional Globe*, 40th Congress, 3rd Session (January 12, 1869), 302.

43 Congressmen proposed numerous bills for the payment of southern claims in the former Confederate states. See *Congressional Globe*, 40th Congress, 2nd Session (June 26, 1868), 3524 for Arkansas; *Congressional Globe*, 40th Congress, 2nd Session (July 20, 1868), 4252 for North Carolina; *Congressional Globe*, 40th Congress, 2nd Session (July 22, 1868), 4335 for Louisiana; *Congressional Globe*, 40th Congress, 2nd Session (July 24, 1868), 4416 for Alabama; *Congressional Globe*, 40th Congress, 3rd Session (December 8, 1868), 13 for Louisiana; *Congressional Globe*, 40th Congress, 3rd Session (January 20, 1869), 467 for South Carolina; *Congressional Globe*, 40th Congress, 3rd Session (January 11, 1869), 281 for North Carolina; *Congressional Globe*, 41st Congress, 1st Session (March 5, 1869),

9 for South Carolina; *Congressional Globe*, 41st Congress, 1st Session (March 15, 1869), 71 for North Carolina and South Carolina; *Congressional Globe*, 41st Congress, 1st Session (March 15, 1869), 73 for Arkansas; *Congressional Globe*, 41st Congress, 1st Session (March 22, 1869), 194 for North Carolina; *Congressional Globe*, 41st Congress, 2nd Session (February 7, 1870), 1087 for Virginia; *Congressional Globe*, 41st Congress, 2nd Session (February 21, 1870), 1458 for Virginia; *Congressional Globe*, 41st Congress, 2nd Session (March 9, 1870), 1813 for Arkansas; *Congressional Globe*, 41st Congress, 2nd Session (March 21, 1870), 2094 for Mississippi and Arkansas; *Congressional Globe*, 41st Congress, 2nd Session (April 27, 1870), 3034 for Alabama; *Congressional Globe*, 41st Congress, 2nd Session (June 6, 1870), 4099 for Louisiana.

44 *Congressional Globe*, 41st Congress, 2nd Session (April 27, 1870), 3020–3021.

45 *Congressional Globe*, 39th Congress, 2nd Session (February 5, 1867), 1000; *Congressional Globe*, 39th Congress, 2nd Session (February 5, 1867), 1000; *Congressional Globe*, 40th Congress, 1st Session (November 26, 1867), 796; Edward I. Renick, "Assignment of Government Claims," *American Law Review* 24 (1890): 442–456; Stanton J. Peele, "History and Jurisdiction of the United States Court of Claims," *Records of the Columbia Historical Society* 9 (1915): 2–21; William M. Wiecek, "The Origin of the United States Court of Claims," *Administrative Law Review* 20 (1968): 387–406; Kyle S. Sinisi, *Sacred Debts: State Civil War Claims and American Federalism, 1861–1880* (New York: Fordham University Press, 2003), 17–18, 25–26.

46 *Congressional Globe*, 41st Congress, 2nd Session (June 6, 1870), 4151.

47 For a list of votes by senators of the 41st Congress, see Appendix A, Tables 1, 2, and 3. For further information on the creation of the Southern Claims Commission, see Bowie, "The Southern Claims Commission," 1–23; Klingberg, *The Southern Claims Commission*, 38–56.

48 *Congressional Globe*, 41st Congress, 3rd Session (March 1, 1871), 1818–1821.

49 *Congressional Globe*, 39th Congress, 1st Session (June 21, 1866), 3308; *Congressional Globe*, 39th Congress, 1st Session (May 4, 1866), 2381–2382, and *Congressional Globe*, 40th Congress, 2nd Session (January 24, 1868), 738.

50 *Congressional Globe*, 40th Congress, 1st Session (July 18, 1867), 717; *Ex Parte Garland* (1866), 71 U.S. 333; *United States v. Padelford* (1869), 76 U.S. 531. The Supreme Court decided *United States v. Klein* (1871), 80 U.S. 128, a similar case, soon after the establishment of the Southern Claims Commission.

51 United States Statutes at Large, 16 (1871), 524–525.

52 For biographical information on the commissioners, see "Memorial Sketch of Hon. Asa Owen Aldis," *Speech before the Vermont Bar Association, October 1903* (Montpelier, VT: Argus and Patriot Company, 1904); *Obituary Notices of Asa Owen Aldis, Robert Stanton Avery, George Bancroft, William Ferrel, Edward T. Fristoe, Julius Erasmus Hilgard, Garrick Mallery, Montgomery Cunningham Meigs, Charles Henry Nichols, James Clarke Welling* (Washington, DC: Philosophical Society of Washington, 1895); Klingberg, *The Southern Claims Commission*, 58–62.

53 The Washington *Daily Morning Chronicle*, March 9, 1871, quoted in Klingberg, *The Southern Claims Commission*, 58.

54 First General Report, 5.

55 J. W. March Order, 1st Assistant Postmaster General, June 10, 1871, Records of the Commissioner of Claims (Southern Claims Commission), 1871–1880, Records of the Division of Captured Property, Claims, and Lands, 1855–1900, General Records of the Department of the Treasury, 1789–1990, Microfilm Publication M87, Record Group 56, National Archives, Washington, DC (hereafter cited as M87), Roll 1; First General Report of the Commissioners of Claims (1871), 42nd Congress, 2nd Session, H. Doc. 16 (hereafter "First General Report), 8; Third General Report of the Commissioners of Claims (1873), 43rd Congress, 1st Session, H. Doc. 23 (hereafter "Third General Report"), 2–3.
56 Second General Report of the Commissioners of Claims (1872), 42nd Congress, 3rd Session, H. Doc. 12 (hereafter, "Second General Report"), 7; Treasury Department to the Commissioners of Southern Claims, Washington, April 14, 1871, Roll 1, Records of the Commissioners of Claims. Congress officially opened the rebel archives to the Commission in April 1871. See the Journal of the Commissioners, Vol. 1, Roll 1, Records of the Commissioners of Claims for a copy of the act approved on April 20, 1871.
57 First General Report, 5; Second General Report, 4; Fifth General Report of the Commissioners of Claims (1875), 44th Congress, 1st Session, H. Doc. 30 (hereafter, "Fifth General Report"), 6–7.
58 First General Report, 2–3.
59 First General Report, 4. See also Klingberg, *The Southern Claims Commission*, 117–118. For studies that examine the property question, see Klingberg, *The Southern Claims Commission*, 117–138; Philip D. Morgan, "The Ownership of Property by Slaves in the Mid-Nineteenth-Century Low Country," *Journal of Southern History* 49, no. 3 (1983): 399–420; Dylan Penningroth, "Slavery, Freedom, and Social Claims to Property Among African Americans in Liberty County, Georgia, 1850–1880," *Journal of American History* 84, no. 2 (1997): 405–435; Dylan C. Penningroth, *The Claims of Kinfolk: African American Property and Community in the Nineteenth-Century South* (Chapel Hill: University of North Carolina Press, 2003); Dylan C. Penningroth, "The Claims of Slaves and Ex-Slaves to Family and Property: A Transatlantic Comparison," *American Historical Review* 112, no. 4 (October 2007): 1039–1069.
60 On property, labor, and citizenship, see Hamilton, "A New Right to Property"; Daniel W. Hamilton, *The Limits of Sovereignty: Property Confiscation in the Union and the Confederacy During the Civil War* (Chicago: University of Chicago Press, 2007); Thomas C. Holt, *The Problem of Freedom: Race, Labor, and Politics in Jamaica and Britain, 1832–1938* (Baltimore: Johns Hopkins University Press, 1992); Frederick Cooper, Thomas C. Holt, and Rebecca J. Scott, eds., *Beyond Slavery: Explorations of Race, Labor, and Citizenship in Postemancipation Societies* (Chapel Hill: University of North Carolina Press, 2000); Demetrius L. Eudell, *The Political Languages of Emancipation in the British Caribbean and the U.S. South* (Chapel Hill: University of North Carolina Press, 2002); Shklar, *American Citizenship*; Glenn, *Unequal Freedom*.
61 "Bragg's Mistake," *Oshkosh Daily Northwestern*, April 22, 1879.
62 Dorris, *Pardon and Amnesty Under Lincoln and Johnson*, 368, 383–392; Hyman, *Era of the Oath*, 256, 264; Burg, "Amnesty, Civil Rights, and the Meaning of Liberal Republicanism, 1862–1872," 37.

63 Andrew L. Slap, *The Doom of Reconstruction: The Liberal Republicans in the Civil War Era* (New York: Fordham University Press, 2006), 205–209.
64 On congressional amnesty, see Dorris, *Pardon and Amnesty Under Lincoln and Johnson*, 362–392. On the support of Liberal Republicans for amnesty, see Burg, "Amnesty, Civil Rights, and the Meaning of Liberal Republicanism, 1862–1872"; Slap, *The Doom of Reconstruction*, 184–186.
65 *Congressional Globe*, 42nd Congress, 2nd Session (December 21, 1871), 287–288.
66 *Congressional Globe*, 42nd Congress, 1st Session (December 21, 1871), 273; *Congressional Globe*, 42nd Congress, 1st Session (March 21, 1871), 209.
67 *Congressional Globe*, 42nd Congress, 1st Session (January 30, 1872), 700.
68 *Congressional Globe*, 42nd Congress, 1st Session (December 21, 1871), 289.
69 *Congressional Globe*, 42nd Congress, 2nd Session (January 23, 1872), 522–524.
70 *Congressional Globe*, 42nd Congress, 2nd Session (January 15, 1872), 386.
71 Congressmen defeated several additional attempts through the 1870s to bestow amnesty without exceptions. Dorris, *Pardon and Amnesty Under Lincoln and Johnson*, 375–386.
72 "The Claims," *Richmond Daily Dispatch*, October 25, 1876.
73 "Rebel War Claims! Grand Raid on the Treasury. How Loyal Men are to be Taxed!! What Democratic Retrenchment Means," Albert and Shirley Small Special Collections Library, University of Virginia, Special Collections, Charlottesville, Virginia.
74 "Yesterday's Proceedings of the Forty-Fourth Congress," *Burlington Daily Hawk-Eye*, July 20, 1876; "A Stroke of Democratic Economy," *Harper's Weekly*, August 12, 1876; "No More Examination of the Rebel Archives," *Waterloo Courier*, August 23, 1876; "The Heated Term," *Harper's Weekly*, October 21, 1876.
75 "Rebel War Claims! Grand Raid on the Treasury. How Loyal Men are to be Taxed!! What Democratic Retrenchment Means," Albert and Shirley Small Special Collections Library, University of Virginia, Special Collections, Charlottesville, Virginia.
76 "Brownlow on the Solid South," *New York Times*, October 30, 1876. See also "The Rebel War Claims," *New York Times*, November 4, 1876.
77 "Rebel Claims: Enormous Payments to be Demanded in Case of Democratic Success," *New York Times*, October 21, 1876. See also "Political Notes," *Cedar Rapids Times*, October 26, 1876; "Rebel War Claims!" *The Advance*, October 26, 1876; "The Rebel Claims," *New York Times*, November 3, 1876.
78 "A Cool Billion Dollars Asked For," *Athens Messenger*, August 24, 1876. See also "What They are Waiting For," *Orrville Crescent*, September 26, 1876; "Rebel Claims: Enormous Payments to be Demanded in Case of Democratic Success," *New York Times*, October 21, 1876; "Tilden's Letter in Virginia," *New York Times*, October 29, 1876; "The Southern Claims," *New York Times*, October 30, 1876; "In the States...," *Athens Messenger*, November 2, 1876; "Startling Presentation of Laws and Decisions," *New York Times*, November 3, 1876.
79 "Rebel Claims: Enormous Payments to be Demanded in Case of Democratic Success," *New York Times*, October 21, 1876; "Rebel Claims," *Cedar Rapids Times*, October 26, 1876.
80 "About Paying Southern Claims," *Milwaukee Daily News*, April 22, 1875.

81 "The Southern Claims," *Edwardsville Intelligencer*, October 25, 1876.
82 "A Letter from Tilden," *New York Times*, October 25, 1876.
83 "Rebel War Claims," *New York Times*, November 2, 1876.
84 "The Southern Claims," *New York Times*, October 30, 1876.
85 "The Southern Claims Issue," *Atlanta Daily Constitution*, July 10, 1878.
86 "Southern Claims: Another Raid on the Treasury," *New York Times*, February 20, 1878.
87 "The House," *Atlanta Daily Constitution*, January 23, 1879; "House," *Titusville Herald*, April 16, 1879; "The Southern Claims Question," *Oshkosh Daily Northwestern*, April 17, 1879.
88 "Stand From Under!" *Harper's Weekly*, January 26, 1878; "Probabilities," *Harper's Weekly*, May 4, 1878.
89 "Mr. Bragg and the War Claims," *New York Times*, April 15, 1879; "'Loyal' War Claims," *New York Times*, February 3, 1879. For earlier criticisms of loyal claims, see "Curiosities of War Claims," *New York Times*, March 6, 1876; "Tilden's Letter in Virginia," *New York Times*, October 29, 1876.
90 "Rebel War Claims: Text of the Proposed Constitutional Amendment Prohibiting Their Payment," *New York Times*, January 28, 1879; "Forty-fifth Congress, Third Session," *New York Times*, January 28, 1879; "Speech by Senator Edmunds," *New York Times*, August 7, 1880.
91 Southerners submitted 22,298 claims, but only 16,995 claimants submitted evidence. Congress barred claims without evidence from compensation. Of the 16,995 claims decided by the commissioners, 7,409 were allowed and 9,589 were disallowed. Including barred claims, southerners petitioned for $60,258,150.44 worth of property and the commissioners allowed $4,636,920.69. The Court of Claims, in comparison, paid out $6,300,436.80, also over ten years. See Klingberg, *The Southern Claims Commission*, 157–175; Tables 4 to 6 in Appendix A.
92 On the extensions of the commission's tenure, see Klingberg, *The Southern Claims Commission*, 70. On Congress's refusal to pay salaries for the commission's personnel, see Editorial, *New York Times*, August 20, 1878.

Chapter 2 Men's Union

1 J. Madison Wells Testimony, March 3, 1874, Adelia E. Casson Disallowed Claim, Rapides Parish, Louisiana, in Records of the United States Court of Claims, 1835–1966, Case Files for General Jurisdiction Cases, 1855–1966, Record Group 123, National Archives, Washington, DC (hereafter cited as Court of Claims), Docket No. 496. Under the Bowman Act of 1883 and the Tucker Act of 1887, rejected claimants before the Southern Claims Commission were allowed to appeal their claims to the Court of Claims. In these cases, all records from the case before the Southern Claims Commission were transferred to the Court of Claims and are therefore deposited among the records of the Court of Claims.

Wells's wartime and postwar biography illustrated white men's complicated allegiances in the postwar South. By the time of his testimony before the Southern Claims Commission in 1874, Wells had served as lieutenant governor and governor during wartime reconstruction, campaigned for governor as a Democrat under postwar Presidential Reconstruction, supported Republican measures such as the Fourteenth

Notes to pp. 39–42

Amendment, been ousted from office as an "impediment to Reconstruction" under Congressional Reconstruction, and acted as chairman of the Republican state election board. On Wells, see Joe Gray Taylor, *Louisiana Reconstructed, 1863–1877* (Baton Rouge: Louisiana State University Press, 1974), 28, 58–59, 126, 140–141; Ted Tunnell, *Crucible of Reconstruction: War, Radicalism, and Race in Louisiana, 1862–1877* (Baton Rouge: Louisiana State University Press, 1984), 22–25, 95–103.

2 Robert S. Heflin Testimony, March 30, 1872, Robert S. Heflin Allowed Claim, Randolph County, Alabama; Summary Report, 1872, ibid. Several witnesses corroborated that Heflin had been a "notorious," "bold," and "independent" Union man who had supported the Union "earnestly and heartily." See Charles S. Cherry Testimony, April 18, 1871, ibid.; John G. Stokes Testimony, April 18, 1871, ibid.; Christopher G. Sheats Testimony, April 18, 1871, ibid.; Robert S. M. Hunter Testimony, March 30, 1872, ibid.

3 For an analysis that divides the Confederacy into zones related to Union occupation, see Stephen V. Ash, *When the Yankees Came: Conflict and Chaos in the Occupied South, 1861–1865* (Chapel Hill: University of North Carolina Press, 1995).

4 The interrogatory read, "At the beginning of the rebellion did you sympathize with the Union cause, or with the rebellion? What were your feelings and what your language on the subject? On which side did you exert your influence and cast your vote? What did you do, and how did you vote? How did you vote on ratifying the ordinance of secession? After the ordinance of secession was adopted in your State, did you adhere to the Union cause, or did you 'go with the State?'" The commissioners later changed their question on sympathies, detaching it from secession and asking, "On which side were your sympathies during the war, and were they on the same side from beginning to end?" See "Standing Interrogatories," 1871, number 33; "Standing Interrogatories," 1872, number 40; "Standing Interrogatories," 1874, number 5 in Appendix B.

5 Joseph E. Segar Testimony, February 26, 1874, Joseph E. Segar Allowed Claim, Elizabeth City County, Virginia; Summary Report, 1874, ibid.

6 *Speech of Mr. Joseph Segar (of Elizabeth City and Warwick) on the Wilmot Proviso, Delivered in the House of Delegates, January 19, 1849* (Richmond: Shepherd & Colin, 1849), 8–9, 22.

7 *Letter of Hon. Joseph Segar, to a Friend in Virginia, in Vindication of his Course in Declining to Follow his State into Secession* (Washington, DC: William H. Moore, Printer, 1862), 5.

8 *Speech of Mr. Joseph Segar, (of Elizabeth City and Warwick,) on the Wilmot Proviso, Delivered in the House of Delegates, January 19, 1849* (Richmond: Shepherd & Colin, 1849), 9, 21, 19. See also *Speech of Joseph Segar on the motion of Mr. Chapman of Monroe to instruct the senators and request the representatives in Congress from the state of Virginia to vote for the immediate recognition of the independence of Texas* (Richmond: Shepherd & Colin Publisher, 1837), 5.

9 *Speech of Joseph Segar, Esq., of the York District, Delivered in the House of Delegates of Virginia, March the 30th, 1861, on the Resolutions of the Senate, Directing the Governor of Virginia to Seize, by Military Force, the U.S. Guns at Bellona Arsenal, and on the Secession of Virginia* (N.p., n.d.), 21.

10 *Letter of Hon. Joseph Segar*, 18–19, 21, 41.

11 On the use of constitutional doctrines of state sovereignty and federal power to protect slavery, see Arthur Bestor, "State Sovereignty and Slavery: A Reinterpretation of Proslavery Constitutional Doctrine, 1846–1860," *Journal of the Illinois State Historical Society* 54 (1961): 117–180.
12 *Speech of Hon. Joseph Segar, on Re-construction, at Hampton, Jul 27, 1867* (N.p, n.d.), 14–15. See also Letter from Joseph Eggleston Segar to John Adams Dix, November 20, 1861, in Letter of Jos. Segar, Esq., to Gen. Dix, *National Intelligencer*, 1861, p. 1–4.
13 In the first two versions of the interrogatories, claimants were asked, "On which side did you exert your influence and cast your vote? What did you do, and how did you vote? How did you vote on ratifying the ordinance of secession?" In their third version, the commissioners slightly altered these questions, limiting claimants to votes after the 1860 presidential election and adding a reference to votes for convention delegates. Their new question read, "After the presidential election of 1860, if of age, did you vote for any candidate or on any questions, during the war, and how did you vote? Did you vote for or against the candidates favoring secession? Did you vote for or against the ratification of the ordinance of secession, or for or against separation in your State?" See number 33 in "Standing Interrogatories," 1871; number 40 in "Standing Interrogatories," 1872; number 44 in "Standing Interrogatories," 1874 in Appendix B.
14 Joel Dendy Allowed Claim, Cherokee County, Alabama; William S. Horsey Claim, Accomack County, Virginia; James B. Kirk Allowed Claim, Culpeper County, Virginia; John W. Hill Allowed Claim, Jefferson County, West Virginia.
15 Aldridge James Testimony, April 17, 1872, Aldridge James Allowed Claim, Fauquier County, Virginia. See also William Ansley Testimony, August 23, 1872, William Ansley Allowed Claim, Fairfax County, Virginia; Charles H. Wilson Testimony, August 19, 1875, Charles H. Wilson Allowed Claim, Dinwiddie County, Virginia; Summary Report, 1877, Joseph H. Kanode Allowed Claim, Jefferson County, West Virginia.
16 In their 1871 and 1872 versions, the commissioners included a question on offices in the U.S. military: "Have you ever held any office in the Army or Navy of the United States? Were you educated by the United States at the Military Academy at West Point, or at the United States Naval Academy?" This question referred to prewar service and probably attempted to sort through the different categories of southerners disfranchised and disabled by various Reconstruction measures. Although the commissioners did not specifically ask claimants about their service in the Union military before 1874, claimants frequently discussed their service when they could do so. See "Standing Interrogatories," 1871, number 30; "Standing Interrogatories," 1872, number 37; "Standing Interrogatories," 1874, number 51 in Appendix B.
17 Melvin B. Carr Testimony, May 21, 1874, Melvin B. Carr Allowed Claim, Cherokee County, Alabama; Willis Carr Testimony, May 21, 1874, ibid.; also corroborated by Elijah C. Carr Testimony, May 21, 1874, ibid. Carr produced his discharge papers as evidence of his Union military service. He later applied for a pension for his service in the Indiana Cavalry, Regiment 8, Company M.
18 First General Report, 8.
19 See Table 7 in Appendix A.

20 See questions for witnesses in "Standing Interrogatories," 1871; questions for witnesses in "Standing Interrogatories," 1872; number 60 in "Standing Interrogatories," 1874 in Appendix B.
21 William Mitchell July 17, 1873, Thomas Nation Allowed Claim, Blount County, Alabama. For other identifications of "Union man," see John Gordon Testimony, October 10, 1872, William O. Winston Allowed Claim, DeKalb County, Alabama; Green M. Haley Testimony, March 27, 1872, Green M. Haley Allowed Claim, Marion County, Alabama; John B. Boggs Testimony, July 12, 1875, Henry M. Hart Allowed Claim, Lauderdale County, Alabama; Jose A. Green Testimony, May 31, 1872, David Young Allowed Claim, Fulton County, Georgia, Fiche 158; William Markham Testimony, January 20, 1873, David Young Allowed Claim, Fulton County, Georgia, Fiche 158; David W. Holmes Testimony, January 26, 1877, Washington Holmes Allowed Claim, Gordon County, Georgia; Isaac E. Casey Testimony, April 25, 1872, Isaac E. Casey Allowed Claim, Murray County, Georgia; Nicholas D. Ingram Testimony, March 20, 1873, T. L. Van Fossen Allowed Claim, Carroll Parish, Louisiana; James Ruth Testimony, February 19, 1875, Abner Ginn Allowed Claim, Beaufort County, South Carolina; David W. Landis Testimony, October 15, 1879, David W. Landis Allowed Claim, Augusta County, Virginia; Robert S. Costin Testimony, May 22, 1875, Robert S. Costin Allowed Claim, Northampton County, Virginia; Robert H. Adams Testimony, October 22, 1872, Robert H. Adams Allowed Claim, Prince George County, Virginia; George W. Joy Testimony, April 11, 1873, George W. Joy Allowed Claim, Washington County, Virginia.
22 John T. Bailey Testimony, July 21, 1877, John T. Bailey Allowed Claim, Cherokee County, Alabama.
23 See, for example, Summary Report, 1877, John T. Bailey Allowed Claim, Cherokee County, Alabama.
24 First General Report, 8.
25 David J. Garber Testimony, October 12, 1871, David J. Garber Allowed Claim, Rockingham County, Virginia.
26 See, for example, Summary Report, 1875, Joel Garber Allowed Claim, Rockingham, County, Virginia; Summary Report, 1876, John Gangwer Allowed Claim, Rockingham County, Virginia. The commissioners excused Joel Garber's vote for the ratification of the ordinance of secession because of the "reign of terror" that existed at his polling place. The conditions that mitigated Joel Garber's actions likely applied to David J. Garber's actions as well. The testimony does not reveal the exact relationship between Joel and David, but they appear to have lived near one another. They served as witnesses for each other on the property question. According to their testimony, they saw each other's property confiscated by General Philip H. Sheridan's men during the Valley Campaign in 1864. According to the census, both Joel and David lived in the same district in Rockingham County. See David J. Garber Testimony, October 12, 1871, Joel Garber Allowed Claim, Rockingham County, Virginia; Joel Garber Testimony, October 12, 1871, David J. Garber Allowed Claim, Rockingham County, Virginia; United States Census, 1860, District No. 1, Rockingham County, Virginia, 101; United States Census, 1860, District No. 1, Rockingham County, Virginia, 62.
27 Summary Report, 1874, David J. Garber Allowed Claim, Rockingham County, Virginia. Garber also appears to have benefited from his status as a Dunkard, a

member of a pacificist religious group. Rockingham County was the home to a number of Dunkards and Mennonites, many of whom submitted claims to the commission as Union men. Garber noted that he had paid the "fine" to escape conscription after his substitute had died and he became liable for conscription again. Dunkards commonly referred to the $500 exemption tax as a "fine." David J. Garber Testimony, October 12, 1871, David J. Garber Allowed Claim, Rockingham County, Virginia.

28 For example, Representative Jacob Benton, a New Hampshire Republican, pointed out: "To show what was his motive, and to explain and prove that he was loyal during the war, what does he do? He turns round and says that his professing to be a rebel and to be in sympathy with the confederate government was all a feint." *Congressional Globe*, 41st Congress, 2nd Session (July 5, 1870), 5198.

29 Senator Lyman Trumbull of Illinois sympathized with "a gentleman ... [who] in fact in his heart has been a Union man all the time," but he suggested that the gentleman's motive altered the "morality" of the act but did not alter the "fact" of the act. *Congressional Globe*, 39th Congress, 1st Session (July 27, 1866), 4214–4215. This fact, as Benjamin F. Wade, an Ohio Republican argued, included that such a man "violated the laws of the United States; he violated his duty as a citizen; he abandoned his allegiance to the Government of the United States; and whatever his motives may have been he was guilty of hostility to this Government." *Congressional Globe*, 39th Congress, 1st Session (July 27, 1866), 4243.

30 For example, Luke P. Poland, a Republican congressman from Vermont, emphasized the foolishness of arguing that a man could be "duressed into an office to hold and exercise the functions of it during a period of four years." He instead favored a definition of duress as "some particular act, some particular time, some particular transaction." *Congressional Globe*, 41st Congress, 2nd Session (July 5, 1870), 5197.

31 Representative Lewis McKenzie, a Conservative from Virginia, argued that "so far as the question of loyalty ... is concerned, it depends very much on how a man feels. If a man is honest and feels in his conscience that he is right, he need not care for the world, the flesh, or the devil." *Congressional Globe*, 41st Congress, 2nd Session (July 5, 1870), 5198. See also *Congressional Globe*, 39th Congress, 1st Session (July 26, 1866), 4168.

32 *Nation*, January 1, 1868.

33 First General Report, 2–3.

34 Kenneth S. Greenberg, *Honor & Slavery: Lies, Duels, Noses, Masks, Dressing as a Woman, Gifts, Strangers, Humanitarianism, Death, Slave Rebellions, the Proslavery Argument, Baseball, Hunting, and Gambling in the Old South* (Princeton, NJ: Princeton University Press, 1996), 3–23.

35 Second General Report, 5. The commissioners finally added a question on coercion in their 1874 version of their interrogatories: "What force, compulsion, or influence was used to make you do anything against the Union cause?" See number 23 in "Standing Interrogatories," 1872 in Appendix B.

36 See number 23 in "Standing Interrogatories," 1872 in Appendix B.

37 For the specific incident mentioned, see Joel Garber Allowed Claim, Rockingham County, Virginia. See also John Gangwer Allowed Claim, Rockingham County, Virginia; Adam R. Gladden Allowed Claim, Rockingham County, Virginia.

38 Second General Report, 5. In determining the "tenor of the claimant's conduct," the commissioners weighed both overt and covert actions on behalf of the Union. The commissioners captured evidence of covert acts of loyalty with general interrogatories, asking whether claimants had ever "contributed anything" or "do[ne] anything" for the Union army or Union civilians. The commissioners granted more weight to assistance to Union soldiers, Unionist civilians, and Confederate deserters who were not related to the claimants because they considered instances in which familial and national interest diverged as the strongest evidence of loyal citizenship. See "Standing Interrogatories," 1871, numbers 21, 22, 23, and 30; "Standing Interrogatories," of 1872, numbers 28, 29, and 37; "Standing Interrogatories," 1874, number 8 in Appendix B. In assessing "sufferings and losses," the commissioners considered actual injury as well as threats to the claimant's person, family, or property. See "Standing Interrogatories," 1871, numbers 18, 19, and 20; "Standing Interrogatories," 1872, numbers 25, 26, and 27; "Standing Interrogatories," 1874, numbers 18 and 21.
39 Summary Report, 1874, Joseph Beery Allowed Claim, Rockingham County, Virginia.
40 Jackson M. Jones Testimony, April 4, 1873, Jackson M. Jones Allowed Claim, Guilford County, North Carolina; Anderson W. Jones Testimony, April 4, 1873, ibid.; Summary Report, 1874, ibid. The commissioners routinely excused religious conscientious objectors like Jones for avoiding conscription by securing substitutes and exemptions. For an example of a Dunkard, see Summary Report, 1876, John J. Garber Allowed Claim, Rockingham County, Virginia. For an example of a Mennonite, see Summary Report, 1876, Jacob Geil Allowed Claim, Rockingham County, Virginia. In other cases, the commissioners considered purchasing a substitute as little different from Confederate service in terms of their determinations of loyal citizenship. In one claim, they commented that "we can make no distinction which would imply that a man of means might hire a substitute to fight against the country and still be accounted loyal, while the poor man who had to do his own fighting from lack of means to hire a substitute must be accounted a rebel." Summary Report, 1871, Noah Flory Disallowed Claim, Rockingham County, Virginia, in P2257.
41 Summary Report, 1872, Martin Miligan Disallowed Claim, Lawrence County, Alabama, in P2257.
42 Summary Report, 1871, James Fiendley Disallowed Claim, Norfolk County, Virginia, in P2257.
43 Summary Report, 1872, Alva Triplett Disallowed Claim, Fauquier County, Virginia, in P2257.
44 Reuben H. J. Garland Testimony, October 4, 1871, Reuben H. J. Garland Disallowed Claim, Upson County, Georgia, in Southern Claims Commission, Barred and Disallowed Claims, 1871–1880, Records of the United States House of Representatives, Microfiche Publication M1407, Record Group 233, National Archives, Washington, DC (hereafter cited as M1407), Fiche 36; Summary Report, 1873, ibid.
45 *Congressional Globe*, 40th Congress, 3rd Session (January 13, 1869), 325.
46 First General Report, 2–3.
47 See "Standing Interrogatories," 1871, numbers 3–18, 23–31, and 33 in Appendix B.

48 Dorris, *Pardon and Amnesty Under Lincoln and Johnson*, 35, 111–112.
49 This figure only includes claims rejected on the loyalty test and not claims rejected on the property test or jurisdictional grounds (as in the case of noncitizens, for example). This estimate is based on an extrapolation of Klingberg's analysis of large claims (more than $10,000), which reveals that the commissioners rejected 144 out of 363 (40 percent) of claimants for evidence of disloyalty. Klingberg, *The Southern Claims Commission*, 162.
50 This figure de-emphasizes the significance of these disloyal acts because it tallies the percentage out of all rejected claimants, including claimants who had been rejected on the property test and jurisdictional grounds and not just on the loyalty question. See Table 8 in Appendix A.
51 For examples of claimants rejected because they had supplied their sons in the Confederate army, see Summary Report, 1873, John V. Nunnally Disallowed Claim, LaFayette County, Mississippi, in P2257; Summary Report, 1874, Ezra B. Towne Disallowed Claim, Madison Parish, Louisiana, in P2257; Summary Report, 1874, William J. Pointevent Disallowed Claim, Hancock County, Mississippi, in P2257. For examples of claimants who had purchased Confederate bonds, see Summary Report, 1873, Sarah A. Price Disallowed Claim, Butler County, Alabama, in P2257; Summary Report, 1872, Clara H. Flower Disallowed Claim, Rapides Parish, Louisiana, in P2257; Summary Report, 1874, Willis Young Disallowed Claim, Scriven County, Georgia, in P2257; Summary Report, 1871, Reuben H. J. Garland Disallowed Claim, Upson County, Georgia, in P2257; Summary Report, 1871, Fielding F. Mathews Disallowed Claim, Upson County, Georgia, in P2257; Summary Report, 1877. Thomas M. Mathews Disallowed Claim, Dallas County, Alabama, in P2257; Summary Report, 1873, Elijah B. Lovett Disallowed Claim, Jefferson County, Alabama, in P2257; Summary Report, 1871, John W. Henderson Disallowed Claim, Henry County, Georgia, in P2257. For examples of claimants rejected for services rendered to the Confederacy, see Summary Report, 1877, Thomas M. Mathews Disallowed Claim, Dallas County, Alabama, in P2257; Summary Report, 1872, Clara H. Flower Disallowed Claim, Rapides Parish, Louisiana, in P2257; Summary Report, 1878, Charles G. Scott Disallowed Claim, Pulaski County, Arkansas, in P2257; Summary Report, 1878, Charles G. Scott Disallowed Claim, Pulaski County, Arkansas, in P2257; Summary Report, 1874, Martha Crane Disallowed Claim, Claiborne County, Mississippi, in P2257; Summary Report, 1874, William J. Pointevent Disallowed Claim, Hancock County, Mississippi, in P2257.
52 Summary Report, 1872, Asa Daniel Disallowed Claim, Monroe County, Mississippi, in P2257.
53 Thomas P. Lewis Testimony, November 23, 1871, Thomas P. Lewis Disallowed Claim, Tuscaloosa County, Alabama, in M1407, Fiche 541. For similar cases, see David Woodruff Testimony, November 23, 1871, Thomas P. Lewis Disallowed Claim, Tuscaloosa County, Alabama, in M1407, Fiche 541; Erasmus L. Houff Testimony, February 15, 1873, and Erasmus L. Houff Testimony, March 6, 1878, Erasmus L. Houff Disallowed Claim, Augusta County, Virginia, in Court of Claims, Docket No. 8,638.
54 Summary Report, 1873, Richard Appling Disallowed Claim, Tuscaloosa County, Alabama, in P2257; Summary Report, 1872, Asa Daniel Disallowed Claim, Monroe County, Mississippi, in P2257.

55 John Hawk Testimony, September 14, 1872, John Hawk Disallowed Claim, Marshall County, Mississippi, in Court of Claims, Docket No. 3,719. See also Summary Report, 1873, Robert Jamison Disallowed Claim, DeSoto County, Mississippi, in P2257.

Other white southerners who received presidential pardons denied any involvement in the rebellion, arguing that they only submitted their petitions as a matter of caution to forestall confiscation proceedings. Massena Beazley insisted that he had requested a presidential pardon because he wanted to save his 400-acre farm from confiscation and because he "did not know whether any discrimination would be made among residents of the southern states, whether friend or foe." Beazley noted, "I had done nothing to aid the rebellion, but had been peaceful, and was a loyal man, and did not believe I came under the purview of the law" but had applied "from prudence, to save my property." Massena Beazley Testimony, June 23, 1871, Massena Beazley Disallowed Claim, Henrico County, Virginia; Summary Report, 1871, ibid.

56 *Congressional Globe*, 40th Congress, 2nd Session (March 2, 1868), 234.

57 Summary Report, 1873, Henry Ormsby Disallowed Claim, Marshall County, Mississippi, in P2257; Summary Report, 1878, John H. Gibbons Disallowed Claim, East Baton Rouge Parish, Louisiana, in P2257. See also Summary Report, 1877, Henry Banks Disallowed Claim, Fulton County, Georgia, in P2257; Summary Report, 1871, Massena Beazley Disallowed Claim, Henrico County, Virginia, in P2257; Summary Report, 1874, Robert Y. Wood Disallowed Claim, Jefferson County, Mississippi, in P2257.

The commissioners included a question on pardons in all three versions of their interrogatories. The commissioners originally asked claimants, "Have you ever taken any amnesty oath; if so, when, where, and under what condition? Have you been pardoned by the President; if so, when and where, and upon what conditions?" The final version asked claimants, "Have you been specially pardoned by the President for participation in the rebellion?" See "Standing Interrogatories," 1871, number 5; "Standing Interrogatories," 1872, number 5; and "Standing Interrogatories," 1874, number 38 in Appendix B.

58 John N. Gatewood Testimony, October 24, 1871, John N. Gatewood Claim, Caroline County, Virginia, in Court of Claims, Docket No. 2,719; John H. Burruss Testimony, October 24, 1871, ibid.; F. S. Tukey Testimony, October 24, 1871, ibid.; Summary Report, 1871, ibid.

59 Joseph T. Mitchell Testimony, February 22, 1875, Joseph T. Mitchell Disallowed Claim, Augusta County, Virginia, in Court of Claims, Docket No. 478. See also Jacob L. Humbert Testimony, September 6, 1872, Jacob L. Humbert Disallowed Claim, Augusta County, Virginia, in M1407, Fiche 471; Benjamin F. Roberson Testimony, August 21, 1872, Benjamin F. Roberson Disallowed Claim, Carteret County, North Carolina, in M1407, Fiche 831.

60 On continued devotion to the Confederacy, see McPherson, *What They Fought For, 1861–1865*; Gallagher, *The Confederate War*; McPherson, *For Cause and Comrades*; Jason Phillips, *Diehard Rebels: The Confederate Culture of Invincibility* (Athens: University of Georgia Press, 2007); Aaron Charles Sheehan-Dean, *Why Confederates Fought: Family and Nation in Civil War Virginia* (Chapel Hill: University of North Carolina Press, 2007). On continued devotion to the Union, see Earl J. Hess, *The Union Soldier in Battle: Enduring the Ordeal of Combat*

(Lawrence: University Press of Kansas, 1997); Gallagher, *The Union War*. On courage, see William Fletcher Thompson, *The Image of War: The Pictorial Reporting of the American Civil War* (New York: T. Yoseloff, 1960); Gerald F. Linderman, *Embattled Courage: The Experience of Combat in the American Civil War* (New York: Collier Macmillan, 1987).

61 Summary Report, 1877, William S. Huggins Disallowed Claim, Coffee County, Tennessee, in P2257; Summary Report, 1875, Daniel Lowry Disallowed Claim, Bartow County, Georgia, in P2257; Summary Report, 1878, Joel H. Dyar Disallowed Claim, Bartow County, Georgia, in P2257.

62 Summary Report, 1878, Erasmus L. Houff Disallowed Claim, Augusta County, Virginia, in Court of Claims, Docket No. 8,638.

63 Adam Fix Testimony, September 14, 1871, Adam Fix Disallowed Claim, Augusta County, Virginia, in M1407, Fiche 458.

64 Nicholas A. Carney Testimony, March 13, 1873, Nicholas A. Carney Disallowed Claim, Washington County, Arkansas, in M1407, Fiche 1,088.

65 John W. Edwards Testimony, November 11, 1875, John W. Edwards Disallowed Claim, Prince George County, Virginia, in M1407, Fiche 3,980.

66 Henry Ambos Testimony, July 11, 1872, Henry Ambos Disallowed Claim, Chatham County, Georgia, in M1407, Fiche 1,595; John W. Edwards Testimony, November 11, 1875, John W. Edwards Disallowed Claim, Prince George County, Virginia, in M1407, Fiche 3,980. See also William Drake Testimony, December 23, 1873, William Drake Disallowed Claim, Southampton County, Virginia, in M1407, Fiche 1,457; James Fiendley Testimony, September 8, 1871, James Fiendley Disallowed Claim, Norfolk County, Virginia, in M1407, Fiche 30; Samuel C. Means Testimony, May 23, 1873, Samuel Orrison Disallowed Claim, Loudon County, Virginia, in M1407, Fiche 1,823.

67 Summary Report, 1879, Logan Osburn Disallowed Claim, Jefferson County, West Virginia, in P2257.

68 Of the thirty-four interrogatories in the 1871 version, forty-three interrogatories in the 1872 version, and fifty-three interrogatories in the 1874 version, only two in each directly queried claimants on their sympathies and only in a vague manner. This count only includes questions directed toward claimants in the loyalty section and excludes questions directed toward claimants in the property section and questions directed toward witnesses. "Standing Interrogatories," 1871; "Standing Interrogatories," 1872; "Standing Interrogatories," 1874 in Appendix B.

69 First General Report, 3.

70 Summary Report, 1871, John Wampler Disallowed Claim, Augusta County, Virginia, in P2257.

71 Summary Report, 1875, Winfield Scott Baugher Disallowed Claim, Rockingham County, Virginia, in Court of Claims, Docket No. 8,736.

72 For examples of claims in which the commissioners emphasized that the claimants had not served in the Union army, see Summary Report, 1878, William Sawyer Disallowed Claim, Pickens County, Georgia, in P2257; Summary Report, 1875, Winfield Scott Baugher Claim, Rockingham County, Virginia, in P2257; Summary Report, 1872, Elijah Kirby Disallowed Claim, Whitfield County, Georgia, in P2257; Summary Report, 1871, John Wampler Disallowed Claim, Augusta County, Virginia, in P2257.

73 Summary Report, 1871, John D. Miller Disallowed Claim, Rockingham County, Virginia, in P2257.
74 Summary Report, 1878, Caroline Lamb, Richard D. Lamb, and Ira M. Lamb Disallowed Claim, Phillips County, Arkansas, in P2257.
75 Summary Report from John B. Keaton Disallowed Claim, Arkansas County, Arkansas, in P2257; Summary Report, 1878, Caroline Lamb, Richard D. Lamb, and Ira M. Lamb Disallowed Claim, Phillips County, Arkansas, in P2257; Summary Report, 1879, Thornton Payne Disallowed Claim, Fauquier County, Virginia, in P2257.
76 For an example of a claimant who escaped Confederate persecution as a result of a "weak mind," see Summary Report, 1878, Hiram Tweedell Allowed Claim, DeKalb County, Georgia, in P2257. For an example of a claimant who escaped Confederate persecution as a result of physical disability, see Summary Report, 1872, Aldridge James Allowed Claim, Fauquier County, Virginia, in P2257. For an example of a claimant who escaped Confederate persecution as a result of his family connections, see Summary Report, 1879, Edward C. Turner Allowed Claim, Fauquier County, Virginia, in P2257.
77 James T. King Testimony, September 22, 1873, James T. King Disallowed Claim, Halifax County, Virginia, in M1407, Fiche 4,018; Peter T. Comer Testimony, September 22, 1873, ibid.; Summary Report, 1879, ibid. The commissioners also criticized King's move from Texas to Virginia, which they identified as "the very hot bed of rebeldom." They also reported that King had briefly served in the home guard, which they excused at least partially in noting that he probably faced "compulsion" in the form of "public opinion, which King a physician and a bachelor he could not well resist."
78 Hugh Young Testimony, September 26, 1871, Hugh Young Allowed Claim, Kershaw County, South Carolina. See also Massena Beazley Testimony, June 23, 1871, Massena Beazley Disallowed Claim, Henrico County, Virginia, in Court of Claims, Docket No. 4,399; William Patterson Testimony, March 29, 1877, William A. Pattie Disallowed Claim, Fauquier County, Virginia, in M1407, Fiche 2713–2714.
79 Reuben Matthews Testimony, August 8, 1872, Reuben Matthews Disallowed Claim, Harnett County, North Carolina, in M1407, Fiche 809.
80 Thomas Nation Testimony, July 17, 1873, Thomas Nation Allowed Claim, Blount County, Alabama. See also Joshua P. Coman Testimony, n.d., Joshua P. Coman Disallowed Claim, Limestone County, Alabama, in M1407, Fiche 1530–1534.
81 Reuben Matthews Testimony, August 8, 1872, Reuben Matthews Disallowed Claim, Harnett County, North Carolina, in M1407, Fiche 809.
82 Thomas Nation Testimony, July 17, 1873, Thomas Nation Allowed Claim, Blount County, Alabama; William Anderton Testimony, July 17, 1873, ibid.; William Mitchell Testimony, July 17, 1873, ibid.; Special Commissioner James H. Bone Remarks, July 17, 1873, ibid.
83 Steven Hahn, *A Nation Under Our Feet: Black Political Struggles in the Rural South from Slavery to the Great Migration* (Cambridge, MA: Harvard University Press, 2005), 265–313.
84 For taxes on slaves, see Crofts, *Reluctant Confederates*, 159–160. For mention of the taxation amendment, see "Ordinance," *Warrenton Flag of 98*, May 9,

1861. Pattie submitted a notarized copy of the amendment in his claim. For the importance of the slavery issue at the Virginia convention in 1861, see William W. Freehling, "The Editorial Revolution, Virginia, and the Coming of the Civil War: A Review Essay," *Civil War History* 16, no. 1 (1970): 64–72.

85 William Bootwright Testimony, July 15, 1875, William Pattie Disallowed Claim, Fauquier County, Virginia, in M1407, Fiche 2713–2714; George C. Round, Brief on Loyalty, November 25, 1876, ibid.

86 Summary Report, 1879, Henry K. Eakle Disallowed Claim, Augusta County, Virginia, in P2257. See also Summary Report, 1873, Thomas P. Lewis Disallowed Claim, Tuscaloosa County, Alabama, in M1407, Fiche 541; Summary Report, 1875, John L. Rogers Disallowed Claim, Whitfield County, Mississippi, in P2257; Summary Report, 1874, George W. Bowen Disallowed Claim, Culpeper County, Virginia, in M1407, Fiche 1,439; Summary Report, 1871, Thaddeus Higgins Disallowed Claim, Hanover County, Virginia, in M1407, Fiche 39; Summary Report, 1871, Massena Beazley Disallowed Claim, Henrico County, Virginia, in P2257; Summary Report, 1879, John Barker Disallowed Claim, New Kent County, Virginia, in P2257; Summary Report, 1873, James Gordon Hughey Disallowed Claim, Gordon County, Georgia, in P2257; Summary Report, 1874, Nicholas A. Carney Disallowed Claim, Washington County, Arkansas, in P2257; Summary Report, 1878, William S. Berry Disallowed Claim, Prince Edward County, Virginia, in P2257; Summary Report, 1874, Anthony Voils Disallowed Claim, Walker County, Georgia, in P2257; Summary Report, 1877, Thomas M. Mathews Disallowed Claim, Dallas County, Alabama, in P2257; Summary Report, 1877, William A. Pattie Disallowed Claim, Fauquier County, Virginia, in M1407, Fiche 2713–2714; Summary Report, 1878, Zara L. Colton Disallowed Claim, Polk County, Arkansas, in P2257; Summary Report, 1873, John J. Fearrington Disallowed Claim, Chatham County, North Carolina, in Court of Claims, Docket No. 6,880; Summary Report, 1879, James T. King Disallowed Claim, Halifax County, Virginia, in M1407, Fiche 4,018; Summary Report, 1875, Joshua P. Coman Disallowed Claim, Limestone County, Alabama, in M1407, Fiche 1530–1534; Summary Report, 1875, Matthew M. Lacy Disallowed Claim, Marshall County, Mississippi, in Court of Claims, Docket No. 776.

87 Friends of Matthew M. Lacy of Mississippi, for example, unsuccessfully called on the commissioners to award him compensation on the basis of his postwar Republican reputation. Summary Report, 1875, Matthew M. Lacy Disallowed Claim, Marshall County, Mississippi, in Court of Claims, Docket No. 776.

88 Terry L. Seip, *The South Returns to Congress: Men, Economic Measures, and Intersectional Relationships, 1868–1879* (Baton Rouge: Louisiana State University Press, 1983); Richard H. Abbott, *The Republican Party and the South, 1855–1877: The First Southern Strategy* (Chapel Hill: University of North Carolina Press, 1986).

89 Simeon Shaw Testimony, April 4, 1877, Simeon Shaw Allowed Claim, Culpeper County, Virginia.

90 James W. Spicer Testimony, April 4, 1877, Simeon Shaw Allowed Claim, Culpeper County, Virginia.

91 Joseph Rozier Testimony, February 19, 1875, Abner Ginn Allowed Claim, Beaufort County, South Carolina. Rozier owned $2,500 in real estate and $900 in personal estate in 1860. Ginn owned $3,000 in real estate and $1,800 in personal estate

in 1860. United States Census, 1860, St. Peters Parish, Beaufort County, South Carolina, 58. See also James W. Spicer Testimony, April 4, 1877, Simeon Shaw Allowed Claim, Culpeper County, Virginia.

92 Thomas Staggs Testimony, October 18, 1874, Thomas Staggs Disallowed Claim, Sumner County, Tennessee, in M1407, Fiche 3908. See also Edward Wadsworth, June 18, 1874, Alfred Agerton Allowed Claim, Chesterfield County, South Carolina; Summary Report, 1877, James Beverly Allowed Claim, Marlboro County, South Carolina; Richard Ennis Testimony, May 10, 1782, Richard Ennis Allowed Claim, Prince William County, Virginia; Joseph Rozier Testimony, February 19, 1875, Abner Ginn Allowed Claim, Beaufort County, South Carolina; Simeon Shaw Testimony, April 4, 1877, Testimony, Simeon Shaw Allowed Claim, Culpeper County, Virginia; Archibald Shaw Testimony, April 4, 1877, ibid.

93 David W. Holmes Testimony, January 26, 1877, Washington Holmes Allowed Claim, Gordon County, Georgia. See also Robert S. Knox Testimony, August 16, 1877, John Thompson Allowed Claim, Murray County, Georgia; Sarah C. Shaw Testimony, April 4, 1877, Simeon Shaw Allowed Claim, Culpeper County, Virginia; Summary Report, 1878, ibid.

94 John J. Pass Testimony, January 30, 1877, John J. Pass Allowed Claim, Gordon County, Georgia. John J. Pass owned $2,000 in real estate and $500 in personal estate in 1860. United States Census, 1860, Calhoun District, Gordon County, Georgia, 275. Only 21% of Gordon County families owned slaves, 16% below the state average. See also Odian Castleberry Testimony, September 1, 1874, Odian Castleberry Allowed Claim, Walker County, Georgia; Levi Crow Testimony, September 30, 1875, Levi Crow Disallowed Claim, Paulding County, Georgia, in Court of Claims, Docket No. 11,325; James Ruth Testimony, February 19, 1875, Abner Ginn Allowed Claim, Beaufort County, South Carolina; Peter P. Perkins Testimony, April 25, 1872, Peter P. Perkins Disallowed Claim, Halifax County, Virginia, in M1407, Fiche 490. For similar claims by white women, see Ferriby Johnson Testimony, December 18, 1872, Ferriby Johnson Allowed Claim, Chesterfield County, South Carolina; John Peterson Testimony, September 5, 1873, and Joseph Dixon Testimony, September 5, 1873, Susan W. Peterson Disallowed Claim, Warren County, Virginia, in Court of Claims, Docket No. 8,707. For former slaveholders on their emancipated slave property, see James L. Roark, *Masters Without Slaves: Southern Planters in the Civil War and Reconstruction* (New York: Norton, 1977), 104–105.

95 John J. Pass Testimony, January 30, 1877, John J. Pass Allowed Claim, Gordon County, Georgia. See also Dillard Young Testimony, September 30, 1875, Levi Crow Disallowed Claim, Paulding County, Georgia, in Court of Claims, Docket No. 11,325.

96 Jacob Brunk Testimony, December 19, 1873, Jacob Brunk Allowed Claim, Rockingham County, Virginia. Jacob Brunk owned $5,000 in real estate and $1,130 in personal estate in 1860. United States Census, 1860, District No. 1, Rockingham County, 277.

97 Allen Ellis Testimony, February 22, 1878, Allen Ellis Allowed Claim, Chatham County, North Carolina. According to the Census of 1860, Ellis owned $330 in real estate and $1,000 in personal estate. United States Census, 1860, Eastern District, Chatham County, North Carolina, 101. See also James Ruth Testimony, February 19, 1875, Abner Ginn Allowed Claim, Beaufort County, South Carolina.

98 George W. Joy Testimony, April 11, 1873, George W. Joy Allowed Claim, Washington County, Virginia.
99 Steven Hahn, *The Roots of Southern Populism: Yeomen Farmers and the Transformation of the Georgia Upcountry, 1850–1890* (New York: Oxford University Press, 1983); McCurry, *Masters of Small Worlds*; William W. Freehling, *The South vs. the South: How Anti-Confederate Southerners Shaped the Course of the Civil War* (Oxford and New York: Oxford University Press, 2001); Martin Crawford, *Ashe County's Civil War: Community and Society in the Appalachian South* (Charlottesville: University Press of Virginia, 2001); Timothy James Lockley, *Lines in the Sand: Race and Class in Lowcountry Georgia, 1750–1860* (Athens: University of Georgia Press, 2001); Harold D. Tallant, *Evil Necessity: Slavery and Political Culture in Antebellum Kentucky* (Lexington: University Press of Kentucky, 2003); Steven Deyle, *Carry Me Back: The Domestic Slave Trade in American Life* (New York: Oxford University Press, 2005), 139; David Brown, *Southern Outcast: Hinton Rowan Helper and the Impending Crisis of the South* (Baton Rouge: Louisiana State University Press, 2006).
100 Joseph Brown Testimony, August 5, 1874, Henry Ambos Disallowed Claim, Chatham County, Georgia, in M1407, Fiche 1,595. Henry Ambos owned no real or personal estate in 1860 and apparently lived with his father who owned $1,850 in real estate and $2,000 in personal estate. See United States Census, 1860, 6th District White Bluff, Chatham County, Georgia, 373.
101 John Hunt Testimony, December 23, 1873, William Drake Disallowed Claim, Southampton County, Virginia, in M1407, Fiche 1,457. William Drake owned $600 in real estate and $450 in personal estate in 1860. See United States Census, 1860, West Side Nottoway River, Southampton County, Virginia, 62. See also James Burwell Testimony, July 10, 1877, Henry Mosby Allowed Claim, Roanoke County, Virginia; George Williams Testimony, August 6, 1872, Ricey E. Edwards Disallowed Claim, Culpeper County, Virginia, in M1407, Fiche 1,458.
102 There is a growing scholarship on interactions between lower-class whites and blacks, including Victoria E. Bynum, *Unruly Women: The Politics of Social and Sexual Control in the Old South* (Chapel Hill: University of North Carolina Press, 1992); Lockley, *Lines in the Sand: Race and Class in Lowcountry Georgia, 1750–1860*; and Joshua D. Rothman, *Notorious in the Neighborhood: Sex and Families Across the Color Line, 1787–1861* (Chapel Hill: University of North Carolina Press, 2003).
103 Summary Report, 1878, Levi Crow Disallowed Claim, Paulding County, Georgia, in P2257.
104 Summary Report, 1871, William Bailey Disallowed Claim, Hanover County, Virginia, in P2257. See also John Hunt Testimony, December 23, 1873, William Drake Disallowed Claim, Southampton County, Virginia, in M1407, Fiche 1,457.
105 William L. Shackleford Testimony, July 10 and 11, 1877, William L. Shackleford Allowed Claim, Prince George County, Virginia.
106 Samuel Norris Testimony, November 26, 1872, Samuel Norris Disallowed Claim, Wake County, North Carolina, in Court of Claims, Docket No. 8,910. See also Henry M. Hart Testimony, July 12, 1875, Henry M. Hart Allowed Claim, Lauderdale County, Alabama. See also John T. Snipes Testimony, March 19,

1872, John T. Snipes Disallowed Claim, Upson County, Georgia, in M1407, Fiche 1,652.

107 P. J. Staudenraus, *The African Colonization Movement, 1816–1865* (New York: Columbia University Press, 1961); Douglas R. Egerton, "'Its Origin Is Not a Little Curious': A New Look at the American Colonization Society," *Journal of the Early Republic* 5, no. 4 (Winter 1985): 463–480; Charles B. Dew, *Apostles of Disunion: Southern Secession Commissioners and the Causes of the Civil War* (Charlottesville: University Press of Virginia, 2001); Eric Burin, *Slavery and the Peculiar Solution: A History of the American Colonization Society* (Gainesville: University Press of Florida, 2005); Adam Rothman, *Slave Country: American Expansion and the Origins of the Deep South* (Cambridge, MA: Harvard University Press, 2005); Lacy K. Ford, *Deliver Us from Evil: The Slavery Question in the Old South* (New York: Oxford University Press, 2009).

108 John H. Bowles Testimony, August 25, 1871, John H. Bowles Disallowed Claim, Goochland County, Virginia, in M1407, Fiche 16. See also John B. Bowen Testimony, October 28, 1878, John B. Bowen Allowed Claim, Jefferson County, Mississippi; Henry M. Hart Testimony, July 12, 1875, Henry M. Hart Allowed Claim, Lauderdale County, Alabama; Patrick Henfrey Testimony, October 2 and 3, 1874, Peter McArdle Disallowed Claim, Hinds County, Mississippi, in Court of Claims, Docket No. 1,013; Samuel Norris Testimony, November 26, 1872, Samuel Norris Disallowed Claim, Wake County, North Carolina, in Court of Claims, Docket No. 8,910; Samuel Watson Testimony, July 31, 1874, Samuel Watson Disallowed Claim, Shelby County, Tennessee, in M1407, Fiche 2,161.

109 David Young Testimony, January 20, 1873, David Young Allowed Claim, Fulton County, Georgia, Fiche 158. See also Patrick Henfrey Testimony, October 2 and 3, 1874, Peter McArdle Disallowed Claim, Hinds County, Mississippi, in Court of Claims, Docket No. 1,013; Robert Austin Testimony, October 2 and 3, 1874, ibid.

110 Anne S. Rubin, *A Shattered Nation: The Rise and Fall of the Confederacy, 1861–1868* (Chapel Hill: University of North Carolina Press, 2005), 158–159.

111 On paternalism and proslavery ideology, see Larry E. Tise, *Proslavery: A History of the Defense of Slavery in America, 1701–1840* (Athens: University of Georgia Press, 1987); John Patrick Daly, *When Slavery Was Called Freedom: Evangelicalism, Proslavery, and the Causes of the Civil War* (Lexington: University Press of Kentucky, 2002); Michael O'Brien, *Conjectures of Order: Intellectual Life and the American South, 1810–1860* (Chapel Hill: University of North Carolina Press, 2004); Ford, *Deliver Us from Evil*; Jeffrey Robert Young, *Domesticating Slavery: The Master Class in Georgia and South Carolina, 1670–1837* (Chapel Hill: University of North Carolina Press, 1999); Eugene D. Genovese, *Roll, Jordan, Roll: The World the Slaves Made* (New York: Pantheon Books, 1974); Deyle, *Carry Me Back*.

112 The portrayal of slavery as a benevolent institution generally arose when former masters and mistresses presented their former slaves to testify to their kindnesses. For example, John Gordon, a former Alabama slave, assessed William O. Winston as a good master. Gordon related Winston's pledge that "as long as he had bread, he would divide with me, but if at any time I wanted to go, that he would do the best he could for me." According to Gordon, twenty-four of Winston's slaves had

opted to stay with him during the war rather than escape with Union troops. Gordon concluded, "he was just as good to us as he could be." Such testimony defended former slaveholders against abolitionist charges of the cruelty of the institution. As in proslavery fiction, slaves' words seemed the most persuasive evidence of the virtues of the institution. John Gordon Testimony, October 10, 1872, William O. Winston Allowed Claim, DeKalb County, Alabama. See also George Morton Testimony, November 11, 1874, Stephanie Chotard Allowed Claim, Concordia Parish, Louisiana; Hector Loadhoaltz Testimony, February 13, 1874, Mary L. Loadholt Disallowed Claim, Beaufort County, South Carolina, in Court of Claims, Docket No. 6,893; Summary Report, 1873, William E. Richardson Disallowed Claim, Dinwiddie County, Virginia, in P2257. Former slaveholders, however, more frequently called on their former slaves to testify to their property holdings than to their loyalties.

113 John Underwood Brown Testimony, December 26, 1872, John Underwood Brown Disallowed Claim, Macon County, Alabama, in Court of Claims, Docket No. 15,622. According to the census of 1860, Brown owned considerable property, including $[3?]7,500 in real estate and $137,100 in personal estate. United States Census of 1860, Northern Division, Macon County, Alabama, 61/873. See also John D. Holt Testimony, July 29, 1873, John D. Holt Disallowed Claim, Limestone County, Alabama, in Court of Claims, Docket No. 1,468; Thomas M. Mills Testimony, August 20, 1873, Thomas M. Mills Disallowed Claim, Orange County, Virginia, in M1407, Fiche 4,033.

114 William C. Lipscomb Testimony, February 18, 1879, William C. Lipscomb Disallowed Claim, Fairfax County, Virginia, in M1407, Fiche 1,587. See also Thomas Kidd Testimony, February 17, 1873, Thomas Kidd Disallowed Claim, Hinds County, Mississippi, in Court of Claims, Docket No. 3,350; Eliza Jane Lindsay Testimony, June 27, 1872, Eliza Jane Lindsay Disallowed Claim, Davidson County, North Carolina, in M1407, Fiche 799; Miles G. Tate Testimony, August 24, 1877, Miles G. Tate Disallowed Claim, Forsyth County, Georgia, in M1407, Fiche 2,954.

115 Wilson H. Dillon Testimony, June 28, 1873, Wilson H. Dillon Disallowed Claim, Hinds County, Mississippi, in Court of Claims, Docket No. 1,157. See John B. Goodwin Testimony, August 30, 1871, John B. Goodwin Disallowed Claim, Rutherford County, Tennessee, in M1407, Fiche 1,352; Thomas Sessions Testimony, September 6, 1876, Thomas Sessions Disallowed Claim, Kershaw County, South Carolina, in M1407, Fiche 333; John W. Vick Testimony, July 14, 1873, John W. Vick Disallowed Claim, Warren County, Mississippi, in M1407, Fiche 2,007.

116 George Markham Testimony, April 22, 1874, George Markham Disallowed Claim, Warren County, Mississippi, in Court of Claims, Docket No. 1,168. For additional information on Markham, see Dyer, *Secret Yankees*. See also James Anderson Testimony, November 21, 1874, James Anderson Disallowed Claim, Wayne County, Tennessee, in Court of Claims, Docket No. 1,399; James Anderson Testimony, February 28, 1879, ibid.; Petition, July 6, 1871, Arthur M. Blake Disallowed Claim, Charleston, South Carolina, in M1407, Fiche 865; Robert Daniel Testimony, November 24 and 25, 1873, Robert Daniel Disallowed Claim, Washington Parish, Louisiana, in M1407, Fiche 3,586.

117 Robert Daniel Testimony, November 24 and 25, 1873, Robert Daniel Disallowed Claim, Washington Parish, Louisiana, in M1407, Fiche 3,586. See also James W. Roberts Testimony, September 3, 1872, James W. Roberts Disallowed Claim, Tensas Parish, Louisiana, in Court of Claims, Docket No. 909; John D. Holt Testimony, July 29, 1873, John D. Holt Disallowed Claim, Limestone County, Alabama, in Court of Claims, Docket No. 1,468.
118 Jennifer L. Weber, *Copperheads: The Rise and Fall of Lincoln's Opponents in the North* (Oxford: Oxford University Press, 2006), 67.
119 Summary Report, 1879, William C. Lipscomb Disallowed Claim, Fairfax County, Virginia, in M1407, Fiche 1,587.
120 "The Union As It Was," *Harper's Weekly*, October 24, 1874.
121 Summary Report, 1874, James Mattox Disallowed Claim, Walker County, Georgia, in P2257. For examples of claims involving male and female claimants who drove their slaves away from the Union army, see Summary Report, 1878, John D. Arbuckle Disallowed Claim, Sebastian County, Arkansas, in P2257; Summary Report, 1874, Roche H. Brabston Disallowed Claim, Warren County, Mississippi, in P2257; Summary Report, 1874, Susan Bowers Disallowed Claim, Beaufort County, South Carolina, in P2257; Summary Report, 1877, George P. Burnett Disallowed Claim, Floyd County, Georgia, in P2257; Summary Report, 1877, James C. Cain Disallowed Claim, East Baton Rouge Parish, Louisiana, in P2257; Summary Report, 1879, William C. Currie Disallowed Claim, Carroll Parish, Louisiana, in P2257; Summary Report, 1877, William C. Davidson Disallowed Claim, Jackson County, Alabama, in P2257; Summary Report, 1879, Samuel M. Dunlap Disallowed Claim, Ouachita County, Arkansas, in P2257; Summary Report, 1872, Richard Fletcher Disallowed Claim, Pulaski County, Arkansas, in P2257; Summary Report, 1874, William H. Gaines Disallowed Claim, Hot Springs County, Arkansas, in P2257; Summary Report, 1879, James Heathman Disallowed Claim, Sunflower County, Mississippi, in P2257; Summary Report, 1877, Jane Hopkins Disallowed Claim, Iberia Parish, Louisiana, in P2257; Summary Report, 1872, John H. Hundley Disallowed Claim, Limestone County, Alabama, in P2257; Summary Report, 1873, Newton Kinnebrew Disallowed Claim, Floyd County, Georgia, in P2257; Summary Report, 1876, Eudora E. Knox Disallowed Claim, Crawford County, Arkansas, in P2257; Summary Report, 1879, Mary A. McGee Disallowed Claim, Crawford County, Arkansas, in P2257; Summary Report, 1874, Theodore H. Phillips Disallowed Claim, Jackson County, Arkansas, in P2257; Nathaniel H. Fish Disallowed Claim, Jefferson County, Arkansas, in P2257; Summary Report, 1874, John H. Ruddell Disallowed Claim, Beaufort County, South Carolina, in P2257; Summary Report, 1878, Charles G. Scott Disallowed Claim, Pulaski County, Arkansas, in P2257; Summary Report, 1874, Ezra B. Towne Disallowed Claim, Madison Parish, Louisiana, in P2257; Summary Report, 1879, Nolen S. Williams Disallowed Claim, Orleans Parish, Louisiana, in P2257; Summary Report, 1878, David Stone Disallowed Claim, Bolivar County, Mississippi, in P2257; Summary Report, 1879, Susan S. Williams Disallowed Claim, Davidson County, Tennessee, in P2257; Summary Report, 1879, Thornton Withers Estate Disallowed Claim, Fauquier County, Virginia, in P2257; Summary Report, 1879, Ann Worthington Disallowed Claim, Washington County, Mississippi, in P2257; Summary Report, 1879, Anna P. Yell (James Yell Estate) Disallowed Claim, Jefferson County, Arkansas, in P2257.

For examples of claims involving legal or economic transactions of slave property, see Summary Report, 1880, Arnold O. Brown Disallowed Claim, Rockdale and Paulding counties, Georgia, in P2257; Summary Report, 1874, William H. Gaines Disallowed Claim, Hot Springs County, Arkansas, in P2257; Summary Report, 1880, Richard Holleman Disallowed Claim, Ouachita County, Arkansas, in P2257; Summary Report, 1874, John D. Magill Estate, Disallowed Claim, Georgetown County, South Carolina, in P2257; Summary Report, 1877, Thomas Stewart Disallowed Claim, Fauquier County, Virginia, in P2257.

The commissioners also applied the same logic in claims by former slaveholders who had submitted their names to the Confederate government for compensation for slaves who escaped with the Union army. See Summary Report, 1879, Silas S. Gregory Disallowed Claim, Camden County, North Carolina, in P2257; Summary Report, 1880, William J. Savage Disallowed Claim, Gates County, North Carolina, in P2257; Summary Report, 1878, Jesse Eason Disallowed Claim, Gates County, North Carolina, in P2257.

Chapter 3 Women's Union

1 Martha M. Wright Testimony, June 1, 1876, and George W. Barrett Testimony, June 1, 1876, Martha M. Wright Disallowed Claim, Claiborne County, Mississippi, in Court of Claims, Docket No. 4,219.
2 Summary Report, 1875, Margaret Brown Disallowed Claim, Greene County, Tennessee, in P2257. For similar identifications of politically minded women as masculine, see LeeAnn Whites, "Strong Minds and Strong Hearts: The Ladies National League and the Civil War as an Intragender War," in *Gender Matters: Civil War, Reconstruction, and the Making of the New South* (New York: Palgrave Macmillan, 2005), 25–26; Kristen L. Streater, "'She-Rebels' on the Supply Line: Gender Conventions in Civil War Kentucky," in *Occupied Women: Gender, Military Occupation, and the American Civil War*, ed. Alecia P. Long and LeeAnn Whites (Baton Rouge: Louisiana State University Press, 2009), 88–102.
3 On coverture and the concept of marital unity, see Norma Basch, "Invisible Women: The Legal Fiction of Marital Unity in Nineteenth-Century America," *Feminist Studies* 5, no. 2 (1979): 346–366; Linda K. Kerber, *Women of the Republic: Intellect and Ideology in Revolutionary America* (Chapel Hill: University of North Carolina Press, 1980); Hartog, "Lawyering, Husbands' Rights, and the Unwritten Law in Nineteenth-Century America"; Linda K. Kerber, *No Constitutional Right to Be Ladies: Women and the Obligations of Citizenship* (New York: Hill and Wang, 1998), 3–46, quotations at 30, 35, and 39; Nancy F. Cott, *Public Vows: A History of Marriage and the Nation* (Cambridge, MA: Harvard University Press, 2000); Hendrik Hartog, *Man and Wife in America: A History* (Cambridge, MA: Harvard University Press, 2000).

On separate spheres, see Barbara Welter, "The Cult of True Womanhood: 1820–1860," *American Quarterly* 18, no. 2 (1966): 151–174; Kathryn Kish Sklar, *Catharine Beecher: A Study in American Domesticity* (New Haven: Yale University Press, 1973); Carroll Smith-Rosenberg, "The Female World of Love and Ritual: Relations Between Women in Nineteenth-Century America," *Signs: Journal of Women in Culture & Society* 1, no. 1 (1975): 1–30; Nancy F. Cott, *The Bonds* of Womanhood: "Woman's Sphere" in New England, 1780–1835 (New Haven: Yale University Press, 1977); Kerber, Women of the Republic; Mary P. Ryan, Cradle of the Middle Class: The Family in Oneida County, New York, 1790–1865 (Cambridge and New York: Cambridge University Press, 1981); Suzanne Lebsock, The Free Women of Petersburg: Status and Culture in a Southern Town, 1784–1860 (New York: Norton, 1984); Cindy Sondik Aron, Ladies and Gentlemen of the Civil Service: Middle-Class Workers in Victorian America (New York: Oxford University Press, 1987); Elizabeth Fox-Genovese, Within the Plantation Household: Black and White Women of the Old South (Chapel Hill: University of North Carolina Press, 1988).

4 Lucretia C. Merry Testimony, November 28, 1873, Lucretia C. Merry Allowed Claim, Fairfax County, Virginia; David L. Finch Testimony, November 28, 1873, ibid.; Summary Report, 1876, ibid.

5 The commissioners only formally required interrogations on a female claimant's loyalty if she owned the property in her own right. They did question female claimants and witnesses about their deceased husband's loyalties if he had owned the property at the time of its appropriation. In these cases, the commissioners judged the loyalty of the husband as the original owner of the property.

6 Harriet J. Carey Testimony, February 8, 1873, Harriet J. Carey Allowed Claim, Hinds County, Mississippi; Harriet J. Carey Testimony, April 21, 1873, ibid.; Edwin W. Cabaniss Testimony, April 24, 1873, ibid.; Summary Report, 1873, ibid. In 1860, Carey owned $10,000 in real estate and $10,000 in personal estate. See United States Census, 1860, Town of Clinton, Hinds County, Mississippi, 89/563. On slaveholding widows and coverture, see Kirsten E. Wood, Masterful Women: Slaveholding Widows from the American Revolution Through the Civil War (Chapel Hill: University of North Carolina Press, 2004), 4, 26.

7 Separate estates did not always guarantee a woman the right to manage her own property. Separate estates, which were increasingly common in the antebellum era, were typically a means by which families protected property from husband's creditors. On separate estates in Virginia, see Lebsock, The Free Women of Petersburg, 54–86.

8 Eliza Woodward Testimony, April 22, 1874, Eliza Woodward Allowed Claim, Fauquier County, Virginia; Summary Report, 1878, ibid.

9 Rachel R. Cole Testimony, November 15, 1876, Rachel R. Cole Allowed Claim, DeKalb County, Alabama; James R. Dorsey Testimony, November 15, 1876, ibid.; Summary Report, 1877, ibid. On the significant social ostracism that divorced women confronted, see David Silkenat, Moments of Despair: Suicide, Divorce, and Debt in Civil War Era North Carolina (Chapel Hill: University of North Carolina Press, 2011), 75–94.

10 Fellman, Inside War, 199–214; Whites, The Civil War as a Crisis in Gender, 143–144; Faust, Mothers of Invention, 198–202.

11 Christine Jacobson Carter, Southern Single Blessedness: Unmarried Women in the Urban South, 1800–1865 (Urbana: University of Illinois Press, 2006), 5–6, 65–94, 118–149.

12 Caroline H. Atkisson Testimony, August 22, 1873, Caroline H. Atkisson Allowed Claim, Colbert County, Alabama; Sarah Atkisson Testimony, August 22, 1873, ibid.; Meredith Thompson Testimony, August 22, 1873, ibid.; Summary Report, 1874, ibid.

13 Lucy A. Weaver Testimony, April 29, 1873, Lucy A. Weaver Disallowed Claim, Chattooga County, Georgia, in Court of Claims, Docket No. 15,794; Summary Report, 1875, ibid.
14 Although states had started passing laws that allowed married women to own property independently of their husbands in the late 1830s, coverture remained the norm. On married women's property laws, see Suzanne Lebsock, "Radical Reconstruction and the Property Rights of Southern Women," *Journal of Southern History* 43, no. 2 (May 1977): 195–216; Basch, "Invisible Women"; Norma Basch, *In the Eyes of the Law: Women, Marriage, and Property in Nineteenth-Century New York* (Ithaca: Cornell University Press, 1982); Richard H. Chused, "Married Women's Property Law: 1800–1850," *Georgetown Law Journal* 71, no. 5 (1983): 1359–1425; Michael B. Dougan, "The Arkansas Married Women's Property Law," *Arkansas Historical Quarterly* 46 (Spring 1987): 3–26; Amy Dru Stanley, "Conjugal Bonds and Wage Labor: Rights of Contract in the Age of Emancipation," *Journal of American History* 75, no. 2 (September 1988): 471–500; Peter W. Bardaglio, *Reconstructing the Household: Families, Sex, and the Law in the Nineteenth-Century South* (Chapel Hill: University of North Carolina Press, 1995), 31–34; Cott, *Public Vows*, 52–55, 65–66, 168–169.
15 For example, Susan P. W. Hall of Virginia submitted a claim for property appropriated by the Union army both before her husband's death, which had legally belonged to him at the time of its appropriation, and after her husband's death, which had legally belonged to her at the time of its appropriation. Because Hall only submitted evidence of her own loyalty and not her husband's, the commissioners only granted compensation for the property that she legally owned at the time of its taking, property taken after her husband's death. See Summary Report, 1878, Susan P. W. Hall Allowed Claim, Culpeper County, Virginia. On the commissioners' procedures in estate claims, see Second General Report, 3. The commissioners' requirement that heirs prove their loyalty differed from the practice in the Court of Claims. See Klingberg, *The Southern Claims Commission*, 148.
16 Of the white female claimants rejected in 1877 on the loyalty question, the commissioners judged 57 percent with their husbands, sons, and other male relatives. This figure is tallied from Summary Reports, 1877, in P2257.
17 The commissioners insisted on proof of title from white female claimants because they suspected that men submitted claims in their wives' names on the assumption that women would be held to less rigorous standards. Confederates had adopted a similar strategy during the war, placing their plantations in their wives' names to take advantage of privileges offered to loyal southerners.
18 White female claimants primarily addressed their loyal actions in response to a question directed at all claimants: "Did you ever voluntarily contribute money, property, or services to the Union cause?" The commissioners complemented this general question with several specific questions for male claimants on votes on secession and service in the military, but they had no comparable questions for white female claimants. For the question directed toward all claimants, see "Standing Interrogatories," 1874, number 11 in Appendix B. For the questions directed toward male claimants, see "Standing Interrogatories," 1874, numbers 44 and 51 in Appendix B.
19 This redundancy only applied to white female claimants. The interrogatories only queried white male claimants about "near relatives" in Confederate service once.

"Standing Interrogatories," 1871, number 23; "Standing Interrogatories," 1872, numbers 30 and 42; and "Standing Interrogatories," 1874, numbers 36 and 69 in Appendix B.

20 Mary L. White Testimony, July 1, 1872, Mary L. White Disallowed Claim, Albemarle County, Virginia, in M1407, Fiche 1,016.

21 Agnes Withers Testimony, March 4, 1878, Thornton Withers Estate Disallowed Claim, Fauquier County, Virginia, in M1407, Fiche 4,084.

22 Mary Elizabeth Finnall Testimony, May 14, 1877, and September 13–19, 1877, Meredith Eskridge Estate Allowed Claim, Fauquier County, Virginia. Finnall's witnesses also testified similarly. Susan Y. Oliver Testimony, May 14, 1877, and September 13–19, 1877, ibid.; William D. Cooper Testimony, May 14, 1877, and September 13–19, 1877, ibid.; Solomon R. Moxley, May 14, 1877, and September 13–19, 1877, ibid.

23 Summary Report, 1874, Anna Dixon Allowed Claim, Fauquier County, Virginia. Dixon's husband's vote for Lincoln is corroborated in other sources. See Eugene M. Scheel, *The Civil War in Fauquier County, Virginia* (Warrenton, VA: Fauquier National Bank, 1985), 12.

24 Summary Report, 1872, Martha A. F. Terrett Allowed Claim, Alexandria County, Virginia. See also Summary Report, 1872, Nancy M. Webb Allowed Claim, Walker County, Alabama; Summary Report, 1876, Lavinia Allen Allowed Claim, Culpeper County, Virginia; Summary Report, 1876, Louisa E. Sparks Allowed Claim, Colbert County, Alabama.

25 The federal government, for example, recognized the patriotic sacrifices of soldiers' wives by providing pensions to widows of Union soldiers. For a discussion of the political importance of "soldiers' wives" in the Confederacy, see McCurry, "Citizens, Soldiers' Wives and 'Hiley Hope Up' Slaves," 95–124.

26 Henrietta Bowden Testimony, June 2, 1872, Henrietta S. Bowden Allowed Claim, Norfolk County, Virginia.

27 Summary Report, 1876, Mary Jane Clem Allowed Claim, Shenandoah County, Virginia. See also Summary Report, 1878, Eliza Robertson Allowed Claim, Gordon County, Georgia; Summary Report, 1876, Parthenia J. Collins Allowed Claim, Prince George County, Virginia.

28 Summary Report, 1879, Nancy Hancock Allowed Claim, Bradley County, Tennessee. See also Summary Report, 1873, Elizabeth Clevenger Allowed Claim, Jefferson County, Tennessee; Summary Report, 1876, Mary Elmore Allowed Claim, Jefferson County, Tennessee; Summary Report, 1878, Meredith Eskridge Estate Allowed Claim, Fauquier County, Virginia; Summary Report, 1879, Betty Ann Hamilton Allowed Claim, Henderson County, North Carolina; Summary Report, 1875, Mary Jones Allowed Claim, Hamilton County, Tennessee; Summary Report, 1874, Ardelia A. Lawson Allowed Claim, Bradley County, Tennessee; Summary Report, 1878, Eliza Robertson Allowed Claim, Gordon County, Georgia; Summary Report, 1880, Mary M. Welborn Allowed Claim, Gibbs County, North Carolina.

29 Amy Murrell Taylor, *The Divided Family in Civil War America* (Chapel Hill: University of North Carolina Press, 2005), 13–62, 91–122, quotations at 119–120.

30 Julia A. Nutt Testimony, March 19, 1874, Stephanie M. Chotard Allowed Claim, Concordia Parish, Louisiana; Major Gen. W. H. Emory to the Commissioners of Southern Claims, February 15, 1872, ibid.; Josiah Winchester Testimony, December

24, 1872, ibid. On Robert J. Walker's brand of southern Unionism, see James Patrick Shenton, *Robert John Walker, A Politician from Jackson to Lincoln* (New York: Columbia University Press, 1961); Frederick Merk, "A Safety Valve Thesis and Texan Annexation," *Mississippi Valley Historical Review* 49, no. 3 (December 1962): 413–436; Pearl T. Ponce, "Pledges and Principles," *Kansas History* 27, no. 1/2 (Summer 2004): 86–99; Paul E. Sturdevant, "Robert John Walker and Texas Annexation: A Lost Champion," *Southwestern Historical Quarterly* 109, no. 2 (October 2005): 188–202.

31 Ellen E. Evans Testimony, April 27, 1874, Ellen E. Evans Disallowed Claim, Henrico County, Virginia, in M1407, Fiche 3,984; C. M. Davis Testimony, April 27, 1874, ibid. Evans' account of her divorce fits with lawmakers' and judges' reluctance to allow divorce on the grounds of political differences. See Taylor, *The Divided Family in Civil War America*, 39. It also fits with the movement among southern judges to grant divorces as remedies for "wronged wives." See Jane Turner Censer, "'Smiling Through Her Tears': Antebellum Southern Women and Divorce," *American Journal of Legal History* 25, no. 1 (January 1981): 24–47; Silkenat, *Moments of Despair*, 77.

32 The commissioners judged white women by their male relatives even when the loyalty of their male relatives was not at issue. For example, of the white female claimants who were rejected in 1877 on the loyalty question and who owned property in their own right, 67 percent found themselves condemned at least partially on the basis of the disloyalty of one or more of their male relatives. Because the women owned the property themselves at the time the Union army had appropriated it, the commissioners technically did not consider the male relatives' loyalties as relevant in and of themselves. They considered them only as indications of the female claimants' loyalties. In many (71 percent) of these cases, the most damning evidence against these white female claimants was the mere fact that they had male relatives who supported the Confederacy, and this evidence sometimes outweighed claimants' identification of what they considered loyal sympathies and contributions. The commissioners cited no evidence that these claimants had possessed any Confederate sympathies or contributed to the Confederacy. These figures are tallied from Summary Reports, 1877, in P2257.

33 For an example of a claim in which the commissioners cited a Confederate husband as evidence against a white female claimant, see Summary Report, 1877, Sarah A. Ganey Disallowed Claim, Wilkinson County, Georgia, in P2257. For an example of a claim in which the commissioners cited a Confederate father, see Summary Report, 1878, Delilia Day Disallowed Claim, Culpeper County, Virginia, in P2257. For an example of a claim in which the commissioners cited a Confederate son in law, see Summary Report, 1877, Hannah Stull Disallowed Claim, Alleghany County, Virginia, in P2257. For an example of claim in which the commissioners cited a Confederate uncle, see Summary Report, 1877, Marthia E. Smith Disallowed Claim, Marborough County, South Carolinia, in P2257.

34 For example, the commissioners ruled against Adam Coe of Tennessee because he had not voted against secession. They noted, "It is remarkable that he did not manifest his loyalty at the elections in Tennessee when the question of secession was distinctly presented, especially in June, 1861. This was the most important

Notes to pp. 76–79

opportunity presented to him for aiding the Union, yet he says he did not vote." See Summary Report, 1880, Adam Coe Disallowed Claim, Davidson County, Tennessee, in P2257.
35 Summary Report, 1875, Stephanie M. Chotard Allowed Claim, Concordia Parish, Louisiana.
36 Summary Report, 1879, Ellen E. Evans Disallowed Claim, Henrico County, Virginia, in M1407, Fiche 3,984.
37 Summary Report, 1877, James L. Coman Disallowed Claim, Limestone County, Alabama, in P2257.
38 Summary Report, 1878, Harriet A. Hart Disallowed Claim, Liberty County, Georgia, in Court of Claims, Docket No. 4,019.
39 Laura F. Edwards, *Gendered Strife & Confusion: The Political Culture of Reconstruction* (Urbana: University of Illinois Press, 1997), 25–31.
40 Eliza A. Clarke Testimony, April 25, 1872, Eliza A. Clarke Disallowed Claim, Roanoke County, Virginia, in M1407, Fiche 443–444; Summary Report, 1872, ibid.
41 Mary Jane Gordon Testimony, November 5, 1875, Mary Jane Covington Disallowed Claim, Amite County, Mississippi, in M1407, Fiche 1,988. See also Summary Report, 1873, Ellen Daniels Disallowed Claim, Washington Parish, Louisiana, in M1407, Fiche 685; Narcissa Monroe Testimony, April and May 1877, Narcissa Monroe Disallowed Claim, Fairfax County, Virginia, in M1407, Fiche 4,036; Martha A. E. Rice Testimony, February 18, 1878, Fleming Rice Estate Disallowed Claim, Floyd County, Georgia, in Court of Claims, Docket No. 3,161.
42 Eliza A. Lively Testimony, November 12, 1872, Eliza A. Lively Disallowed Claim, Elizabeth City, Virginia, in M1407, Fiche 1,478.
43 Mary E. Jennings Testimony, February 27, 1873, Joseph L. Jennings Estate Allowed Claim, Fauquier County, Virginia. See also Nancy Jones Testimony, January 21, 1873, Nancy Jones Disallowed Claim, Wake County, North Carolina, in Court of Claims, Docket No. 8,977; Eliza M. Parrott Testimony, May 17, 1878, Eliza M. Parrott Disallowed Claim, West Baton Rouge County, Louisiana, in M1407, Fiche 2,978.
44 Mary Jane Gordon Testimony, November 5, 1875, Mary Jane Covington Disallowed Claim, Amite County, Mississippi, in M1407, Fiche 1,988. See also Eliza A. Cochran Testimony, July 15, 1876, Eliza A. Cochran Disallowed Claim, Orleans Parish, Louisiana, in Court of Claims, Docket No. 1,945; Bethany Gray Testimony, September 29, 1873, Bethany Gray Allowed Claim, Lauderdale County, Alabama; Mary Lowe Testimony, February 25, 1878, Mary Lowe Disallowed Claim, Arkansas County, Arkansas, in M1407, Fiche 4,118–4,119; Harriet Lunceford Testimony, December 21 to 22, 1877, Harriet Lunceford Disallowed Claim, Fauquier County, Virginia, in M1407, Fiche 4,025.
45 Margaret Johnson Testimony, May 5, 1873, Margaret Johnson Disallowed Claim, Warren County, Mississippi, in M1407, Fiche 1,696. See also Tabitha Courter Testimony, June 6, 1873, Tabitha Courter Disallowed Claim, Chatham County, Georgia, in Court of Claims, Docket No. 4,031; Julia M. Wilburn Testimony, September 28 and 29, 1875, Julia M. Wilburn Allowed Claim, Benton County, Mississippi.
46 Tabitha Courter Testimony, June 6, 1873, Tabitha Courter Disallowed Claim, Chatham County, Georgia, in Court of Claims, Docket No. 4,031.

47 Harriet Lunceford Testimony, December 21 to 22, 1877, Harriet Lunceford Disallowed Claim, Fauquier County, Virginia, in M1407, Fiche 4,025. See also Eliza A. Cochran Testimony, July 15, 1876, Eliza A. Cochran Disallowed Claim, Orleans Parish, Louisiana, in Court of Claims, Docket No. 1,945.

48 Mary J. Ellison Testimony, August 14, 1872, Mary J. Ellison Disallowed Claim, Whitfield County, Georgia, in M1407, Fiche 1,142. For an additional example, see Susan W. Peterson Testimony, September 5, 1873, Susan W. Peterson Disallowed Claim, Warren County, Virginia, in Court of Claims, Docket No. 8,707.

49 Drew Gilpin Faust, *Mothers of Invention: Women of the Slaveholding South in the American Civil War* (Chapel Hill: University of North Carolina Press, 1996), 20–23.

50 Narcissa Monroe Testimony, April and May 1877, Narcissa Monroe Disallowed Claim, Fairfax County, Virginia, in M1407, Fiche 4,036; Jane C. Vandiver Testimony, May 18, 1872, Jane C. Vandiver Disallowed Claim, Floyd County, Georgia, in Court of Claims, Docket No. 9,462; Eliza White Testimony, May 7, 1872, Eliza White Disallowed Claim, Jefferson County, Arkansas, in M1407, Fiche 3,409–3,410; Summary Report, 1876, Sarah M. Thomas Disallowed Claim, Adams or Hinds County, Mississippi, in P2257. On providentialism, see Steven E. Woodworth, *While God Is Marching On: The Religious World of Civil War Soldiers* (Lawrence: University Press of Kansas, 2001), 27–39; Mark A. Noll, *The Civil War as a Theological Crisis* (Chapel Hill: University of North Carolina Press, 2006), 75–94; George C. Rable, *God's Almost Chosen Peoples: A Religious History of the American Civil War* (Chapel Hill: University of North Carolina Press, 2010), 54–55, 248, 345.

51 Summary Report, 1872, Victoria E. Essex Disallowed Claim, Fauquier County, Virginia, in M1407, Fiche 454.

52 Summary Report, 1876, Mary Jane Covington Disallowed Claim, Amite County, Mississippi, in M1407, Fiche 1,988.

53 Summary Report, 1873, Jane C. Vandiver Disallowed Claim, Floyd County, Georgia, in Court of Claims, Docket No. 9,462.

54 On northern women, see Jeanie Attie, *Patriotic Toil: Northern Women and the American Civil War* (Ithaca, NY: Cornell University Press, 1998); Carol Faulkner, *Women's Radical Reconstruction: The Freedmen's Aid Movement* (Philadelphia: University of Pennsylvania Press, 2004); Nina Silber, *Daughters of the Union: Northern Women Fight the Civil War* (Cambridge, MA: Harvard University Press, 2005), 123–221. On southern women, see George C. Rable, *Civil Wars: Women and the Crisis of Southern Nationalism* (Urbana: University of Illinois Press, 1989), 144–151; LeeAnn Whites, *The Civil War as a Crisis in Gender: Augusta, Georgia, 1860–1890* (Athens: University of Georgia Press, 1995), 41–63, 132–159; Faust, *Mothers of Invention*, 9–29, 80–113, 248–254; Elizabeth R. Varon, *We Mean to Be Counted: White Women & Politics in Antebellum Virginia* (Chapel Hill: University of North Carolina Press, 1998), 71–177.

55 Southern Claims Commission Memorandum, January 19, 1880, Martha W. Dunbar Allowed Claim, Adams County, Mississippi; Martha D. Claiborne Testimony, October 12, 1876, ibid.; Summary Report, 1880, ibid. On the link between rights and obligations as they apply to women, see Kerber, *No Constitutional Right to Be Ladies*, xxi.

56 Summary Report, 1880, Milly Wilson Allowed Claim, DeKalb County, Georgia.

57 See Summary Report, 1876, Harriet Howard Allowed Claim, Baldwin County, Georgia; Summary Report, 1878, Mary E. Davis Allowed Claim, Fauquier County, Virginia; Summary Report, 1879, Mary Brogdon Allowed Claim, Effingham County, Georgia; Summary Report, 1879, Nancy Russell Allowed Claim, Bartow County, Georgia; Summary Report, 1878, Mary McDonald Allowed Claim, Bartow County, Georgia; Summary Report, 1880, Martha W. Dunbar Allowed Claim, Adams County, Mississippi.

58 Summary Report, 1878, Mary E. Davis Allowed Claim, Fauquier County, Virginia.

59 Martha W. Taylor Testimony, October 3, 1872, Martha W. Taylor Disallowed Claim, Shelby County, Tennessee, in Court of Claims, Docket No. 927; Chatham Adams Testimony, October 3, 1872, ibid.; Summary Report, 1879, ibid.

60 Gordon S. Wood, *The Radicalism of the American Revolution* (New York: Knopf, 1992); Elizabeth B. Clark, "'The Sacred Rights of the Weak': Pain, Sympathy, and the Culture of Individual Rights in Antebellum America," *Journal of American History* 82, no. 2 (1995): 463–493; Gregg D. Crane, "Dangerous Sentiments: Sympathy, Rights, and Revolution in Stowe's Antislavery Novels," *Nineteenth-Century Literature* 51, no. 2 (1996): 176–204; Andrew Burstein, "The Political Character of Sympathy," *Journal of the Early Republic* 21, no. 4 (2001): 601–632; Hoffert, *When Hens Crow*, 49.

61 See "Standing Interrogatories," 1871, number 33; "Standing Interrogatories," 1872, number 40; and "Standing Interrogatories," 1874, number 5 in Appendix B.

62 Amanda Davis Testimony, January 24, 1873, Amanda Davis Disallowed Claim, Washington County, Georgia, in M1407, Fiche 2,862; Amanda Davis to C. W. Bennett, January 6, 1878, ibid.; Amanda Davis Testimony, February 26, 1878, ibid. See also Mary S. Adams Testimony, November 27, 1872, Mary S. Adams Disallowed Claim, Franklin County, Arkansas, in M1407, Fiche 1,080; Elizabeth A. Anderson Testimony, March 6, 1878, Elizabeth A. Anderson Disallowed Claim, Bibb County, Georgia, in M1407, Fiche 3,420; Agnes Cauthen Testimony, n.d., Agnes Cauthen Disallowed Claim, Lancaster County, South Carolina, in Court of Claims, Docket No. 3,512; Martha J. Pyeatt Testimony, February 13, 1873, Martha J. Pyeatt Disallowed Claim, Washington County, Arkansas in Court of Claims, Docket No. 9,135; Amelia B. Taylor Testimony, January 2, 1873, Amelia B. Taylor Disallowed Claim, Richland County, South Carolina, in M1407, Fiche 1,739.

63 Adele Currin Testimony, January 23, 1872, Adele Currin Disallowed Claim, Rutherford County, Tennessee, in Court of Claims, Docket No. 8,577. See also Susan Davis Testimony, February 22, 1878, Susan Davis Disallowed Claim, Lumpkin County, Georgia, in Court of Claims, Docket No. 6,821; Elizabeth Dillard Testimony, December 1 and 2, 1874, Elizabeth Dillard Disallowed Claim, Jackson County, Alabama, in Court of Claims, Docket No. 9,360; Mattie Jarnigan Testimony, June 21, 1877, Mattie H. Jarnigan Disallowed Claim, Bolivar County, Mississippi, in Court of Claims, Docket No. 10,377; Eliza M. Parrott Testimony, May 17, 1878, Eliza M. Parrott Disallowed Claim, West Baton Rouge County, Louisiana, in M1407, Fiche 2978; Amelia B. Taylor Testimony, January 2, 1873, Amelia B. Taylor Disallowed Claim, Richland County, South Carolina, in M1407, Fiche 1,739.

64 James Freeman Testimony, February 25, 1878, James Freeman Disallowed Claim, Gates County, North Carolina, in M1407, Fiche 3,023.
65 Summary Report, 1874, Fanny Green Disallowed Claim, Shelby County, Tennessee, in M1407, Fiche 1,354.
66 Nancy H. Fair Testimony, May 5, 1873, Nancy H. Fair Disallowed Claim, Benton County, Arkansas, in M1407, Fiche 560–561. See also Ann Estes Testimony, August 21, 1873, Ann Estes Disallowed Claim, Orange County, Virginia, in Court of Claims, Docket No. 14,264; Martha A. E. Rice Testimony, February 18, 1878, Fleming Rice Estate Disallowed Claim, Floyd County, Georgia, in Court of Claims, Docket No. 3,161. For examples of white female claimants who submitted testimony that they had tried to influence their husbands' politics, see Rhoda H. Deane Testimony, February 22, 1878, Josiah C. Deane Disallowed Claim, Amherst County, Virginia, in M1407, Fiche 3,171; Josiah C. Deane Testimony, February 22, 1878, ibid.
67 Summary Report, 1878, Josiah C. Deane Disallowed Claim, Amherst County, Virginia, in M1407, Fiche 3,171; Summary Report, 1874, Martha Crane Disallowed Claim, Claiborne County, Mississippi, in P2257.
68 Robert Ayres to Elizabeth A. Anderson, November 21, 1873, Elizabeth A. Anderson Disallowed Claim, Bibb County, Georgia, in M1407, Fiche 3,420.
69 Summary Report, 1875, Susan W. Peterson Disallowed Claim, Warren County, Virginia, in Court of Claims, Docket No. 8,707.
70 Summary Report, 1875, Jane Prince Disallowed Claim, Panola County, Mississippi, in P2257.
71 Annie Horton Testimony, September 4, 1871, Annie Horton Disallowed Claim, Wake County, North Carolina, in M1407, Fiche 278.
72 Martha A. E. Rice Testimony, February 18, 1878, Fleming Rice Estate Disallowed Claim, Floyd County, Georgia, in Court of Claims, Docket No. 3,161. See also Ellen Daniels Testimony, March 1, 1873, Ellen Daniels Disallowed Claim, Washington Parish, Louisiana, in M1407, Fiche 685.
73 Summary Report, 1875, Lucy A. Weaver Disallowed Claim, Chattooga County, Georgia, in P2257.
74 Louisa Gooch Testimony, February 26, 1878, Louisa Gooch Disallowed Claim, Wake County, North Carolina, in M1407, Fiche 3,027. See also Summary Report, 1872, Annie Horton Disallowed Claim, Wake County, North Carolina, in P2257; Summary Report, 1878, Eliza and George Savoy Disallowed Claim, Warren County, Mississippi, in P2257; Summary Report, 1877, Nancy E. Wilson Disallowed Claim, Fulton County, Georgia, in P2257.
75 Mary S. Darden Testimony, July 14, 1874, Mary S. Darden Disallowed Claim, Hinds County, Mississippi, in Court of Claims, Docket No. 785. See also Agnes Cauthen Testimony, n.d., Agnes Cauthen Disallowed Claim, Lancaster County, South Carolina, in Court of Claims, Docket No. 3,512.
76 "Standing Interrogatories," 1874, number 69 in Appendix B.
77 Summary Report, 1874, Carrie E. Hambrick Disallowed Claim, DeKalb County, Georgia, in P2257.
78 Mary Sims Testimony, July 10, 1874, Clifford and Mary Sims Disallowed Claim, Desha, Arkansas, in M1407, Fiche 1,914.
79 Summary Report, 1876, Clifford and Mary Sims Disallowed Claim, Desha, Arkansas, in M1407, Fiche 1,914.

Notes to pp. 88–93

80 Amelia B. Taylor Testimony, January 2, 1873, Amelia B. Taylor Disallowed Claim, Richland County, South Carolina, in M1407, Fiche 1,739; Summary Report, 1875, ibid.

Chapter 4 Former Slaves' Union

1 C. W. Dudley to the Commissioners of Southern Claims, Bennettsville, South Carolina, April 20, 1871, in M87, Roll 2.
2 For an insightful discussion of slave agency, see Walter Johnson, "On Agency," *Journal of Social History* 37, no. 1 (2003): 113–124.
3 This chapter covers former slaves who had gained their freedom as a result of the war. Black southerners who had gained their freedom through purchase or manumission or who had been born free are addressed in Chapter 5.
4 Johnson Gary Testimony, April 22, 1872, James T. Ayler Disallowed Claim, Nansemond County, Virginia, in M1407, Fiche 3, 949–3,950.
5 For examples of the conflation of possible claimants with white southerners, see *Congressional Globe*, 40th Congress, 3rd Session (December 15, 1868), 88; *Congressional Globe*, 40th Congress, 3rd Session (January 11, 1869), 278. For an attempt to include slave property in compensation efforts, see *Congressional Globe*, 37th Congress, 2nd Session (May 15, 1862), 2154–2155. For a rare instance of black southerners mentioned as possible claimants, see *Congressional Globe*, 41st Congress, 2nd Session (June 13, 1870), 4411.
6 W. B. Figures to Charles F. Benjamin, July 26, [1871], in M87, Roll 2.
7 See "Standing Interrogatories," 1871, numbers 33, 9–10, 30, 7, 27–28; "Standing Interrogatories," 1872, numbers 40, 9–15, 37, 7, 34–35 in Appendix B.
8 E. H. Stiles to Charles F. Benjamin, April 16, 1874, in M87, Roll 5.
9 According to the technical wording of the interrogatories, former slaves answered questions reserved for male and female claimants. The commissioners, however, were primarily thinking of white claimants when they devised their sections for men and women. The section for male claimants included questions on several disloyal acts, many of which did not apply to black men, including voting in elections and participating in vigilance committees. The section for female claimants asked questions intended for white women, including whether they belonged to "any sewing-society organized to make clothing for confederate soldiers or their families." Also, because many special commissioners reserved the male and female sections of the interrogatories for white claimants, in much of the testimony taken under the 1874 version, former slaves were never asked about their loyalties. See "Standing Interrogatories," 1874, numbers 44–51; "Standing Interrogatories," 1874, number 69 in Appendix B.
10 Major Middleton Testimony, January 27, 1873, Major Middleton Allowed Claim, Chatham County, Georgia. See also Diana Cummings Testimony, June 17, 1873, Diana Cummings Allowed Claim, Chatham County, Georgia; Samuel McIver Testimony, November 21, 1872, Samuel McIver Allowed Claim, Chatham County, Georgia; Alexander Steele Testimony, August 17, 1872, Alexander Steele Allowed Claim, Chatham County, Georgia.
11 James Burwell Testimony, July 10, 1877, Henry Mosby Allowed Claim, Roanoke County, Virginia. See also Ephraim Wynn Testimony, February 6, 1873, Ephraim Wynn Allowed Claim, Dinwiddie County, Virginia.

12 Charles Jess Testimony, March 12, 1873, Mary Jess Allowed Claim, Chatham County, Georgia.
13 W. E. B. DuBois, *Black Reconstruction in America*, 1935; repr., (New York: Atheneum, 1992), 55–86; Benjamin Quarles, *The Negro in the Civil War* (Boston: Little, Brown, 1953); Benjamin Quarles, *The Negro in the American Revolution* (New York: Norton, 1961); Herbert Aptheker, *American Negro Slave Revolts* (New York: Columbia University Press, 1943); Kenneth Wiggins Porter, *The Negro on the American Frontier* (New York: Arno Press, 1971); J. Leitch Wright, *Creeks & Seminoles: The Destruction and Regeneration of the Muscogulge People* (Lincoln: University of Nebraska Press, 1986); Sylvia R. Frey, *Water from the Rock: Black Resistance in a Revolutionary Age* (Princeton, NJ: Princeton University Press, 1991); Jane Landers, *Black Society in Spanish Florida* (Urbana: University of Illinois Press, 1999); Claudio Saunt, *A New Order of Things: Property, Power, and the Transformation of the Creek Indians, 1733–1816* (Cambridge and New York: Cambridge University Press, 1999); Christopher Brown and Philip D. Morgan, eds., *Arming Slaves: From Classical Times to the Modern Age* (New Haven: Yale University Press, 2006); Steven Hahn, *The Political Worlds of Slavery and Freedom* (Cambridge, MA: Harvard University Press, 2009); Watson W. Jennison, *Cultivating Race: The Expansion of Slavery in Georgia, 1750–1860* (Lexington: University Press of Kentucky, 2012).
14 John Cuthbert Testimony, April 15, 1873, John Cuthbert Allowed Claim, Chatham County, Georgia.
15 Edward Harper Testimony, January 3, 1873, Edward Harper Allowed Claim, Elbert County, Georgia. See also Littleton Barber Allowed Claim, Adams County, Mississippi; Johnson Boyd Testimony, November 21, 1872, Johnson Boyd Disallowed Claim, Sebastian County, Arkansas, in M1407, Fiche 1568; Noah Brown Testimony, July 10, 1873, Noah Brown Allowed Claim, Adams County, Mississippi; Richard Dorsey Testimony, July 8, 1873, Richard Dorsey Allowed Claim, Adams County, Mississippi; Richard Freeman Testimony, September 5, 1871, Richard Freeman Allowed Claim, Norfolk County, Virginia; Edward W. Whitehurst Testimony, July 31, 1877, Edward W. Whitehurst Allowed Claim, Elizabeth City County, Virginia; Ephraim Wynn Testimony, February 6, 1873, Ephraim Wynn Allowed Claim, Dinwiddie County, Virginia.
16 Summary Report, Richard Dorsey Allowed Claim, Adams County, Mississippi. See also Summary Report, Mary Cowling Allowed Claim, Norfolk County, Virginia; Summary Report, Richard Freeman Allowed Claim, Norfolk County, Virginia; Summary Report, Edward Whitehurst Allowed Claim, Elizabeth City County, Virginia.
17 Summary Report, Edward Harper Allowed Claim, Elbert County, Georgia.
18 Jerry Brown Testimony, December 19, 1873, Jerry Brown Allowed Claim, Chatham County, Georgia; Stephen Gildersleeve Testimony, December 19, 1873, ibid.; Summary Report, 1876, ibid.
19 Charles Bromfield Testimony, January 17, 1874, William Anderson Allowed Claim, Chatham County, Georgia; William Harris Testimony, November 19, 1872, William Harris Allowed Claim, Chatham County, Georgia; Stephen Carter Testimony, December 26, 1873, Stephen Carter Allowed Claim, Chatham County, Georgia; Phebe Carter Testimony, December 26, 1873, Stephen Carter Allowed

Claim, Chatham County, Georgia. See also Rachel Bromfield Testimony, January 8, 1873, Rachel Bromfield Allowed Claim, Chatham County, Georgia; Francis Keaton Testimony, April 8, 1873, Francis Keaton Allowed Claim, Chatham County, Georgia; Henry Murray Testimony, February 28, 1873, Henry Murray Allowed Claim, Muscogee County, Georgia.

20 James Carter Testimony, March 31, 1874, Katherine S. Minor Allowed Claim, Adams County, Mississippi. See George W. Carter Testimony, July 8, 1873, Richard Dorsey Allowed Claim, Adams County, Mississippi, for the high estimate of sixty. See also Winthrop D. Jordan, *Tumult and Silence at Second Creek: An Inquiry into a Civil War Slave Conspiracy* (Baton Rouge: Louisiana State University Press, 1993); Anthony E. Kaye, *Joining Places: Slave Neighborhoods in the Old South* (Chapel Hill: University of North Carolina Press, 2007).

21 James K. Hyman Testimony, July 8, 1873, Richard Dorsey Allowed Claim, Adams County, Mississippi.

22 Jerry Myres Testimony, March 18, 1875, Straffon Herb Allowed Claim, Chatham County, Georgia.

23 Rebecca Williams Testimony, June 3, 1873, Alfred Barnard Allowed Claim, Chatham County, Georgia. See also Lafayette DeLegal Testimony, July 11, 1872, Lafayette DeLegal Allowed Claim, Liberty County, Georgia.

24 Judy Rose Testimony, January 20, 1873, Judy Rose Allowed Claim, Chatham County, Georgia.

25 Littleton Barber Testimony, August 17, 1873, Littleton Barber Allowed Claim, Adams County, Mississippi; James K. Hyman Testimony, July 8, 1873, Richard Dorsey Allowed Claim, Adams County, Mississippi; and Henry Farrar Testimony, July 15, 1873, Butler Williams Disallowed Claim, Adams County, Mississippi, in M1407, Fiche 3,663.

26 George Corprew Testimony, September 7, 1871, George Corprew Allowed Claim, Norfolk County, Virginia.

27 On spreading rumors as political acts, see Hahn, *A Nation Under Our Feet*, 116–159. For an analysis of slave communication networks using the Southern Claims Commission records, see Justin Behrend, "Rebellious Talk and Conspiratorial Plots: The Making of a Slave Insurrection in Civil War Natchez," *Journal of Southern History* 77, no. 1 (February 2011): 17–52. On the role of rumor in sustaining Confederate will to fight, see Jason Phillips, "The Grape Vine Telegraph: Rumors and Confederate Persistence," *Journal of Southern History* **74**, no. 4 (November 2006): 753–788.

28 Peter Miller Testimony, June 10, 1873, Peter Miller Allowed Claim, Chatham County, Georgia; Mary Hall Testimony, March 19, 1875, Straffon Herb Allowed Claim, Chatham County, Georgia; James K. Hyman Testimony, July 8, 1873, Richard Dorsey Allowed Claim, Adams County, Mississippi. See also Mary Anderson Testimony, William Anderson Allowed Claim, Chatham County, Georgia; Charles Bromfield Testimony, January 17, 1874, William Anderson Allowed Claim, Chatham County, Georgia; David Combs Testimony, July 16, 1873, David Combs Allowed Claim, Adams County, Mississippi; John Smith Testimony, July 16, 1873, David Combs Allowed Claim, Adams County, Mississippi; Diana Cummings Testimony, June 17, 1873, Diana Cummings Allowed Claim, Chatham County, Georgia; Lafayette DeLegal Testimony, July 11, 1872, Lafayette DeLegal Allowed

Claim, Liberty County, Georgia; Richard Freeman Testimony, September 5, 1871, Richard Freeman Allowed Claim, Norfolk County, Virginia; William Harris Testimony, November 19, 1872, William Harris Allowed Claim, Chatham County, Georgia; Cato Keating Testimony, June 26, 1873, Cato Keating Allowed Claim, Chatham County, Georgia.

29 John Ford Testimony, January 17, 1872, Benjamin Sterling Turner Allowed Claim, Dallas County, Alabama. See also Edward Mordic Testimony, March 17, 1873, Edward Mordic and Jacob Hicks Allowed Claim, Chatham County, Georgia.

30 Joseph Bacon Testimony, August 12, 1873, Joseph Bacon Allowed Claim, Liberty County, Georgia.

31 Clarence L. Mohr, *On the Threshold of Freedom: Masters and Slaves in Civil War Georgia* (Athens: University of Georgia Press, 1986), 120–148, 160, 172; James H. Brewer, *The Confederate Negro: Virginia's Craftsmen and Military Laborers, 1861–1865* (Tuscaloosa: University of Alabama Press, 2007), 9–11.

32 Benjamin Sterling Turner Testimony, April 21, 1871, Benjamin Sterling Turner Allowed Claim, Dallas County, Alabama. See also William Holland Testimony, June 30, 1873, William Holland Allowed Claim, Fulton County, Georgia; Peter Storrs Testimony, February 7, 1872, Peter Storrs Allowed Claim, Hanover County, Virginia.

33 Adrien Croizet Testimony, February 22, 1874, Adrien Croizet Allowed Claim, Pointe Coupée Parish, Louisiana. See also Crawford Monroe Testimony, June 13, 1874, Crawford Monroe Allowed Claim, Fulton County, Georgia.

34 William Jackson Testimony, April 22, 1874, George Markham Disallowed Claim, Warren County, Mississippi, in Court of Claims, Docket No. 1,168.

35 D. H. Bragonier to Charles Benjamin, March 17, 1874, in M87, Roll 5.

36 For examples when the commissioners ignored the issue of loyalty in their reports to Congress, see Summary Report, 1879, Ephraim Wynn Allowed Claim, Dinwiddie County, Virginia; Summary Report, 1878, William L. Ashton Allowed Claim, Fairfax County, Virginia; Summary Report, 1878, William James Allowed Claim, Henrico County, Virginia; Summary Report, 1873, Peter Pintler Allowed Claim, Norfolk County, Virginia; Summary Report, 1878, Henry Mosby Allowed Claim, Roanoke County, Virginia. For an example when the commission noted that loyalty had been established by the testimony, see Summary Report, 1874, Littleton Barber Allowed Claim, Adams County, Mississippi.

37 Summary Report, 1876, James S. Dean Disallowed Claim, Fauquier County, Virginia, in P2257.

38 Summary Report, 1874, John Patterson Disallowed Claim, Mobile County, Alabama, in P2257. See also Summary Report, 1879, Martha Gibbs Disallowed Claim, Warren County, Mississippi, in P2257; Summary Report, 1879, Elizabeth Lyman Disallowed Claim, Louisa County, Virginia, in P2257; Summary Report, 1879, Henry Lecount Disallowed Claim, Liberty County, Georgia, in P2257. For other dismissals of the capabilities of former slaves, see Summary Report, 1875, Levi J. Thompson Disallowed Claim, Chatham County, Georgia, in P2257; Summary Report, 1874, Benjamin Y. Trotter Disallowed Claim, Monroe County, Arkansas, in P2257.

39 R. B. Avery Report, July 1, 1878, Thomas Butler Allowed Claim, Chatham County, Georgia.

40 Charles Benjamin of the Office of the Commissioners of Claims to [illegible], February 20, 1877, Blucher Hudnall Allowed Claim, Fauquier County, Virginia.
41 Henry Beedles Testimony, July 8, 1873, Henry and Polly Beedles Allowed Claim, Fulton County, Georgia; Polly Beedles Testimony, July 8, 1873, ibid. See also Tillman Rhew Testimony, August 17, 1873, Littleton Barber Allowed Claim, Adams County, Mississippi; Charles Jess Testimony, March 12, 1873, Mary Jess Allowed Claim, Chatham County, Georgia; Mary Ann Pollard Testimony, November 29, 1876, Reuben Pollard Estate Allowed Claim, Fauquier County, Virginia.
42 Historians generally focus on the political uses of friendship as white men moved from subjects to citizens. Lizabeth Cohen, *Making a New Deal: Industrial Workers in Chicago, 1919–1939* (Cambridge: Cambridge University Press, 1990); Alan Taylor, *William Cooper's Town: Power and Persuasion on the Frontier of the Early American Republic* (New York: A. A. Knopf, 1995); Caleb Crain, *American Sympathy: Men, Friendship, and Literature in the New Nation* (New Haven: Yale University Press, 2001); Ivy Schweitzer, *Perfecting Friendship: Politics and Affiliation in Early American Literature* (Chapel Hill: University of North Carolina Press, 2006); Richard Godbeer, *The Overflowing of Friendship: Love Between Men and the Creation of the American Republic* (Baltimore: Johns Hopkins University Press, 2009).
43 Ira Berlin, *Slaves No More: Three Essays on Emancipation and the Civil War* (Cambridge and New York: Cambridge University Press, 1992); Rothman, *Slave Country*; Gallagher, *The Union War*.
44 Benjamin Sterling Turner Testimony, April 21, 1871, Benjamin Sterling Turner Allowed Claim, Dallas County, Alabama. Turner served as a representative from Alabama in the 42nd Congress from March 4, 1871, to March 3, 1873. As a congressman, Turner supported amnesty for former Confederates, proposing one bill to remove the disabilities imposed by the Fourteenth Amendment and several additional bills to remove disabilities from white Alabamans. For further information on Turner, see Stephen Middleton, ed., *Black Congressmen During Reconstruction: A Documentary Sourcebook* (Westport, CT: Greenwood Press, 2002), 349–356.
45 For more on the assertion of this mythical Union, see Blight, "'For Something Beyond the Battlefield'" 1156–1178.
46 Thomas Williams Testimony, August 28, 1873, Pleasant B. Barton Disallowed Claim, Colbert County, Alabama, in Court of Claims, Docket No. 8,220. See also Rodney Morrell Testimony, November 12, 1872, Thomas Butler Allowed Claim, Chatham County, Georgia; David Moses Testimony, March 25, 1873, David Moses Allowed Claim, Chatham County, Georgia.
47 Bryant Wallace Testimony, October 9, 1875, Edmund Boone Disallowed Claim, Washington County, Arkansas, in M1407, Fiche 2,794.
48 Abraham Johnston Testimony, August 12, 1872, Abraham Johnston Allowed Claim, Chatham County, Georgia. See also Thomas Steward Testimony, January 8, 1873, Rachel Bromfield Allowed Claim, Chatham County, Georgia; Paul Jackson Testimony, September 12, 1872, Harriett Dallas Allowed Claim, Chatham County, Georgia; George Gardner Testimony, November 15, 1872, George Gardner Disallowed Claim, Chatham County, Georgia, in M1407, Fiche 3,467.
49 Summary Report, 1880, Levi Allain Allowed Claim, Pointe Coupée Parish, Louisiana; Levi Allain Testimony, November 6, 1876, ibid. See also Antoine

Baptiste Testimony, March 3, 1874, Antoine Baptiste Disallowed Claim, Pointe Coupée Parish, Louisiana, in M1407, Fiche 2,409.

50 Joseph Proctor Testimony, July 9, 1872, Celia Boisfeillet Allowed Claim, Chatham County, Georgia. See also Andrew Montgomery Testimony, July 8, 1873, Henry and Polly Beedles Allowed Claim, Fulton County, Georgia; Charles Harris Testimony, December 6, 1872, Charles Harris Disallowed Claim, Crawford County, Arkansas, in M1407, Fiche 1,575; Mary Hall Testimony, March 19, 1875, Straffon Herb Allowed Claim, Chatham County, Georgia; Delia Rivers Testimony, April 3, 1873, Georgiana Kelley Allowed Claim, Chatham County, Georgia.

51 This contrasts with the commissioners' key events as stressed in their interrogatories: "the battle of Bull Run or Manassas, the capture of New Orleans, the fall of Vicksburgh, and the final surrender of the confederate forces." "Standing Interrogatories," 1874, number 14 in Appendix B.

52 For scholars who stress the agency of Abraham Lincoln and Union soldiers, see James M. McPherson, "Who Freed the Slaves?" in *Drawn with the Sword: Reflections on the American Civil War* (New York: Oxford University Press, 1996), 192–207; Manning, *What This Cruel War Was Over*. For scholars who stress the agency of slaves themselves, see DuBois, *Black Reconstruction in America*, 55–86; Berlin, *Slaves No More*; Ira Berlin, "Who Freed the Slaves? Emancipation and Its Meaning," in *Union and Emancipation: Essays on Politics and Race in the Civil War Era*, ed. David W. Blight and Brooks D. Simpson (Kent, OH: Kent State University Press, 1997), 105–121.

53 Others have noted that former slaves before the Southern Claims Commission did not credit themselves with emancipation, but they did not explore possible benefits of doing so. See, for example, Medford, "'I Was Always a Union Man'"; Kaye, "Slaves, Emancipation, and the Powers of War." On the assertion of a mythical abolition Union to argue for the extension of equality to former slaves, see Blight, "'For Something Beyond the Battlefield,'" 1156–1178.

54 David Combs Testimony, July 16, 1873, David Combs Allowed Claim, Adams County, Mississippi. See also David Thompson Testimony, March 31, 1877, William L. Ashton Allowed Claim, Fairfax County, Virginia; David Combs Testimony, July 16, 1873, David Combs Allowed Claim, Adams County, Mississippi; Jasper Ampey Testimony, February 6, 1873, Ephraim Wynn Allowed Claim, Dinwiddie County, Virginia.

55 Historians have relied on the Southern Claims Commission records to explore black propertyholding. See Morgan, "The Ownership of Property by Slaves in the Mid-Nineteenth-Century Low Country"; Penningroth, "Slavery, Freedom, and Social Claims to Property Among African Americans in Liberty County, Georgia, 1850–1880"; Penningroth, *The Claims of Kinfolk*; Penningroth, "The Claims of Slaves and Ex-Slaves to Family and Property."

56 Nancy Jones Testimony, February 18, 1876, Nancy Jones Allowed Claim, Madison County, Alabama. See also James Cusbert Testimony, October 6, 1877, James Cusbert Disallowed Claim, Liberty County, Georgia, in M1407, Fiche 2,860; Thomas S. Garrett Testimony, September 20, 1871, Thomas Garrett Allowed Claim, Chatham County, Georgia; Stephen Geldersleeve Testimony, December 18, 1873, Stephen Geldersleeve Allowed Claim, Chatham County, Georgia; Josiah H. Grant Testimony, January 6, 1873, Josiah H. Grant Allowed Claim, Chatham County, Georgia.

57 Mary Jess Testimony, March 12, 1873, Mary Jess Allowed Claim, Chatham County, Georgia.
58 James Miller Testimony, January 22, 1873, James Miller Disallowed Claim, Chatham County, Georgia, in M1407, Fiche 2,912. See also Josiah H. Grant Testimony, January 6, 1873, Josiah H. Grant Allowed Claim, Chatham County, Georgia.
59 Prince Ponder Testimony, June 15, 1874, Prince Ponder Allowed Claim, Fulton County, Georgia.
60 Special Commissioner Virgil Hillyer Remarks, September 12, 1872, Harriett Dallas Allowed Claim, Chatham County, Georgia. Hillyer's remarks made in the claim of a free black woman applied to both free blacks and former slaves.
61 Claude F. Oubre, *Forty Acres and a Mule: The Freedmen's Bureau and Black Land Ownership* (Baton Rouge: Louisiana State University Press, 1978).
62 "Standing Interrogatories," 1874, number 70 in Appendix B.
63 Summary Report, 1878, Houston Booby Disallowed Claim, Liberty County, Georgia, in P2257.
64 See, for example, Summary Report, 1878, James Miller Disallowed Claim, Chatham County, Georgia, in P2257; Summary Report, 1878, Limerick Murray Disallowed Claim, Effingham County, Georgia, in P2257. On the slave economy, see Betty Wood, Women's Work, Men's Work: The Informal Slave Economies of Lowcountry Georgia (Athens: University of Georgia Press, 1995).
65 Summary Report, 1877, Morocco D. Smith Disallowed Claim, Phillips County, Arkansas, in P2257.
66 They rejected only 42 percent of former slaves compared with 56 percent of white southerners. However, nearly all of the 42 percent of former slaves were denied payment because the commissioners doubted their property ownership. In contrast, nearly all of the 56 percent of white southerners were rejected because the commissioner suspected their loyalty. See Summary Reports, 1871–1880, in P2257. On slaves' and former slaves' ability to work independently, see Drew Gilpin Faust, ed., *The Ideology of Slavery: Proslavery Thought in the Antebellum South, 1830–1860* (Baton Rouge: Louisiana State University Press, 1981); Hartman, *Scenes of Subjection*; Eudell, *The Political Languages of Emancipation in the British Caribbean and the U.S. South*; Cooper et al., *Beyond Slavery*.
67 The commissioners also suspected that Gordon had not owned the claimed property. June R. Gordon Testimony, January 18, 8173, June R. Gordon Disallowed Claim, McIntosh County, Georgia, in M1407, Fiche 623; Summary Report, 1873, ibid.
68 This figure was obtained by reading the commissioners' summary reports to Congress in all 9,589 disallowed claims.
69 Miranda M. Kellogg, *Sketch of the Life of Asa Aldis by His Daughter*, Bailey Library, University of Vermont, 76–77. Although Miranda M. Kellogg primarily penned the "sketch" (c. 1870), her brother Asa Owen Aldis included his contribution on Chloe at the end.
70 Francis Pendleton Gaines, *The Southern Plantation: A Study in the Development and the Accuracy of a Tradition* (New York: Columbia University Press, 1925); Blight, *Race and Reunion*, 211–254.
71 Joseph Jefferson Testimony, September 9, 1871, Joseph Jefferson Disallowed Claim, Warren County, Mississippi, in M1407, Fiche 709; Summary Report, 1873, ibid.

See also Robert Casey Testimony, August 9, 1873, Robert Casey Disallowed Claim, Lauderdale County, Alabama, M1407, Fiche 1,030; Special Commissioner John H. Price, Remarks, August 9, 1873, ibid.; Enos Richmond Report, April 11, 1874, ibid.; Alexander Steele Testimony, August 17, 187[?], Alexander Steele Allowed Claim, Chatham County, Georgia.

72 "Dem Good Ole Times," 1874, Sam DeVincent Collection of Illustrated American Sheet Music, National Museum of American History.

73 On the meaning of slavery, see Igor Kopytoff and Suzanne Miers, eds., *Slavery in Africa: Historical and Anthropological Perspectives* (Madison: University of Wisconsin Press, 1977); Orlando Patterson, *Slavery and Social Death: A Comparative Study* (Cambridge, MA: Harvard University Press, 1982); Orlando Patterson, *Freedom in the Making of Western Culture* (New York: Basic Books, 1991); Cooper et al., *Beyond Slavery*; Johnson, "On Agency," 113–124; Kaye, *Joining Places*.

74 Summary Report, 1873, Israel Smith Disallowed Claim, Richland County, South Carolina, in P2257. Smith's case was appealed before the Court of Claims, Docket No. 4,505. The full context of Smith's admission that he had entered the Confederate service is unknown because his file is missing from the Court of Claims records in the National Archives in Washington, DC. Only the commissioners' Summary Report remains in the records of the Southern Claims Commission.

75 George Gardner Testimony, November 15, 1872, George Gardner Disallowed Claim, Chatham County, Georgia, in M1407, Fiche 3,467; George Gardner Testimony, June 21, 1878, ibid.; R. B. Avery Report, July 1878, ibid.; Summary Report, 1879, ibid.

76 One witness, another former slave, also reported that some slaves had suspected that Boone had favored the Confederate side, but the commissioners did not remark on this testimony in their report. Edmund Boone Testimony, August 20, 1875, Edmund Boone Disallowed Claim, Washington County, Arkansas, in M1407, Fiche 2,794; Lafayette Boone Testimony, August 20, 1875, ibid.; Summary Report, 1878, ibid.; Bryant Wallace Testimony, October 9, 1875, ibid. See also Summary Report, 1873, June R. Gordon Disallowed Claim, MacIntosh County, Georgia, in P2257; Summary Report, 1877, William H. Riley Disallowed Claim, Beaufort County, South Carolina, in P2257.

77 James S. Dean Testimony, November 14, 1873, James S. Dean Disallowed Claim, Fauquier County, Virginia, in Court of Claims, Docket No. 9,415; Jane Dean Testimony, November 14, 1873, ibid.; Charlotte Arnold Testimony, November 14, 1873, ibid.; Summary Report, 1876, ibid.

Chapter 5 The Colored Union

1 Racial descriptors carry inherent shortcomings. For the sake of brevity, I use the term "free black," despite its problems as an accurate descriptor, to refer to people of African descent who gained their freedom before the war (distinguished from slaves who gained their freedom as a result of the war as discussed in Chapter 4) and who were born free. Free black, in my usage, does not indicate skin color, as it includes both black and light-skinned people. I use the term "free people of color" for free people of African descent who emphasized their white ancestry or otherwise distinguished themselves from other free people of African descent.

2 Gilbert Moyers, Brief on Loyalty, c. March 15, 1887, Carroll Jones Disallowed Claim, Natchitoches Parish, Louisiana, in Court of Claims, Docket No. 810.
3 Dallas's husband may be Moses Dallas, mentioned in Mohr, *On the Threshold of Freedom*, 289–290. Harriet Dallas Testimony, September 12, 1872, Harriet Dallas Allowed Claim, Chatham County, Georgia; Alice Marshall Testimony, September 12, 1872, ibid.; Special Agent Enos Richmond, Report, June 1873, ibid.; Summary Report, 1874, ibid.

In 1801, the Georgia legislature reserved the right of manumission to itself, voiding all other deeds of manumission. For a brief period, from 1815 to 1818, state law allowed owners to free their slaves by will. Harriet Dallas does not appear in Georgia's acts and resolutions as a slave granted her freedom. "Georgia Legislative Documents," accessed June 7, 2012, http://www.galileo.usg.edu/express?link=zlgl. On manumission law in Georgia, see Ralph Betts Flanders, *Plantation Slavery in Georgia* (Chapel Hill: The University of North Carolina Press, 1933), 249; Jennison, *Cultivating Race*, 300.

The commissioners generally accepted a claimant's word on his or her status as enslaved or free. This chapter analyzes claims by black southerners that the commissioners accepted as free blacks. Many of the free blacks analyzed in this chapter identified themselves as free, understood themselves as free, and were recognized as free by others, but may not have been legally free and may have arranged for their freedom after the passage of laws in their states that prohibited the practice.
4 Ira Berlin, *Slaves Without Masters: The Free Negro in the Antebellum South* (New York: Pantheon Books, 1974), 188–190, 369–380.
5 Green Puckett identified himself as free before the commissioners, but his name does not appear in Georgia's acts and resolutions as a slave granted his freedom. "Georgia Legislative Documents." Green Puckett Testimony, May 26, 1874, Green Puckett Allowed Claim, Newton County, Georgia. See also Mary Blackburn Testimony, September 6, 1871, Mary Blackburn Allowed Claim, Augusta County, Virginia; Margaret Butler Testimony, October 25, 1873, Margaret Butler Allowed Claim, Shelby County, Alabama; Jesse Win Testimony, December 12, 1876, Jack Winn Allowed Claim, Tuscaloosa County, Alabama.
6 Abraham Johnston Testimony, August 12, 1872, Abraham Johnston Allowed Claim, Chatham County, Georgia. See also Elizabeth Wingfield Testimony, February 20, 1873, Elizabeth Wingfield Allowed Claim, Dinwiddie County, Virginia; Susan Denslow Testimony, March 31, 1873, Amos Denslow Disallowed Claim, Chatham County, Georgia, in M1407, Fiche 2,864.
7 Phil Sewell Testimony, June 21, 1871, Phil Sewell and Phil Sewell, Jr., Allowed Claim, Dinwiddie County, Virginia; Phil Sewell, Jr., Testimony, June 21, 1871, ibid.
8 Brewer, *The Confederate Negro*, 6, 11–14, 145, 159.
9 Benjamin Summers Testimony, February 6, 1872, Benjamin Summers Allowed Claim, Norfolk County, Virginia; Summary Report, 1879, ibid. For other attempts to resist coerced labor for the Confederacy, see John T. Gibbs Testimony, September 5, 1871, John T. Gibbs Allowed Claim, Norfolk County, Virginia.
10 James Dennison Testimony, May 27, 1872, James Dennison Allowed Claim, Chatham County, Georgia; James Symes Testimony, May 27, 1872, ibid.; A. M. Stone Testimony, May 27, 1872, ibid. James Dennison's name does not appear in Georgia's acts and resolutions as a slave granted his freedom. "Georgia Legislative Documents." For additional examples of claimants who discussed problems

securing their freedom, see Patrick Rose Testimony, January 29, 1872, Claiborne Scott and Patrick Rose Allowed Claim, Campbell County, Virginia; Job Mayzeck Testimony, March 11, 12, 13, 1873, Job Mayzeck Disallowed Claim, Georgetown County, South Carolina, in M1407, Fiche 4,183–4,185.

11 Richard D. Arnold, *Letters of Richard D. Arnold, M.D., 1808–1876, Mayor of Savannah, Georgia, First Secretary of the American Medical Association*, ed. Richard Harrison Shryock (New York: AMS Press, 1970), 32, 65–67, 164; Whittington Bernard Johnson, *Black Savannah, 1788–1864* (Fayetteville: University of Arkansas Press, 1996), 148, 161, 166. There is no reference to Kelley's status as a mulatto in the Southern Claims Commission testimony, but it is likely that Kelley was light skinned with both white and black ancestry. The census taker in 1860 left Georgianna Kelly's race blank, which was the typical practice for whites. See United States Census, 1860, Savannah, Fourth District, Chatham County, Georgia, 272.

12 Georgiana Kelley Testimony, April 3, 1873, Allowed Claim, Chatham County, Georgia; Delia Rivers Testimony, April 3, 1873, ibid.; Richard Rivers Testimony, April 3, 1873, ibid.; Henry Fields Testimony, April 3, 1873, ibid. Kelley chose several former slaves who visited her house to testify both to her loyalty and her property ownership. The commissioners, doubtful that Kelley's friends could accurately report her property ownership, sent a special agent to investigate. The special agent interviewed the daughter and son-in-law of her guardian, Dr. Arnold, who provided, in the commissioners' estimation, stronger evidence of her propertyholdings. See Ellen N. Cosens Testimony, August 3, 1876, ibid.; W. W. Paine Report, August 5, 1876, ibid.

13 Summary Report, 1875, Green Puckett Allowed Claim, Newton County, Georgia. See also Summary Report, 1876, Delia Logwood Allowed Claim, Lawrence County, Alabama.

14 Summary Report, 1873, Woodson Armistead Allowed Claim, Lauderdale County, Alabama. See also Summary Report, 1873, Margaret J. Butler Allowed Claim, Shelby County, Alabama; Summary Report, 1879, Allen Campbell Allowed Claim, Monroe County, Alabama; Summary Report, 1879, Abraham Johnson Allowed Claim, Chatham County, Georgia; Summary Report, 1874, John M. Dogans Allowed Claim, Page County, Virginia; Summary Report, 1875, Mary Blackburn Allowed Claim, Augusta County, Virginia; Summary Report, 1877, Claiborne Scott and Patrick Rose Allowed Claim, Campbell County, Virginia.

15 Summary Report, 1876, Georgiana Kelley Allowed Claim, Chatham County, Georgia.

16 Brown, like several of his free black neighbors, marked his deposition with an "X," underscoring the denial of education that he complained about in his testimony. Joseph Brown Testimony, March 13, 1874, Joseph Brown Allowed Claim, New Kent County, Virginia; George Tucker Report, April 21, 1876, ibid.; William Wilkerson Testimony, March 1, 1877, ibid.; Beverly Dixon Testimony, March 1, 1877, ibid.

17 George Tucker, the special agent who investigated his claim, described Hord as a "colored man" with "nothing in his complection or his general appearance which would indicate to a stranger that he has in his veins any Affrican blood." Commissioner Orange Ferris saw this for himself when Hord testified in Washington in 1874. When appearance failed to indicate Hord's race, Ferris referred to the

submitted evidence: "I see from these papers you have here that it was alleged that you were a colored man." Samuel Hord Testimony, October 19, 1874, Samuel Hord Allowed Claim, Fauquier County, Virginia; Special Agent George Tucker, Report, August 7, 1875, ibid.

18 James C. Muschett Deposition, August 9, 1879, James C. Muschett Disallowed Claim, Prince William County, Virginia, in Court of Claims, Docket No. 7,513.

19 See George Tucker, Report, April 21, 1876, Joseph Brown Allowed Claim, New Kent County, Virginia; Enos Richmond Report, February 28, 1876, Jean Conant Allowed Claim, Natchitoches Parish, Louisiana; Emily Atkins Deposition, February 24, 1873, Isaac Pleasants Allowed Claim, Henrico County, Virginia.

20 Beverly Matteur Testimony, September 19, 1874, Beverly Matteur Allowed Claim, Appomattox County, Virginia. See also Mitchel P. Boisfeillet Testimony, July 9, 1872, Celia Boisfeillet Allowed Claim, Chatham County, Georgia; William Wilkerson Testimony, March 1, 1877, Joseph Brown Allowed Claim, New Kent County, Virginia; Ann Maria Jackson Testimony, September 9, 1872, Ann Maria Jackson Disallowed Claim, Amelia County, Virginia, in M1407, Fiche 2,688; William James Testimony, March 20, 1872, William James Allowed Claim, Henrico County, Virginia; William Riley Testimony, April 29, 1873, William Riley Allowed Claim, Fauquier County, Virginia.

21 George W. Carter Testimony, July 8, 1873, Richard Dorsey Allowed Claim, Adams County, Mississippi. See also Joseph Brown Testimony, March 13, 1874, Joseph Brown Allowed Claim, New Kent County, Virginia; Sarah Carter Testimony, June 19, 1873, Allen and Mary Frazer Allowed Claim, Fulton County, Georgia; Nicholas Rue Testimony, November 15, 1871, Martin Decoux Allowed Claim, Pointe Coupée Parish, Louisiana; Westward Hudnall Testimony, March 3, 1873, Westward Hudnall Allowed Claim, Fauquier County, Virginia; William Peters Testimony, June 16, 1875, William Peters Allowed Claim, Rockingham County, Virginia.

22 Milton Copeland Testimony, January 6, 1872, Milton Copeland Allowed Claim, Norfolk County, Virginia.

23 William James Testimony, March 20, 1872, William James Allowed Claim, Henrico County, Virginia. See also Mitchel P. Boisfeillet Testimony, July 9, 1872, Celia Boisfeillet Allowed Claim, Chatham County, Georgia; Jane Dent Testimony, January 18, 1872, Jane Dent Allowed Claim, Adams County, Mississippi; John Coleman Testimony, February 6, 1873, John Coleman Allowed Claim, Dinwiddie County, Virginia; Robert Elliott Testimony, September 6, 1871, William and Robert Elliott Allowed Claim, Norfolk County, Virginia; Henry Escridge Testimony, June 18, 1877, Henry Escridge Allowed Claim, Fairfax County, Virginia; William Riley Testimony, April 29, 1873, William Riley Allowed Claim, Fauquier County, Virginia.

24 Cornelius Donato Testimony, December 8, 1876, Dubriel Olivier Estate Allowed Claim, St. Landry Parish, Louisiana. Michael P. Johnson and James L. Roark describe the increasing hostility faced by free people of color in South Carolina. See Michael P. Johnson and James L. Roark, *Black Masters: A Free Family of Color in the Old South* (New York: Norton, 1984), 233–338.

25 Cornelius Donato Testimony, December 8, 1876, Dubriel Olivier Estate Allowed Claim, St. Landry Parish, Louisiana. See also James P. Anderson, September 9, 1872,

James P. Anderson Disallowed Claim, Amelia County, Virginia, in Court of Claims, Docket No. 746; Alexander Anderson Testimony, September 9, 1872, Alexander Anderson Disallowed Claim, Amelia County, Virginia, in M1407, Fiche 2,660; Joseph Atkins Testimony, February 24, 1873, Joseph Atkins Disallowed Claim, Henrico County, Virginia, in M1407, Fiche 2,662; Joseph Brown Testimony, March 13, 1874, Joseph Brown Allowed Claim, New Kent County, Virginia; Mitchel P. Boisfeillet Testimony, July 9, 1872, Celia Boisfeillet Allowed Claim, Chatham County, Georgia; Jean Conant Testimony, August 31, 1874, Jean Conant Allowed Claim, Natchitoches Parish, Louisiana; Henry F. Harrison Testimony, September 11, 1872, Henry F. Harrison Disallowed Claim, Amelia County, Virginia, in M1407, Fiche 2,682; William James Testimony, March 20, 1872, William James Allowed Claim, Henrico County, Virginia.

26 Sarah Carter Testimony, June 19, 1873, Allen and Mary Frazer Allowed Claim, Fulton County, Georgia. See also Ann Maria Jackson Testimony, September 9, 1872, Ann Maria Jackson Disallowed Claim, Amelia County, Virginia, in M1407, Fiche 2,688.

27 Summary Report, 1880, Nicholas Rue Disallowed Claim, Pointe Coupée Parish, Louisiana, in P2257; Summary Report, 1874, Sawyer Watkins Allowed Claim, Norfolk County, Virginia, in P2257.

28 Summary Report, 1877, Lucy Green Allowed Claim, Charles City County, Virginia, in P2257.

29 Summary Report, 1879, Samuel Hord Allowed Claim, Fauquier County, Virginia, in P2257.

30 François Bouligny Testimony, March 4, 1874, François Bouligny Disallowed Claim, Pointe Coupée Parish, Louisiana, in Court of Claims, Docket No. 11,592. Bouligny owned approximately thirty-five to forty slaves prior to the war. For discussions of Bouligny's slaveholdings and his opinions on slavery, see the testimony taken before the Court of Claims.

31 Summary Report, 1879, François Bouligny Disallowed Claim, Pointe Coupée Parish, Louisiana, in Court of Claims, Docket No. 11,592.

32 The commissioners did not tally the number of free blacks they found disloyal. This figure was obtained by reading the commissioners' summary reports to Congress in all 9,589 disallowed claims. Altogether, they judged 52 blacks disloyal, approximately 4 percent of the total of 1,355 claims, a miniscule figure relative to white claimants. The commissioners rejected approximately 60 percent of claims overall. See Klingberg, *The Southern Claims Commission*, 157.

33 See Summary Report, 1879, Stokein Dedrich Disallowed Claim, Charleston County, South Carolina, in P2257; Summary Report, 1879, Archibald Jackson Disallowed Claim, Beaufort County, South Carolina, in P2257; Summary Report, 1879, Josiah Jackson Disallowed Claim, Beaufort County, South Carolina, in P2257; Summary Report, 1877, William H. Pettipher Disallowed Claim, Craven County, North Carolina, in P2257; Summary Report, 1878, F. Azenor Metoyer Disallowed Claim, Natchitoches Parish, Louisiana, in P2257; Summary Report, 1879, Adam Sheftall Estate Disallowed Claim, Chatham County, Georgia, in P2257.

34 Emmanuel Sheftall Testimony, November 20, 1872, Adam Sheftall Estate Disallowed Claim, Chatham County, Georgia, in M1407, Fiche 3,541.

35 James Goin Testimony, June 7, 1877, James Goin Disallowed Claim, Lauderdale County, Alabama, in M1407, Fiche 2,261.

36 George A. King to the Commissioners of Southern Claims, November 29, 1876, Archibald Jackson Disallowed Claim, Hampton County, South Carolina, in M1407, Fiche 3,752.
37 Archibald Jackson Testimony, September 21, 1878, Josiah Jackson Disallowed Claim, Beaufort County, South Carolina.
38 Summary Report, 1879, Archibald Jackson Disallowed Claim, Beaufort County, South Carolina, in in M1407, Fiche 3,752.
39 Summary Report, 1877, Joseph Blake Disallowed Claim, Dallas County, Alabama, in Court of Claims, Docket No. 4,964.
40 Summary Report, 1879, Susan Carrier Disallowed Claim, Chatham County, Georgia, in Court of Claims, Docket No. 6,820; Summary Report, 1879, Stokein Dedrich Disallowed Claim, Charleston County, South Carolina, in Court of Claims, Docket No. 14,656; Summary Report, 1877, James Goin Disallowed Claim, Lauderdale County, Alabama, in P2257; Summary Report, 1879, Jackson B. Sheftall Disallowed Claim, Chatham County, Georgia, in P2257.
41 The central question examined by most historians who focus on slaveholders of color is whether they were benevolent or exploitative masters and mistresses. This question essentially seeks to categorize slaveholders of color like other black southerners or like white southerners or, alternatively, a third class in between. Benevolent slaveholders of color purchased family members to free them but kept them in bondage in compliance with state laws that prevented manumission. Exploitative slaveholders of color held slaves, whom they considered racially different, to generate profits and, in these respects, were similar to other slaveholders. Scholarship suggests that although most black slaveholders were benevolent, substantial numbers were exploitative. Moreover, most slaves owned by free blacks were owned by exploitative masters. Exploitative black slaveholders, defined as those owning four or more slaves, comprised 27 percent of total black slaveholders and owned 66 percent of all slaves owned by black slaveholders. See David L. Lightner and Alexander L. Ragan, "Were African American Slaveholders Benevolent or Exploitative? A Quantitative Approach," *Journal of Southern History* 71, no. 3 (August 2005): 535–558. Much of the scholarship on black slaveholders consists of statistical analyses of the slaveholder census. The few studies that examine case studies of black slaveholders reveal very little about how black slaveholders understood their slaveholding and their relationships to white slaveholders and to their slave property as a result of evidentiary silences. The records of the commission provide such evidence. For published primary sources authored by slaveholders of color, see William Johnson, *William Johnson's Natchez: The Ante-bellum Diary of a Free Negro*, ed. William Ransom Hogan and Edwin Adams Davis (Baton Rouge: Louisiana State University Press, 1951); Michael P. Johnson and James L. Roark, eds., *No Chariot Let Down: Charleston's Free People of Color on the Eve of the Civil War* (Chapel Hill: University of North Carolina Press, 1984).
42 Alfred Anderson Testimony, September 9, 1872, Alfred Anderson Disallowed Claim, Amelia County, Virginia, in Court of Claims, Docket No. 1,912. According to the 1860 census, Anderson owned $5,600 in real estate and held $18,604 in personal estate. Anderson ran a thriving plantation. In 1860, his 700-acre farm (with a little less than half in cultivation) yielded 12,000 pounds of tobacco, 200 bushels of wheat, 650 bushels of corn, 480 bushels of oats, and 40 hogs. See United States Census, 1860, Free Schedules, Magisterial District No. 5, Amelia County,

Virginia, 23/171; Luther Porter Jackson, *Free Negro Labor and Property Holding in Virginia, 1830–1860* (New York: Atheneum, 1969), 128.

43 According to the census of 1860, he had owned $46,000 worth of property. Heluter Taunoir Testimony, May 18, 1874, Heluter Taunoir Disallowed Claim, Pointe Coupée Parish, Louisiana, in Court of Claims, Docket No. 16,082; United States Census, 1860, Pointe Coupée Parish, Louisiana, 82. There are several alternate spellings for this name: Tounoir, Tonnier, and Taunoir. He is listed in the 1860 census as Heluter Tounoir. He is listed in Gary B. Mills' published index of the commission as Heluter Tonnier. I have used the "Taunoir" spelling in line with his signature on his deposition in his claim before the Southern Claims Commission. Taunoir may have wished to distance himself from the name "Tounoir," which may have been a truncation of the French "tout noir," meaning "all black." See Gary B. Mills, *Southern Loyalists in the Civil War: The Southern Claims Commission* (Baltimore: Genealogical Publishing Co., 1994), 600.

44 Summary Report, 1877, Alfred Anderson Disallowed Claim, Amelia County, Virginia, in Court of Claims, Docket No. 1,912.

45 Summary Report, 1879, Heluter Taunoir Disallowed Claim, Pointe Coupée Parish, Louisiana, in Court of Claims, Docket No. 16,082.

46 Summary Report, 1877, Alfred Anderson Disallowed Claim, Amelia County, Virginia, in Court of Claims, Docket No. 1,912; Summary Report, 1879, Heluter Taunoir Disallowed Claim, Pointe Coupée Parish, Louisiana, in Court of Claims, Docket No. 16,082; Summary Report, 1875, Joseph Balquais Allowed Claim, St. Landry Parish, Louisiana; Summary Report, 1877, Dubriel Olivier Estate Allowed Claim, St. Landry Parish, Louisiana.

47 Adelphia Miles Testimony, July 24, 1877, Archie Miles Allowed Claim, King William County, Virginia.

48 For a general overview of Indians in the South, see Theda Perdue and Michael D. Green, *The Columbia Guide to American Indians of the Southeast* (New York: Columbia University Press, 2001), 125–135.

49 For general overviews of Indians during the Civil War, see Laurence M. Hauptman, *Between Two Fires: American Indians in the Civil War* (New York: Free Press, 1995), 65–122; Anne J. Bailey, *Invisible Southerners: Ethnicity in the Civil War* (Athens: University of Georgia Press, 2006), 24–46.

50 R. Alton Lee, "Indian Citizenship and the Fourteenth Amendment," *South Dakota History* 4, no. 2 (Spring 1974): 198–221; Stephen D. Bodayla, "'Can An Indian Vote?': Elk V. Wilkins, A Setback for Indian Citizenship," *Nebraska History* 67, no. 4 (December 1986): 373; Vine Deloria and David E. Wilkins, *Tribes, Treaties, and Constitutional Tribulations* (Austin: University of Texas Press, 1999), 141–148; David E. Wilkins, *American Indian Politics and the American Political System* (Lanham, MD: Rowman & Littlefield, 2002), 60–66, 103–110, quotation on 61–62.

51 Adelphia Miles Testimony, July 24, 1877, Archie Miles Allowed Claim, King William County, Virginia; Thomas Cook Testimony, October 23, 1871, Thomas Cook Allowed Claim, King William County, Virginia; Thomas Sampson Testimony, October 23, 1871, Thomas Cook Allowed Claim, King William County, Virginia; John Langston Testimony, January 17, 1874, Holt Langston Allowed Claim, King William County, Virginia; Thomas Bradby Testimony, January 17, 1874,

Holt Langston Allowed Claim, King William County, Virginia; Lambert C. Page Testimony, October 30, 1871, Lambert C. Page Allowed Claim, King William County, Virginia.

Claimants with Pamunkey ancestry who lived off the reservation presented contrasting claims to loyal citizenship. They had left the reservation either temporarily or permanently and lived just off the reservation in New Kent County. Called by scholars "nonreservation Indians" and "detribalized Indians," these individuals retained a tradition of their Indian ancestry, but they refrained from making public claims as Indians. See Helen C. Rountree, *Pocahontas's People: The Powhatan Indians of Virginia Through Four Centuries* (Norman: University of Oklahoma Press, 1990), 189–191. This is evident in their testimony before the commission. Members of the New Kent community claimed Indian ancestry but did not explicitly call themselves Pamunkeys or Indians. See Frank Sweat Testimony, July 21, 1877, Frank Sweat Allowed Claim, New Kent County, Virginia; William C. Langston Testimony, March 18, 1874, William C. Langston Allowed Claim, New Kent County, Virginia. Some did not acknowledge their Indian ancestry at all. See William H. Brisby Testimony, July 19, 1877, William C. Langston Allowed Claim, New Kent County, Virginia. Brisby's mother, Miranda Brisby, was a Pamunkey Indian. For a recent official recognition of William H. Brisby as an African American that notes his Pamunkey ancestry, see Senate Joint Resolution No. 13 recognizing the African-American members elected to the Virginia Constitutional Convention of 1867 to 1868 and members elected to the Virginia General Assembly during Reconstruction on Virginia General Assembly, Legislative Information System, accessed February 17, 2012, http://leg1.state.va.us/lis.htm.

52 For claimants who performed services to the Confederacy, sometimes for wages, see Terrill Bradby Testimony, October 30, 1871, Terrill Bradby Allowed Claim, King William County, Virginia; Thomas Bradby Testimony, January 17, 1874, Thomas Bradby Allowed Claim, King William County, Virginia; Holt Langston Testimony, January 17, 1874, Holt Langston Allowed Claim, King William County, Virginia; William Wheely Testimony, March 2, 1875, William Wheely Allowed Claim, King William County, Virginia. For other stories of Pamunkeys in Union service, see Thomas Bradby Testimony, January 17, 1874, Thomas Bradby Allowed Claim, King William County, Virginia; Terrill Bradby Testimony, November 26, 1873, Archie Miles Allowed Claim, King William County, Virginia; Adelphia Miles Testimony, July 24, 1877, ibid.; Terrill Bradby Testimony, July 25, 1877, Isaac Miles Disallowed Claim, King William County, Virginia, in M1407, Fiche 2,697; John Langston Testimony, July 25, 1877, ibid.; Jacob J. Miles Testimony, July 25, 1877, ibid.; Lambert C. Page Testimony, October 30, 1871, Lambert C. Page Allowed Claim, King William County, Virginia; Thomas Cook Testimony, October 30, 1871, ibid.

53 Brewer, *The Confederate Negro*, 7, 8, 139.

54 Lambert C. Page Testimony, October 30, 1871, Lambert C. Page Allowed Claim, King William County, Virginia. For other stories of Pamunkeys in Union service, see Terrill Bradby Testimony, October 30, 1871, Terrill Bradby Allowed Claim, King William County, Virginia; Thomas Bradby Testimony, January 17, 1874, Thomas Bradby Allowed Claim, King William County, Virginia; Terrill Bradby Testimony, November 26, 1873, Archie Miles Allowed Claim, King William County, Virginia;

Adelphia Miles Testimony, July 24, 1877, Archie Miles Allowed Claim, King William County, Virginia; Terrill Bradby Testimony, July 25, 1877, Isaac Miles Disallowed Claim, King William County, Virginia; John Langston Testimony, July 25, 1877, Isaac Miles Disallowed Claim, King William County, Virginia; Jacob J. Miles Testimony, July 25, 1877, Isaac Miles Disallowed Claim, King William County, Virginia; Thomas Cook Testimony, October 30, 1871, Lambert C. Page Allowed Claim, King William County, Virginia.

55 Terrill Bradby Testimony, October 30, 1871, Terrill Bradby Allowed Claim, King William County, Virginia; Terrill Bradby Testimony, July 23, 1877, Nancy Langston Allowed Claim, King William County, Virginia; for the quotation, see Thomas Cook Testimony, October 23, 1871, Thomas Cook Allowed Claim, King William County, Virginia.

56 Terrill Bradby Testimony, July 13, 1872, Edward Bradby Allowed Claim, King William County, Virginia. See also Terrill Bradby Testimony, July 23, 1877, Nancy Langston Allowed Claim, King William County, Virginia; Terrill Bradby Testimony, July 24, 1877, Caroline Cook Allowed Claim, King William County, Virginia; Terrill Bradby Testimony, July 25, 1877, Isaac Miles Disallowed Claim, King William County, Virginia; William Wheely Testimony, March 2, 1875, William Wheely Allowed Claim, King William County, Virginia.

57 Terrill Bradby Testimony, October 30, 1871, Terrill Bradby Allowed Claim, King William County, Virginia. For additional references to voting for the Republican ticket after the war, see Testimony of John H. Langston, March 18, 1874, William C. Langston Allowed Claim, New Kent County, Virginia; Lambert C. Page Testimony, October 30, 1871, Lambert C. Page Allowed Claim, King William County, Virginia.

58 Thomas Cook Testimony, October 23, 1871, Thomas Cook Allowed Claim, King William County, Virginia; Thomas Cook Testimony, October 30, 1871, Lambert C. Page Allowed Claim, King William County, Virginia.

59 Helen C. Rountree, "Ethnicity Among the 'Citizen' Indians of Tidewater Virginia, 1800–1930," in *Strategies for Survival: American Indians in the Eastern United States*, ed. Frank W. Porter (New York: Greenwood Press, 1986), 174–178; Hauptman, *Between Two Fires*, 66.

60 James Mooney, "The Powhatan Confederacy, Past and Present," *American Anthropologist* 9, no. 1 (January 1, 1907): 145; Rountree, *Pocahontas's People*, 197–198; Hauptman, *Between Two Fires*, 68–69.

61 For Lumbee claimants' identification of themselves as "colored," see Hugh Oxendine Testimony, November 19, 1874, Hugh Oxendine Allowed Claim, Robeson County, North Carolina; Solomon Oxendine Testimony, November 19, 1874, Solomon Oxendine Allowed Claim, Robeson County, North Carolina.

62 Nancy Sampson Testimony, February 19, 1878, Henry Sampson Allowed Claim, Robeson County, North Carolina.

63 Karen I. Blu, *The Lumbee Problem: The Making of an American Indian People* (New York: Cambridge University Press, 1980), 36–48; Malinda Maynor Lowery, *Lumbee Indians in the Jim Crow South: Race, Identity, and the Making of a Nation* (Chapel Hill: University of North Carolina Press, 2010), 4–6, 14.

64 Blu, *The Lumbee Problem*, 56–64.

65 For examples of claimants who had offered few or no contributions to the Union and who admitted that they had worked on Confederate fortifications, see Hugh

Oxendine Allowed Claim, Robeson County, North Carolina; Solomon Oxendine Allowed Claim, Robeson County, North Carolina; Henry Sampson Allowed Claim, Robeson County, North Carolina. For an example of a rote recitation of negative responses to the interrogatories, see Testimony of Neill Galbreth, November 19, 1874, Hugh Oxendine Allowed Claim, Robeson County, North Carolina. For additional examples, see Neill Nevils Testimony, November 19, 1874, Hugh Oxendine Allowed Claim, Robeson County, North Carolina; Neill Galbreth Testimony, November 19, 1874, Solomon Oxendine Allowed Claim, Robeson County, North Carolina; Neill Nevils Testimony, November 19, 1874, Solomon Oxendine Allowed Claim, Robeson County, North Carolina.

66 William McKee Evans, *To Die Game: The Story of the Lowry Band, Indian Guerrillas of Reconstruction* (Baton Rouge: Louisiana State University Press, 1971), 38–241; Blu, *The Lumbee Problem*, 51–55; Lowery, *Lumbee Indians in the Jim Crow South*, 15–16.

67 The Sampson family was connected to the Lowrys through the marriage of two daughters. Maria Sampson married Calvin Lowry, and Flora Sampson married Andrew Strong. Both marriages linked Sampson to Henry Berry Lowry himself. Calvin Lowry was his brother and Andrew Strong's sister Rhoda Strong was his wife. Solomon and Hugh Oxendine, who were cousins, were likely related to Henderson Oxendine, a member of the band.

68 "The North Carolina Bandits," *Harper's Weekly*, March 30, 1872; Evans, *To Die Game*; Blu, *The Lumbee Problem*, 51–53.

69 Commissioners of Claims, Memorandum, June 26, 1878, Henry Sampson Allowed Claim, Robeson County, North Carolina.

Conclusion

1 Summary Report, 1873, John Hawk Disallowed Claim, Marshall County, Mississippi, in Court of Claims, Docket No. 3,719.

2 Speech of Hon. Orange Ferriss of New York, March 2, 1868, Congressional Globe, Appendix, 235.

3 On black southerners' continuing political activism, see Steven Hahn, *A Nation Under Our Feet*, and Michael W. Fitzgerald, *Urban Emancipation: Popular Politics in Reconstruction Mobile, 1860–1890* (Baton Rouge: Louisiana State University Press, 2002).

4 *Congressional Record*, 55th Congress, 2nd Session (May 12, 1898), 5404–5505.

5 *Congressional Globe*, Appendix, 40th Congress, 2nd Session (March 2, 1868), 235.

Bibliography

Primary Sources

Court of Claims, Committee on Claims, and Southern Claims Commission Records

General Records of the Department of the Treasury, 1789–1990. Records of the Division of Captured Property, Claims, and Lands, 1855–1900. Records of the Commissioner of Claims (Southern Claims Commission), 1871–1880. Microfilm Publication M87. Record Group 56. National Archives, Washington, DC.

Records of the Accounting Officers of the Department of the Treasury, 1775–1927. Records of the Land, Files, and Miscellaneous Division. Southern Claims Commission, Allowed Claims, 1871–1880. Record Group 217. National Archives, Washington, DC.

Records of the United States Court of Claims, 1835–1966. Case Files for General Jurisdiction Cases, 1855–1966. Record Group 123. National Archives, Washington, DC.

Records of the United States House of Representatives, 1789–1990. Records of Committees Relating to Claims, 1794–1946. Petitions and Memorials Referred to the Committee on Claims, 37th through 39th Congresses. Record Group 233. National Archives, Washington, DC.

Records of the United States House of Representatives, 1789–1990. Southern Claims Commission, 1871–1880. Summary Reports of the Commissioners of Claims in All Cases Reported to Congress as Disallowed Under the Act of March 3, 1871. Microfilm Publication P2257. Record Group 233. National Archives, Washington, DC.

Records of the United States House of Representatives, 1789–1990. Southern Claims Commission, Barred and Disallowed Claims, 1871–1880. Microfiche Publication M1407. Record Group 233. National Archives, Washington, DC.

United States Congress. House. Eighth General Report of the Commissioners of Claims. 45th Cong., 3d sess., 1878. H. Doc. 6.

United States Congress. House. Fifth General Report of the Commissioners of Claims. 44th Cong., 1st sess., 1875. H. Doc. 30.

United States Congress. House. First General Report of the Commissioners of Claims. 42d Cong., 2d sess., 1871. H. Doc. 16.
United States Congress. House. Fourth General Report of the Commissioners of Claims. 43d Cong., 2d sess., 1874. H. Doc. 18.
United States Congress. House. Ninth General Report of the Commissioners of Claims. 46th Cong., 2d sess., 1879. H. Doc. 10.
United States Congress. House. Second General Report of the Commissioners of Claims. 42d Cong., 3d sess., 1872. H. Doc. 12.
United States Congress. House. Seventh General Report of the Commissioners of Claims. 45th Cong., 2d sess., 1877. H. Doc. 4.
United States Congress. House. Sixth General Report of the Commissioners of Claims. 44th Cong., 2d sess., 1876. H. Doc. 4.
United States Congress. House. Tenth General Report of the Commissioners of Claims. 46th Cong., 2d sess., 1880. H. Doc. 30.
United States Congress. House. Third General Report of the Commissioners of Claims. 43d Cong., 1st sess., 1873. H. Doc. 23.

Supreme Court Cases

Armstrong v. United States (1871)
Congressional Globe, 1861–1898
Ex Parte Garland (1866)
Pargoud v. United States (1868)
Pargoud v. United States (1871)
United States Census, 1860 and 1870
United States v. Klein (1871)
United States v. Padelford (1869)

Newspapers and Periodicals

Athens Messenger, 1876
Atlanta Daily Constitution, 1878
Burlington Daily Hawk-Eye, 1876
Cedar Rapids Times, 1876
Charleston Daily Courier, 1872
DeBow's Review, 1851, 1855
Douglass' Monthly, 1861
Edwardsville Intelligencer, 1876
Harpers' Weekly, 1860–1880
Milwaukee Daily News, 1875
National Intelligencer, 1861
New York Times, 1860–1800
Orrville Crescent, 1876
Oshkosh Daily Northwestern, 1879
Richmond Daily Dispatch, 1861, 1876
Richmond Enquirer, 1861
Richmond Whig, 1861
The Advance, 1876

Titusville Herald, 1879
Warrenton Flag of 98, 1861
Warrenton True Index, 1870–1881
Warrenton Weekly Whig, 1861
Waterloo Courier, 1876

Other Primary Sources

Adams, John Quincy. *Narrative of the Life of John Quincy Adams, When in Slavery, and Now as a Freeman*. Harrisburg, PA: Sieg, Printer & Stationer, 1872.
Arnold, Richard D. *Letters of Richard D. Arnold, M.D., 1808–1876, Mayor of Savannah, Georgia, First Secretary of the American Medical Association*. Edited by Richard Harrison Shryock. New York: AMS Press, 1970.
Avins, Alfred, ed. *The Reconstruction Amendments' Debates: The Legislative History and Contemporary Debates in Congress on the 13th, 14th, and 15th Amendments*. Richmond: Virginia Commission on Constitutional Government, 1967.
Berlin, Ira, Barbara J. Fields, Steven F. Miller, Joseph P. Reidy, Leslie S. Rowland. *Free at Last: A Documentary History of Slavery, Freedom, and the Civil War*. New York: New Press, 1992.
Brownlow, William Gannaway. *Sketches of the Rise, Progress, and Decline of Secession: With a Narrative of Personal Adventures Among the Rebels*. Philadelphia: Applegate & Co., 1862.
Diffley, Kathleen, ed. *Where My Heart is Turning Ever: Civil War Stories and Constitutional Reform, 1861–1875*. Athens: University of Georgia Press, 1992.
Faust, Drew Gilpin, ed. *The Ideology of Slavery: Proslavery Thought in the Antebellum South, 1830–1860*. Baton Rouge: Louisiana State University Press, 1981.
Fleming, Walter L., ed. *Documentary History of Reconstruction: Political, Military, Social, Religious, Educational, and Industrial, 1865 to the Present Time*. Gloucester, MA: Peter Smith, 1960.
Gates, Henry Louis, Jr., ed. *The Classic Slave Narratives*. New York: Mentor Books, 1987.
"Georgia Legislative Documents." Accessed June 7, 2012. http://www.galileo.usg.edu/express?link=zlgl.
Helper, Hinton R. *The Impending Crisis: How to Meet It*. New York: A. B. Burdick, 1857.
Hyman, Harold M., ed. *The Radical Republicans and Reconstruction, 1861–1870*. Indianapolis: The Bobbs-Merrill Company, 1967.
Johnson, Michael P., and James L. Roark, eds. *No Chariot Let Down: Charleston's Free People of Color on the Eve of the Civil War*. Chapel Hill: University of North Carolina Press, 1984.
Johnson, William. *William Johnson's Natchez: The Ante-bellum Diary of a Free Negro*. Edited by William Ransom Hogan and Edwin Adams Davis. Baton Rouge: Louisiana State University Press, 1951.
Keckley, Elizabeth Hobbs. *Behind the Scenes, or, Thirty Years a Slave and Four Years in the White House*. New York: G. W. Carleton, 1868.
Kellogg, Miranda M. *Sketch of the Life of Asa Aldis by His Daughter*. Bailey Library, University of Vermont. Brattlesboro, VT: s.n., 1972.

Matthews, James M., ed. Confederate States of America, *The Statutes at Large of the Provisional Government of the Confederate States of America, from the Institution of the Government, February 8, 1861, to its Termination, February 18, 1862, Inclusive; Arranged in Chronological Order. Together with the Constitution for the Provisional Government, and the Permanent Constitution of the Confederate States, and the Treaties Concluded by the Confederate States with Indian Tribes.* Richmond, VA: R. M. Smith, 1864.

"Memorial Sketch of Hon. Asa Owen Aldis." Speech before the Vermont Bar Association, October 1903. Montpelier, VT: Argus and Patriot Company, 1904.

Middleton, Stephen, ed., *Black Congressmen During Reconstruction: A Documentary Sourcebook.* Westport, CT: Greenwood Press, 2002.

Mills, Gary B. *Civil War Claims in the South: An Index of Civil War Damage Claims Filed Before the Southern Claims Commission, 1871–1880.* Laguna Hills, CA: Aegean Park Press, 1980.

—— *Southern Loyalists in the Civil War: The Southern Claims Commission.* Baltimore, MD: Genealogical Pub. Co., 1994.

Moore, Frank, ed. *The Rebellion Record: A Diary of American Events with Documents, Narratives, Illustrative Incidents, Poetry, Etc.,* vol. 1. New York: O.P. Putnam, 1862.

Naron, Levi H. *Chickasaw, a Mississippi Scout for the Union: The Civil War Memoir of Levi H. Naron.* Edited by Michael B. Ballard, Thomas D. Cockrell, and R. W. Surby. Baton Rouge: Louisiana State University Press, 2005.

Sam DeVincent Collection of Illustrated American Sheet Music, 1790–1987, National Museum of American History, Washington DC.

Segar, Joseph E. *Letter of Hon. Joseph Segar, to a Friend in Virginia, in Vindication of his Course in Declining to Follow His State into Secession.* Washington, DC: William H. Moore, Printer, 1862.

—— *Speech of Hon. Joseph Segar, on Re-construction, at Hampton, Jul 27, 1867.* N.p, n.d.

—— *Speech of Joseph Segar on the motion of Mr. Chapman of Monroe to instruct the senators and request the representatives in Congress from the state of Virginia to vote for the immediate recognition of the independence of Texas.* Richmond, VA: Shepherd & Colin Publisher, 1837.

—— *Speech of Mr. Joseph Segar (of Elizabeth City and Warwick) on the Wilmot Proviso, Delivered in the House of Delegates, January 19, 1849.* Richmond, VA: Shepherd & Colin, 1849.

—— *Speech of Joseph Segar, Esq., of the York District, Delivered in the House of Delegates of Virginia, March the 30th, 1861, on the Resolutions of the Senate, Directing the Governor of Virginia to Seize, by Military Force, the U.S. Guns at Bellona Arsenal, and on the Secession of Virginia.* N.p., n.d.

Stephens, Alexander. *A Constitutional View of the Late War Between the States,* vol. 1. Philadelphia: National Publishing Company, 1868.

Wakelyn, Jon L., ed. *Southern Pamphlets on Secession, November 1860 to April 1861.* Chapel Hill: University of North Carolina Press, 1996.

Wish, Harvey. *Antebellum Writings of George Fitzhugh and Hinton Rowan Helper on Slavery.* New York: Capricorn Books, 1960.

Bibliography

Secondary Sources

Abbott, Richard H. *The Republican Party and the South, 1855–1877: The First Southern Strategy*. Chapel Hill: University of North Carolina Press, 1986.

Allen, Theodore W. *The Invention of the White Race*. London: Verso, 1994.

Aptheker, Herbert. *American Negro Slave Revolts*. New York: Columbia University Press, 1943.

Aron, Cindy Sondik. *Ladies and Gentlemen of the Civil Service: Middle-Class Workers in Victorian America*. New York: Oxford University Press, 1987.

Ash, Stephen V. *When the Yankees Came: Conflict and Chaos in the Occupied South, 1861–1865*. Chapel Hill: University of North Carolina Press, 1995.

Attie, Jeanie. *Patriotic Toil: Northern Women and the American Civil War*. Ithaca, NY: Cornell University Press, 1998.

Ayers, Edward L. "Narrating the New South." *Journal of Southern History* 61, no. 3 (August 1995): 555–566.

The Promise of the New South: Life After Reconstruction. New York: Oxford University Press, 1992.

Bailey, Anne J. *Invisible Southerners: Ethnicity in the Civil War*. Athens: University of Georgia Press, 2006.

Bardaglio, Peter W. *Reconstructing the Household: Families, Sex, and the Law in the Nineteenth-Century South*. Chapel Hill: University of North Carolina Press, 1995.

Basch, Norma. *In the Eyes of the Law: Women, Marriage, and Property in Nineteenth-Century New York*. Ithaca: Cornell University Press, 1982.

"Invisible Women: The Legal Fiction of Marital Unity in Nineteenth-Century America." *Feminist Studies* 5, no. 2 (1979): 346–366.

Behrend, Justin. "Rebellious Talk and Conspiratorial Plots: The Making of a Slave Insurrection in Civil War Natchez." *Journal of Southern History* 77, no. 1 (February 2011): 17–52.

Belz, Herman. *Emancipation and Equal Rights: Politics and Constitutionalism in the Civil War Era*. New York: Norton, 1978.

Reconstructing the Union: Theory and Policy During the Civil War. Ithaca, NY: Cornell University Press, 1969.

Benedict, Michael Les. *A Compromise of Principle: Congressional Republicans and Reconstruction, 1863–1869*. New York: Norton, 1974.

Bercaw, Nancy. *Gendered Freedoms: Race, Rights, and the Politics of Household in the Delta, 1861–1875*. Gainesville: University Press of Florida, 2003.

Beringer, Richard E., Herman Hattaway, Archer Jones, and William N. Still. *Why the South Lost the Civil War*. Athens: University of Georgia Press, 1986.

Berlin, Ira. *Slaves No More: Three Essays on Emancipation and the Civil War*. Cambridge and New York: Cambridge University Press, 1992.

Slaves Without Masters: The Free Negro in the Antebellum South. New York: Pantheon Books, 1974.

"Who Freed the Slaves? Emancipation and Its Meaning." In *Union and Emancipation: Essays on Politics and Race in the Civil War Era*, edited by David W. Blight and Brooks D. Simpson, 105–121. Kent, OH: Kent State University Press, 1997.

Bestor, Arthur. "State Sovereignty and Slavery: A Reinterpretation of Proslavery Constitutional Doctrine, 1846–1860." *Journal of the Illinois State Historical Society* 54 (1961): 117–180.
Blatt, Martin Henry, Thomas J. Brown, and Donald Yacovone, eds. *Hope & Glory: Essays on the Legacy of the Fifty-Fourth Massachusetts Regiment*. Amherst: University of Massachusetts Press, 2001.
Blight, David W. "Fifty Years of Freedom: The Memory of Emancipation at the Civil War Semi-Centennial, 1911–15." *Slavery & Abolition* 21, no. 2 (2000): 117–134.
——— "'For Something Beyond the Battlefield': Frederick Douglass and the Struggle for the Memory of the Civil War." *Journal of American History* 75, no. 4 (1989): 1156–1178.
——— *Race and Reunion: The Civil War in American Memory*. Cambridge, MA: Harvard University Press, 2001.
——— "The Meaning or the Fight: Frederick Douglass and the Memory of the Fifty Fourth Massachusetts." *Massachusetts Review* 36, no. 1 (1995): 141–153.
——— "'What Will Peace Among the Whites Bring?': Reunion and Race in the Struggle over the Memory of the Civil War in American Culture." *Massachusetts Review* 34, no. 3 (1993): 393–410.
Blu, Karen I. *The Lumbee Problem: The Making of an American Indian People*. New York: Cambridge University Press, 1980.
Bodayla, Stephen D. "'Can an Indian Vote?': Elk V. Wilkins, a Setback for Indian Citizenship." *Nebraska History* 67, no. 4 (December 1986): 372–380.
Bowie, Benjamin E. "The Southern Claims Commission." Master's Thesis, University of Mississippi, 1949.
——— "The Southern Claims Commission, 1871–1880." *Journal of Mississippi History* 12 (April 1950): 105–115.
Brandwein, Pamela. *Reconstructing Reconstruction: The Supreme Court and the Production of Historical Truth*. Durham: Duke University Press, 1999.
Brewer, James H. *The Confederate Negro: Virginia's Craftsmen and Military Laborers, 1861–1865*. Tuscaloosa: University of Alabama Press, 2007.
Brock, William R. *An American Crisis: Congress and Reconstruction, 1865–1867*. New York: St. Martin's Press, 1963.
Brown, Christopher, and Philip D. Morgan, eds. *Arming Slaves: From Classical Times to the Modern Age*. New Haven: Yale University Press, 2006.
Brown, David. *Southern Outcast: Hinton Rowan Helper and the Impending Crisis of the South*. Baton Rouge: Louisiana State University Press, 2006.
Brown, Kathleen M. *Good Wives, Nasty Wenches, and Anxious Patriarchs: Gender, Race, and Power in Colonial Virginia*. Chapel Hill: University of North Carolina Press, 1996.
Buck, Paul H. *The Road to Reunion, 1865–1900*. Boston: Little, Brown, 1937.
Burg, Robert W. "Amnesty, Civil Rights, and the Meaning of Liberal Republicanism, 1862–1872." *American Nineteenth Century History* 4, no. 3 (Fall 2003): 29–60.
Burin, Eric. *Slavery and the Peculiar Solution: A History of the American Colonization Society*. Gainesville: University Press of Florida, 2005.
Burstein, Andrew. "The Political Character of Sympathy." *Journal of the Early Republic* 21, no. 4 (2001): 601–632.
Bynum, Victoria E. *The Free State of Jones: Mississippi's Longest Civil War*. Chapel Hill: University of North Carolina Press, 2001.

Unruly Women: The Politics of Social and Sexual Control in the Old South. Chapel Hill: University of North Carolina Press, 1992.

Carney, Court. "The Contested Image of Nathan Bedford Forrest." *Journal of Southern History* 67, no. 3 (2001): 601–630.

Carter, Christine Jacobson. *Southern Single Blessedness: Unmarried Women in the Urban South, 1800–1865*. Urbana: University of Illinois Press, 2006.

Carter, Dan T. *When the War Was Over: The Failure of Self-Reconstruction in the South, 1865–1867*. Baton Rouge: Louisiana State University Press, 1985.

Censer, Jane Turner. "'Smiling Through Her Tears': Antebellum Southern Women and Divorce." *American Journal of Legal History* 25, no. 1 (January 1981): 24–47.

Chused, Richard H. "Married Women's Property Law: 1800–1850." *Georgetown Law Journal* 71, no. 5 (1983): 1359–1425.

Cimprich, John. *Fort Pillow, a Civil War Massacre, and Public Memory*. Baton Rouge: Louisiana State University Press, 2005.

Clark, Elizabeth B. "'The Sacred Rights of the Weak': Pain, Sympathy, and the Culture of Individual Rights in Antebellum America." *Journal of American History* 82, no. 2 (1995): 463–493.

Clark, Kathleen. "Celebrating Freedom: Emancipation Day Celebrations and African American Memory in the Early Reconstruction South." In *Where These Memories Grow: History, Memory, and Southern Identity*, edited by W. Fitzhugh Brundage, 107–132. Chapel Hill: University of North Carolina Press, 2000.

Cohen, Lizabeth. *Making a New Deal: Industrial Workers in Chicago, 1919–1939*. Cambridge: Cambridge University Press, 1990.

Connelly, Thomas L., and Barbara L. Bellows. *God and General Longstreet: The Lost Cause and the Southern Mind*. Baton Rouge: Louisiana State University Press, 1982.

The Marble Man: Robert E. Lee and His Image in American Society. New York: Knopf, 1977.

Cooper, Frederick, Thomas C. Holt, and Rebecca J. Scott, eds. *Beyond Slavery: Explorations of Race, Labor, and Citizenship in Postemancipation Societies*. Chapel Hill: University of North Carolina Press, 2000.

Cott, Nancy F. *Public Vows: A History of Marriage and the Nation*. Cambridge, MA: Harvard University Press, 2000.

The Bonds of Womanhood: "Woman's Sphere" in New England, 1780–1835. New Haven: Yale University Press, 1977.

Cox, Karen L. *Dixie's Daughters: The United Daughters of the Confederacy and the Preservation of Confederate Culture*. Gainesville: University Press of Florida, 2003.

Cox, LaWanda, and John H. Cox. "Negro Suffrage and Republican Politics: The Problem of Motivation in Reconstruction Historiography." *Journal of Southern History* 33, no. 3 (August 1967): 303–330.

Crain, Caleb. *American Sympathy: Men, Friendship, and Literature in the New Nation*. New Haven: Yale University Press, 2001.

Crane, Gregg D. "Dangerous Sentiments: Sympathy, Rights, and Revolution in Stowe's Antislavery Novels." *Nineteenth-Century Literature* 51, no. 2 (1996): 176–204.

Crawford, Martin. *Ashe County's Civil War: Community and Society in the Appalachian South*. Charlottesville: University Press of Virginia, 2001.

Crofts, Daniel W. *Reluctant Confederates: Upper South Unionists in the Secession Crisis*. Chapel Hill: University of North Carolina Press, 1989.

Dailey, Jane Elizabeth. *Before Jim Crow: The Politics of Race in Postemancipation Virginia*. Chapel Hill: University of North Carolina Press, 2000.

Daly, John Patrick. *When Slavery Was Called Freedom: Evangelicalism, Proslavery, and the Causes of the Civil War*. Lexington: University Press of Kentucky, 2002.

Dawson, Joseph G. *Army Generals and Reconstruction: Louisiana, 1862–1877*. Baton Rouge: Louisiana State University Press, 1982.

Deloria, Vine, and David E. Wilkins. *Tribes, Treaties, and Constitutional Tribulations*. Austin: University of Texas Press, 1999.

Dew, Charles B. *Apostles of Disunion: Southern Secession Commissioners and the Causes of the Civil War*. Charlottesville: University Press of Virginia, 2001.

Deyle, Steven. *Carry Me Back: The Domestic Slave Trade in American Life*. New York: Oxford University Press, 2005.

Dick, Anthony. "The Substance of Punishment Under the Bill of Attainder Clause." *Stanford Law Review* 63 (May 2011): 1177–1211.

Dorris, Jonathan T. *Pardon and Amnesty Under Lincoln and Johnson: The Restoration of the Confederates to Their Rights and Privileges, 1861–1898*. Chapel Hill: University of North Carolina Press, 1953.

Dougan, Michael B. "The Arkansas Married Women's Property Law." *Arkansas Historical Quarterly* 46 (Spring 1987): 3–26.

Dresser, Rebecca M. "Kate and John Minor: Confederate Unionists of Natchez." *Journal of Mississippi History* 64, no. 3 (2002): 188–216.

DuBois, Ellen Carol. *Feminism and Suffrage: The Emergence of an Independent Women's Movement in America, 1848–1869*. Ithaca: Cornell University Press, 1978.

DuBois, W. E. B. *Black Reconstruction in America*. 1935; repr. New York: Atheneum, 1992.

Dudden, Faye E. *Fighting Chance: The Struggle over Woman Suffrage and Black Suffrage in Reconstruction America*. New York: Oxford University Press, 2011.

Dunn, Durwood. *Cades Cove: The Life and Death of a Southern Appalachian Community, 1818–1937*. Knoxville: University of Tennessee Press, 1988.

Durrill, Wayne K. *War of Another Kind: A Southern Community in the Great Rebellion*. New York: Oxford University Press, 1990.

Dyer, Thomas G. *Secret Yankees: The Union Circle in Confederate Atlanta*. Baltimore: Johns Hopkins University Press, 1999.

Edwards, Laura F. *Gendered Strife & Confusion: The Political Culture of Reconstruction*. Urbana: University of Illinois Press, 1997.

Egerton, Douglas R. "'Its Origin Is Not a Little Curious': A New Look at the American Colonization Society." *Journal of the Early Republic* 5, no. 4 (Winter 1985): 463–480.

Escott, Paul D. *"What Shall We Do with the Negro?": Lincoln, White Racism, and Civil War America*. Charlottesville: University of Virginia Press, 2009.

Eudell, Demetrius L. *The Political Languages of Emancipation in the British Caribbean and the U.S. South*. Chapel Hill: University of North Carolina Press, 2002.

Evans, William McKee. *To Die Game: The Story of the Lowry Band, Indian Guerrillas of Reconstruction*. Baton Rouge: Louisiana State University Press, 1971.

Fahs, Alice, and Joan Waugh, eds. *The Memory of the Civil War in American Culture*. Civil War America. Chapel Hill: University of North Carolina Press, 2004.

Faulkner, Carol. *Women's Radical Reconstruction: The Freedmen's Aid Movement.* Philadelphia: University of Pennsylvania Press, 2004.
Faust, Drew Gilpin. "Altars of Sacrifice: Confederate Women and the Narratives of War." *Journal of American History* 76, no. 4 (1990): 1200–1228.
  Mothers of Invention: Women of the Slaveholding South in the American Civil War. Chapel Hill: University of North Carolina Press, 1996.
Fellman, Michael. *Inside War: The Guerrilla Conflict in Missouri During the American Civil War.* New York: Oxford University Press, 1989.
Fisher, Dennis. "'We Have Our Memories and Our Present Grievances': African-Memory During the Great War, 1917–1919." *Journal of the American Studies Association of Texas* 36 (2005): 23–44.
Fitzgerald, Michael W. *Urban Emancipation: Popular Politics in Reconstruction Mobile, 1860–1890.* Baton Rouge: Louisiana State University Press, 2002.
Flanders, Ralph Betts. *Plantation Slavery in Georgia.* Chapel Hill: University of North Carolina Press, 1933.
Fleche, Andre. "'Shoulder to Shoulder as Comrades Tried': Black Men and White Union Veterans and Civil War Memory." *Civil War History* 51, no. 2 (2005): 175–201.
Foner, Eric. *Reconstruction: America's Unfinished Revolution, 1863–1877.* New York: Harper & Row, 1988.
  The Fiery Trial: Abraham Lincoln and American Slavery. New York: W.W. Norton, 2010.
Ford, Lacy K. *Deliver Us from Evil: The Slavery Question in the Old South.* New York: Oxford University Press, 2009.
Foster, Gaines M. *Ghosts of the Confederacy: Defeat, the Lost Cause, and the Emergence of the New South, 1865 to 1913.* New York: Oxford University Press, 1987.
Fox-Genovese, Elizabeth. *Within the Plantation Household: Black and White Women of the Old South.* Chapel Hill: University of North Carolina Press, 1988.
Freehling, William W. "The Editorial Revolution, Virginia, and the Coming of the Civil War: A Review Essay." *Civil War History* 16, no. 1 (March 1970): 64–72.
  The South vs. the South: How Anti-Confederate Southerners Shaped the Course of the Civil War. Oxford and New York: Oxford University Press, 2001.
Frey, Sylvia R. *Water from the Rock: Black Resistance in a Revolutionary Age.* Princeton, NJ: Princeton University Press, 1991.
Fuke, Richard P. *Imperfect Equality: African Americans and the Confines of White Racial Attitudes in Post-Emancipation Maryland.* New York: Fordham University Press, 1999.
Gaines, Francis Pendleton. *The Southern Plantation: A Study in the Development and the Accuracy of a Tradition.* New York: Columbia University Press, 1925.
Gallagher, Gary W. *Causes Won, Lost, and Forgotten: How Hollywood and Popular Art Shape What We Know About the Civil War.* Chapel Hill: University of North Carolina Press, 2008.
  Jubal A. Early, the Lost Cause, and Civil War History: A Persistent Legacy. Milwaukee, WI: Marquette University Press, 1995.
  Lee and His Generals in War and Memory. Baton Rouge: Louisiana State University Press, 1998.
  The Confederate War. Cambridge, MA: Harvard University Press, 1997.
  The Union War. Cambridge, MA: Harvard University Press, 2011.

Gallagher, Gary W., and Alan T. Nolan. *The Myth of the Lost Cause and Civil War History*. Bloomington: Indiana University Press, 2000.
Geertz, Clifford. "Thick Description: Toward an Interpretive Theory of Culture." In *The Interpretation of Cultures*, 6–20. New York: Basic Books, 1973.
Genovese, Eugene D. *Roll, Jordan, Roll: The World the Slaves Made*. New York: Pantheon Books, 1974.
Glenn, Evelyn Nakano. *Unequal Freedom: How Race and Gender Shaped American Citizenship and Labor*. Cambridge, MA: Harvard University Press, 2002.
Godbeer, Richard. *The Overflowing of Friendship: Love Between Men and the Creation of the American Republic*. Baltimore: Johns Hopkins University Press, 2009.
Goldfield, David R. *Still Fighting the Civil War: The American South and Southern History*. Baton Rouge: Louisiana State University Press, 2002.
Goodman, James E. *Stories of Scottsboro*. New York: Pantheon Books, 1994.
Greenberg, Kenneth S. *Honor & Slavery: Lies, Duels, Noses, Masks, Dressing as a Woman, Gifts, Strangers, Humanitarianism, Death, Slave Rebellions, the Proslavery Argument, Baseball, Hunting, and Gambling in the Old South*. Princeton, NJ: Princeton University Press, 1996.
Grimsley, Mark. *The Hard Wand of War: Union Military Policy Toward Southern Civilians, 1861–1865*. Cambridge: Cambridge University Press, 1995.
Gross, Ariela. "'Of Portuguese Origin': Litigating Identity and Citizenship Among the 'Little Races' in Nineteenth-Century America." *Law & History Review* 25, no. 3 (Fall 2007): 467–512.
Hahn, Steven. *A Nation Under Our Feet: Black Political Struggles in the Rural South from Slavery to the Great Migration*. Cambridge, MA: Harvard University Press, 2005.
The Political Worlds of Slavery and Freedom. Cambridge, MA: Harvard University Press, 2009.
The Roots of Southern Populism: Yeomen Farmers and the Transformation of the Georgia Upcountry, 1850–1890. New York: Oxford University Press, 1983.
Hale, Grace Elizabeth. *Making Whiteness: The Culture of Segregation in the South, 1890–1940*. New York: Pantheon Books, 1998.
Halttunen, Karen. "'Domestic Differences': Competing Narratives of Womanhood in the Murder Trial of Lucretia Chapman." In *The Culture of Sentiment: Race, Gender and Sentimentality in Nineteenth-Century America*, edited by Shirley Samuels, 39–57. New York: Oxford University Press, 1992.
Hamilton, Daniel W. "A New Right to Property: Civil War Confiscation in the Reconstruction Supreme Court." *Journal of Supreme Court History* 29, no. 3 (November 2004): 254–285.
The Limits of Sovereignty: Property Confiscation in the Union and the Confederacy During the Civil War. Chicago: University of Chicago Press, 2007.
Harris, William C. *With Charity for All: Lincoln and the Restoration of the Union*. Lexington: University Press of Kentucky, 1997.
Harrison, Noel G. "Atop an Anvil: The Civilians' War in Fairfax and Alexandria Counties, April 1861-April 1862." *Virginia Magazine of History & Biography* 106, no. 2 (1998): 133–164.
Hartman, Saidiya V. *Scenes of Subjection: Terror, Slavery, and Self-Making in Nineteenth-Century America*. New York: Oxford University Press, 1997.

Hartog, Hendrik. "Lawyering, Husbands' Rights, and the Unwritten Law in Nineteenth-Century America." *Journal of American History* 84 (June 1997): 67–96.

Man and Wife in America: A History. Cambridge, MA: Harvard University Press, 2000.

Hatfield, Eugene A. "Stephen Green Dorsey and the Southern Claims Commission: A Question of Loyalty." *Atlanta Historical Journal* 29, no. 2 (1985): 19–29.

Hauptman, Laurence M. *Between Two Fires: American Indians in the Civil War*. New York: Free Press, 1995.

Haynes, Dennis E. *A Thrilling Narrative: The Memoir of a Southern Unionist*. Edited by Arthur W. Bergeron. Fayetteville: University of Arkansas Press, 2006.

Hersh, Blanche Glassman. *The Slavery of Sex: Feminist-Abolitionists in America*. Urbana: University of Illinois Press, 1978.

Hess, Earl J. *The Union Soldier in Battle: Enduring the Ordeal of Combat*. Lawrence: University Press of Kansas, 1997.

Hoffert, Sylvia D. *When Hens Crow: The Woman's Rights Movement in Antebellum America*. Bloomington: Indiana University Press, 1995.

Holt, Thomas C. *Black Over White: Negro Political Leadership in South Carolina During Reconstruction*. Urbana: University of Illinois Press, 1977.

The Problem of Freedom: Race, Labor, and Politics in Jamaica and Britain, 1832–1938. Baltimore: Johns Hopkins University Press, 1992.

Honey, Michael K. "The War Within the Confederacy: White Unionists of North Carolina." *Prologue* 18, no. 2 (1986): 75–93.

Hyman, Harold M. *Era of the Oath: Northern Loyalty Tests During the Civil War and Reconstruction*. Philadelphia: University of Pennsylvania Press, 1954.

The Radical Republicans and Reconstruction, 1861–1870. Indianapolis: Bobbs-Merrill, 1967.

To Try Men's Souls: Loyalty Tests in American History. Berkeley: University of California Press, 1959.

Hyman, Harold Melvin. *A More Perfect Union: The Impact of the Civil War and Reconstruction on the Constitution*. New York: Knopf, 1973.

Hyman, Harold Melvin, and William M. Wiecek. *Equal Justice Under Law: Constitutional Development, 1835–1875*. New York: Harper & Row, 1982.

Inscoe, John C., and Robert C. Kenzer, eds. *Enemies of the Country: New Perspectives on Unionists in the Civil War South*. Athens: University of Georgia Press, 2001.

Inscoe, John C., and Robert C. Kenzer, and Gordon B. McKinney. *The Heart of Confederate Appalachia: Western North Carolina in the Civil War*. Chapel Hill: University of North Carolina Press, 2000.

Jackson, Luther Porter. *Free Negro Labor and Property Holding in Virginia, 1830–1860*. New York: Atheneum, 1969.

Jameson, Frederic. *The Political Unconscious: Narrative as a Socially Symbolic Act*. Ithaca, NY: Cornell University Press, 1981.

Janney, Caroline E. *Burying the Dead But Not the Past: Ladies' Memorial Associations and the Lost Cause*. Chapel Hill: University of North Carolina Press, 2008.

Jennison, Watson W. *Cultivating Race: The Expansion of Slavery in Georgia, 1750–1860*. Lexington: University Press of Kentucky, 2012.

Johnson, Michael P., and James L. Roark. *Black Masters: A Free Family of Color in the Old South*. New York: Norton, 1984.

Johnson, Walter. "On Agency." *Journal of Social History* 37, no. 1 (2003): 113–124.
Johnson, Whittington Bernard. *Black Savannah, 1788–1864*. Fayetteville: University of Arkansas Press, 1996.
Jordan, Winthrop D. *Tumult and Silence at Second Creek: An Inquiry into a Civil War Slave Conspiracy*. Baton Rouge: Louisiana State University Press, 1993.
Kachun, Mitchell A. *Festivals of Freedom: Memory and Meaning in African American Emancipation Celebrations, 1808–1915*. Amherst: University of Massachusetts Press, 2003.
Kaczorowski, Robert J. *The Politics of Judicial Interpretation: The Federal Courts, Department of Justice and Civil Rights, 1866–1876*. New York: Oceana, 1985.
Kaser, James A. *At the Bivouac of Memory: History, Politics, and the Battle of Chickamauga*. New York: P. Lang, 1996.
Kaye, Anthony E. *Joining Places: Slave Neighborhoods in the Old South*. Chapel Hill: University of North Carolina Press, 2007.
   "Slaves, Emancipation, and the Powers of War: Views from the Natchez District of Mississippi." In *The War Was You and Me: Civilians in the American Civil War*, edited by Joan E. Cashin, 60–84. Princeton, NJ: Princeton University Press, 2002.
Kerber, Linda K. *No Constitutional Right to Be Ladies: Women and the Obligations of Citizenship*. New York: Hill and Wang, 1998.
   Women of the Republic: Intellect and Ideology in Revolutionary America. Chapel Hill: University of North Carolina Press, 1980.
Kettner, James H. *The Development of American Citizenship, 1608–1870*. Chapel Hill: University of North Carolina Press, 1978.
Keyssar, Alexander. *The Right to Vote: The Contested History of Democracy in the United States*. New York: Basic Books, 2000.
Klingberg, Frank W. *The Southern Claims Commission*. Berkeley: University of California Press, 1955.
   "The Southern Claims Commission: A Postwar Agency in Operation." *Mississippi Valley Historical Review* 32, no. 2 (1945): 195–214.
Kopytoff, Igor, and Suzanne Miers, eds. *Slavery in Africa: Historical and Anthropological Perspectives*. Madison: University of Wisconsin Press, 1977.
Landers, Jane. *Black Society in Spanish Florida*. Urbana: University of Illinois Press, 1999.
Laqueur, Thomas Walter. *Making Sex: Body and Gender from the Greeks to Freud*. Cambridge, MA: Harvard University Press, 1990.
Larson, Sarah. "Records of the Southern Claims Commission." *Prologue* 12, no. 4 (1980): 207–218.
Lebsock, Suzanne. "Radical Reconstruction and the Property Rights of Southern Women." *Journal of Southern History* 43, no. 2 (May 1977): 195–216.
   The Free Women of Petersburg: Status and Culture in a Southern Town, 1784–1860. New York: Norton, 1984.
Lee, R. Alton. "Indian Citizenship and the Fourteenth Amendment." *South Dakota History* 4, no. 2 (Spring 1974): 198–221.
Lightner, David L., and Alexander L. Ragan. "Were African American Slaveholders Benevolent or Exploitative? A Quantitative Approach." *Journal of Southern History* 71, no. 3 (August 2005): 535–558.

Linderman, Gerald F. *Embattled Courage: The Experience of Combat in the American Civil War*. New York: Collier Macmillan, 1987.
Lockley, Timothy James. *Lines in the Sand: Race and Class in Lowcountry Georgia, 1750–1860*. Athens: University of Georgia Press, 2001.
Logan, Wayne A. "The Ex Post Facto Clause and the Jurisprudence of Punishment." *American Criminal Law Review* 35 (Summer 1998): 1261–1318.
Lowery, Malinda Maynor. *Lumbee Indians in the Jim Crow South: Race, Identity, and the Making of a Nation*. Chapel Hill: University of North Carolina Press, 2010.
Maltz, Earl M. *Civil Rights, the Constitution, and Congress, 1863–1869*. Lawrence: University Press of Kansas, 1990.
  The Fourteenth Amendment and the Law of the Constitution. Durham, NC: Carolina Academic Press, 2003.
Manning, Chandra. *What This Cruel War Was Over: Soldiers, Slavery, and the Civil War*. New York: Alfred A. Knopf, 2007.
McConnell, Stuart Charles. *Glorious Contentment: The Grand Army of the Republic, 1865–1900*. Chapel Hill: University of North Carolina Press, 1992.
McCurry, Stephanie. "Citizens, Soldiers' Wives and 'Hiley Hope Up' Slaves: The Problem of Political Obligation in the Civil War South." In *Gender and the Southern Body Politic*, edited by Nancy Bercaw, 95–124. University Press of Mississippi, 2000.
  Masters of Small Worlds: Yeoman Households, Gender Relations, and the Political Culture of the Antebellum South Carolina Low Country. New York: Oxford University Press, 1995.
McKinney, Gordon B. "Layers of Loyalty: Confederate Nationalism and Amnesty Letters from Western North Carolina." *Civil War History* 51, no. 1 (2005): 5–22.
McKitrick, Eric L. *Andrew Johnson and Reconstruction*. Chicago: University of Chicago Press, 1960.
McPherson, James M. *For Cause and Comrades: Why Men Fought in the Civil War*. New York: Oxford University Press, 1997.
  "Long-Legged Yankee Lies: The Southern Textbook Crusade." In *The Memory of the Civil War in American Culture*, edited by Alice Fahs and Joan Waugh, 64–78. Chapel Hill: University of North Carolina Press, 2004.
  The Struggle for Equality: Abolitionists and the Negro in the Civil War and Reconstruction. Princeton: Princeton University Press, 1964.
  What They Fought For, 1861–1865. Baton Rouge: Louisiana State University Press, 1995.
  "Who Freed the Slaves?" In *Drawn with the Sword: Reflections on the American Civil War*, 192–207. New York: Oxford University Press, 1996.
Medford, Edna Greene. "'I Was Always a Union Man': The Dilemma of Free Blacks in Confederate Virginia." *Slavery & Abolition* 15, no. 3 (1994): 1–16.
Merk, Frederick. "A Safety Valve Thesis and Texan Annexation." *Mississippi Valley Historical Review* 49, no. 3 (December 1962): 413–436.
Michot, Stephen S. "'War Is Still Raging in This Part of the Country': Oath-Taking, Conscription, and Guerrilla War in Louisiana's Lafourche Region." *Louisiana History* 38, no. 2 (1997): 157–184.
Mohr, Clarence L. *On the Threshold of Freedom: Masters and Slaves in Civil War Georgia*. Athens: University of Georgia Press, 1986.

Mooney, James. "The Powhatan Confederacy, Past and Present." *American Anthropologist* 9, no. 1 (January 1, 1907): 129–152.
Moore, John Hammond. "Getting Uncle Sam's Dollars: South Carolinians and the Southern Claims Commission, 1871–1880." *South Carolina Historical Magazine* 82, no. 3 (1981): 248–262.
——— "In Sherman's Wake: Atlanta and the Southern Claims Commission, 1871–1880." *Atlanta Historical Journal* 29, no. 2 (1985): 5–18.
——— "Richmond Area Residents and the Southern Claims Commission, 1871–1880." *Virginia Magazine of History & Biography* 91, no. 3 (1983): 285–295.
——— "Sherman's 'Fifth Column': A Guide to Unionist Activity in Georgia." *Georgia Historical Quarterly* 68, no. 3 (1984): 382–409.
Morgan, Edmund S. *American Slavery, American Freedom: The Ordeal of Colonial Virginia*. New York: Norton, 1975.
Morgan, Philip D. "The Ownership of Property by Slaves in the Mid-Nineteenth-Century Low Country." *Journal of Southern History* 49, no. 3 (1983): 399–420.
Nabers, Deak. *Victory of Law: The Fourteenth Amendment, the Civil War, and American Literature, 1852–1867*. Baltimore: Johns Hopkins University Press, 2006.
Neff, John R. *Honoring the Civil War Dead: Commemoration and the Problem of Reconciliation*. Lawrence: University Press of Kansas, 2005.
Nelson, William E. *The Fourteenth Amendment: From Political Principle to Judicial Doctrine*. Cambridge, MA: Harvard University Press, 1988.
Ngai, Mae M. *Impossible Subjects: Illegal Aliens and the Making of Modern America*. Princeton, NJ: Princeton University Press, 2004.
Noe, Kenneth W. "Red String Scare: Civil War Southwest Virginia and the Heroes of America." *North Carolina Historical Review* 69, no. 3 (1992): 301–322.
Nolan, Alan T. *Lee Considered: General Robert E. Lee and Civil War History*. Chapel Hill: University of North Carolina Press, 1991.
Noll, Mark A. *The Civil War as a Theological Crisis*. Chapel Hill: University of North Carolina Press, 2006.
O'Brien, Michael. *Conjectures of Order: Intellectual Life and the American South, 1810–1860*. Chapel Hill: University of North Carolina Press, 2004.
Olick, Jeffrey K., and Joyce Robbins. "Social Memory Studies: From 'Collective Memory' to the Historical Sociology of Mnemonic Practices." *Annual Review of Sociology* 24 (1998): 105–140.
Ong, Aihwa. *Buddha Is Hiding: Refugees, Citizenship, the New America*. Berkeley: University of California Press, 2003.
——— "Cultural Citizenship as Subject-Making: Immigrants Negotiate Racial and Cultural Boundaries in the United States." *Current Anthropology* 37, no. 5 (1996): 737–762.
Osterweis, Rollin G. *The Myth of the Lost Cause, 1865–1900*. Hamden: Archon Books, 1973.
Oubre, Claude F. *Forty Acres and a Mule: The Freedmen's Bureau and Black Land Ownership*. Baton Rouge: Louisiana State University Press, 1978.
Paludan, Phillip Shaw. *A Covenant with Death: The Constitution, Law, and Equality in the Civil War Era*. Urbana: University of Illinois Press, 1975.
——— *Victims: A True Story of the Civil War*. Knoxville: University of Tennessee Press, 1981.

Patterson, Orlando. *Freedom in the Making of Western Culture*. New York: Basic Books, 1991.
  Slavery and Social Death: A Comparative Study. Cambridge, MA: Harvard University Press, 1982.
Peele, Stanton J. "History and Jurisdiction of the United States Court of Claims." *Records of the Columbia Historical Society* 9 (1915): 2–21.
Penningroth, Dylan C. "Slavery, Freedom, and Social Claims to Property Among African Americans in Liberty County, Georgia, 1850–1880." *Journal of American History* 84, no. 2 (1997): 405–435.
  The Claims of Kinfolk: African American Property and Community in the Nineteenth-Century South. Chapel Hill: University of North Carolina Press, 2003.
  "The Claims of Slaves and Ex-Slaves to Family and Property: A Transatlantic Comparison." *American Historical Review* 112, no. 4 (October 2007): 1039–1069.
Perdue, Theda, and Michael D. Green. *The Columbia Guide to American Indians of the Southeast*. New York: Columbia University Press, 2001.
Phillips, Jason. *Diehard Rebels: The Confederate Culture of Invincibility*. Athens: University of Georgia Press, 2007.
  "The Grape Vine Telegraph: Rumors and Confederate Persistence." *Journal of Southern History* 74, no. 4 (November 2006): 753–788.
Pollard, John Garland. *Pamunkey Indians of Virginia*. Washington, DC: U.S. Government Printing Office, 1894.
Ponce, Pearl T. "Pledges and Principles." *Kansas History* 27, no. 1/2 (Summer 2004): 86–99.
Porter, Kenneth Wiggins. *The Negro on the American Frontier*. New York: Arno Press, 1971.
Quarles, Benjamin. *The Negro in the American Revolution*. New York: Norton, 1961.
  The Negro in the Civil War. Boston: Little, Brown, 1953.
Rable, George C. *Civil Wars: Women and the Crisis of Southern Nationalism*. Urbana: University of Illinois Press, 1989.
  God's Almost Chosen Peoples: A Religious History of the American Civil War. Chapel Hill: University of North Carolina Press, 2010.
Reardon, Carol. *Pickett's Charge in History and Memory*. Chapel Hill: University of North Carolina Press, 1997.
Renick, Edward I. "Assignment of Government Claims." *American Law Review* 24 (1890): 442–456.
Richards, David A. J. *Conscience and the Constitution: History, Theory, and Law of the Reconstruction Amendments*. Princeton, NJ: Princeton University Press, 1993.
Roark, James L. *Masters Without Slaves: Southern Planters in the Civil War and Reconstruction*. New York: Norton, 1977.
Robertson, Cara W. "Representing 'Miss Lizzie': Cultural Convictions in the Trial of Lizzie Borden." *Yale Journal of Law and the Humanities* 8 (1996): 351–416.
Roediger, David R. *The Wages of Whiteness: Race and the Making of the American Working Class*. London: Verso, 1991.
Renato Rosaldo. "Cultural Citizenship in San Jose, Califomia." *Polar* 17 (2008): 57–63.

Rosen, Hannah R. *Terror in the Heart of Freedom: Citizenship, Sexual Violence, and the Meaning of Race in the Postemancipation South*. Chapel Hill: University of North Carolina Press, 2009.

Rothman, Adam. *Slave Country: American Expansion and the Origins of the Deep South*. Cambridge, MA: Harvard University Press, 2005.

Rothman, Joshua D. *Notorious in the Neighborhood: Sex and Families Across the Color Line in Virginia, 1787–1861*. Chapel Hill: University of North Carolina Press, 2003.

Rountree, Helen C. "Ethnicity Among the 'Citizen' Indians of Tidewater Virginia, 1800–1930." In *Strategies for Survival: American Indians in the Eastern United States*, edited by Frank W. Porter, 172–209. New York: Greenwood Press, 1986.

Pocahontas's People: The Powhatan Indians of Virginia Through Four Centuries. Norman: University of Oklahoma Press, 1990.

Rountree, Helen C. and E. Randolph Turner. *Before and After Jamestown: Virginia's Powhatans and Their Predecessors*. Gainesville: University Press of Florida, 2002.

Rubin, Anne S. *A Shattered Nation: The Rise and Fall of the Confederacy, 1861–1868*. Chapel Hill: University of North Carolina Press, 2005.

Ryan, Mary P. *Cradle of the Middle Class: The Family in Oneida County, New York, 1790–1865*. Cambridge and New York: Cambridge University Press, 1981.

Sarris, Jonathan Dean. *A Separate Civil War: Communities in Conflict in the Mountain South*. Charlottesville: University of Virginia Press, 2006.

Saunt, Claudio. *A New Order of Things: Property, Power, and the Transformation of the Creek Indians, 1733–1816*. Cambridge and New York: Cambridge University Press, 1999.

Savage, Kirk. *Standing Soldiers, Kneeling Slaves: Race, War, and Monument in Nineteenth-Century America*. Princeton, NJ: Princeton University Press, 1997.

Saville, Julie. *The Work of Reconstruction: From Slave to Wage Laborer in South Carolina, 1860–1870*. New York: Cambridge University Press, 1994.

Scheel, Eugene M. *The Civil War in Fauquier County, Virginia*. Warrenton, VA: Fauquier National Bank, 1985.

Schwalm, Leslie A. *A Hard Fight for We: Women's Transition from Slavery to Freedom in South Carolina*. Urbana: University of Illinois Press, 1997.

Schweitzer, Ivy. *Perfecting Friendship: Politics and Affiliation in Early American Literature*. Chapel Hill: University of North Carolina Press, 2006.

Scott, Joan Wallach. *Gender and the Politics of History*. New York: Columbia University Press, 1988.

Scott, Rebecca J., Thomas C. Holt, and Frederick Cooper, eds. *Societies After Slavery: A Select Annotated Bibliography of Printed Sources on Cuba, Brazil, British Colonial Africa, South Africa, and the British West Indies*. Pittsburgh: University of Pittsburgh Press, 2002.

Seip, Terry L. *The South Returns to Congress: Men, Economic Measures, and Intersectional Relationships, 1868–1879*. Baton Rouge: Louisiana State University Press, 1983.

Sheehan-Dean, Aaron Charles. *Why Confederates Fought: Family and Nation in Civil War Virginia*. Chapel Hill: University of North Carolina Press, 2007.

Shenton, James Patrick. *Robert John Walker, a Politician from Jackson to Lincoln*. New York: Columbia University Press, 1961.

Shklar, Judith N. *American Citizenship: The Quest for Inclusion.* Cambridge, MA: Harvard University Press, 1991.
Silber, Nina. *Daughters of the Union: Northern Women Fight the Civil War.* Cambridge, MA: Harvard University Press, 2005.
  The Romance of Reunion: Northerners and the South, 1865–1900. Chapel Hill: University of North Carolina Press, 1993.
Silkenat, David. *Moments of Despair: Suicide, Divorce, and Debt in Civil War Era North Carolina.* Chapel Hill: University of North Carolina Press, 2011.
Simpson, John A. *S. A. Cunningham and the Confederate Heritage.* Athens: University of Georgia Press, 1994.
Sinisi, Kyle S. *Sacred Debts: State Civil War Claims and American Federalism, 1861–1880.* New York: Fordham University Press, 2003.
Sklar, Kathryn Kish. *Catharine Beecher: A Study in American Domesticity.* New Haven: Yale University Press, 1973.
Slap, Andrew L. *The Doom of Reconstruction: The Liberal Republicans in the Civil War Era.* New York: Fordham University Press, 2006.
Smith, Mark M. *How Race Is Made: Slavery, Segregation, and the Senses.* Chapel Hill: University of North Carolina Press, 2006.
Smith, Rogers M. *Civic Ideals: Conflicting Visions of Citizenship in U.S. History.* New Haven, CT: Yale University Press, 1997.
Smith-Rosenberg, Carroll. "The Female World of Love and Ritual: Relations Between Women in Nineteenth-Century America." *Signs: Journal of Women in Culture & Society* 1, no. 1 (1975): 1–30.
Spaulding, Norman W. "The Discourse of Law in Time of War: Politics and Professionalism During the Civil War and Reconstruction." *William & Mary Law Review* 46 (April 2005): 2001–2109.
Stanley, Amy Dru. "Conjugal Bonds and Wage Labor: Rights of Contract in the Age of Emancipation." *Journal of American History* 75, no. 2 (September 1988): 471–500.
  "Instead of Waiting for the Thirteenth Amendment: The War Power, Slave Marriage, and Inviolate Human Rights." *American Historical Review* 115, no. 3 (June 2010): 732–765.
Staudenraus, P. J. *The African Colonization Movement, 1816–1865.* New York: Columbia University Press, 1961.
Steiner, Ashley M. "Remission of Guilt or Removal of Punishment? The Effects of a Presidential Pardon." *Emory Law Journal* 46 (Spring 1997): 959–1003.
Storey, Margaret M. "Civil War Unionists and the Political Culture of Loyalty in Alabama, 1860–1861." *Journal of Southern History* 69, no. 1 (2003): 71–106.
  Loyalty and Loss: Alabama's Unionists in the Civil War and Reconstruction. Baton Rouge: Louisiana State University Press, 2004.
Streater, Kristen L. "'She-Rebels' on the Supply Line: Gender Conventions in Civil War Kentucky." In *Occupied Women: Gender, Military Occupation, and the American Civil War*, edited by Alecia P. Long and LeeAnn Whites, 88–102. Baton Rouge: Louisiana State University Press, 2009.
Sturdevant, Paul E. "Robert John Walker and Texas Annexation: A Lost Champion." *Southwestern Historical Quarterly* 109, no. 2 (October 2005): 188–202.

Sutherland, Daniel E. *Guerrillas, Unionists, and Violence on the Confederate Home Front*. Fayetteville: University of Arkansas Press, 1999.
  Seasons of War: The Ordeal of a Confederate Community, 1861–1865. New York: Simon & Schuster, 1995.
Tallant, Harold D. *Evil Necessity: Slavery and Political Culture in Antebellum Kentucky*. Lexington: University Press of Kentucky, 2003.
Taylor, Alan. *William Cooper's Town: Power and Persuasion on the Frontier of the Early American Republic*. New York: A.A. Knopf, 1995.
Taylor, Amy Murrell. *The Divided Family in Civil War America*. Chapel Hill: University of North Carolina Press, 2005.
Taylor, Joe Gray. *Louisiana Reconstructed, 1863–1877*. Baton Rouge: Louisiana State University Press, 1974.
Thompson, Elizabeth Lee. "Reconstructing the Practice: The Effects of Expanded Federal Judicial Power on Postbellum Lawyers." *American Journal of Legal History* 43, no. 3 (July 1999): 306–330.
Thompson, William Fletcher. *The Image of War: The Pictorial Reporting of the American Civil War*. New York: T. Yoseloff, 1960.
Tise, Larry E. *Proslavery: A History of the Defense of Slavery in America, 1701–1840*. Athens: University of Georgia Press, 1987.
Tripp, Steven. *Yankee Town, Southern City: Race and Class Relations in Civil War Lynchburg*. New York: New York University Press, 1997.
Tunnell, Ted. *Crucible of Reconstruction: War, Radicalism, and Race in Louisiana, 1862–1877*. Baton Rouge: Louisiana State University Press, 1984.
VanDeburg, William L. "The Battleground of Historical Memory: Creating Alternative Culture Heroes in Postbellum America." *Journal of Popular Culture* 20, no. 1 (1986): 49–62.
Varon, Elizabeth R. *We Mean to Be Counted: White Women & Politics in Antebellum Virginia*. Chapel Hill: University of North Carolina Press, 1998.
Vogel, Jeffrey E. "Redefining Reconciliation: Confederate Veterans and the Southern Responses to Federal Civil War Pensions." *Civil War History* 51, no. 1 (2005): 67–93.
Vorenberg, Michael. *Final Freedom: The Civil War, the Abolition of Slavery, and the Thirteenth Amendment*. Cambridge and New York: Cambridge University Press, 2001.
Wald, Priscilla. *Constituting Americans: Cultural Anxiety and Narrative Form*. Durham: Duke University Press, 1995.
Washington, Reginald. "The Southern Claims Commission: A Source for African-American Roots." *Prologue* 27, no. 4 (1995): 374–382.
Weber, Jennifer L. *Copperheads: The Rise and Fall of Lincoln's Opponents in the North*. Oxford: Oxford University Press, 2006.
Weeks, James P. "A Different View of Gettysburg: Play, Memory, and Race at the Civil War's Greatest Shrine." *Civil War History* 50, no. 2 (2004): 175–191.
Welter, Barbara. "The Cult of True Womanhood: 1820–1860." *American Quarterly* 18, no. 2 (1966): 151–174.
Whites, LeeAnn. "Strong Minds and Strong Hearts: The Ladies National League and the Civil War as an Intragender War." In *Gender Matters: Civil War, Reconstruction, and the Making of the New South*, 25–44. New York: Palgrave Macmillan, 2005.

The Civil War as a Crisis in Gender: Augusta, Georgia, 1860–1890. Athens: University of Georgia Press, 1995.

Wiecek, William M. "The Origin of the United States Court of Claims." *Administrative Law Review* 20 (1968): 387–406.

Wiener, Jonathan M. *Social Origins of the New South: Alabama, 1860–1885.* Baton Rouge: Louisiana State University Press, 1978.

Wilkins, David E. *American Indian Politics and the American Political System.* Lanham, MD: Rowman & Littlefield, 2002.

Wilson, Charles Reagan. *Baptized in Blood: The Religion of the Lost Cause, 1865–1920.* Athens: University of Georgia Press, 1980.

Wood, Betty. *Women's Work, Men's Work: The Informal Slave Economies of Lowcountry Georgia.* Athens: University of Georgia Press, 1995.

Wood, Gordon S. *The Radicalism of the American Revolution.* New York: Knopf, 1992.

Wood, Kirsten E. *Masterful Women: Slaveholding Widows from the American Revolution Through the Civil War.* Chapel Hill: University of North Carolina Press, 2004.

Woodworth, Steven E. *While God Is Marching On: The Religious World of Civil War Soldiers.* Lawrence: University Press of Kansas, 2001.

Wright, Gavin. *Old South, New South: Revolutions in the Southern Economy Since the Civil War.* New York: Basic Books, 1986.

Wright, J. Leitch. *Creeks & Seminoles: The Destruction and Regeneration of the Muscogulge People.* Lincoln: University of Nebraska Press, 1986.

Yellin, Jean Fagan. *Women and Sisters: The Antislavery Feminists in American Culture.* New Haven, CT: Yale University Press, 1989.

Young, Jeffrey Robert. *Domesticating Slavery: The Master Class in Georgia and South Carolina, 1670–1837.* Chapel Hill: University of North Carolina Press, 1999.

Zebley, Kathleen Rosa. "Rebel Salvation: The Story of Confederate Pardons." PhD Dissertation, University of Tennessee, 1999.

Index

Abercrombie, Mary, 87
Alabama, 17, 22, 34, 40–41, 43, 44, 48, 50, 55, 56, 62, 70–71, 92, 97–98, 100, 101, 104, 122, 125, 197–198, 213
Aldis, Asa Owen, 24, 28, 79, 107
Allain, Levi, 103
Ambos, Henry, 53, 59
Amnesty Act of 1872, 30–31, 136
Amnesty Act of 1898, 136–137
amnesty and pardon, 4, 7, 13–14, 15–16, 23, 29–31, 33, 38, 50–51, 54, 135, 136–137, 191
Anderson, Alfred, 124–125
Anderson, Elizabeth A., 85
Arkansas, 17, 31, 41, 52, 85, 87–88, 106, 109–110
Arnold, Richard D., 116–117
Atkisson, Caroline H., 70–71
Avery, R. B., 98, 109

Bacon, Joseph, 97
Bailey, John T., 44
Barrett, George W. 67
Barton, Elias, 59
Beedles, Henry, 99
Beedles, Polly, 99
Beery, Joseph, 47
Benjamin, Charles, 98–99
Blackburn, Mary, 1–2
Boone, Edmund, 109–110
Boone, Lafayette, 109
Bouligny, François, 121
Bowden, Henrietta S., 74
Bowles, John H., 61
Bradby, Edward, 127

Bradby, Terrill, 127, 129
Bragg, Edward S., 34
Brown, Jerry, 95
Brown, John Underwood, 62
Brown, Joseph (of Georgia), 59
Brown, Joseph (of Virginia), 118
Brunk, Jacob, 58
Burwell, James, 93

Carey, Harriet J., 69
Carney, Nicholas A., 52
Carr, Melvin B., 43
Carter, James, 96
Carter, Sarah, 120
Chotard, Henry, 75
Chotard, Stephanie, 75–76
citizenship
  active, 6–7, 40, 42–44, 54–57, 69–70, 74–75, 84–88, 93–95, 96–99, 114, 115–116, 127, 134, 135
  former Confederates, 13–17, 19, 29
  ideological, 2, 6, 41–42, 54–57, 61–65, 93, 99–104, 106, 111, 115, 131, 134–135
  limitations according to loyalty, 3, 13–19
  national, 3
  official, 7, 13–19, 43–48, 49–51, 52, 53, 54, 56–57, 59–60, 64–65, 71, 72, 74–77, 80–82, 84–88, 94–95, 98, 110–111, 117–118, 120–121, 123, 124–125, 129, 131, 174
  particularized, 6–7, 9–11, 27, 28, 132, 134, 135, 136
  race or gender exclusions, 2, 3, 12, 91–92, 135

247

citizenship (cont.)
  reciprocal obligations, 99, 106
  rights and privileges, 4
  subject, 51–54, 79–80, 81–82, 98
  vernacular, 2, 4, 6, 7, 41–43, 46, 50–53,
    55–56, 57–59, 61–64, 69–71, 73–74,
    78–80, 84–88, 93–94, 95–98, 115,
    119–120, 127–129, 174–175
Claiborne, Martha D., 81–82
Clarke, Eliza A., 78
Clem, Mary Jane, 74
Cole, Cornelius, 22, 141
Cole, Rachel R., 70
Combs, David, 104
Congress
  on amnesty, 29–31
  attacks on Southern Claims Commission,
    31, 33–34
  on black suffrage, 16–19
  creation of Southern Claims
    Commission, 19–25
  on duress, 45–46, 188
  on fraud, 21–22, 23, 34, 49
  on loyalty and citizenship, 12–38
  on obligations, 45–46
  restoration of former Confederates, 136–137
  on sympathies, 45–46
  views on black southerners, 92
  views on Indians, 126
conscientious objectors, 47–48
Cook, Thomas, 127–129
Copeland, Milton, 119
Corprew, George, 97
courage, 23, 44, 51–52, 54, 79, 137
Courter, Tabitha, 79
coverture, 28, 67–69, 71–78
Croizet, Adrien, 98
Currin, Adele, 84
Cuthbert, John, 94

Dallas, Harriet, 105, 114
Daniel, Asa, 50
Daniel, Robert, 63–64
Darden, Mary S., 86–87
Davis, Garrett, 19, 139
Davis, Henry Winter, 14
Davis, Jefferson, 126
Davis, Mary E., 82
Dean, James S., 110
Dennison, James, 116
dependence, 2, 48, 51–54, 65, 67–68, 71–82,
  88–89, 90, 95–99, 107, 109–110, 131,
  132, 135–136

Dillon, Wilson H., 63
disfranchisement, 6, 16–19, 29, 100, 130, 136
Dixon, Anna, 74
Donato, Cornelius, 120
Drake, William, 59
Dudley, C. W., 90
Dunbar, Martha W. 81–82
duress, 39, 45–49, 87, 95–96, 97–98, 110,
  115–116, 122–123, 188

Edmunds, George F., 22, 34, 140
Edwards, John W., 53
Ellis, Allen, 58
Ellis, Ezekial J., 34
Ellison, Mary J., 79
emancipation, 3–4, 8, 18, 19, 39, 42, 58–59,
  60–65, 93, 100–104, 106, 107–108, 115,
  117, 124
Emancipation Proclamation, 63, 65, 100, 103
Evans, Ellen E., 76, 77
Ex Parte Garland, 16, 24

Fair, Nancy H., 85
Ferriss, Orange, 24–25, 27, 28, 50–51, 134, 137
Fifteenth Amendment, 3, 17
Figures, W. B., 92
Finck, William E., 15
Finnall, Mary Elizabeth, 73–74
Fix, Adam, 52
Florida, 17, 94
foraging, 20
Ford, John, 97
Fourteenth Amendment, 3, 7, 17, 29, 30, 136,
  149, 157, 164, 185, 213
free blacks (former)
  contributions to Confederacy, 115–116,
    121–123
  contributions to Union, 115
  decisions by Southern Claims Commission,
    117–118, 120–121, 123, 124–125
  distinctions from slaves, 118–121
  enslaved relatives, 115, 116
  expectation for rights under Union, 120
  experience of coercion, 115–116, 122–123
  failure to pass loyalty test before Southern
    Claims Commission, 121–125
  nominal freedom, 114–121
  privileges, 116–117, 119–120
  similiarities with slaves, 114–118
  slaveholdings, 123–124, 221
  sympathies with Union, 115, 122
  treatment under Confederacy, 115–116,
    119–120

Index

views on emancipation, 115
white racial ancestry, 118–119
Freeman, James, 84

Garber, David J., 45, 187–188
Gardner, George, 108–109
Garland, Reuben H. J., 49
Gary, Johnson, 91–92
Gatewood, John N., 51
Georgia, 17, 22, 40, 43, 49, 53, 58, 59, 61–62, 71–72, 79–80, 85, 86, 93, 94, 95, 96, 97, 99, 103, 105, 106–107, 108–109, 114, 115, 116–117, 120, 122, 217
Goin, James, 122, 125
Gooch, Louisa, 86
Gordon, June R., 106–107
Gordon, Mary Jane, 78, 79
Grant, Ulysses S., 4, 24

Harper, Edward, 94
Hawk, John, 50–51
Hayes, Rutherford B., 136
Heflin, Robert S., 40–41
Holmes, Washington, 58
honor, 46
Hord, Samuel, 118–119
Horton, Annie, 86
Howard, Jacob M., 21, 140
Howell, James B., 24 25, 26, 27, 28, 140
Hunt, John, 59
Hyman, James K., 96

impressment, 20, 53, 115, 127
independence, 2, 40–45, 49–51, 65, 68–71, 90, 91–95, 107, 108–109, 121–125, 132
Indians
  alliance with Confederacy, 126
  alliance with Union, 126
  classification with blacks, 126, 129–130, 131
  Confederate policy regarding, 126
  contributions to Confederacy, 127, 130
  contributions to Union, 127, 130–131
  decisions by Southern Claims Commission, 129, 131
  experience of coercion, 127
  Lumbees, 129–131
  official citizenship status of, 126
  Pamunkeys, 125–129, 223
  removal, 126
  status as indigenous peoples, 126–127, 130
  status as sovereign peoples, 127–129
  sympathies for Union, 127

Union policy regarding, 126
votes for Republican party, 127
internal slave trade, 2, 116
ironclad oath, 13–14, 55, 178

Jackson, Archibald, 122–123, 125
James, Aldridge, 43
James, William, 119
Jefferson, Joseph, 107–108
Jennings, Mary E., 78–79
Johnson, Andrew, 15–16, 51, 17, 25, 33, 61, 65
Johnson, Margaret, 79
Johnston, Abraham, 115
Jones, Carroll, 113
Jones, Catharine, 113
Jones, Jackson M., 47–48
Jones, Nancy, 104
Joy, George W., 58

Kelley, Georgiana, 116–117
King, James T., 54–55
Ku Klux Klan, 30, 49, 55–56, 65, 130

Ladies' Memorial Societies, 8
Lee, Robert E., 22
Levy, William M., 31
Lewis, Thomas P., 50
Liberal Republicans, 29–30, 54
limiting act, 20
Lincoln, Abraham, 13–15, 61, 63, 100, 103, 126
Lipscomb, William C., 62–63
Lively, Eliza A., 78
Loring, George B., 15
Louisiana, 17, 31, 34, 39, 63–64, 75–76, 94, 98, 103, 113, 119–120, 121, 124, 125
Lowry, Henry Berry, 130, 225
loyalty
  geography of, 22, 41
  obligations, 6, 40, 42–44, 54–57, 59, 69–70, 74–75, 84–88, 91–92, 93–95, 96–99, 108–111, 113, 114, 115–116, 121–123, 124–125, 127, 134, 135, 136
  past vs. future or wartime vs. postwar, 4, 8, 13–19, 50–51, 54–57
  public vs. private, 40, 44, 51–54, 65, 68, 71, 82–88
  sympathies, 6, 41–42, 45–46, 53, 55, 56, 57–59, 61–65, 69, 73–74, 76–77, 78–79, 80, 83–84, 91–92, 93, 99, 100, 106, 107–108, 115
Lunceford, Harriet, 79

Markham, George, 63
Matteur, Beverly, 119
Matthews, Reuben, 55
McClellan, George B., 100
McCreery, Thomas C., 22, 139
memory, 5–6, 8, 176
Merry, Lucretia C., 68, 71
Middleton, Major, 93
Miles, Adelphia, 125–126
Miligan, Martin, 48
Military Reconstruction Acts, 3, 17
Miller, James, 104–105
Mississippi, 17, 50, 63, 67, 69, 78, 79, 86–87, 93, 104, 107–108, 126
Mitchell, John T., 51–52
Mitchell, William, 44
Morton, Oliver P., 30, 140
Mosby, John S., 55
Myres, Jerry, 96

Nast, Thomas, 32, 34, 35, 36, 64
Nation, Thomas, 55, 56
neutrality, 5, 11, 47, 51–54, 63, 78–82, 98, 130–131
Norris, Samuel, 61
North Carolina, 17, 22, 41, 47–48, 55, 58, 61, 84, 86, 126, 129–131
Nye, James W., 23, 141

Page, Lambert C., 127
Parker, Isaac, 30
Pass, John J., 58
paternalism, 62
Pattie, William A., 56
pensions, 4, 13, 89
persecution, 6, 8, 21, 22, 39, 40, 44, 45–49, 51, 53–54, 55–56, 65, 66, 70–71, 74, 96, 115–116, 120, 135
Phillips, Wendell, 12
Ponder, Prince, 105
Proctor, Joseph, 103
Puckett, Green, 115

reconciliation, 8, 22, 29, 33, 37, 66, 133, 135, 137
Reid, William, 20
reputation, 40, 44, 65, 68, 71, 82, 87
Rice, Martha A. E., 86
Risk, Harvey, 1–2
Rose, Judy, 96
Rozier, Joseph, 57

Sampson, Nancy, 129
Sawyer, Frederick, 29–30, 140
Schurz, Carl, 30, 139
secession, 16, 22, 23, 27, 40, 41–42, 43, 44, 47, 49, 50, 51, 52, 53, 54, 55, 56, 57, 60, 62, 63, 66, 67, 69, 71, 73, 78, 79, 80, 82, 84, 87, 92, 95, 131, 134, 135, 137
Segar, Joseph E., 41–42
separate spheres, 67–68
Sewell, Phil, 115
Seymour, Horatio, 63
Shackleford, William L., 60
Shaw, Simeon B., 57
Sheftall, Emmanuel, 122
Shelley, Charles M., 34
Sherman, William T., 94, 109
slaveholders (former)
    antislavery sympathies, 61, 69
    decisions by Southern Claims Commission, 64–65
    defense of slaveholding, 62, 124, 197–198
    views on emancipation, 61–64, 124, 200
slavery
    abuses of, 96, 97–98, 109–110
    antithesis of, 108
    defense of, 42, 62, 124
    opposition to, 54–57, 61, 69, 91–92, 93–94, 96–97, 99, 100, 115, 120
slaves (former)
    chronology of Civil War, 103
    contributions to Confederacy, 97–98, 106–107, 108–110
    contributions to Union, 90, 94, 96–97
    criticism of freedom, 107–108
    decisions by Southern Claims Commission, 94–95, 98, 110–111
    denigration of, 16, 18, 98–99
    entitlement to compensation, 90, 105
    experience of coercion, 95–96, 97–98, 109–110
    failure to pass loyalty test before Southern Claims Commission, 105
    lack of agency, 98
    property appropriated by the Union army, 104
    resistance, 93–95, 96–97
    sympathies for Union, 93, 99–100
    treatment by Union soldiers, 104–105
    treatment under enslavement, 95–96, 97–98, 109–110
    viewed as loyal to owner, 107, 109–110
    views on emancipation, 93, 100–104

Index

votes for Republican Party, 104
  as witnesses, 59–60, 81
Smith, Israel, 108
South Carolina, 17, 29–30, 55, 57, 87–88, 90, 94, 108, 122–123, 125, 129
Southern Claims Commission
  appointment of commissioners, 24–25
  compensation for special commissioners, 1
  congressional attacks on, 31, 33–34
  creation, 19–25
  denigration of blacks, 98–99
  as a dialogue between commissioners and claimants, 5–7, 133
  on duress, 46–47, 98, 110, 123
  end of tenure, 37
  exemptions from standards, 2, 82, 98–99, 111–112, 114, 117–118, 120–121, 129, 131, 132, 134, 135
  extension, 31, 33, 37
  general procedures, 4–5
  identification of blacks as property, 124–125
  implicit masculinity of standards, 6, 74, 92–93, 94–95, 134, 136
  implicit whiteness of standards, 6, 91–93, 136
  interrogatories, 1–2, 4, 5, 6, 26, 27, 28, 46, 47, 49, 50, 57, 59, 60–61, 68–69, 72, 83, 84, 87, 88–89, 92–93, 95, 105, 129, 130, 131, 134, 135
  on marital disunity, 76, 77, 87–88
  on marital unity, 74–75, 76–77, 87–88
  mode of collecting evidence, 4–5, 26–27
  on obligations, 6, 43–44, 51, 59–60, 64–65, 67–68, 74–75, 80, 81–82, 86–88, 94–95, 98–99, 108–111, 120–121, 124–125, 134, 136, 189
  on persecution, 44–45, 54, 56, 120–121, 189
  procedures for black claimants, 92–93
  procedures for white female claimants, 68–69, 72–73
  on property, 27–28, 65, 72, 201, 202
  on reputation, 44–45
  rulings on black claimants, 94–95, 98, 110–111, 117–118, 120–121, 123, 124–125, 132
  rulings on Indian claimants, 129, 131
  rulings on white female claimants, 68, 71–72, 78, 80–83, 84, 85–88
  rulings on white male claimants, 40–41, 43–45, 46–47, 49–51, 52, 53, 54, 55, 56–57, 59–60, 64–65
  special agents, 5

special commissioners, 4
  on sympathies, 6, 53, 59–60, 64–65, 67–68, 84, 94–95, 98, 120–121
  total claims before, 37
  views on black incapability, 111–112
Southern Historical Society, 8
Staggs, Thomas, 57
Stanton, Elizabeth Cady, 19
Stephens, Alexander, 16
Stiles, E. H., 93
suffrage
  blacks, 14, 16–19, 29, 118–119, 120
  former Confederates, 17, 19, 29
  Indians, 127, 130
  white women, 19
Summers, Benjamin, 115–116
Sumner, Charles, 30, 140
Supreme Court, 16, 24, 38, 136

Taunoir, Heluter, 124, 125
Taylor, Alexander R., 87–88
Taylor, Amelia B., 87–88
Taylor, Martha W., 82–83
Tennessee, 22, 41, 57, 82–83, 84
Terrett, Martha A. F., 74
Texas, 17, 54
Thirteenth Amendment, 3, 100
Tilden, Samuel J., 33
Trumbull, Lyman, 21, 140, 188
Turner, Benjamin Sterling, 97–98, 100, 101, 102

Union
  anti-secession, 6, 41, 134
  antislavery, 2, 54–57, 61–62, 63, 64–65, 93, 99–104, 106, 111, 115, 131, 134
  proslavery, 62–64, 134–135
United Confederate Veterans, 8, 177–178
United Daughters of the Confederacy, 8, 177–178

Virginia, 17, 20, 22, 41–42, 43, 45, 47, 51, 52, 53, 54–55, 56, 57, 58, 59, 60, 61, 62–63, 68, 69–70, 71, 73–74, 76, 77, 78–79, 82, 91–92, 93, 94, 97, 110, 115–116, 118–119, 124, 125-128, 187, 189, 193, 218–219

Wade, Benjamin, 14
Walker, Robert, 75
Warner, Willard, 22, 139
Weaver, Lucy A., 71–72
Wells, J. Madison, 39, 184–185
West Virginia, 21, 41

White, Mary L., 73
Willey, Waitman, 21, 139
Williams, George H., 49, 141
Williams, Thomas, 101
Wilshire, William W., 31

Withers, Agnes, 73
Woodward, Eliza, 69–70
Wright, Martha M., 67

Young, David, 61